THE EUROPEAN PARLIAMENT AND DELEGATED LEGISLATION

This book revisits the Treaty of Lisbon's promise to further parliamentarise the EU's functioning by looking into the Treaty-law framework governing the delegation of legislative power in the EU. In this field, the Lisbon Treaty formally greatly strengthened the position of the European Parliament vis-à-vis both the European Commission and the Council. The book explores whether Parliament's formally reinforced role is reflected in the actual balance of powers in the area of delegated legislation and executive rule-making. It does so by assessing how both the law and practice of decision-making at the legislative level, looking at specific case studies, and the sub-legislative level, examining the scrutiny over delegated legislation, has crystallised in the ten years following the entry into force of the Lisbon Treaty. This rigorous study gives a fascinating insight into one of the most significant developments in European parliamentary law-making, which EU constitutional lawyers will find required reading.

Volume 8 in the series Parliamentary Democracy in Europe

Parliamentary Democracy in Europe

The European Union is founded on the idea of 'representative democracy'. Its citizens are directly represented in the European Parliament, but Union democracy is equally based on indirect forms of representation especially through the European Council and the Council – two Union institutions whose members will be democratically accountable to their national parliaments. The good functioning of the Union democracy assumes, therefore, the good functioning of the democratic institutions of each Member State.

What is the role and relationship between the European and the national parliaments in the democratic functioning of the Union? Do they exercise distinct or complementary functions? Has the European Parliament adopted a structure similar to national parliaments; and how do national parliaments assume their 'European' functions? These questions have gained particular relevance in recent years. Not only has the Lisbon Treaty conferred new functions upon national parliaments, especially concerning the scrutiny on the compliance with the subsidiarity principle (the so called 'Early Warning System'), the coordination of fiscal and economic policies at the European level has led to significant restrictions of national parliamentary powers.

The new Hart Series on 'Parliamentary Democracy in Europe', encompassing both monographs and edited collections, aims to answer some of these questions. The series offers new insights into rules and conventions shaping parliaments and parliamentary democracy in Europe. Its aim is to provide a better understanding of the role parliaments are playing in European constitutional law and its idea of 'representative democracy'.

Series Editors

Nicola Lupo
Robert Schütze

Interparliamentary Cooperation in the Composite European Constitution
Edited by Nicola Lupo and Cristina Fasone

The Italian Parliament in the European Union
Edited by Nicola Lupo and Giovanni Piccirilli

The Principle of Subsidiarity and its Enforcement in the EU Legal Order: The Role of National Parliaments in the Early Warning System
Katarzyna Granat

Parliamentary Oversight of the Executives: Tools and Procedure in Europe
Elena Griglio

The Internationalisation of Constitutional Law: A View from the Venice Commission
Sergio Bartole

Executive-legislative (Im)balance in the European Union: (Im)balance in the European Union
Edited by Diane Fromage and Anna Herranz-Surrallés

Germany's Dual Constitution: Parliamentary Democracy in the Federal Republic
Florian Meinel

The European Parliament and Delegated Legislation: An Institutional Balance Perspective
Merijn Chamon

The European Parliament and Delegated Legislation

An Institutional Balance Perspective

Merijn Chamon

•HART•
OXFORD • LONDON • NEW YORK • NEW DELHI • SYDNEY

HART PUBLISHING

Bloomsbury Publishing Plc

Kemp House, Chawley Park, Cumnor Hill, Oxford, OX2 9PH, UK

1385 Broadway, New York, NY 10018, USA

29 Earlsfort Terrace, Dublin 2, Ireland

First published in Great Britain 2022

A catalogue record for this book is available from the British Library.

A catalogue record for this book is available from the Library of Congress.

Library of Congress Control Number: 2022944283

ISBN: HB: 978-1-50993-185-9
ePDF: 978-1-50993-187-3
ePub: 978-1-50993-186-6

Typeset by Compuscript Ltd, Shannon

CONTENTS

TABLE OF CASES

Judgments of the Court of Justice

Opinions of Advocates General

Judgments of the General Court

LIST OF FIGURES

LIST OF TABLES

1

Introduction

This monograph explores the law and practice of 'delegated legislation' from an institutional balance perspective. The backdrop of this enquiry is that on paper, the Lisbon Treaty radically reformed the EU legal framework governing the delegation of rulemaking powers to the executive (ie delegated legislation). It did so very much to the benefit of the European Parliament, or as Christiansen and Lange note, Lisbon 'recalibrated a historical imbalance in favour of the executive' that had characterised the pre-Lisbon system.[1] Whether or not there was indeed an *im*balance pre-Lisbon and whether it has now been properly corrected is ultimately a political question which this enquiry will not look into. Instead, this study stays on firmer legal ground, looking into the actual post-Lisbon law and practice in this field since it has been amply noted in scholarship that the Lisbon Treaty's (general) promise of parliamentarising the functioning of the EU has not necessarily been completely fulfilled.[2] To know whether the European Parliament truly has greater control over, or can keep a greater check on, delegated legislation, we need to determine how the relevant legal framework has evolved post-Lisbon and, crucially, how it is applied/respected in practice.

Since only now the dust has settled, some 10 years after the entry into force of the Lisbon Treaty, the conditions are right to pursue these questions. While the vantage point is that of delegated legislation, the enquiry will deal with this topic in its context: the Treaty Articles dealing with delegated legislation in a strict sense (Articles 290 and 291 TFEU), should not be assessed in isolation but should instead be appreciated as part of a broader constitutional framework governing executive rulemaking which must be included in the analysis. As noted, the prism through which this enquiry will be pursued is the institutional balance which requires the EU institutions to 'act within the limits of the powers conferred on [them] in the Treaties, and in conformity with the procedures, conditions and objectives set out in them'.[3] Taking the entry into force of the Lisbon Treaty as a watershed moment for the European Parliament's position vis-à-vis executive rulemaking implies that the pre-Lisbon institutional balance in this area was fundamentally redefined by the Lisbon Treaty. As will be shown, on paper this is indeed the case. Two more specific questions

[1] Thomas Christiansen and Sabina Lange, 'Executive-Legislative Relations and Delegated Powers in the European Union' in Diane Fromage and Anna Herranz-Surrallés (eds), *Executive-Legislative (Im)balance in the European Union* (Oxford, Hart Publishing, 2020) 69. More neutrally, Türk notes that the 'avenues for the adoption of non-legislative norms have evolved from the prevailing comitology model dominated by executive actors, to accommodate at sub-legislative level the increasing importance of the European Parliament in the law-making process'. See Alexander Türk, 'Legislative, delegated acts, comitology and interinstitutional conundrum in EU law – configuring EU normative spaces' (2020) 26 *European Law Journal* 418.

[2] See in the present series eg Diane Fromage and Anna Herranz-Surrallés, 'Introduction: Executive-Legislative (Im)balance in the European Union' in Fromage and Herranz-Surrallés (eds), *Executive-Legislative (Im)balance* (2020) 4–9.

[3] See Art 13(2) TEU.

follow from this premise: (i) how does the post-Lisbon institutional balance in executive rulemaking compare to the pre-Lisbon institutional balance; and (ii) how should the post-Lisbon institutional *practice* be assessed in light of the formal post-Lisbon institutional balance. Specifically for the European Parliament, then, the question arises whether its prerogatives under the institutional balance are indeed fully respected when the EU's executive institutions and bodies engage in rulemaking. Approaching this issue from a more political perspective, this raises the question whether, in the aftermath of the Lisbon Treaty's entry into force, the Parliament has indeed lost the implementation game as Christiansen and Dobbels claimed.[4]

I. A Primer: Operationalising Institutional Balance as a Yardstick for Assessing Institutional Developments

A key assumption on which the present enquiry rests is that the notion of institutional balance, which is to be found in Article 13(2) TEU,[5] can be qualified as a constitutional principle of EU law. While the Court of Justice confirmed the institutional balance's status as such,[6] some scholars have questioned this,[7] and often the Court in its case law does not treat it as a principle but simply relies on the notion of 'institutional balance' as a shorthand for the (Treaty-defined) rules governing the relations between the institutions.[8] However, if the institutional balance is a *genuine* principle and not just 'a court-made device to give a veneer of rationality to the often chaotic allocation of powers to institutions and organs laid down by the Treaty text',[9] it must have its own *stable* purpose and meaning.[10] If we are to construe the institutional balance as a constitutional principle of EU law, its purpose could be to protect the fundamental elements in the institutional system of the EU, ie a function of systemic protection,[11] or the protection of pre-existing

[4] Thomas Christiansen and Mathias Dobbels, 'Comitology and delegated acts after Lisbon: How the European Parliament lost the implementation game' (2012) 16 *European Integration Online Papers* Art 13.

[5] Confirming that Treaty provision as the normative foundation of the principle, see eg Case C-425/13, *Commission v Council*, ECLI:EU:C:2015:483 [69]; Case C-73/14, *Council v Commission*, ECLI:EU:C:2015:663 [61]; Case C-687/15, *Commission v Council*, ECLI:EU:C:2017:803 [40].

[6] For the first time in Case C-133/06, *Parliament v Council*, ECLI:EU:C:2008:257 [57].

[7] Armin von Bogdandy, *Europäische Verfassungsrecht* (Berlin, Springer, 2003) 199. Krajewski even refers to the institutional balance as an 'empty shell'; see Michał Krajewski, *Relative authority of judicial and extra-judicial review* (Oxford, Hart Publishing, 2021) 41.

[8] See on this already Damian Chalmers, 'Justifying Institutional Accommodation' (2008) 33 *European Law Review* 456; Bruno de Witte, 'Institutional Principles: A Special Category of General Principles of EC Law' in Ulf Bernitz and Joakim Nergelius (eds), *General Principles of European Community Law* (The Hague, Kluwer Law International, 2000) 150–51.

[9] Bruno de Witte, 'The role of the Court of Justice in shaping the institutional balance in the EU' in Joana Mendes and Ingo Venzke (eds), *Allocating authority – Who should do what in European and international law?* (Oxford, Hart Publishing, 2018) 144.

[10] Engaging only with French doctrine, Bertrand for instance notes that the legal nature of the institutional balance remains unclear and that it lacks an autonomous function; see Brunessen Bertrand, 'Institutions européennes – Le principe de l'équilibre institutionnel : la double inconstance' (2016) 6 *Europe* 5–10.

[11] Fabien Le Bot, 'Le principe de l'équilibre institutionnel en droit de l'union européenne' (Paris, Université Panthéon-Assas, 2012, PhD thesis) 243. Identifying a possibly different function, AG Trstenjak suggested that the principle's function is to ensure that the Union's 'functions are … exercised by the organs which are best placed to perform them under the Treaties'. See Opinion of AG Trstenjak in Case C-101/08, *Audiolux ea*, ECLI:EU:C:2009:410 [104].

competences.[12] This protection would be necessary because the EU Treaties constitute *traités cadres* which set out (ambitious) objectives and set up and empower institutions tasked with realising these objectives.[13] Undermining this carefully crafted institutional system is then tantamount to frustrating that aim, making it impossible to implement the process of integration which in itself is the *raison d'être* of the EU.[14]

This essentially means that the principle of institutional balance would also be inward-looking and self-referential to the EU legal system as created by the EU Treaties.[15] Its self-referential nature further means that the institutional balance does not require the institutions' powers to be in an actual state of equilibrium.[16] To illustrate this often overlooked point: if the *Herren der Verträge* at the occasion of a future Treaty revision were to strip the European Commission of all its powers, a Commission with no powers at all would be perfectly balanced from the perspective of the institutional balance. Legally, the institutional balance as defined in the Treaties is always perfectly valid, since it is part of primary law. Politically, however, one can of course disagree on how the institutional balance *ought* to be.[17] In the conceptualisation of the institutional balance presented here, that disagreement would then turn on the question how the institutional system of the EU should ideally look in order to implement the process of integration.[18] These considerations will then be relevant when the Treaties are revised and, realistically speaking, also when the Court, in a dispute turning on the precise powers and prerogatives of the EU institutions, is asked for clarification. Adhering to the legal fiction established by the Court in *Denkavit*, however, the Court will not 'choose' from different possible institutional balances; instead it merely

This function allows for an exogenous perspective as to which organ is 'best placed' to perform a certain function, regardless of what the Treaties themselves prescribe. However, if the institutional balance is laid down in the Treaties (as confirmed by the Court in *Chernobyl*; see Case C-70/88, *Parliament v Council*, ECLI:EU:C:1990:217 [21]), the institutional balance cannot be exogenously determined. Such an exogenous perspective would only come into play during Treaty revisions when the institutional balance can operate as a political principle, as noted by Lenaerts and Verhoeven, see Koen Lenaerts and Amaryllis Verhoeven, 'Institutional Balance as a Guarantee for Democracy in EU Governance' in Christian Joerges and Renaud Dehousse (eds), *Good Governance in Europe's Integrated Market* (Oxford, OUP, 2002) 47ff.

[12] David Yuratich, 'Article 13(2) TEU: Institutional Balance, Sincere Co-Operation, and Non-Domination During Lawmaking?' (2017) 18 *German Law Journal* 102.

[13] Panos Koutrakos, 'Institutional balance and sincere cooperation in treaty-making under EU law' (2019) 68 *International and Comparative Law Quarterly* 6.

[14] See Opinion 2/13 re the EU's accession to the ECHR, ECLI:EU:C:2014:2454 [172].

[15] Understanding the institutional balance as endogenous to the Treaties shows the difficulty in the argument made by Blumann in relation to the Lisbon Treaty: '*En matière d'exécution, la séparation des pouvoirs, … connaît une montée en puissance au détriment du principe d'équilibre institutionnel*'. See Claude Blumann, 'Le système normatif de l'Union européenne vingt ans après le traité de Maastricht' (2012) *Revue des affaires européennes* 256. The fact that the principle would be self-referential may also explain why Conway finds that the normative basis of the institutional balance in the Court's case law is unclear. See Gerard Conway, 'Recovering a Separation of Powers in the European Union' (2011) 17 *European Law Journal* 321.

[16] See also fn 56 below. Christiansen ignores this when he notes that 'Institutional balance, in a basic understanding of the term, is about the absence of any single institution among these three having fundamentally more weight and influence in the politics of the Union than the other two'. See Thomas Christiansen, 'The European Union after the Lisbon Treaty: An Elusive "Institutional Balance"?' in Andrea Biondi and Piet Eeckhout (eds), *EU Law after Lisbon* (Oxford, OUP, 2012) 228.

[17] This is where the conceptualisation of the principle by AG Trstenjak may come into play (see n 11).

[18] Differently, Lenaerts and Verhoeven note that it raises the question how the institutions and the interactions between them should be shaped so that 'each interest and constituency present in the Union is duly represented and co-operates with others in the frame of an institutionalised debate geared towards the formulation of the common good'. See Lenaerts and Verhoeven, 'Institutional Balance as a Guarantee for Democracy' (2002) 47.

clarifies and defines the meaning and scope of Treaty provisions as they must be or ought to have been understood and applied from the time of their coming into force.[19]

Defining its function as one of systemic protection is important since it means that while upholding the institutional balance may also further democracy or the republican value of non-domination,[20] that is not its ultimate function.[21] Of course, these values can still be promoted incidentally. Especially in the pre-Maastricht years, the Court reinforced the position of the European Parliament (and as a result strengthened the EU's democratic credentials) through its institutional balance jurisprudence. For instance, in *Isoglucose*, the Court relied on a teleological reading of the Parliament's advisory role in the consultation procedure to find that the Council cannot claim to have consulted the Parliament simply because it had asked for the Parliament's opinion (without receiving it). To arrive at this conclusion, the Court interpreted the Parliament's consultative role as an expression of 'the fundamental democratic principle that the peoples should take part in the exercise of power through the intermediary of a representative assembly'.[22] By opting for a teleological, rather than a textual, reading of the Treaty provision prescribing the Parliament's consultative role, and by identifying the furtherance of democratic decision-making as the telos, enforcing the institutional balance also reinforced democracy. However, equating both generally would be wrong.[23] *Isoglucose* also shows how it would be equally wrong to speak of *the* institutional balance.[24] This also follows clearly from the Court's case law, since it held in *Commission v Council* that the powers of the institutions and the conditions on their exercise do not follow from one overarching provision or idea but instead 'derive from various specific provisions of the Treaty,' subtly noting that 'the differences between those provisions … are not always based on consistent criteria'.[25] Earlier, in *France, Italy & UK v Commission*, the Court had rejected the argument that there is a single general principle from which the limits to the powers conferred on the institutions can be inferred and that instead these limits must be deduced 'from an interpretation of the particular wording of the provision in question, … analysed in the light of its purpose and its place in the scheme of the Treaty'.[26] How the competences and prerogatives of the institutions are concretely defined thus varies between policy areas and between different phases in the policy cycle,[27] meaning that *the* institutional

[19] Case 61/79, *Denkavit*, ECLI:EU:C:1980:100 [16].

[20] Advancing such a reading, see Desmond Johnson, 'Institutional Balance as Constitutional Dialogue: A Republican Paradigm for the EU' in Mattias Derlén and Johan Lindholm (eds), *The Court of Justice of the European Union: Multidisciplinary Perspectives* (Oxford, Hart Publishing, 2018) 115–40.

[21] Le Bot, 'Le principe de l'équilibre institutionnel' (2012) 243.

[22] Case 138/79, *SA Roquette Frères v Council*, ECLI:EU:C:1980:249 [33].

[23] The Court's *MFA* judgment is a case in point. On the question of the existence and limits to the Commission's power to revoke legislative proposals, the Court enforced an institutional balance that was largely inspired by the Community method, rather than by the principle of democracy. See Case C-409/13, *Council v Commission*, ECLI:EU:C:2015:217. Criticising this, see Dominique Ritleng, 'Does the European Court of Justice take democracy seriously? Some thoughts about the Macro-Financial Assistance case' (2016) 53 *Common Market Law Review* 11–33.

[24] Confirming the idea that the institutional balance varies from one policy area to the next. See Marise Cremona, 'The Two (or Three) Treaty Solution: The New Treaty Structure of the EU' in Biondi, Eeckhout and Ripley, *EU Law after Lisbon* (2012) 50; de Witte, 'The role of the Court of Justice in shaping the institutional balance' (2018) 146.

[25] Case 242/87, *Commission v Council*, ECLI:EU:C:1989:217 [13].

[26] Joined cases 188 to 190/80, *France, Italy & UK v Commission*, ECLI:EU:C:1982:257 [6].

[27] Noting this explicitly in relation to the Economic and Monetary Union, see Opinion of AG Pitruzella in Joined Cases C-597/18 P, C-598/18 P, C-603/18 P and C-604/18 P, *Council v Chrysostomides*, ECLI:EU:C:2020:390 [44].

balance cannot be determined in the abstract.[28] Its substance, ie the concrete rules derived from it, which will give specific expression to the idea contained in Article 13(2) TEU, are thus to be determined ad hoc.

This point also helps in understanding the relation between the institutional balance and both the Community Method and the separation of powers. As noted elsewhere,[29] the Community method is not defined in the Treaties, but it is generally juxtaposed with the intergovernmental method. It is often used as a synecdoche to describe the EU's unique *legislative* process,[30] but in essence the Community method captures the rather unique (compared to other international organisations) supranational features of EU decision-making. Clearly, however, the Community method does not characterise all EU decision-making, the area of the Common Foreign and Security Policy (CFSP) being one notable exception. Put differently, the institutional balance in the CFSP does not (at all) reflect the ideal of the Community method. When arguments are made to do away with the unanimity requirement in the CFSP,[31] this effectively comes down to arguing that the CFSP institutional balance should be recalibrated to reflect (to a greater extent) the Community method. The latter therefore does not give expression to the institutional balance,[32] but instead the different institutional balances in the TEU and TFEU may reflect to a greater or lesser degree the Community method ideal type.[33]

Likewise, while there is no denying that there is a *functional* separation of powers in the EU (as in any system),[34] the EU's uniqueness partially results from the fact that this functional separation is not matched with an institutional separation (entrusting the three different functions to three different branches or institutions).[35] Just like the Community method, the (institutional) separation of powers is an ideal type, exogenous to the EU Treaties. The institutional balance tells us how powers are separated at the EU level, but it is not the EU's equivalent to the principle of separation of powers. Instead, the latter may

[28] See Koen Lenaerts and José Gutiérrez-Fons, 'A Constitutional Perspective' in Robert Schütze and Takis Tridimas (eds), *Oxford Principles of European Union Law: The European Union Legal Order*, Volume I (Oxford, OUP, 2018) 124.

[29] Merijn Chamon, 'Institutional balance and Community method in the implementation of EU legislation following the Lisbon Treaty' (2016) 53 *Common Market Law Review* 1504–05.

[30] See inter alia Jerzy Kranz, 'Gibt es ein Demokratiedefizit in der Europäischen Union?' (2013) 51 *Archiv des Völkerrechts* 411; Alexandra Gatto, 'Governance in the European Union: A Legal Perspective' (2006) 12 *Columbia Journal of European Law* 491; Armin von Bogdandy, Felix Arndt and Jürgen Bast, 'Legal Instruments in European Union Law and their Reform: A Systematic Approach on an Empirical Basis' (2004) 23 *Yearbook of European Law* 124.

[31] See eg European Parliament resolution of 13 February 2019 on the state of the debate on the future of Europe, OJ [2020] C 449/90 [9].

[32] Arguing as such, see René Barents, 'De post-Lissabon-rechtspraak over het institutioneel evenwicht' (2019) 67 *Tijdschrift voor Europees en economisch recht* 328.

[33] See in this sense also the analysis by Müller Gómez, Wessels and Wolters, who identify three possible institutional balances characterising the relationship between the European Parliament and the European Council, depending on the ideal type of EU governance which one pursues: intergovernmentalist, federalist or a fusion. Johannes Müller Gómez, Wolfgang Wessels and Johannes Wolters, 'The European Parliament and the European Council: A Shift in the Balance of Power?' in Olivier Costa (ed), *The European Parliament in Times of EU Crisis – Dynamics and Transformations* (Springer, 2019) 56–59, available at doi.org/10.1007/978-3-319-97391-3.

[34] Koen Lenaerts, 'Some Reflections on the Separation of Powers in the European Community' (1991) 28 *Common Market Law Review* 14.

[35] More elaborately on separation of powers, see Merijn Chamon, *EU Agencies: Legal and Political Limits to the Transformation of the EU Administration* (Oxford, OUP, 2016) 259–68.

function both as a yardstick and an inspiration: we can assess in how far the (different) institutional balance(s) in the EU measure up to the separation of powers,[36] and when the Treaties are revised, proposals can be put forward to rebalance the inter-institutional relations more in line with the traditional (organic) separation of powers as understood at the national level.

Turning back to the function of the principle institutional balance, it should be noted that often the fundamental elements of the EU's institutional system will be sufficiently clarified and protected by explicit Treaty provisions defining the competences and prerogatives of the EU institutions. In those cases, there is no need to rely on the institutional balance and the principle will not come into play. As Prechal suggested, in other situations the explicit Treaty provisions governing the competences and prerogatives of the EU institutions are silent or insufficiently clear, in which case the institutional balance will serve its purpose as a 'gap filling' principle.[37] As developed elsewhere,[38] two typical situations may arise in which the institutional balance may then be relied upon to determine the legality of a given institutional claim for (in)action. First there are the cases where, often following a new Treaty (amendment), the Treaties only lay down abstract rules and no consensus on how these rules should be understood is reached. A second type of situation is when a given institutional practice or development does not find its origins in the Treaties but finds itself in a 'grey zone' for which it needs to be determined whether the institutional (in)action is either *praeter* or *contra legem*.[39]

It is in this light and by adhering to the *Denkavit* fiction noted above that the discussion on whether the institutional balance constitutes a dynamic or static principle needs to be understood. In between Treaty revisions, the institutional balance must *by definition* be static since the institutional balance is defined in the Treaties and only the Treaty authors can alter it.[40] That is not to say that the principle cannot have dynamic effects: when it is enforced by the Court, the Court will have to pick the single correct interpretation from a series of rivalling interpretations (typically) advanced by the political EU institutions. This may then have very real dynamic effects in so far as (established) institutional practice may have to be adapted to be in line with the institutional balance as ultimately clarified by the Court. Yet, explicating that the *principle* of institutional balance may produce such dynamic effects arguably amounts to a pleonasm. After all, if a principle would not have such (possible) dynamic effects it would not serve a purpose and it would not be a principle at all.

What then finally of the principle's scope? Which bodies' prerogatives are protected under the institutional balance; who is bound to respect the institutional balance; and who can invoke the institutional balance as an actionable principle? Also on these issues, the Court's jurisprudence has not fully crystallised, but the view taken here is that in light of the

[36] See Conway, 'Recovering a Separation of Powers in the European Union' (2011) 308–18.

[37] Sacha Prechal, 'Institutional Balance: A Fragile Principle with Uncertain Contents' in Ton Heukels, Niels Blokker and Marcel Brus (eds), *The European Union after Amsterdam* (The Hague, Kluwer Law International, 1998) 277–78.

[38] Chamon, *EU Agencies* (2016) 285ff.

[39] Merijn Chamon, 'The Institutional Balance, an Ill-Fated Principle of EU Law?' (2015) 21 *European Public Law* 385–386.

[40] This follows from the *Chernobyl* case in which the Court noted that 'the institutional balance [is] created by the Treaties'. See Case 70/88, *Parliament v Council*, ECLI:EU:C:1990:217 [21]. In this sense, see also Lenaerts and Gutiérrez-Fons, 'A Constitutional Perspective' (2018) 124.

principle's proposed function, it is only the formal institutions' prerogatives (or at least those bodies foreseen by primary law),[41] that merit protection. Going against earlier suggestions in both case law and doctrine,[42] the function of the principle of institutional balance set out above shows how the powers of subsidiary bodies or the Member States as such do not merit its protection.[43] Instead, both subsidiary bodies and Member States (and of course the institutions themselves) are obliged to respect the institutional balance.[44] While the *Vreugdenhil* case law, in which the Court held that the institutional balance in itself is not a superior rule of law protecting individuals,[45] would seem to preclude this,[46] it would have to be accepted, in light of the principle's function, that any party should be able to rely on an infringement of the institutional balance before the EU courts. This especially since institutional practice (that might undermine the institutional balance) is often buttressed by an inter-institutional consensus.[47]

[41] In the classification originally set out by Hilf, this means that the institutional balance safeguards the prerogatives of the bodies of the first (and second, depending on the detail of the relevant primary law provisions) organisational layer(s) of the EU. According to Hilf the primary structure of the EU is laid down by the Member States in the Treaties. The EU's secondary structure is elaborated by the EU institutions themselves based on specific provisions in the Treaties authorising the institutions to do so, while for the EU's tertiary structure the Treaties do not contain any explicit authorisations. See Meinhard Hilf, *Die Organisationsstruktur der Europäischen Gemeinschaften* (Berlin, Springer Verlag, 1982) 4.

[42] Some case law suggests that the institutional balance also protects EU agencies, see Case T-165/06, *Elio Fiorucci v OHIM*, ECLI:EU:T:2009:157 [67]; Case T-135/08, *Schniga v CPVO*, ECLI:EU:T:2010:397 [85]. For a suggestion that also the Member States enjoy protection under the institutional balance, see Ellen Vos, 'The Rise of Committees' (1997) 3 *European Law Journal* 223; Opinion of AG Mengozzi in Case C-443/05 P, *Common Market Fertilizers SA v Commission*, ECLI:EU:C:2007:127 [106]. Germany also tried to argue to this effect in *Germany v ECHA*, but its suggestion that the Member States are also protected by the institutional balance (*in casu* because of their membership in a committee of the European Chemicals Agency) was not accepted by the General Court. See Case T-755/17, *Germany v ECHA*, ECLI:EU:T:2019:647 [136] and [141].

[43] For an argument in favour of a Member State-oriented institutional balance see Annalisa Volpato, *Delegation of Powers in the EU Legal System* (London, Routledge, 2022) 26–27. A special case which illustrates the point made here are the governors of the national central banks. The Court in *Rimšēvičs v Latvia* confirmed that they enjoy protection under the institutional balance (against their own Member States), but this precisely because of their function in the ECB and the European System of Central Banks. See Joined Cases C-202/18 and C-238/18, *Rimšēvičs v Latvia*, ECLI:EU:C:2019:139 [72]. Simply put, Member State(s) (actors) will only come within the scope of the institutional balance if EU primary law specifically entrusts them with a task or function. Generally, see Koen Lenaerts, Piet Van Nuffel and Tim Corthaut, *EU Constitutional Law* (Oxford, OUP, 2021) 504–16.

[44] That this is so for Member States can be read into *Pringle*, where the Court held that if the EU Member States conclude *inter se* agreements they can confer new tasks on the EU institutions through the *inter se* agreement, but these new tasks cannot alter the essential character of the powers conferred on the institutions by the EU Treaties. See Case C-370/12, *Pringle*, ECLI:EU:C:2012:756 [162]. Contra this reading of *Pringle*, see Sébastien Platon, 'The Principle of Institutional Balance: Rise, Eclipse and Revival of a General Principle of EU Constitutional Law' in Katja Ziegler, Päivi Neuvonen and Violata Moreno-Lax (eds), *Research Handbook on General Principles in EU Law* (Cheltenham, Edward Elgar, 2022) 136–55.

[45] Case C-282/90, *Vreugdenhil v Commission*, ECLI:EU:C:1992:124 [20]–[22]. Criticising this case law, see Opinion of AG Bot in Case C-221/10 P, *Artegodan GmbH v Commission*, ECLI:EU:C:2011:744 [40]–[44].

[46] Platon rightly notes however that *Vreugdenhil* was ruled in an action for damages, where a litigant needs to show that an EU institution breached a rule of law *intended to confer rights on individuals*, not just that an institution acted illegally (as under Art 263 TFEU proceedings). See Platon, 'The Principle of Institutional Balance' (2022) 136–55. Recently the Court of Justice itself stressed that the 'purpose of that restriction is, *without prejudice to the rules applicable to the assessment of the legality of a Union act*, to limit liability to situations where the unlawful conduct of Union institutions, bodies, offices and agencies has caused damage to an individual by prejudicing his or her interests specifically protected by Union law' (emphasis added). See Case C-615/19 P, *Dalli v Commission*, ECLI:EU:C:2021:133 [128].

[47] Chamon, 'The Institutional Balance' (2015) 386.

A. Devising an Institutional Balance Test

The institutional balance test which can be applied in those cases where the explicit Treaty provisions are insufficiently clear consists of two steps. As a preliminary step it of course needs to be determined whether recourse to the institutional balance is at all necessary. If the relevant Treaty provisions give sufficient explicit guidance, there is no need to rely on the principle of institutional balance. Only when there is a genuine gap to be filled should one turn to the institutional balance. Where those situations present themselves, the issue will typically revolve around a claim to a certain power (by an EU institution, Member State or even other actor) that (in)directly affects the legal position of one of the EU institutions. As a first step, an institutional balance test would then require the contested power to be put into the legal context as it results from the Treaties. Here the typical methods of interpretation employed by the Court of Justice, including the purposive interpretation,[48] will come into play.[49] Putting the contested power in its legal context might already exceptionally result in a finding that it cannot be upheld in light of the principle of institutional balance. Most of the time, however, a second step will be needed to assess what the repercussions would be on the independence and the competences and prerogatives of the EU institution whose legal position would be (in)directly affected if the contested power were to be upheld. The institutional balance test would then only be met if the contested power does not unduly interfere with the institution's independence, competences and prerogatives.

Two recent cases before the Court of Justice serve to illustrate the rather abstract test set out above. Both cases dealt with the Commission's prerogative of legislative initiative, whereby the questions involved related to the extent of the Commission's discretion, first, where an admissible European Citizen's Initiative (ECI) had been tabled and, second, where the social partners had achieved an agreement under Article 155 TFEU. To be entirely clear, it is not argued here that the Court actually followed the test presented above, but merely that following the latter would also produce the outcome at which the Court arrived. What is in any event clear is that the Advocate Generals (AGs), reasoning more elaborately than the Court, indeed largely followed the approach of the institutional balance test (without being explicit on the different steps).

Turning to the relevant legal provisions, the ECI was introduced by the Lisbon Treaty while the possibility to implement agreements reached between the social partners at EU

[48] Even if AG Bobek has rightly noted the problematic features of this method of interpretation: 'such reasoning … may lead one to anywhere one wishes it to lead, based on the purpose that one decides to embrace'. See Opinion of AG Bobek in Joined Cases C-59/18 and C-182/18 and Case C-743/19, *Italy and Milan v Council & Parliament v Council*, ECLI:EU:C:2021:812 [130]. While this risk is not denied here, the present enquiry will still rely on the purposive method of interpretation and will leave it to the reader whether the purposes identified were indeed the purposes pursued by the (primary) legislator when drafting (Treaty) provisions.

[49] See Gunnar Beck, *The Legal Reasoning of the Court of Justice of the EU* (Oxford, Hart Publishing, 2013) 187–233. Next to the purposive or teleological interpretation already mentioned, there are the technique of systemic interpretation and 'genetic' and historical methods of interpretation by relying on the genesis of Treaty provisions and the *travaux préparatoires*. Lenaerts and Gutiérrez-Fons classify these latter methods under the contextual method of interpretation; see Koen Lenaerts and José Gutiérrez-Fons, *Les méthodes d'interprétation de la Cour de justice de l'Union européenne* (Bruxelles, Bruylant, 2020) 27.

level has been part of EU law since the Single European Act. The relevant Treaty provisions are also markedly different. Article 11(4) TEU inter alia provides that:

> Not less than one million citizens who are nationals of a significant number of Member States may take the initiative of *inviting the European Commission*, within the framework of its powers, to submit any appropriate proposal on matters where citizens consider that a legal act of the Union is required for the purpose of implementing the Treaties. (emphasis added)

In contrast, Article 155(2) TFEU inter alia provides that:

> Agreements concluded at Union level *shall be implemented* either in accordance with the procedures and practices specific to management and labour and the Member States or, in matters covered by Article 153, at the joint request of the signatory parties, by a Council decision on a proposal from the Commission. The European Parliament shall be informed. (emphasis added)

The meaning of both provisions may seem clear at first sight, but in the two cases concerned, the Court was confronted with the claim that the Commission is *obliged* to submit a proposal once a ECI has been successfully lodged or once an agreement between the social partners is submitted to the Commission. In *Puppinck*, AG Bobek explored the genesis of Article 11(4) TEU and the systemic and institutional context in which the ECI needs to be placed.[50] This the AG confronted with the Commission's quasi-monopoly over the legislative initiative whereby he also stressed the original purpose of this prerogative being bestowed on the Commission.[51] Assessing what would be the impact of confirming an obligation for the Commission to act on a successful ECI, the AG noted:

> [The] essential features of the [Commission's] power of initiative, encompassing the choice to present a proposal, its objective and its content, are fundamental elements of the EU decision-making system. They form the bedrock of the independence of the Commission and its mandate to pursue the general interest of the European Union. The interpretation advocated by the Appellants would conflict with the mandate of the Commission, enshrined in Article 17(1) TEU, to promote the general interest of the European Union and to take the appropriate initiatives to that end. It would also imply a departure from the general obligation of the Commission to act with complete independence in the exercise of its power of initiative, in accordance with Article 17(3) TEU.[52]

The Court essentially followed the same reasoning and came to the same conclusion: accepting such a power for the proponents of an ECI and, conversely, such a limitation on the Commission's power of initiative would interfere with the institutional balance laid down by the Treaties.[53]

If the outcome of this case might seem predictable in light of the wording of Article 11(4) TEU, this was different in the *EPSU* case where the margin of discretion for the Commission not to propose to the Council that an agreement reached by the European social partners be implemented at EU level was at issue. AG Pikamäe looked into a literal, genetic, systemic and teleological interpretation of Article 155 TFEU.[54] According to the AG, none

[50] See subsections 1 and 2 of his analysis of the first plea, Opinion of AG Bobek in Case C-418/18 P, *Puppinck e.a. v Commission*, ECLI:EU:C:2019:640 [33]–[62].

[51] Opinion of AG Bobek in Case C-418/18 P, *Puppinck e.a. v Commission*, ECLI:EU:C:2019:640 [46].

[52] ibid [49]–[50].

[53] Case C-418/18 P, *Puppinck ea v Commission*, CLI:EU:C:2019:1113 [62].

[54] See sections 1, 2, 3 and 4 respectively of his substantive analysis of the first plea, ibid [46]–[76].

of these interpretations supported the reading of Article 155 TFEU advanced by EPSU and specifically in light of a systemic, combined, reading of Articles 155 TFEU and 17 TEU, the AG noted that confirming EPSU's interpretation would run counter to the institutional balance since it would give the specific interests of the social partners precedence over the general interests which the Commission is required to promote and for which it was granted the prerogative of legislative initiative.[55] Also in this case, the Court followed the lead of its AG and held that EPSU's reading of Article 155 TFEU would undermine the prerogatives of the Commission and therefore the institutional balance.[56]

Both cases show how (a limitation on) the powers of an EU institution may be assessed by first testing that claim through an interpretation of the Treaty text relying on the full plethora of interpretative techniques and by subsequently testing the repercussions of upholding that claim on the prerogatives of the institution involved and the other institutions.

B. Applying the Institutional Balance Test to Identify Constitutional Modifications

The legal test set out and illustrated in the preceding section can be used to assess how the Lisbon Treaty's reform of the framework governing executive rulemaking has subsequently been operationalised by the political and judicial EU institutions. As will be discussed below, the new framework defined by the Lisbon Treaty raised more questions than it settled and for each of these issues which the Lisbon Treaty did not exhaustively settle in an explicit manner, the institutions had a choice between many different rivalling solutions or interpretations. For each of the solutions opted for or interpretations settled upon, an institutional balance test may be pursued to determine whether post-Lisbon institutional practice is in line with the institutional balance as (re)defined by the Lisbon Treaty. In those cases where the institutional practice is not in line with the institutional balance, an instance of constitutional modification presents itself, ie a situation in which the key constitutional assumptions underlying the Lisbon schema has been sidelined or even undermined.[57] The legal assessment underpinning such a finding may also be linked with the political science literature on institutional change.[58] From that perspective, instances of constitutional modification are the legally problematic cases of interstitial change.

[55] Opinion of AG Pikamäe in Case C-928/19 P, *EPSU v Commission*, ECLI:EU:C:2021:38 [71]–[72].

[56] Case C-928/19 P, *EPSU v Commission*, ECLI:EU:C:2021:656 [48]–[49]. Interestingly, however, the Court also observed that recognising a power for the social partners to force the Commission to submit proposals to the Council would breach the institutional balance since it would give them a power which even the Parliament and Council do not possess. See Case C-928/19 P, *EPSU v Commission*, ECLI:EU:C:2021:656 [63]. Taken at face value, that finding of the Court is misguided since the institutional balance does not imply or require that EU institutions (and here the social partners and the EU institutions) stand on an equal footing. See Lenaerts and Gutiérrez-Fons (n 28) 124.

[57] See Paul Craig, 'Comitology, Rulemaking and the Lisbon Settlement – Tensions and Strains' in Carl Fredrik Bergström and Dominique Ritleng (eds), *Rulemaking by the European Commission – The New System for Delegation of Powers* (Oxford, OUP, 2016) 173.

[58] See Gretchen Helmke and Steven Levitsky, 'Informal Institutions and Comparative Politics: A Research Agenda' (2004) 2 *Perspectives on Politics* 725–740.

On the latter, Farrel and Héritier have noted how Treaty ambiguity may produce such change,[59] since the institutions will have to resolve that Treaty ambiguity by developing new or additional rules. These new institutional rules, adopted between formal Treaty revisions, may be of a formal or informal nature and may converge or diverge from the Treaty sanctioned rules. While the focus of the enquiry in political science is typically to study interstitial change to determine the balance of power and relationships between the institutions,[60] the focus of the present, legal, enquiry is normative. Both formal (eg judgments of the EU courts, legislation, inter-institutional agreements) and informal interstitial change (simply resulting from practice) may be either in line with the institutional balance or diverge from it. Evidently, only in case of divergence will the interstitial change in question be a legally problematic instance of constitutional modification. In line with the general theme of this series, the overarching question of this monograph then is whether, following the Lisbon Treaty which generally strengthened the position of the European Parliament on paper, interstitial change has occurred in the area of executive rulemaking and whether any such interstitial change amounts to constitutional modification. When such modification is found, the circle may be squared by verifying in how far this goes at the expense of the European Parliament's (formally strengthened) prerogatives.

II. Structure of the Enquiry

In pursuing the enquiry, this study will first recall the main features of the Lisbon Treaty's reform and very briefly comment on the road that led to the Lisbon Treaty. Having set the scene, the developments in institutional practice will be thematically addressed, identifying interstitial change and assessing whether that change aligns with or infringes the institutional balance defined by the Lisbon Treaty. The first development that will be addressed is the exponential multiplication of delimitation problems, given the increase in the types of executive acts. Following on from that, the institutional practice on delegated and implementing acts will be assessed. This will be done in a holistic manner, integrating the practice of the political institutions with the post-Lisbon jurisprudence of the courts. Since an important part of interstitial change accrues based on practice and conventions developed in the legislative process, a final chapter before the conclusion will test and develop earlier findings from Brandsma and Blom-Hansen by retracing the negotiations on executive empowerments in the General Data Protection Regulation and the Data Governance Act.

[59] See Henry Farrell and Adrienne Héritier, 'Introduction: Contested competences in the European Union' (2007) 30 *West European Politics* 228.

[60] Adrienne Héritier, Catherine Moury, Carina Bischoff and Carl-Fredrik Bergström, 'Theory and hypotheses' in Adrienne Héritier, Catherine Moury, Carina Bischoff and Carl-Fredrik Bergström (eds), *Changing Rules of Delegation: A Contest for Power in Comitology* (Oxford, OUP, 2013) 19–21.

2

A Formal Reading of the Lisbon Treaty

While stories are most often told from beginning to end, some tales lend themselves more to a reverse chronology, and for others still, such as the present one, it is better to start *in medias res*. To best understand the role of the European Parliament in executive rulemaking, it indeed seems advisable to first sketch the black letter law as we find it in the present EU Treaties, before briefly looking into where we come from and, subsequently, what the current 'living law' is. This chapter will thus set out how the framework for delegated legislation and executive rulemaking is defined in the TEU and the TFEU.

I. The Formal Catalogue of Acts

One of the many novelties of the Lisbon Treaty was that it introduced a typology of acts in addition to the already existing typology of instruments. The latter is to be found in Article 288 TFEU and lists the typical binding *instruments* of EU law, viz the regulation, directive and decision. It goes back to the Rome Treaty under the original Article 189 EEC. In contrast, the Lisbon Treaty's typology of *acts* is not neatly listed in one Article but is spread out over Articles 289–291 TFEU. The first of these Articles introduced for the first time the idea of formal legislation into EU law.[1] AG Lagrange's Opinion in *Costa v Enel* makes clear why this introduction was already remarkable, since he found that 'Community regulations, even the most important ones, are not legislative measures nor even, as is sometimes said, 'quasi-legislative measures' but rather measures emanating from an executive power (Council or Commission)'.[2] The consideration that the Council might constitute the legislative branch at EU level was not entertained at the time and this was also reflected in how the acts adopted at EU level were qualified. As will be noted in section 3.II, the Court only made a distinction between basic acts and implementing acts.

Article 289(3) TFEU thus introduces the concept of legislative act and defines legislation in a straightforward and procedural manner: '[l]egal acts adopted by legislative procedure shall constitute legislative acts'.[3] Article 290 TFEU then introduces the delegated

[1] As noted by Liisberg, before the Treaty of Lisbon, the term 'legislation' was not found in the Treaties but was used as a term of convenience by the Court (and the political institutions). See Jonas Bering Liisberg, 'The EU Constitutional Treaty and its distinction between legislative and non-legislative acts – Oranges into apples?' Jean Monnet Working Paper 01/06, 6ff. Lenaerts and Van Nuffel, for instance, qualified all acts based directly on the Treaties as legislation. See Koen Lenaerts and Piet Van Nuffel, *Europees Recht* (Antwerpen, Maklu, 2003) 513.

[2] Opinion of AG Lagrange in Case 6/64, *Costa*, ECLI:EU:C:1964:51, p 604. See also Karine Caunes, 'Et la fonction exécutive européenne créa l'administration à son image … Retour vers le futur de la comitologie' (2007) 43 *Revue trimestrielle de droit européen* 309–10.

[3] See Art 289(3) TFEU.

act. Defined in both a material and functional way, it is an act of general application that amends or supplements formal legislation. In a material sense the delegated act is legislative in nature,[4] but since it has not been adopted pursuant to a legislative procedure, it cannot be qualified as formal legislation. Finally, Article 291 TFEU introduced the notion of the implementing act, which is defined functionally as an act that implements a legally binding Union act under uniform conditions.

Just like there is no hierarchy between the different instruments of the Union, there is no formal hierarchy between the different acts.[5] While it seems natural to read Articles 289–291 TFEU as implying a hierarchy in the order of legislative act > delegated act > implementing act,[6] no such hierarchy is explicitly prescribed in the Treaties. While a specific delegated or implementing act will, by necessity, be inferior to the specific act on which it is based,[7] the Treaties do not contain any further statements on any abstract hierarchy between these acts.[8] If one were to argue that the Treaties lay down an implicit hierarchy between these acts it would then have to result from a separate norm. One obvious candidate in this respect would be the democracy principle, enshrined inter alia in Articles 2 and 10 TEU, since the different acts in question differ considerably in terms of their democratic pedigree. In this regard one could point to the evident but imperfect correlation with the role that the European Parliament plays in the adoption of legislative, delegated and implementing acts (see further). So far, however, the Court has not taken a position on this point.

II. The Lisbon Treaty's 'Atypical' Acts

A discussion of the Lisbon Treaty's new catalogue of acts usually ends here. But even making abstraction of the acts adopted under the Common Foreign and Security Policy (CFSP),[9] the account presented so far would only give a partial picture.

Firstly, a significant part of EU rulemaking is done at the international level when the EU concludes international agreements. Since Council decisions on the signature, provisional application or conclusion of international agreements[10] are not formally adopted

[4] This since Art 290 TFEU requires delegated acts to be of general application.

[5] Bast, for instance, notes that 'the Treaty does not provide for a hierarchical distinction between delegated and implementing acts'. See Jürgen Bast, 'New categories of acts after the Lisbon reform: Dynamics of parliamentarization in EU law' (2012) 49 *Common Market Law Review* 924. Contra, see Alexander Türk, 'Lawmaking after Lisbon in Andrea Biondi, Piet Eeckhout and Stefanie Ripley (eds), *EU Law after Lisbon* (Oxford, OUP, 2012) 66; Vihar Georgiev, 'Too much executive power? Delegated law-making and comitology in perspective' (2013) 20 *Journal of European Public Policy* 536.

[6] See eg Carl Fredrik Bergström, *Comitology – Delegation of Powers in the European Union and the Committee System* (Oxford, OUP, 2005) 355.

[7] Koen Lenaerts and Marlies Desomer, 'Towards a Hierarchy of Legal Acts in the European Union? Simplification of Legal Instruments and Procedures' (2005) 11 *European Law Journal* 765–66; René Barents, 'De post-Lissabon-rechtspraak over het institutioneel evenwicht' (2019) 67 *Tijdschrift voor Europees en economisch recht* 338.

[8] In past IGCs, suggestions had been made to introduce such a hierarchy. See Carlos-Manuel Alves, 'La hiérarchie du droit dérivé unilatéral à la lumière de la Constitution européenne: révolution juridique ou sacrifice au nominalisme?' (2004) 40 *Cahiers de droit européen* 695–97.

[9] Given its peculiar position, the CFSP largely falls outside the scope of the present enquiry. On the CFSP from a constitutional perspective, see Graham Butler, *Constitutional Law of the EU's Common Foreign and Security Policy* (Oxford, Hart Publishing, 2019).

[10] See Art 218(5)–(6) TFEU.

pursuant to a legislative procedure, they cannot be legislative acts.[11] However, neither are they delegated acts or implementing acts since they are adopted based directly on the Treaties. Similarly, the decisions which the Council adopts pursuant to Article 218(9) TFEU to establish the positions to be adopted on the EU's behalf in an international forum are executive acts falling outside the framework of Articles 290–291 TFEU.[12]

Secondly, there are a significant number of legal bases in the Treaties that confer a competence to adopt acts that might appear legislative in a material sense, but since those legal bases do not qualify the procedure which they prescribe as being legislative in nature, these acts cannot be considered legislative in the sense of Article 289 TFEU.[13] Instead, these legal bases give expression to an autonomous executive competence conferred on the (European) Council, Commission or ECB.[14] In total there are around 70 legal bases conferring autonomous executive powers. In a sense these are the remnants of these institutions' original competences from the time that the notion of 'legislation' was alien to E(E)C primary law and there was only the distinction between 'basic instruments' based directly on the Treaty and the measures implementing these basic instruments (see below section 3.II). While the Treaty of Lisbon introduced the notion of legislation, not all legal bases that allow for the adoption of generally applicable acts prescribe a (special or the ordinary) legislative procedure for their adoption. This is a feature which the Lisbon Treaty took over from the Constitutional Treaty (see section 3.III.C). As Otto notes, this 'leftover' group is incredibly diverse – he identifies more than 30 different procedural constellations[15] – and substantively

[11] As noted in section 4.I.A, the suggestion of the General Court and of AG Wathelet in the *Front Polisario* cases to treat decisions concluding international agreements as legislative acts was effectively overruled by the Court, albeit not in the actual appeal in that case; see Michał Krajewski, *Relative authority of judicial and extra-judicial review* (Oxford, Hart Publishing, 2021) 149.

[12] The decisions which the Council adopts pursuant to this legal basis are not subject to the same material limits as those applicable to the delegated and implementing acts. In *COTIF I*, Germany argued that the Council could thereby undermine the legislative prerogatives of the European Parliament, but the Court did not engage with this argument. See Case C-600/14, *Germany v Council*, ECLI:EU:C:2017:935 [70]–[71].

[13] See Joined Cases C-643/15 and C-647/15, *Slovakia & Hungary v Council*, ECLI:EU:C:2017:631 [62]–[64].

[14] The following draws on Otto's work. He identified the following legal bases conferring an autonomous executive power which the institution concerned exercises wholly on its own: for the Commission, Arts 44(2), 45(3)d, 105(2), 105(3), 106(3), 108(2), 108(4), 114(6) and 143(3) TFEU; for the Council, Arts 143(2), 143(3), 243, 337 (through qualified majority voting (QMV)) and 342 (through unanimity) TFEU; for the ECB, Arts 132(1) first indent, 132(1) second indent TFEU; for the European Council, Arts 236(a) and 236(b) TFEU. Other legal bases provide that the Council will decide by QMV following a proposal by the Commission: Arts 31, 43(3), 75(2), 122(1), 126(6), 126(9), 126(12), 213 and 300(5) second sentence TFEU; that the Council will decide with unanimity following a Commission proposal, see Art 203 first sentence TFEU; that the Commission or Council (with unanimity) decide based on a request by a Member State, see Arts 65(4) and 108(2) TFEU; that the Council decides (with unanimity) on a proposal from the Court, see Art 252(1) second sentence TFEU, or with QMV on a proposal from the President of the Court, see Art 252(2) first and second sentences TFEU; that the Council will decide with QMV after consulting the Parliament, see Arts 150(1) and 160(1) TFEU; that the Council decides with simple majority after consulting the Commission, see Art 242 TFEU; that the Commission may act on its own initiative or at the request of a Member State, after hearing that Member State, see Arts 95(4) and 96(2) TFEU. Still other legal bases provide for autonomous executive acts, prescribing procedures involving more than two actors. Thus, the following legal bases prescribe that the Council acts through QMV pursuant to a Commission proposal and after consulting the Parliament: Arts 78(3), 103(1) 109, 125(2), 126(14)3 and 349(1) first sentence TFEU. Others prescribe the same procedure but only foresee that the Parliament is informed, rather than consulted, see Arts 122(2) and 126(11) TFEU. Under Art 352(1) first sentence TFEU, the Council acts through unanimity pursuant to a proposal by the Commission and subject to the consent of the Parliament. One specific legal basis prescribes that the Council acts through QMV pursuant to a Commission proposal but that the Parliament may object and veto the act, see Art 315(2) TFEU. For a full overview, see Annex I.

[15] See Nicholas Otto, *Die Vielfalt unionaler Rechtsetzungsverfahren: Eine verfassungs- und verfahrenstheoretische Rekonstruktion der Funktions- und Organisationslogiken des Rechtsetzungsverfahrensrechts der Europäischen Union* (Tübingen, Mohr Siebeck, 2022) 112.

autonomous executive powers are used to take decisions ranging from the appointment of EU officials to developing substantive EU policy (such as competition policy).

Bergström noted that these types of autonomous executive acts were largely absent from the original draft Constitutional Treaty and were added in the 2004 Intergovernmental Conference (IGC),[16] but it should be noted that the Draft Constitution (as sent to the IGC) already contained more than 30 legal bases allowing the Council or Commission to adopt 'European regulations or decisions'.[17] Similarly to the special legislative procedure, the precise procedure through which these autonomous executive competences are exercised is determined ad hoc in each legal basis. In terms of roles played by the institutions, some of these procedures may be completely identical to a special legislative procedure.[18] However, legal (and practical) differences still remain, since the requirements prescribed for legislative decision-making will not apply for autonomous executive acts.[19] As a result, proposals by the Commission need not be sent to national parliaments pursuant to Protocol No 1;[20] the national parliaments' subsidiarity scrutiny pursuant to Protocol No 2 is not applicable;[21] the deliberations in the Council are not public;[22] and the balance between the confidentiality and transparency of the decision-making procedure, when assessing requests for access to documents, will tilt more in favour of the former.[23] In addition, the qualification of these acts may also have repercussions for the jurisdiction of the European Ombudsman. The latter has accepted that she can only review *administrative* acts for instances of maladministration.[24] In the case of a delegated act, she accepted that in so far as the Commission's act was (implicitly) confirmed by the legislators this constituted an act of quasi-legislative nature which also fell outside her mandate.[25] A fortiori all acts that are formally legislative in nature would fall outside her mandate, but for the autonomous executive acts, it could mean that the Ombudsman would have to verify in every instance whether she is competent to review their content. These significant differences between legislative and autonomous executive acts become especially critical for the (admittedly limited number of) Treaty Articles that provide two alternative legal bases (one legislative, one executive) for the adoption of identical measures: Articles 203, 349, first paragraph; and 352(1) TFEU appear to leave the choice

[16] Carl Fredrik Bergström, *Comitology – Delegation of Powers in the European Union and the Committee System* (Oxford, OUP, 2005) 353–54.

[17] See Draft Treaty establishing a Constitution for Europe, OJ [2003] C 169/1. As Liisberg notes, very few members of the Convention seemed preoccupied with these numerous non-legislative legal bases. See Jonas Bering Liisberg, 'The EU Constitutional Treaty and its distinction between legislative and non-legislative acts – Oranges into apples?' Jean Monnet Working Paper 01/06, 22ff.

[18] Criticising this and noting that this suggests that some special legislative procedures should not be considered as genuine legislative (since the procedure is identical to a non-legislative procedure), see Türk, 'Lawmaking after (2012) 71.

[19] Stressing this, see Opinion of AG Bot in Joined cases C-643/15 and C-647/15, *Slovakia & Hungary v Council*, ECLI:EU:C:2017:618 [58]; Joined Cases C-643/15 and C-647/15, *Slovakia & Hungary v Council*, ECLI:EU:C:2017:631 [59].

[20] Article 2 of Protocol No 1 provides that draft legislative acts are forwarded to the national parliaments.

[21] Like Protocol No 1, the requirements imposed on the Commission and the *droit de regard* conferred on national parliaments pursuant to Protocol No 2 only applies to draft legislative acts.

[22] Article 16(8) TEU provides that 'The Council shall meet in public when it deliberates and votes on a draft legislative act. To this end, each Council meeting shall be divided into two parts, dealing respectively with deliberations on Union legislative acts and non-legislative activities'.

[23] See Case C-156/21, *Hungary v Parliament & Council*, ECLI:EU:C:2022:97 [58].

[24] Decision of the European Ombudsman in Case 417/2015/NF [24].

[25] ibid [35].

between legislative and autonomous action in the hands of the institutions (de facto the Council),[26] although in post-Lisbon practice all the acts relying on these legal bases were adopted pursuant to a special legislative procedure.[27]

To summarise, while the Lisbon Treaty's aim was to simplify the EU's functioning – and it indeed constituted a rationalisation of the acts through which the EU realises its objectives – the catalogue of acts in Articles 289–291 TFEU could never have presented a complete and accurate picture of the arsenal of EU acts.[28] Crucially, the Treaties do not contain any clue on how the autonomous executive powers of the (European) Council, Commission and ECB relate to and how they are functionally different (or not) from the legislative powers conferred on the EU.[29] That there is no clear logic in the distinction between both has been criticised,[30] with Türk noting that the differentiation simply 'seems to be driven by the desire of Member States to remove certain areas from the ambit of legislative acts'.[31] And the fact that this category was created at all in the Lisbon Treaty was deplored by De Witte as more than 'an aesthetic failing of the simplification effort'.[32] While that may be the case, the legal bases conferring autonomous executive powers are taken as a given for the purposes of the present enquiry since they are part of the Treaty framework and therefore also an integral part of the institutional balance which they Treaty authors intended to lay down.

III. The Distinction between Delegated and Implementing Acts: A Cursory Reading of the TFEU

Given their inclusion in the formal catalogue of acts (see section 2.I above) the distinction introduced by the Treaty of Lisbon between delegated and implementing acts in Articles 290

[26] This will de facto be the Council for the measures adopted pursuant to Arts 203 and 352 TFEU. These legal bases prescribe recourse to unanimity in the Council in any event. Since the Council can amend Commission proposals with unanimity (pursuant to Art 293(1) TFEU), there is no impediment to the Council changing a Commission proposal for a legislative act into an executive act. For proposals pursuant to Art 349 TFEU this is different since that legal basis prescribes QMV.

[27] See eg Council Decision 2021/1764 on the association of the Overseas Countries and Territories with the European Union including relations between the European Union on the one hand, and Greenland and the Kingdom of Denmark on the other, OJ [2021] L 355/6; Council Regulation 2020/1785 opening and providing for the administration of autonomous Union tariff quotas for imports of certain fishery products into the Canary Islands from 2021 to 2027, OJ [2020] L 403/1; Council Regulation 2022/555 amending Regulation (EC) No 168/2007 establishing a European Union Agency for Fundamental Rights, OJ [2022] L 108/1.

[28] Barents has qualified the resulting situation as 'disordered', see Barents, 'De post-Lissabon-rechtspraak over het institutioneel evenwicht' (2019) 336.

[29] Alexander Türk, *The concept of legislation in European community law: a comparative perspective* (Den Haag, Kluwer Law International, 2006) 231.

[30] Armin von Bogdandy, Felix Arndt and Jürgen Bast, 'Legal Instruments in European Union Law and their Reform: A Systematic Approach on an Empirical Basis' (2004) 23 *Yearbook of European Law* 135–36. Paolo Stancanelli, 'Le système décisionnel de l'Union' in Giuliano Amato, Hervé Bribosia and Bruno de Witte (eds), *Genèse et destinée de la constitution européenne: commentaire du traité établissant une Constitution pour l'Europe à la lumière des travaux préparatoires et perspectives d'avenir* (Bruxelles, Bruylant, 2007) 517–19.

[31] Türk, *The concept of legislation in European community law* (2006) 231. As critical so many years later, see Türk (n 5) 70–71.

[32] See Bruno de Witte, 'Legal Instruments and Law-Making in the Lisbon Treaty' in Stefan Griller and Jacques Ziller (eds), *The Lisbon Treaty: EU Constitutionalism without a Constitutional Treaty* (Wien, Springer, 2008) 100–02. See also Paolo Stancanelli, 'Le système décisionnel de l'Union' in Amato, Bribosia and de Witte, *Genèse et destinée de la constitution européenne* (2007) 517–19.

and 291 TFEU is one of the Treaty's most visible changes in the area of EU decision-making. In essence, the novelty boiled down to the introduction of the delegated act and its carving-out of the larger notion of implementation. That latter notion indeed already existed in EU law prior to the entry into force of the Lisbon Treaty, but it was conceived broadly and was simply juxtaposed with 'the measures directly based on the Treaty itself',[33] ie 'basic acts or instruments'.[34] The broad conceptualisation meant that pre-Lisbon implementing acts could apply, implement or adapt those 'basic instruments'.[35] By prescribing that delegated acts are to be used to adapt (ie supplement or amend) legislative acts, the notion of implementation concomitantly shrunk. While post-Lisbon delegated and implementing acts thus correspond to the pre-Lisbon implementing acts, the same cannot be said of post-Lisbon legislative acts and the pre-Lisbon basic acts. After all, some (pre-Lisbon) basic acts are now (post-Lisbon) autonomous executive acts. The *rationalisation* brought by the Lisbon Treaty therefore did not equate with a *simplification*, as Figure 2.1 shows.

Figure 2.1 Rationalisation of acts under the Lisbon Treaty

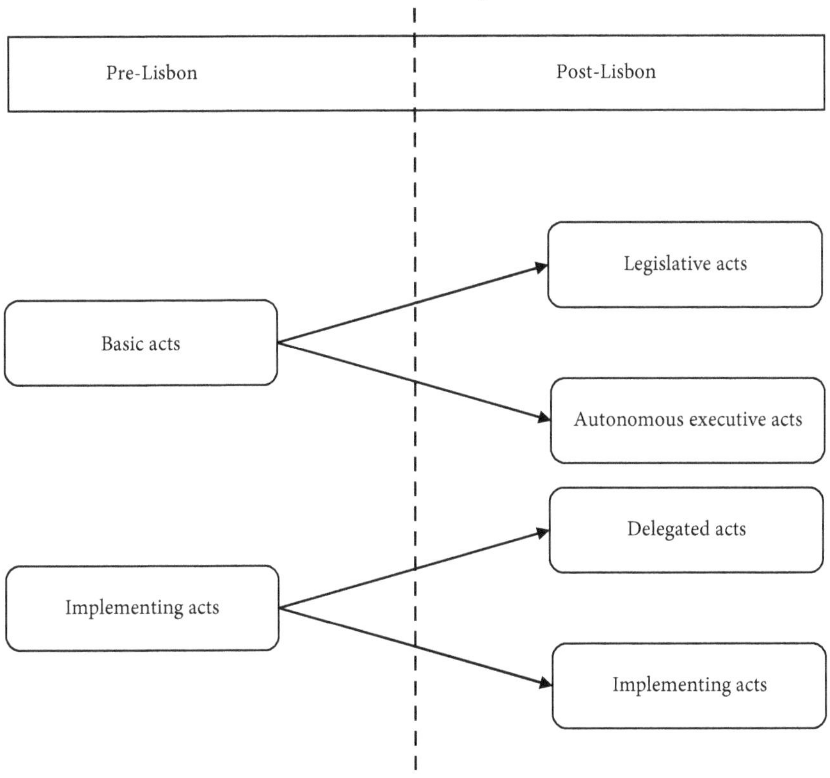

[33] Case 25/70, *Köster*, ECLI:EU:C:1970:115 [6].

[34] Noting that the Court typically did not refer to these instruments as legislative in nature, see Türk (n 29) 2–3.

[35] See Art 2 of Council Decision 1999/468 laying down the procedures for the exercise of implementing powers conferred on the Commission, OJ [1999] L 184/23.

In a way, this need not surprise. Behind the laudable ideal of simplification[36] there are clear vertical (EU-Member States) and horizontal (inter-institutional) power struggles which will frustrate any simplification exercise.

Before looking in detail into how the EU institutions (including the Court) have interpreted and applied the new Treaty provisions, and how this affects the inter-institutional relations and notably the position of the Parliament, it is useful to present the key features of Articles 290 and 291 TFEU and to briefly qualify what is at stake when we are referring to executive rulemaking. The two figures below are drawn from data available on Eur-Lex,[37] and show the rough proportions in terms of quantitative importance of the Commission's implementing acts and delegated acts, the Council's autonomous executive and implementing acts and the formal legislative acts (adopted under the ordinary and special legislative procedures).

Figure 2.2 Number of legislative and executive acts adopted

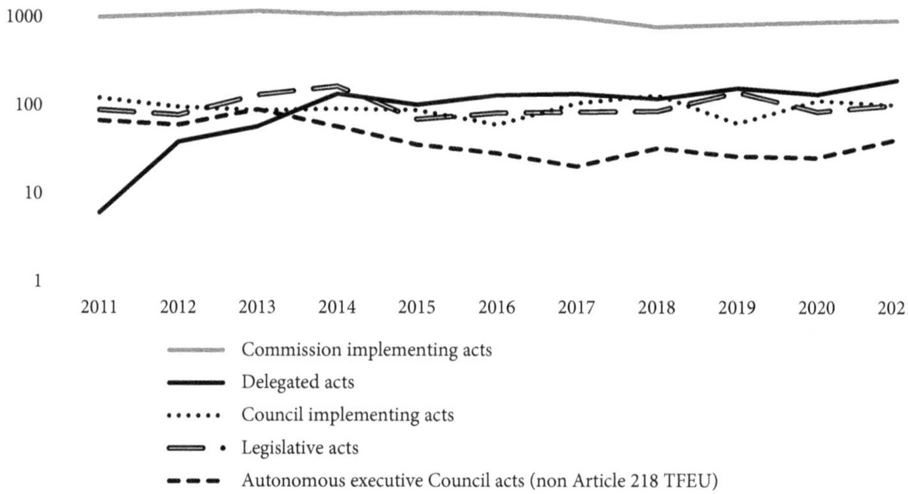

Figure 2.2 (which uses a logarithmic scale on the Y axis) immediately makes clear that the greatest normative output of the EU institutions is not through formal legislative acts but through Commission implementing acts (discussed in chapter 6), of which it adopts many more than its delegated acts (discussed in chapter 5); and that the Council retains an important autonomous executive function (discussed in section 4.I) and is still conferred numerous implementing powers in secondary legislation (discussed in section 6.III).

[36] On the Lisbon Treaty's simplification objective, going back to the Convention and the Laeken Declaration, see de Witte, 'Legal Instruments and Law-Making' (2008) 84–86.

[37] For this reason, the figures are just provided to give a sense of proportion. In line with Art 297 TFEU, not all binding acts are published on Eur-Lex, which partially explains the discrepancy between the Commission implementing acts available on Eur-Lex and those reported by the Commission in its annual comitology reports (see Figure 6.3 in section 6.V.C). In addition, there are the inevitable coding errors on Eur-Lex where acts are assigned to wrong categories.

As noted in section 2.II, the Council, Commission and ECB may exercise an autonomous executive function. In so far as they relate to monetary policy and banking supervision (ECB) or competition policy (Council and Commission) they will not be the focus of this horizontal enquiry given their intimate connection with only one specific policy field. Also the autonomous executive powers of the Council and Commission in pursuing the EU's external relations fall outside the scope of the present enquiry, given the distinct character of the legal framework governing the EU's external relations. Still, and to get a sense of proportion, it may be noted that quantitatively, the Council's autonomous executive acts adopted pursuant to the legal bases contained in Article 218 TFEU are typically more numerous than those adopted pursuant to other Treaty legal bases (see Figure 2.3).

Figure 2.3 Council autonomous executive acts

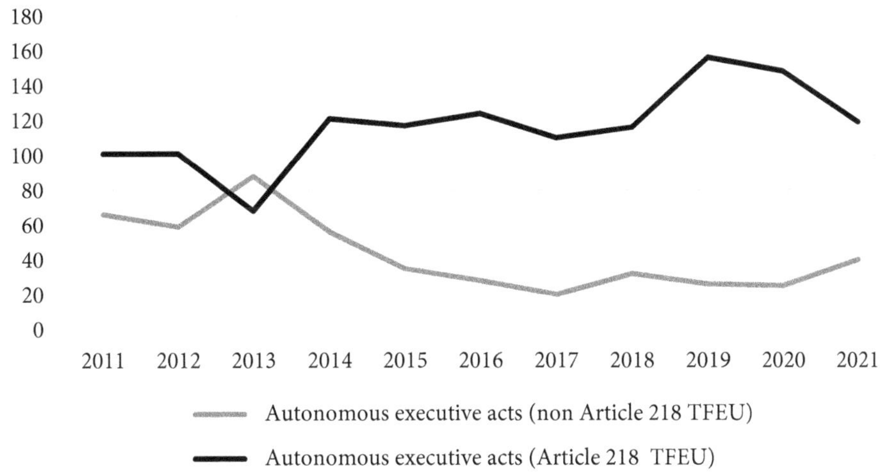

Quantitatively, the Council's autonomous executive function is for the greatest part an external relations' power. The peak for 'internal' autonomous executive acts noticeable in 2013 is then explained by the accession of Croatia to the EU, and the special empowerment which the Council receives under the acts of accession of new Member States to update the existing acquis to accommodate the entry of a new EU member.[38] Having illustrated the (quantitative) importance of executive rulemaking, let us now look at the key features of the delegated and implementing acts introduced by the Lisbon Treaty.

A. Key Features of Article 290 TFEU

> Article 290
>
> 1. A legislative act may delegate to the Commission the power to adopt non-legislative acts of general application to supplement or amend certain non-essential elements of the legislative act.

[38] See Art 50 of the Act of Accession of Croatia, OJ [2013] L 112/21.

> The objectives, content, scope and duration of the delegation of power shall be explicitly defined in the legislative acts. The essential elements of an area shall be reserved for the legislative act and accordingly shall not be the subject of a delegation of power.
>
> 2. Legislative acts shall explicitly lay down the conditions to which the delegation is subject; these conditions may be as follows:
>
> (a) the European Parliament or the Council may decide to revoke the delegation;
> (b) the delegated act may enter into force only if no objection has been expressed by the European Parliament or the Council within a period set by the legislative act.
>
> For the purposes of (a) and (b), the European Parliament shall act by a majority of its component members, and the Council by a qualified majority.
>
> 3. The adjective 'delegated' shall be inserted in the title of delegated acts.

Article 290(1) TFEU provides that a legislative act *may* delegate a power to the Commission to adopt non-legislative acts of general application (ie material legislation) which amends or supplements the legislative act. However, only the non-essential elements may thus be amended or supplemented, and the legislator must be explicit on the objectives, content, scope and duration of the delegation. Unpacking the first paragraph of Article 290 TFEU, it should thus be stressed that there is an option, but no requirement, for the legislator to delegate powers to the Commission; that delegated acts must always be of general (and not individual) application; that a delegated power may either amend or supplement its parent legislative act; that there is a non-delegation doctrine in that the legislator must itself lay down the essential elements and that a delegation must be explicitly circumscribed. The latter two requirements may be referred to as the essentiality and specificity requirements,[39] and while only the former is imposed on both the legislator and the Commission,[40] whereas textually the specificity requirement is only imposed on the legislator,[41] both requirements by necessity work in both ways: also the Commission is bound by the specificity requirement since any acts which it adopts pursuant to a delegated power are only lawful if they accord to the objectives, content, scope and duration of the delegation as defined by the legislator.[42]

In comparative perspective, Article 290(1) TFEU thus prescribes an essential elements doctrine that may also be found in some national legal systems although at the national level these typically result from jurisprudence rather than being prescribed by the constitution.[43] While Article 290(1) TFEU clearly reflects a hierarchic relationship between the EU legislator and the Commission, EU primary law in general reflects a relation between the legislator and the executive in a manner markedly different from national legal systems

[39] Daniel Kollmeyer, *Delegierte Rechtsetzung in der EU – Eine Analyse der Art. 290 und 291 AEUV* (Baden-Baden, Nomos, 2015) 259.

[40] Article 290(1) TFEU refers to a power (for the Commission) to amend or supplement non-essential elements and the essential elements being reserved to the legislature (resulting in a duty to lay down the essential elements).

[41] Article 290(1) TFEU only provides that objectives, content, scope and duration be defined in the legislative act.

[42] Merijn Chamon, 'Granting powers to EU decentralised agencies, three years following Short-selling' (2018) 18 *ERA Forum* 597–609.

[43] See eg the *Wesentlichkeitstheorie* in Germany, the essential elements doctrine in Belgium and in very diluted form the intelligible principle in the US. See German Federal Administrative Court, *Krankenversicherung* [2004] 121 BVerwGE 103; Belgian Council of State, 25 March 2020, *Covid 19*, Advice 67.142/AV; US Supreme Court, *Hampton & Co v US* [1928] 276 US 394.

such as the French one, where the realm of the legislator is exhaustively defined in Article 34 of the Constitution and a general autonomous executive power is laid down in Article 37 for 'matters other than those coming under the scope of formal legislation'. Under the EU Treaties no such subordinate relationship exists: the legislative and autonomous executive powers are laid down specifically for each matter, neither of both being the rule or exception.[44] Textually, Article 290(1) TFEU then very much resembles Article 80(1) of the German *Grundgesetz* (GG) and Article 76 of the Italian Constitution. The latter provides: 'The exercise of the legislative function may not be delegated to the Government unless principles and criteria have been established and then only for a limited time and for specified purposes'. The former inter alia provides that '[the government] may be authorised by a law to issue statutory instruments. The content, purpose and scope of the authority conferred shall be specified in the law'. Yet, unlike Article 80(1) GG, the possibility to subdelegate is not explicitly foreseen in Article 290 TFEU.

On the other hand, just like Article 80(2) GG, Article 290(2) TFEU continues by prescribing the control regime, requiring the legislator to exercise control.[45] It seemingly leaves a choice in this regard since the control regime *may* consist of a right of revocation of the (co-)legislator(s) and the requirement that delegated acts may only enter into force if there is no objection to the draft by the (co-)legislator(s). Finally, since all three binding instruments listed in Article 288 TFEU can be of legislative or non-legislative nature, Article 290(3) TFEU prescribes, for reasons of transparency, that delegated acts should also formally be qualified as such in their title.

B. Key Features of Article 291 TFEU

> Article 291
>
> 1. Member States shall adopt all measures of national law necessary to implement legally binding Union acts.
>
> 2. Where uniform conditions for implementing legally binding Union acts are needed, those acts shall confer implementing powers on the Commission, or, in duly justified specific cases and in the cases provided for in Articles 24 and 26 of the Treaty on European Union, on the Council.
>
> 3. For the purposes of paragraph 2, the European Parliament and the Council, acting by means of regulations in accordance with the ordinary legislative procedure, shall lay down in advance the rules and general principles concerning mechanisms for control by Member States of the Commission's exercise of implementing powers.
>
> 4. The word 'implementing' shall be inserted in the title of implementing acts.

Article 291(1) TFEU lays down the basic rule in the EU's executive federalism. Differently from Article 290 TFEU, which only relates to formal legislation, Article 291 TFEU concerns the implementation of all binding EU law. The fact that Member States are the default authorities to implement EU law has been qualified, in the literature, both as a

[44] See section 2.II.

[45] After all, Art 290(2) TFEU provides that '[l]egislative acts shall explicitly lay down the conditions to which the delegation is subject'.

Member State prerogative[46] and as an EU duty imposed on Member States.[47] The latter reading would stress that Article 291(1) TFEU was introduced by the Lisbon Treaty and is a (now) specific expression of the duty of sincere cooperation in Article 4(3) TEU (pre-Lisbon Article 10 EC). A subsidiarity-inspired federalist perspective supports the first view, however, since the EU should only involve itself in the implementation of EU law when it is shown that Member States cannot ensure a proper implementation thereof on their own. This is indeed what Article 291(2) TFEU hints at and which, together with Article 291(3) TFEU, is a further development of Article 202 EC. However, regardless of which of both interpretations is followed,[48] it should be clear that the Member States are an integral part of the system of implementation of EU law and that when the EU legislator wishes to see its legislation implemented it should (first) be done by the Member States and only in the alternative by the Commission (or Council).[49] To further compare how Article 291 TFEU constitute as a further development of Article 202 EC, it is useful to juxtapose these provisions, highlighting the different terms employed in the TFEU.

Table 2.1 Comparison of Article 202 EC and Article 291 TFEU

Article 202 EC	Article 291(2)–(3) TFEU
[T]he Council shall, in accordance with the provisions of this Treaty: ... confer on the Commission, in the acts which the Council adopts, powers for the implementation of the rules which the Council lays down. The Council may impose certain requirements in respect of the exercise of these powers. The Council may also reserve the right, in specific cases, to exercise directly implementing powers itself. The procedures referred to above must be consonant with principles and rules to be laid down in advance by the Council, acting unanimously on a proposal from the Commission and after obtaining the opinion of the European Parliament.	Where uniform conditions for implementing legally binding Union acts are needed, those [legally binding Union acts] shall confer implementing powers on the Commission, or, in duly justified specific cases and in the cases provided for in Articles 24 and 26 of the Treaty on European Union, on the Council. For the purposes of paragraph 2, the European Parliament and the Council, acting by means of regulations in accordance with the ordinary legislative procedure, shall lay down in advance the rules and general principles concerning mechanisms for control by Member States of the Commission's exercise of implementing powers.

[46] Jean-Paul Jacqué, 'L'éternel retour – Réflexion sur la comitologie' in G Vandersanden (ed), *Mélanges en hommage à Jean-Victor Louis* (Bruxelles, Editions de l'Université de Bruxelles, 2003) 214–16; Caunes, 'Et la fonction exécutive européenne créa l'administration à son image' (2007) 298; Michel Waelbroeck, 'The Emergent Doctrine of Community Pre-emption, Consent and Re-delegation' in Terrance Sandalow and Eric Stein (eds), *Courts and Free Markets: Perspectives from the United States and Europe*, Vol II (New York, Clarendon Press, 1982) 577; Zamira Xhaferri, 'Delegated Acts, Implementing Acts, and Institutional Balance Implications Post-Lisbon' (2013) 20 *Maastricht Journal of European and Comparative Law* 565.

[47] See Koen Lenaerts, Piet Van Nuffel and Tim Corthaut, *EU Constitutional Law* (Oxford, OUP, 2021) 512. Dubos sees Art 291(1) TFEU as a competence conferred on Member States by the EU. See Olivier Dubos, 'Objectif d'efficacité de l'exécution du droit de l'union européenne: la tectonique des compétences' in Eleftheria Neframi (ed), *Objectifs et compétences dans l'Union européenne* (Bruxelles, Bruylant, 2012) 293–314.

[48] Greiner even combines the two and refers to both an obligation and claim of the Member States to implement EU law; see Jakob Greiner, *Die Reform der Komitologie durch den Vertrag von Lissabon: Delegierte Rechtsetzung und Durchführungsrechtsetzung nach Art. 290 und Art. 291 AEUV* (Tübingen, Mohr Siebeck, 2018) 142.

[49] In contrast, Brandsma and Blom-Hansen note that they 'do not consider the member states alternative to the Commission as an agent of delegated rule-making'. Yet this finding results from the premise that they aim to 'study the more specific issue of delegation of tertiary regulation'. By defining their object of enquiry as

While purely textually it might seem significant that Article 202 EC only referred to Council acts, the Court of Justice (pre-Lisbon) had already clarified that this is not limited to acts adopted only by the Council.[50] The general reference to 'legally binding Union acts' in Article 291 TFEU was therefore welcome but not in itself a significant change. Potentially more important is the reference in Article 291(2) TFEU to the need for uniform conditions, since no such 'triggering condition' existed in Article 202 EC. Because the verb 'shall'[51] has remained, the Council (or legislator) arguably has no discretion anymore in conferring or not implementing powers: when the condition of 'uniform conditions' is met, a requirement to confer implementing powers is created.[52] This arguably strengthened the position of the Commission,[53] as did the change in language on the possibility for the Council to reserve implementing powers to itself. In addition to the general rule that the Common Foreign and Security Policy is implemented by the Council, the exception of Council implementation is now reserved to 'duly justified specific cases', rather than to 'specific cases'. Article 291(3) TFEU, differently from Article 202 EC, further prescribes that the comitology procedures shall be laid down in advance, whereas Article 202 EC provided that the Council *may* impose procedural requirements on the Commission. This suggests that there is no choice for the legislator (Council): control must be ensured *ex ante*,[54] and it is the Member States controlling the Commission. Also this was significant since it further undermined the logic of the pre-Lisbon comitology procedures whereby a committee could take a file out of the hands of the Commission and entrust it to the Council (see section 3.I).[55] Article 291(3) TFEU, finally, also prescribes that the instrument creating the framework is now established by Parliament and Council under the ordinary legislative procedure rather than by the Council on its own, following an opinion from the Parliament.

Like Article 202 EC, however, Article 291(3) TFEU leaves open the exact status of the horizontal comitology instrument: it is to be adopted pursuant to the ordinary legislative

'tertiary regulation', which can only be adopted by the EU institutions, it logically follows that whatever Member States do cannot be considered as an alternative. See Gijs Jan Brandsma and Jens Blom-Hansen, *Controlling the EU executive? The politics of delegation in the European Union* (Oxford, OUP, 2017) 26–27.

[50] See Case C-259/95, *Parliament v Council*, ECLI:EU:C:1997:454 [26], which dealt with a power of the Council to update EU legislation (adopted by Parliament and Council) in light of the fourth enlargement and which the Court transposed, without any further reasoning also to Art 202 EC in Case C-378/00, *Commission v Parliament & Council*, ECLI:EU:C:2003:42 [40].

[51] This is the same in other language versions of the Treaties, which, using the present indicative, prescribed in Art 202 EC that the Council *verleent, überträgt, conferisce, confère* and in Art 291 TFEU that the implementing powers, *worden … toegekend, werden … übertragen* and that binding acts *conferiscono, confèrent* implementing powers.

[52] Blumann argued that this obligation was already created under the Single European Act when the legal basis for comitology, beforehand implicit under Art 155 EEC was created in Art 145 EEC (later Art 202 EC). See Claude Blumann, 'La Comitologie: l'exercice de la fonction exécutive dans la Communauté européenne' in C Engel and W Wessels (eds), *From Luxembourg to Maastricht: institutional change in the European Community after the Single European Act* (Bonn, Europa Union, 1992) 100. But clearly the Lisbon Treaty enhanced this obligation by objectifying the triggering condition. See also Claude Blumann, 'Un nouveau départ pour la Comitologie. Le règlement n° 182/2011 du 16 février 2011' (2011) 47 *Cahiers de droit européen* 25.

[53] According to Jacqué and Kortenberg, executive power at EU level lay with the Council, not the Commission. See Jacqué, 'L'éternel retour' (2003) 212–13; Helmut Kortenberg, 'Comitologie: le retour' (1998) 34 *Revue trimestrielle de droit européen* 3 317.

[54] In this sense, see also Caunes (n 2) 328–29.

[55] According to Kortenberg, the possibility for the Council to reclaim implementing powers (following the intervention of a comitology committee) was essential to ensure the unity in EU law. Kortenberg, 'Comitologie' (1998) 320.

procedure, but how does it relate to other basic acts adopted pursuant to the Treaties? Arguably it is of equal rank to other legislative acts, but what would be the purpose of a horizontal comitology framework (adopted in the form of a legislative act) if the EU legislator would not be bound by that framework when it takes the decision to confer implementing powers on the Commission? Pre-Lisbon, the Parliament had argued against the comitology decision as being an act of 'organic law',[56] which was understandable because it would have meant that the Parliament would be bound by an act which the Council had adopted on its own. Now that the Comitology Regulation is adopted through the ordinary legislative procedure, that political consideration has changed. Lastly, analogously to Article 290(3) TFEU, Article 291(4) TFEU requires implementing acts to be qualified as such in their titles.

IV. Parliamentary Control Over Post-Lisbon Executive Acts

That the role of the European Parliament (and that of national parliaments) in the EU legislative process was strengthened, was a widely welcomed feature of the Lisbon Treaty,[57] although, of course, the ordinary legislative procedure is still not the *default* legislative procedure let alone the *only* legislative procedure. The question of the parliaments' role in the adoption and/or scrutiny of the new executive acts was less commented. A first point to be made here is that, unlike in the legislative process, national parliaments are formally not involved in the adoption of autonomous executive, delegated and implementing acts.[58] Indeed, under Article 12 TEU and the Protocol on the role of national Parliaments in the European Union, national parliaments only have a formal role following the proposition of draft legislative acts which the Protocol defines as proposals or any other document for the adoption of legislative acts.[59] Given the Treaties' formal definition of legislative acts in Article 289 TFEU this means that (typically) the Commission is not required to forward draft autonomous executive, delegated or implementing acts to national parliaments. The only exception here is the autonomous executive acts adopted pursuant to Article 352 TFEU, which in accordance with Article 352(2) TFEU are subjected to the national parliaments' subsidiarity review. Parliamentary scrutiny over or involvement in the adoption of EU executive acts therefore is a matter for the European Parliament. Any role played by national parliaments will be indirect, ie depending on the 'particular constitutional organisation and practice of each Member State',[60] national parliaments may be involved by scrutinising, at national level, their national governments that are represented in the Council, comitology committees and working parties.

In terms of scrutiny or involvement of the European Parliament a first distinction has to be made between the autonomous executive acts and delegated acts on the one hand and

[56] See Opinion of AG Geelhoed in Case C-378/00, *Commission v Parliament & Council*, EU:C:2002:561 [39]. The AG, however, sided with the Commission and found the comitology decision to be organic in nature (see [82]). The Court did not take an explicit position on the matter. See also section 6.V.B.i below.

[57] European Parliament resolution on the Treaty establishing a Constitution for Europe, OJ [2005] C247E/88; Jean-Claude Piris, *The Lisbon Treaty – A Legal and Political Analysis* (Cambridge, CUP, 2010) 118–22.

[58] On the role of national parliaments in EU decision-making generally, see Katarzyna Granat, *The Principle of Subsidiarity and its Enforcement in the EU Legal Order – The Role of National Parliaments in the Early Warning System* (Oxford, Hart Publishing, 2018).

[59] See Art 2 of Protocol No 2; see also Art 3 of Protocol No 3.

[60] See the Preamble to Protocol No 2.

the implementing acts on the other hand. For the former, the control regime is laid down in the Treaties themselves, while for the implementing acts, the Parliament's involvement or control depends on the horizontal instrument, ie the Comitology Regulation, adopted pursuant to Article 291(3) TFEU. Next to the instrument in which the control regime is laid down (and its resulting place in the hierarchy of norms), a distinction can be made between the nature of the control regime(s). In this regard, the control regimes in place for delegated and implementing acts are both horizontal in nature: one coherent norm sets out the mechanisms of control and scrutiny that apply whenever a delegated or implementing act is adopted. For the former, this is to be found in Article 290(2) TFEU, for the latter it is again to be found in the Comitology Regulation. This contrasts with the control regimes applicable to the adoption of autonomous executive acts. These are determined ad hoc, by each specific legal basis granting an autonomous executive power. Focusing purely on the European Parliament,[61] some legal bases provide no role for it at all,[62] while other legal bases prescribe the Parliament is merely informed,[63] or that is consulted,[64] that it may veto a decision[65] or, finally, that its consent is required.[66]

Table 2.2 Control regimes over executive rulemaking

Executive power	Control regime laid down in	Control regime established in
Autonomous executive acts	Primary law	Ad hoc manner
Delegated acts	Primary law	Horizontal manner
Implementing acts	Secondary law	Horizontal manner

As noted above (see section 2.II) the idea behind the autonomous executive powers goes back to the Convention where it was assumed that some decisions are not really legislative in nature and therefore should not be adopted in the form of laws or framework laws. The fact that for some of these executive acts, parliamentary consultation or even consent is prescribed does reveal, however, that the need for greater democratic legitimacy of such acts was somehow accepted. Yet, a perusal of the relevant legal bases does not indicate a very clear philosophy behind the Parliament's (non-)involvement. Evidently the decision to appoint certain members to advisory bodies can be qualified as executive and arguably does not require parliamentary involvement,[67] and the same goes for derogations or exemptions granted to Member States.[68] But if the dividing line between autonomous executive legal bases and legislative legal bases is that only the latter allow for measures that imply basic policy choices (see section 4.II), it is firstly not entirely clear why measures such as

[61] In total there are more than 30 different procedures through which autonomous executive acts can be adopted since both the author of the act may vary ((European) Council, Commission, ECB) as well as the institutions or bodies being involved in a consultative capacity (Parliament, ECB, Court of Auditors, Committee of the Regions, European Economic and Social Committee, European Economic and Financial Committee) and whether or not the act must be adopted based on a Commission proposal.

[62] See the legal bases listed in rows 1, 2, 3, 4, 5, 6, 7, 8, 9, 10, 11, 13, 14, 20, 22 and 31 in Annex I.

[63] See the legal bases listed in rows 16, 21 and 25 in Annex I.

[64] See the legal bases listed in rows 12, 15, 19, 23, 24, 26, 27, 29, 30 and 32 in Annex I.

[65] See the legal basis listed in row 18 in Annex I.

[66] See the legal bases listed in rows 17, 28, 33 and 34 in Annex I.

[67] See eg Arts 302 and 305 TFEU.

[68] See eg Arts 65, 92 and 108(2) TFEU.

the common customs tariffs, the Basic Competition Regulation and the definition of additional 'other particularly serious crimes' on which the EU can legislate, are adopted through executive acts; and secondly why for the first there is no involvement of the Parliament at all, whereas for the second the Parliament needs to be consulted, while the third requires Parliament's consent.

This contrasts with the horizontal control regimes that apply to the delegated and implementing acts. Under Article 290 TFEU the Parliament's control may (at least) exist in two forms: it may, independently from the Council, block any draft delegated act by the Commission or it may, again independently from the Council, revoke a delegation granted to the Commission.[69] As we will see, an open question is whether the legislator, when delegating powers, may prescribe further control requirements than the powers to object or revoke. At least the text of Article 290 TFEU itself seems to suggest that further requirements are indeed possible.[70] This will be explored in section 5.IV.B.

Differently from Article 202 EC, Article 291(3) TFEU prescribes that the horizontal comitology instrument is to be adopted pursuant to the co-decision procedure. This greatly strengthened the position of the Parliament, which is inter alia illustrated by the fact that post-Lisbon the Parliament was successfully ensured that the implementation of the Common Commercial Policy (which pre-Lisbon did not come under the horizontal comitology regime) was subjected to the standard comitology rules.[71] While Article 291(3) TFEU refers to the 'mechanisms for control by Member States', the Comitology Regulation[72] also provides for a control power by the Parliament and Council. Its Article 11 creates a *droit de regard* for both institutions, allowing them to signal to the Commission that a draft implementing act which the Commission intends to adopt, to implement a legislative act adopted pursuant to the ordinary legislative procedure, exceeds the limits to the Commission's power. This in essence replicates a power which the Parliament already held under Article 8 of the second comitology decision.[73] How it has been relied upon by the Parliament will be discussed in section 6.V.D. With the presentation of the current Treaty law out of the way, the enquiry can now move to the origins of comitology.

[69] Of course, this only applies in so far as the basic legislative act granting a delegated power to the Commission has been adopted pursuant to the ordinary legislative procedure. See Bart Driessen, 'Delegated legislation after the Treaty of Lisbon: an analysis of Article 290 TFEU' (2010) 35 *European Law Review* 843. As discussed in section 5.IV, the actor exercising the control depends on the actors involved in the adoption of the legislative act. In contrast, no legislative act exists (yet) whereby only the Parliament may control the Commission, since the legal bases prescribing a special legislative procedure in which the Parliament adopts the legislative act are limited and deal with the Parliament's internal functioning or the Ombudsman; see Arts 223(2), 226 and 228(4) TFEU.

[70] This is also the position of the Parliament; see Resolution of 5 May 2010 on the power of legislative delegation, OJ [2011] C 81E/6, point 3. *Contra*, see the Council Legal Service Opinion on the Application of Arts 290 (delegated acts) and 291 (implementing acts) TFEU, 11 April 2011, 8970/11, point 20. See also Michael Dougan, 'The Convention's draft Constitutional Treaty: bringing Europe closer to its lawyers?' (2003) 28 *European Law Review* 785–86. An argument in favour of the control mechanisms in Art 290 TFEU constituting an exhaustive list may be found in the *travaux préparatoires* of the constitutional treaty. During the Convention an additional control mechanism had been suggested but not retained. See the Presidency's 'Projet d'articles 24 à 33 du Traité constitutionnel', 26/02/2003, CONV 571/03 7.

[71] For a discussion, see Jacques Bourgeois and Merijn Chamon, 'The Integration of EU Trade Defence in the Horizontal Comitology Regime' in Michael Hahn and Guillaume Van der Loo (eds), *Law and Practice of the Common Commercial Policy – The first 10 years after the Treaty of Lisbon* (Leiden, Brill, 2020) 512–30.

[72] Regulation 182/2011 of the European Parliament and of the Council laying down the rules and general principles concerning mechanisms for control by Member States of the Commission's exercise of implementing powers, OJ [2011] L 55/13.

[73] See Council Decision 1999/468 laying down the procedures for the exercise of implementing powers conferred on the Commission, OJ [1999] L 184/23.

3

The Road Leading Up to the Lisbon Treaty

Since the history of comitology has already been amply discussed and analysed elsewhere,[1] no extensive historical discussion will be presented here. Still, this chapter will sketch the origins and major phases in the development of comitology since these are key in order to properly understand both the provisional culmination, in the Lisbon Treaty, of the coming of age of comitology and the significance of the post-Lisbon constitutional modifications discussed in chapters four to six.

I. Comitology's Origins and Original Sin

While the origins of comitology are often traced to the Common Agricultural Policy (CAP), the very first comitology committee, in terms of function, was in fact established in the framework of the EEC's social policy. Article 27 of Regulation No 9 regarding the European social fund instituted the committee of the European social fund, which, according to Article 29 had to be consulted inter alia for all implementing measures necessary for the application of the Regulation.[2] Admittedly, the committee was not yet a traditional comitology committee in terms of composition, since it included not only representatives of the Member States but also representatives of the social partners. The first comitology committee in terms of both function and composition can then indeed be traced back to the CAP, notably Regulation No 19 on the common market organisation in cereals.[3] Differently from Regulation No 9, it did not prescribe a mere advisory procedure but instead incarnated what would come to be known as the management procedure: the Commission could adopt its draft measures regardless of whether the opinion of the committee (adopted with qualified majority voting; QMV) was positive or negative, but in case of a negative opinion the file could be taken over by the Council. While a management

[1] See inter alia Carl Fredrik Bergström, *Comitology – Delegation of Powers in the European Union and the Committee System* (Oxford, OUP, 2005) 38–320; Gijs Jan Brandsma and Jens Blom-Hansen, *Controlling the EU executive? The politics of delegation in the European Union* (Oxford, OUP, 2017) 39–54; Daniela Corona, 'The Adoption of Secondary Legislation through Comitology in the EU: Some Reflections on the Regulation (EU) 182/2011 in Comparison with the Pre-Lisbon Reform' (2014) 2 *The Theory and Practice of Legislation* 89–97.

[2] See Règlement No 9 du Conseil concernant le Fonds social européen, JO [1960] 1189/60.

[3] See Règlement No 19 du Conseil portant établissement graduel d'une organisation commune des marchés dans le secteur des céréales, JO [1962] 933/62.

procedure allows for more control by the Member States and Council (compared to the advisory procedure), it still left the Commission with a lot of freedom since it required a double qualified majority to overrule the Commission: once in the committee to disagree with a draft, and once in the Council to agree on an alternative measure.[4] This mechanism to implement the CAP, ie procedures hence to be known as comitology, was then a compromise between the two extreme positions defended by The Netherlands on the one hand and France on the other. The former was notably in favour of a broad delegation of powers to the Commission whereas the latter had argued for the creation of independent agencies (in which Commission and Member State officials would be represented) to manage the CAP.[5]

What followed was a learning process for both the Member States and the Commission that did not always go smoothly. For example, in June 1967 the Commission submitted a proposal for a new directive creating a framework for the use of additives in animal feed which included an empowerment of the Commission to adopt implementing measures.[6] However, in the final Directive 70/524, the Council only retained those provisions which provided for Council implementing powers.[7] Part of the learning process was also the realisation that conferring implementing powers on the Commission, even if Member States might be wary of doing so, is often a matter of simple necessity. Indeed, the same Directive 70/524 was amended in 1973 by introducing provisions which ultimately did confer implementing powers on the Commission,[8] albeit not subject to the management procedure. Instead, a third type of committee was created. The Council decided to prescribe the regulatory procedure as it had done earlier in 1971 when Directive 64/432 on animal health issues relating to trade in cattle and pigs had been updated.[9] Originally, that Directive also did not provide for an authorisation for the Commission to adopt implementing measures. However, the 1971 amendment[10] added an Article 12 and prescribed that the Commission could only adopt its draft following a *positive* opinion in the committee. A negative or no opinion would result in the file being sent to the Council, which had three months to adopt an alternative decision. If it failed to do so the Commission could adopt its original draft unless the Council objected with simple majority.

[4] And as Piris noted, it did happen that even if four out of five Member States in the committee opposed a measure, the Commission went on and adopted it since the Council could not muster a QMV in favour of an alternative measure. See Jean-Claude Piris, 'La comitologie: Vers l'épilogue d'une longue saga?' in Gérard Cohen-Jonathan, Vlad Constantinesco, Valérie Michel, Jean-Claude Piris and Patrick Wachsmans (eds), *Chemins d'Europe: Mélanges en l'honneur de Jean Paul Jacqué* (Paris, Dalloz, 2010) 550, fn 9. The so-called 1975 aérosol declaration to which Piris refers is the Commission declaration in which it committed to try and not go against a dominant position within the committee.

[5] Jean-Victor Louis, *Les règlements de la Communauté économique européenne* (Bruxelles, Presses Universitaires de Bruxelles, 1969) 25.

[6] Commission européenne, Proposition d'une directive du Conseil concernant les additifs dans l'alimentation des animaux, JO [1967] 254/55.

[7] See Arts 6 and 7 of Council Directive 70/524 concerning additives in feeding-stuffs, OJ [1970] L 270/1.

[8] See the new Arts 16a and 16b introduced by Council Directive 73/103 amending the Directive of 23 November 1970 concerning additives in feeding-stuffs, OJ [1973] L 124/17.

[9] Council Directive 64/432 on animal health problems affecting intra-Community trade in bovine animals and swine, OJ [1964] 1977/64.

[10] See the new Art 12 introduced by Council Directive 71/285 amending the Directive of 26 June 1964 on animal health problems affecting intra-Community trade in bovine animals and swine, OJ [1971] L 179/1.

A simple juxtaposition of the management and regulatory procedure shows the dynamics at play between the Commission, Council and the Member States:

Table 3.1 Pre-Lisbon comitology procedures: management vs regulatory procedure

Management procedure	Regulatory procedure
'Draft adopted' is the default position since Committee must vote (QMV) against draft	'Draft not adopted' is the default position since Committee must vote (QMV) in favour of draft
Commission can adopt draft even if opinion is negative	Commission may only immediately adopt draft if opinion is positive
Council may only block Commission draft if it musters a QMV in favour of alternative measure	Council may block Commission draft if it musters simple majority against draft[11] Council may adopt alternative measures with QMV

The overview above is in itself already a simplification. After all, since there was no horizontal instrument governing the comitology procedures and committees, these being each time laid down ad hoc, *the* advisory, *the* management or *the* regulatory procedure did not exist, and instead secondary legislation was littered with many variations on the ideal types presented above. Still a common trait in all of them, and comitology's original sin, was the complete absence of the European Parliament, which did not have any role in the process.

In a way this was a logical corollary to the Parliament not having any significant role in the adoption of the basic instruments granting implementing powers. Still, while not significant, the Parliament typically did have an advisory role in the adoption of basic instruments and therefore did itself see the constitutional significance of the new comitology phenomenon, objecting strongly against it. Already in 1962 it opposed the intention of the Council 'de réduire le rôle de la Commission exécutive au bénéfice d'un nouvel organe administrative dont l'avis conforme serait nécessaire et déterminant'.[12] A key document in this respect was the 1967 Jozeau-Marigné report, in which the Legal Affairs Committee of the Parliament analysed many of the legal questions which we still face today. The report stressed that the Parliament should be attentive and should only allow implementing measures to deal with straightforward technical execution since otherwise the normative function undertaken can no longer be qualified as implementation and the measures in question should be laid down in the basic instrument for which the Parliament has an advisory role.[13] In its conclusion, the committee expressed its concern over a development of which it noted that it could not conclusively say that it was *legally* unsound, but which it at least found *politically* problematic.[14] Indeed, while the Treaties did not contain an explicit legal basis allowing

[11] This possibility did not exist in all regulatory procedures. If the Member States in the Council did not have this option, the *filet* variant was applicable (simple *safety net*, since the committee can stop the Commission). When the possibility to block a draft measure by simple majority, even if there was no qualified majority for an alternative measure, was applicable, this was qualified as the *contre-filet* variant (*double safety net*).

[12] See Résolution du Parlement européen sur les attributions de la Commission européenne dans la mise en œuvre de la politique agricole commune, JO [1962] 72/62.

[13] Jozeau-Marigné rapport nopens de communautaire procedures ter uitvoering van het afgeleide gemeenschapsrecht, PE Doc 115/68, para 19.

[14] ibid, para 45.

for the establishment of the comitology system, it could not be outright qualified as *contra legem*, and instead comitology developed *praeter legem*.[15]

II. Judicial Sanctioning of Comitology and the Commission's Broad Implementing Powers

Determining the constitutional legality of the comitology system is one of the instances which required an institutional balance assessment. Without being explicitly foreseen or allowed by the Treaties, an institutional practice had developed which had repercussions for the powers and prerogatives of the different EU institutions. The question of the constitutionality of this institutional practice was first addressed by the Court in the *Köster* case. The Commission had imposed the requirement of a deposit securing the export of agricultural products in the measures implementing Regulation No 19 (see section 3.I) although Regulation No 19 only explicitly foresaw a system of guarantees for imports (not exports) of agricultural products. When the Köster company saw its export guarantee of DM 2,400 withheld by the German market regulation office, it challenged this decision before the German administrative court. The latter then queried the Court of Justice both on the legality of the Commission imposing these substantive conditions through an implementing measure and on the procedural legality of the management procedure prescribed by Regulation No 19 for the adoption of the implementing measure.

On the question of the delegation and the management committee's involvement in the work of the Commission, the Court noted that this touched upon the fundamental question of the relationship between the Council and Commission.[16] In order to arrive at an answer, the Court therefore also placed this problem in its broader context. The Court noted that it was recognised in the Treaty itself (Article 155 EEC) and in the legal systems of all Member States that the 'legislator' cannot deal with all the details of regulation.[17]

What had to be regulated in Regulation No 19 were the main issues or the essential elements with regard to the common organisation of the market for cereals, whereby the Court in later case law clarified that the essential elements are those that 'give concrete shape to the fundamental guidelines of [EU] policy'.[18] Ancillary matters or non-essential elements on the other hand could be settled through implementing measures. With regard

[15] See also Atilla Vincze, 'Delegation versus Implementation: a deconstruction of the promise of the Lisbon Treaty' in Eljalill Tauschinsky and Wolfgang Weiß (eds), *The Legislative Choice Between Delegated and Implementing Acts in EU Law* (Cheltenham, Edward Elgar, 2018) 21.

[16] According to Advocate General Dutheillet de Lamothe, in the oral proceedings the impact of the management committee procedure on Parliament's prerogatives had also been extensively debated. See Opinion of AG Dutheillet de Lamothe in Cases 11/70, 25/70, 26/70 & 30/70, *International Handelsgesellschaft*, ECLI:EU:C:1970:100 1142.

[17] Case 25/70, *Köster*, ECLI:EU:C:1970:115 [6]. Vincze criticises the Court on this point, correctly observing that the different national legal systems have not given one single answer to the problem of delegation. See Atilla Vincze, 'Delegation versus Implementation: a deconstruction of the promise of the Lisbon Treaty' in Tauschinsky and Weiß, *The Legislative Choice* (2018) 35–36 Yet, when the EU legislator delegates powers it is not further (sub) delegating these after having received them from the Member States: the EU legal order is autonomous and its institutions are vested with their own original powers. These powers can be delegated, drawing inspiration from national legal systems, but under the conditions set specifically for the EU legal order.

[18] See Case C-240/90, *Germany v Commission*, ECLI:EU:C:1992:408 [37] (finding that a sanctions regime is not necessarily an essential element to be foreseen in the basic act).

to the latter, the Court in *Köster* noted that both the Council itself and the Commission could adopt these.[19] The Court held that Regulation No 19 indeed regulated all essential elements and that the Commission had therefore not acted outside its competence.[20] As regards the participation of the management committee, which, according to Köster, would endanger the independence of the Commission, the Court referred back to the provision in Article 155 EEC. Since this Article merely gave the Council the possibility to delegate to the Commission certain powers which it could also reserve to itself, the Council was also free to impose conditions on such an authorisation (*qui peut le plus, peut le moins*).[21] Furthermore, the Court emphasised that the management committee only had an advisory function and could never adopt measures in place of the Commission or the Council. The Court thus approved the comitology procedure as Article 155 EEC was sufficiently open to it.[22] Without explicitly referring to an institutional balance test, the Court's approach thus aligned well with the test set out in section 1.I.A. Article 155 EEC did not explicitly regulate the institutional development of comitology, requiring the Court to look beyond the literal text of the provision, putting it in context to devise its meaning. Subsequently, the Court checked whether the involvement of the management committee indeed kept the prerogatives of the Council and Commission intact.

Turning to the substantive question whether the Commission could 'extend', through implementing measures, the guarantee system to exports, where the basic act only prescribed this for imports, the Court noted that the basic act's enabling clause had to be read not on its own but in light of the scheme and objectives of the regime which the basic regulation had only partially fleshed out and of the regulation as a whole.[23] This meant that the Commission could adopt 'all provisions intended to supplement the partial measures laid down in [the basic regulation], according to the pattern of that [partially worked out regime]'.[24] In *Rey Soda* the Court further rejected the claim that the implementing competences of the Commission ought to be interpreted restrictively in order to safeguard the institutional balance between the Council and Commission. Instead, the Court ruled that it followed from the context of the Treaty and from practical necessities that 'the concept of implementation must be given a wide interpretation',[25] involving 'wide powers of discretion'.[26] In addition, the Court held that the limits to that implementing power are not to be derived from a literal reading of the enabling clause in the basic act but must be based on the latter's basic general objectives.[27] While it is sometimes cautioned that this broad interpretation of implementing powers in the field of the CAP cannot simply be transposed to other policy fields,[28] no coherent picture (creating a clear link between the

[19] Case 25/70, *Köster*, ECLI:EU:C:1970:115 [6].
[20] ibid [9].
[21] ibid.
[22] ibid.
[23] ibid [16].
[24] ibid [18].
[25] Case 23/75, *Rey Soda*, ECLI:EU:C:1975:142 [10].
[26] ibid [11].
[27] ibid [14].
[28] Alexander Türk, 'Lawmaking after Lisbon' in Andrea Biondi, Piet Eeckhout and Stefanie Ripley (eds), *EU Law after Lisbon* (Oxford, OUP, 2012) 78; Herwig Hofmann, 'Legislation, Delegation and Implementation under the Treaty of Lisbon: Typology Meets Reality' (2009) 15 *European Law Journal* 490–91.

scope of implementing powers and the policy field concerned) emerges from the Courts' pre-Lisbon case law.[29]

Following *Köster*, the idea that the basic acts (adopted directly on the Treaties) should merely define the essential elements of the matter to be regulated was sanctioned, as was the constitutionality of the management procedure. But what about the regulatory procedure which, after all, further weakened the position of the Commission? Again, in a case concerning the CAP, the Court ruled that also this procedure (even in its *contre-filet* variant)[30] posed no problem. Indeed, in *Tedeschi*, the Court noted that even if this procedure allows the Council to block a draft Commission measure without adopting an alternative measure itself, the Commission is not paralysed and is left with sufficient discretion to develop implementing measures.[31] Having been developed *praeter legem*, these series of rulings put comitology on sufficiently sound constitutional footing until primary law was updated with an explicit legal basis in the Single European Act (SEA).

III. From the Single European Act to the 2006 Revision of the Second Comitology Decision

The developments between the SEA and the entry into force of the Lisbon Treaty can be summarised as three concepts: codification; parliamentarisation; and increasing transparency.[32] Institutional practice became codified in both primary and secondary law, whereby the Parliament continuously pushed for greater influence in an area still dominated by the Council and Commission. Logically, Parliament thereby claimed to fight for greater transparency and democratic legitimacy of executive rulemaking. Likewise, the Commission tried to strengthen its executive position by proposing reforms inspired by simplification and rationalisation.[33] The second comitology decision in particular proved

[29] Hofmann (ibid) refers to the *Vreugdenhil* case, but that case presented the specific problem of the Commission using implementing powers conferred by a basic act related to the CAP to de facto amend a basic act of a different policy area where that second basic act did not confer any implementing powers on the Commission. The Court's finding that the 'wide interpretation of the Commission's powers can be accepted only in the specific framework of the rules on agricultural markets. It cannot be relied upon in support of provisions adopted by the Commission on the basis of its implementing powers in agricultural matters where the purpose of the provision in question lies outside that sphere but within a sector subject to an exhaustive set of rules laid down by the Council which, moreover, do not confer any implementing powers on the Commission', must thus be interpreted against this background and can arguably not be read as the Court suggesting that the Commission may be granted a broader implementing power in the CAP compared to other policy areas. See Case 22/88, *Vreugdenhil*, ECLI:EU:C:1989:277 [17]. Türk (ibid) refers to *Central-Import Münster*, but that is also a CAP case and the Court's emphasis on a 'sufficiently specific enabling clause' in that case might simply have resulted from how the referring (German) judge worded the request for a preliminary ruling. See Case 291/86, *Central-Import Münster*, ECLI:EU:C:1988:361 [8] and [13]. Türk also refers to the *Alliance for Natural Health* case, which indeed falls outside the field of the CAP, but in that case the Court questionably amalgamated the strict delegation requirements for private bodies imposed by *Meroni* with the more generous *Köster* requirements for delegations to the Commission. For a critique, see Merijn Chamon, *EU Agencies: Legal and Political Limits to the Transformation of the EU Administration* (Oxford, OUP, 2016) 222–24.

[30] See above n 11.

[31] Case 5/77, *Tedeschi*, ECLI:EU:C:1977:144 [55]–[56].

[32] For a more elaborate discussion of the historic developments up until the second comitology decision, see Georg Haibach, 'The History of Comitology' in Mads Andenas and Alexander Türk (eds), *Delegated Legislation and the Role of Committees in the EC* (The Hague, Kluwer Law International, 2000) 185–215.

[33] See notably the Commission's ideas for the EU's institutional architecture set out during the Convention and the informal Penelope proposal (drafted at the request of the Commission). These included suggestions to the effect

key in increasing the transparency of comitology as a whole and of the individual decision-making procedures by requiring information to be sent to the Parliament and by requiring the Commission to publish yearly reports on the functioning of the committees.[34]

A. Codification: The SEA and the First Comitology Decision

The SEA of 1986 was the first major revision of the 1957 Treaty of Rome. Its main purpose was to enable the realisation of the internal market, but as far as comitology is concerned, the SEA is also of great importance, since it enshrined the comitology system in the Treaties.[35] Article 145 EEC, which listed the powers of the Council, was amended through the addition of the following provision:

> [The Council shall] confer on the Commission, in the acts which the Council adopts, powers for the implementation of the rules which the Council lays down. The Council may impose certain requirements in respect of the exercise of these powers. The Council may also reserve the right, in specific cases, to exercise directly implementing powers itself. The procedures referred to above must be consonant with principles and rules to be laid down in advance by the Council, acting unanimously on a proposal from the Commission and after obtaining the Opinion of the European Parliament.[36]

Whereas Article 155 EEC (which was not amended by the Single European Act)[37] left the Council with complete freedom to decide whether or not to empower the Commission (as confirmed in *Köster*; see section 3.II), Article 145 EEC seemed to suggest that the Council *should* confer implementing powers on the Commission and could only exceptionally retain them itself.[38] The control function of comitology was however also anchored in the Treaties, as Article 145 EEC explicitly stated that conditions could be imposed on the Commission when it exercised its implementing powers. Finally, the possibility of rationalising comitology was created, since the Council was deprived of the freedom to devise such conditions

that only the Commission should implement EU law at EU level; that only the advisory comitology procedure should remain in place; that the Commission could adopt delegated legislation; etc. See European Commission, For the European Union: peace, freedom, solidarity – Communication of the Commission on the institutional architecture, COM(2002) 728 final; European Commission, Feasibility Study – Contribution to a Preliminary Draft Constitution of the European Union – Working Document, 4 December 2002. It has thus been noted that the Commission's continued efforts to simplify and democratise EU decision-making also served to cement its control of the executive function in the EU. See Karine Caunes, 'Et la fonction exécutive européenne créa l'administration à son image … Retour vers le futur de la comitologie' (2007) 43 *Revue trimestrielle de droit européen* 335, fn 177.

[34] See Giuseppe Ciavarini Azzi, 'Comitologie: le voile se lève …' (2001) *Revue des affaires européennes* 19–20.

[35] For a more in-depth discussion of the changes brought by the SEA, see Hans-Joachim Glaesner, 'The Single European Act: Attempt at an Appraisal' (1987) 10 *Fordham International Law Journal* 468–70; Claude Blumann, 'Le pouvoir exécutif de la commission à la lumière de l'Acte unique européen' (1988) 24 *Revue trimestrielle de droit européen* 23–66.

[36] See Art 10 of the SEA, OJ [1986] L 169/1.

[37] Jacqué notes that the Commission had proposed an amendment of Art 155 EEC but following a suggestion by the Netherlands, Art 145 EEC was amended instead. See Jean-Paul Jacqué, 'L'acte Unique Européen' (1986) 22 *Revue trimestrielle de droit européen* 594–95.

[38] Supporting this reading, see Kieran St Bradley, 'Comitology and the law: through a glass, darkly' (1992) 29 *Common Market Law Review* 713; Blumann, 'Le pouvoir exécutif de la Commission' (1988) 24 *Revue trimestrielle de droit européen* 30–32. In four of the seven procedures foreseen in the decision, the last word was reserved to the Council, however. This was one of the reasons why the Parliament tried to challenge the decision before the Court of Justice. See Action brought on 2 October 1987 in Case 302/87, *Parliament v Council*, OJ [1987] C 321/4.

on an ad hoc basis. Instead, the procedures had to be laid down in advance in an act adopted through an advisory procedure (unanimity in the Council and opinion by the Parliament).

Article 145 EEC served as the legal basis for the first comitology decision of 1987.[39] This decision introduced a number of standard procedures that would apply (only) from then on[40] whenever the Council conferred implementing powers on the Commission. The proliferation of ad hoc procedures was thus halted, as 'only' seven procedures would remain in the future: the advisory procedure; the management procedure (with two variants); the regulatory procedure (with two variants); and a procedure for adopting safeguard measures (again with two variants).[41]

B. A Call for Parliamentarisation and the Second Comitology Decision

Although the first comitology decision represented a rationalisation of comitology, and the Commission, pursuant to the Plumb-Delors agreement of 1988, had committed to forward to the Parliament all draft normative measures presented to a comitology committee,[42] Parliament was quick to call for a new revision, after its legal challenge against the comitology decision was rejected by the Court.[43] After all, with the Maastricht Treaty, Parliament's powers had further accrued given the introduction of the co-decision procedure where it was put on an (almost)[44] equal footing with the Council.[45] In practice, this meant that Parliament could veto a basic act which conferred implementing powers (still in the broad sense) to the Commission. At the same time this put comitology's original sin in even

[39] See Council Decision 87/373 laying down the procedures for the exercise of implementing powers conferred on the Commission, OJ [1987] L 197/33. For a discussion of the adoption of the decision, see Walter Meng, 'Die Neuregulung der EG-Verwaltungsauschüsse – Streit um die Comitologie' (1988) 48 *Zeitschrift für ausländisches öffentliches Recht und Völkerrecht* 208–28; Claus-Dieter Ehlermann, 'Compétences d'exécution conférées à la Commission: la nouvelle décision-cadre du Conseil' (1988) 31 *Revue du Marché Commun* 232–39.

[40] That the decision did not immediately do away with the existing cacophony of committees and procedures was another reason for the Parliament to challenge the legality of the decision; see Action brought on 2 October 1987 in Case 302/87, *Parliament v Council*, OJ [1987] C 321/4.

[41] Very critical of the decision and rejecting the idea that it simplified or rationalised comitology, see Karel De Gucht, *Besluitvorming in de Europese Unie* (Antwerpen, Maklu, 1994) 77–85. For a more positive contemporary assessment, see Alain Van Solinge, 'La Commission – Agent d'exécution du droit communautaire – La comitologie' in J-V Louis and D Waelbroeck (eds), *La Commission au coeur du système institutionnel des Communautés européennes* (Bruxelles, Editions de l'Université de Bruxelles, 1989) 71–77.

[42] In contrast, measures of day-to-day management and those of limited duration or importance were expressly excluded from this commitment. See Letter of President Delors to President Plumb, SG (88) D/03026.

[43] At the time the Parliament did not have active *locus standi* in the action for annulment. The Court rejected the challenge on admissibility grounds without going into the merits of the case. See Case 302/87, *Parliament v Council*, ECLI:EU:C:1988:461.

[44] Under Art 189b(6) of the EEC Treaty, the Council could adopt a basic act in third reading if the conciliation committee failed to produce a compromise. Rather than requiring the agreement of the Parliament in such cases, the Maastricht version of the co-decision procedure only foresaw that the Parliament could veto the Council's decision with an absolute majority of its members. See OJ [1992] C 224/1.

[45] In addition to comitology undermining the idea that Parliament and Council are on equal footing, the Parliament in particular also took issue with the *contre-filet* variant of the regulatory procedure (on this see fn 11 above) since it allowed the Council to decide with simple majority whereas the Council (when adopting the basic act) needed to muster a QMV to act. See Ciavarini Azzi, 'Comitologie' (2001) 17.

starker terms: Parliament now had 'full' control over the substance of basic acts, but it was (still) completely excluded from the process whereby those basic acts were subsequently implemented.[46] Given the Court's generous interpretation of the notion of implementation (see section 3.II), it is readily apparent why the Parliament increasingly objected to comitology remaining a private affair between the Commission, Member States and Council. Early on, following the entry into force of the Maastricht Treaty, the Parliament therefore even tried to argue that comitology could not apply to basic acts adopted pursuant to the co-decision procedure.[47] In the end, however, it accepted that comitology would (continue to) apply generally and a *Modus Vivendi*[48] was agreed pacifying the conflict until the next Treaty revision.[49] Under that *Modus Vivendi* of 1994 the institutions agreed to keep Parliament informed of the draft general measures implementing basic acts adopted pursuant to Article 189b EEC. In addition, in the *Modus Vivendi*, the Commission and Council agreed to take into account the comments received by the Parliament before adopting any relevant implementing measures. Crucially, the institutions agreed that the issue would be reviewed at the intergovernmental conference which would eventually lead to the Treaty of Amsterdam. As Bergström explains, the terms of the *Modus Vivendi* were not fully adhered to by the Commission, resulting in the Parliament using its budgetary powers to starve the comitology system of funding, putting pressure on the Commission.[50] Under the subsequent Samland–Williamson agreement, which pacified the conflict, the Commission agreed to provide the Parliament with the agenda's and voting results of the committee meetings.[51]

Despite the earlier commitment to do so, however, the Amsterdam Treaty did not alter Article 145 EEC in the end.[52] The reason for this can be traced back to the Westendorp Reflection Group set up in the wake of the 1994 Corfu European Council.[53] In its report, the group noted that there was only a (large) majority in favour of simplifying existing

[46] Of course, this problem was not new. In the 1990s, the Parliament also went to court to safeguard its prerogatives in the consultation procedure. Since it would only be consulted on the basic act and not on subsequent implementing acts, it challenged both the legality of enabling clauses and specific implementing acts. See Case C-156/93, *Parliament v Commission*, ECLI:EU:C:1995:238 (unsuccessfully challenging an implementing measure); Case C-417/93, *Parliament v Council*, ECLI:EU:C:1995:127 (unsuccessfully challenging an enabling clause); and Case C-303/94, *Parliament v Council*, ECLI:EU:C:1996:238 (successfully challenging an implementing measure).

[47] Jean-Paul Jacqué, 'L'éternel retour – Réflexion sur la comitologie' in Georges Vandersanden (ed), *Mélanges en hommage à Jean-Victor Louis* (Bruxelles, Editions de l'Université de Bruxelles, 2003) 213. The legal argument for this was that Art 145 EEC referred to the Council conferring implementing powers on the Commission (and not the Council and Parliament). The Maastricht Treaty had not updated this provision in light of the introduction of the co-decision procedure. The Court later clarified, however, that where the Treaties referred to 'acts of the Council' this includes those acts 'adopted by that institution, either alone or together with the Parliament under the co-decision procedure'. See Case C-259/95, *Parliament v Council*, ECLI:EU:C:1997:454 [26].

[48] See OJ [1996] C 102/1.

[49] Claude Blumann, 'Le Parlement européen et la comitologie: une complication pour la conférence intergouvernementale de 1996' (1996) 32 *Revue trimestrielle de droit européen* 11–24. Unsurprisingly, the application of the *Modus Vivendi* quickly showed different readings of this IIA by the Parliament and Commission.

[50] Bergström, *Comitology* (2005) 240–43.

[51] See OJ [1996] C 347/134.

[52] In discussions on the Amsterdam Treaty, the Commission proposed to delete Art 145 EEC and update Art 155 EEC with a reference to implementing powers conferred by Council or Council and Parliament, further proposing that the horizontal comitology instrument be adopted through the co-decision procedure. See Secretariat of the IGC, Non-Paper sur la comitologie par la Commission, 29 April 1997, CONF/3900/97.

[53] See Presidency Conclusions of the European Council at Corfu, 24–25 June 1994.

comitology, but for this it noted that a Treaty revision was not required and a revision of the comitology decision would suffice.[54] The more ambitious proposals in the group did not muster sufficient support but were already indicative for the debate in the Convention: proponents of a clearer hierarchy of norms suggested that executive powers should rest squarely with the Commission, controlled by the Parliament and Council; proponents of the status quo wished to maintain the institutional balance and the Council's executive powers but simplify and streamline the system; lastly a compromise was suggested whereby the Commission would remain subject to committee control but whereby Parliament and Council would receive veto powers.[55]

As noted, these more fundamental reform proposals did not make it to the Intergovernmental Conference (IGC), which limited itself to renumbering Article 145 EC as Article 202 EC. A declaration (No 31) was instead adopted instructing the Commission to submit a proposal to review the first comitology decision. The reform sought by the Parliament could therefore only take place through secondary law, within the framework provided for in Article 202 EC. This reform resulted in the second comitology decision of 1999, which repealed and replaced the first comitology decision of 1987.

The second comitology decision strengthened Parliament's role,[56] especially regarding the transparency of procedures, and also reduced the number of procedures to four: the advisory procedure; the management procedure; the regulatory procedure, and a procedure for safeguard measures, all without variants. Yet, the second comitology decision did not automatically align the old procedures to the new ones and instead this had to be done ad hoc for each basic instrument.[57] As the new procedures have now in turn be repealed, they will not further be discussed in detail. Although the second comitology decision strengthened the position of the Parliament, comitology procedures remained dominated by the Commission, Member States and the Council and the mismatch with the legislative role of the Parliament further increased as the Amsterdam and Nice Treaties further generalised the co-decision procedure.

It was only during the Convention on the Future of Europe and the subsequent IGC, that the decision to radically reform the comitology system, something that had already been envisaged for the 1996 IGC, but which had failed at the time, was definitely made.

[54] Rapport du Groupe de réflexion, SN 520/1/95 REV 1, para 128.

[55] Rapport du Groupe de réflexion, SN 520/1/95 REV 1, para 127. This third solution was also preferred by the Parliament itself; see Resolution on the functioning of the Treaty on European Union with a view to the 1996 Intergovernmental Conference – Implementation and development of the Union, OJ [1995] C 151/56 [32(ii)]; Resolution embodying (i) Parliament's opinion on the convening of the Intergovernmental Conference, and (ii) an evaluation of the work of the Reflection Group and a definition of the political priorities of the European Parliament with a view to the Intergovernmental Conference, OJ [1996] C 96/77 [21.6].

[56] However, not as much as the Commission had originally proposed. For instance, the Commission had advanced a regulatory procedure which did not result in a referral to the Council in case of a negative or no opinion, but simply the inability for the Commission to adopt the draft act. The Commission foresaw that in such cases, the legislator (Council or Parliament and Council) would have to be involved, ensuring an equality between the two arms of the legislature See Art 5 and recital 6 of European Commission, COM (1998) 380 final. On the reform introduced by the second comitology decision, see Ciavarini Azzi (n 34) 16–28.

[57] See the Declaration of the Commission and Council at the occasion of the adoption of the second comitology decision, OJ [1999] C 203/1.

C. The Constitution and the Amendment of the Second Comitology Decision

Since the Lisbon framework essentially goes back to Articles I-34 to I-37 of the Constitution (Articles I-33 and I-36 of the draft Constitutional Treaty),[58] it is useful to briefly discuss[59] the work of the Convention, specifically on the two issues of creating a new framework for the adoption of executive acts based on secondary legislation (comitology) and of defining the notion of legislation.

The Convention's fourth plenary session was devoted to the legitimacy and efficiency of how the EU fulfils its mission.[60] In order to prepare for this plenary session, a study on the system of the EU's legal instruments then in force was circulated.[61] The study noted that '[l]egislative power is not defined by the treaties; they merely define, on a case-by-case basis, the respective roles of the institutions involved'[62] and that the competence to implement and apply EU legislation in principle resides with the Member States whereby the Commission 'exercises such competences in a subsidiary capacity only, in particular where it is necessary to ensure some degree of homogeneity in applying secondary legislation.'[63] In addition, the note observed that Articles 202 and 211 EC conceptualised the notion of implementation in a broad sense, covering both regulatory powers and the power to adopt individual measures.[64] Anticipating the work of the Convention, the note suggested that the relationship between legislation and implementation could be clarified by introducing a hierarchy of norms.[65] The note fed into the work of the plenary, where a number of Members argued that such a hierarchy of norms should be introduced with a clearer separation of powers.[66] A further general consensus then seemed to emerge on the need to tackle the opaqueness and complexity of the comitology system, with some members arguing in favour of creating new mechanisms of control for the legislator over the Commission.[67]

From this debate, the presidency concluded that it was necessary to set up a dedicated working group on 'the simplification of legislative procedures, and instruments'.[68] As its name implies, the working group's mandate was not focused exclusively on reforming comitology or on clarifying the relationship between legislative and non-legislative acts. Before the working group commenced its activities, the eighth plenary session of the Convention

[58] For the final text of the Constitution, see OJ [2004] C 310/1; for the draft text resulting from the Convention and submitted to the IGC, see OJ [2003] C 169/1.

[59] For a more extensive discussion, see Bergström (n 1) 335–63; Jonas Bering Liisberg, 'The EU Constitutional Treaty and its distinction between legislative and non-legislative acts – Oranges into apples?', Jean Monnet Working Paper 01/06; Paolo Stancanelli, 'Le système décisionnel de l'Union' in Giuliano Amato, Hervé Bribosia and Bruno de Witte (eds), *Genèse et destinée de la constitution européenne: commentaire du traité établissant une Constitution pour l'Europe à la lumière des travaux préparatoires et perspectives d'avenir* (Bruxelles, Bruylant, 2007) 485–528.

[60] See Secretariat of the Convention, Note on the plenary meeting – Brussels, 23 and 24 May 2002, CONV 60/02.

[61] See Secretariat of the Convention, The legal instruments: present system, CONV 50/02.

[62] ibid 3.

[63] ibid 13.

[64] ibid 13–14. The latter point was clarified by the Court in Case 16/88, *Commission v Council*, ECLI:EU:C:1989:397 [11].

[65] See Secretariat of the Convention, The legal instruments: present system, CONV 50/02, 15.

[66] See Secretariat of the Convention, The legal instruments: present system, CONV 162/02, 20.

[67] ibid 21.

[68] See Secretariat of the Convention, Working groups: second wave, CONV 206/02.

was exclusively dedicated to the topic of simplification. One of the four questions identified by the presidency and debated by the plenary queried whether it was 'necessary to establish a clear classification of legal instruments based on their hierarchical position (hierarchy of legislation)?'[69] In light thereof, the working group's specific mandate was further clarified. In addition to the ideas of introducing a formal hierarchy of norms and the necessary reform of the comitology regime, it was proposed to also come to a definition of the 'legislative' sphere in EU decision-making.[70] As noted above (see chapter two), these lofty ambitions were not realised in the Lisbon Treaty and this was not a result of that Treaty's 'deconstitutionalisation' of the Constitutional Treaty. Instead, the latter also failed to establish a clear legislative sphere and hierarchy of norms.[71]

Turning to comitology, or the issue of non-legislative acts adopted pursuant to secondary legislation, the third of the working group's seven meetings, seems to have been key. In that meeting, the working group took testimony from the then Director-Generals of the Commission and Council (Messrs Petite and Piris) as well as from the current president of the Court of Justice, Lenaerts (then judge at the General Court). Piris mainly focused on simplifying the plethora of instruments and only limitedly commented on the acts adopted by the EU. On the latter he cautioned against any ill-considered simplification, but conceded that indicating the legislative or executive nature of an act in its title could contribute to greater transparency.[72] The Director-General of the Commission Legal Service was rather conservative in his suggestions on the implementation of EU law by proposing that the Commission ought to implement EU law (if it is not implemented by the Member States) and that it should be subject to control by the EU legislator.[73] In contrast, the origins of the reform as eventually introduced by the Lisbon Treaty seem more inspired by the intervention by Lenaerts who argued for 'a clear distinction between the legislative and executive acts of the Union. This distinction, based not on the identity of the author of the act, but on the type of procedure followed for its adoption'.[74] This latter point ultimately won over the members, since within the Working Group, there initially seemed to be a preference for defining legislative acts in a material sense, rather than procedurally.[75]

Within the executive acts, Lenaerts made a distinction between so-called 'delegated legislation' and 'executive acts stricto sensu'. For the former he suggested a 'heavy comitology procedure' and a strict control by the Parliament, while the 'executive acts stricto sensu' could do with an advisory comitology procedure, leaving the ultimate responsibility to the

[69] See Secretariat of the Convention, Summary Report on the plenary session – Brussels, 12 and 13 September 2002, CONV 284/02, 4.

[70] Secretariat of the Convention, Mandate of Working Group IX on the simplification of legislative procedures and instruments, CONV 271/02, 8.

[71] See Carlos-Manuel Alves, 'La hiérarchie du droit dérivé unilatéral à la lumière de la Constitution européenne: révolution juridique ou sacrifice au nominalisme?' (2004) 40 *Cahiers de droit européen* 691–726.

[72] See Secretariat of the Convention, Simplification of legislative procedures and instruments – Paper by Mr Jean-Claude Piris, Working Group IX, Working Document 06, 21.

[73] See Secretariat of the Convention, Simplifying Legislative Procedures and Instruments – Paper by Mr Michel Petite, Working Group IX, Working Document 08, 7. Unsurprisingly, he thereby did not diverge from the suggestions made earlier by the Commission as an institution, see above fn 33.

[74] See Secretariat of the Convention, Simplifying Legislative Procedures and Instruments – Paper by Prof Koen Lenaerts, Working Group IX, Working Document 07, 2.

[75] Secretariat of the European Convention, Working Document 13 of the WG on simplification, 6 November 2002.

Commission, under the general political control of the Parliament.[76] While Lenaerts thus argued to differentiate the acts in terms of the procedure used for their adoption, the control over delegated and implementing acts only differed in their intensity. Yet the idea that also the actors controlling the Commission should be different depending on the type of act being adopted appeared to be a further clear preference in the working group,[77] which in a logic of path dependency much influenced the final outcomes of the Convention and the IGC as highlighted by Bergström.[78] In addition, at least for the working group itself, the purpose of the introduction of the delegated act also really was to 'encourage the legislator to look *solely* to the essential elements' of its legislation.[79]

Liisberg further notes that little attention in the working group (or Convention) was devoted to the issue of non-legislative acts based directly on the Treaties.[80] The autonomous executive acts were recognised by the working group as autonomous *legislation*,[81] and 'limited' to the following cases: internal organisational measures; appointments; technical decisions by the Commission or ECB to implement the EU's competition and monetary policies; and 'cases where the Institutions exercise executive functions and develop in detail the policy choices already expressed in the Treaty in a particular area'.[82] In the working group, the Commission did not propose to do away with them, but rather to restrict their use.[83] While the existence of and logic behind these legal bases was criticised (see section 2.II), Liisberg explains how the Convention arrived at the result that ultimately ended up in the Lisbon Treaty: starting from the status quo of the Nice Treaty[84] the Convention members used a procedural criterion and found that all legal bases already prescribing the co-decision procedure would be turned into legislative legal bases and, conversely, all legal bases granting competences to the Commission, could not be legislative legal bases. For the remainder of the legal bases in the Nice Treaty, a material criterion[85] was used and it was assessed

[76] ibid 4–5. Lenaerts also suggested to do away with the legal bases granting autonomous executive powers to the Council and the Commission, requalifying these as either formal legislative acts or executive acts (in the strict sense or as delegated legislation), but clearly this suggestion was not followed.

[77] The Commission's representative, Paolo Ponzano, borrowed the language of the different types of acts proposed by Lenaerts, but insisted that for executive acts *stricto sensu* 'a regular control of the Commission (or the Member States) by the Legislature does not appear justified'. See Secretariat of the Convention, Proposal from the Commission's representative in the Working group to distinguish legislative and executive functions in the institutional system of the European Union, Working Group IX, Working Document 16, 2. Further, Spanish MP Cisneros in particular vigorously stressed that in comitology, the Council does not act in its legislative capacity and the Member States are involved because they are in principle responsible to implement EU law. For him this meant that only the Member States, but not the European Parliament, ought to control the Commission in its task of implementing EU law. See Secretariat of the Convention, Simplification des procedures – propositions de M. Gabriel Cisneros, Working Group IX, Working Document 05, 2–3.

[78] Bergström (n 1) 342.

[79] Secretariat of the European Convention, Final report of Working Group IX on Simplification, CONV 424/02, 9 (emphasis added).

[80] Jonas Bering Liisberg, 'The EU Constitutional Treaty and its distinction between legislative and non-legislative acts – Oranges into apples?', Jean Monnet Working Paper 01/06, 26–27.

[81] See Secretariat of the European Convention, Working Document 10 of the WG on simplification, 24 October 2002.

[82] Secretariat of the European Convention, Final report of Working Group IX on Simplification, CONV 424/02, 13.

[83] Secretariat of the European Convention, Working Document 16 of the WG on simplification, 7 November 2002.

[84] For the working group's inventory of all the legal bases under the Nice Treaty, see Secretariat of the European Convention, Working Document 3 of the WG on simplification, 1 October 2002.

[85] This was also in line with the suggestion made by Lenaerts, see Secretariat of the European Convention, Working Document 7 of the WG on simplification, 6 November 2002, 4–5.

whether the Council had been given a power to make policy choices, in which case legislation was at issue, or whether it was merely empowered to execute a policy choice already made in primary law, in which case an autonomous executive power was at issue.[86]

Both the draft Constitution and the final text of the Constitution, then distinguished between legislation (European laws and framework laws) (Article I-34), autonomous executive acts (European regulations and decisions) (Article I-35), 'delegated European regulations', which the Commission could adopt in order to supplement or amend the non-essential elements of European laws and framework laws (Article I-36), and 'implementing acts', which the Commission (or, exceptionally, the Council) could adopt if legally binding acts of the EU had to be implemented under uniform conditions (Article I-37).

The system as elaborated in the Constitution is very similar to the system as finally introduced by the Lisbon Treaty. Articles I-36 and I-37 are even identical to Articles 290 and 291 TFEU, with the exception of the constitutional terminology that the Lisbon Treaty eliminated. Article I-34 of the Constitution returned as Article 289 TFEU, but Article I-35, which explicitly clarified the existence of non-legislative acts, was largely abolished. This was unfortunate since, as noted above, the legal bases granting autonomous executive powers themselves were not abolished, making their existence in the Lisbon Treaty more obscure.

Given the Constitution's blueprint for the Lisbon Treaty, it is further useful to compare the latter with the Parliament's initial proposal adopted during the Convention. In its resolution dedicated to a 'typology of acts and hierarchy of legislation in the European Union' it had proposed that *all* acts adopted pursuant to the Treaties should be legislation adopted following the co-decision procedure, thus doing away with any autonomous executive acts and special legislative procedures. In terms of implementation (in a broad sense), the Parliament had suggested a distinction between 'executive provisions' and 'delegated regulations'.[87] The latter would be used to supplement (but not amend) legislation while the former were narrowly construed and would only serve to lay down the procedural conditions for implementing legislation. For both types of powers, Parliament and Council would be on an equal footing both in terms of their conferral and control. The control would have consisted of a right of objection which would automatically trigger the initiation of a legislative procedure through which Parliament and Council could also amend 'delegated regulations' themselves. Interestingly, the Parliament envisaged that also EU agencies would be able to adopt 'delegated regulations' (but not 'executive provisions') in which case not just the Parliament and Council but also the Commission would be granted a right of objection.

Despite the Lisbon Treaty (and the Constitution) significantly reinforcing the Parliament's position, it clearly still was a long way off the Parliament's original wish list summarised above: under the Lisbon framework, Parliament cannot block implementing measures (see section 6.V.D), it cannot amend delegated acts (see section 5.IV.B), it cannot grant a delegated power to EU agencies (see section 5.I) and its broad notion of supplementation (at the expense of implementation through 'executive provisions') has not materialised (see section 4.III). Yet, while after the 2004 IGC the Parliament still regretted that the IGC 'left out some proposals, notably of the European Parliament and of the Convention, that

[86] Jonas Bering Liisberg, 'The EU Constitutional Treaty and its distinction between legislative and non-legislative acts – Oranges into apples?', Jean Monnet Working Paper 01/06, 26–27.

[87] See European Parliament resolution on the typology of acts and the hierarchy of legislation in the European Union, OJ [2004] C31E/126 [18].

would have, in the view of their authors, brought further improvements to the Union',[88] the Parliament quickly had to reconsider its priorities.

The failed ratification of the European Constitution (following negative referenda in France and The Netherlands in 2005) meant that the new 'delegated European regulations', one of the biggest prizes of the Constitutional Treaty, would not see the light in the near future. As the Parliament's hopes of strengthening its position through primary law were again dashed (as with earlier IGCs), it insisted on adapting the second comitology decision as a short-term alternative and in anticipation of a new treaty that would finally introduce the 'delegated European regulations'. As a result, in 2006, the regulatory procedure with scrutiny (or PRAC, from the French acronym *procédure de réglementation avec contrôle*) was added to the procedures already provided for in the second comitology decision.[89] The PRAC was prescribed as the method to be used for the adoption of 'measures of general scope designed to amend non-essential elements of a basic instrument adopted in accordance with [the] co-decision procedure, including by deleting some of those elements or by supplementing the instrument by the addition of new non-essential elements'. The PRAC was (and is; see section 4.III.C) anything but a simple procedure, and although it strengthened Parliament's role (compared to the ordinary regulatory procedure), it was still not the Council's equal.[90] Still, for the Parliament it was important as a temporary *Ersatz* to the delegated act which would become unlocked with the entry into force of the Lisbon Treaty.

IV. A Recalibrated Institutional Balance

This section finalises the discussion of the developments up until the entry into force of the Lisbon Treaty. The discussion above has shown how the Lisbon Treaty's redefinition of the legal framework governing executive rulemaking resulted in a recalibration of the inter-institutional power relationships, Arguably, the institutional balance in the field of executive rule-making as defined by the Lisbon Treaty was therefore more closely aligned to the traditional community method (compared to the pre-Lisbon institutional balance),[91] since the more supranational institutions gained clout over the Council: in terms of granting executive powers to the Commission and scrutinising their exercise, the Parliament gained complete equality with the Council under both Articles 290 and 291 TFEU; the Commission was indicated as the sole executive authority that may amend or supplement legislation in Article 290 TFEU; and the exceptional policy implementation by the Council under Article 291(2) TFEU was arguably further restricted.

[88] See European Parliament resolution on the Treaty establishing a Constitution for Europe, OJ [2005] C247E/88.

[89] It may be noted that the Commission had already proposed in 2002 to introduce the PRAC 'given the relatively long period which will elapse before the new Treaty [prepared by the Convention] comes into force'. See European Commission, COM (2002) 719 final, 2.

[90] For a more elaborate discussion of the (introduction of the) PRAC, see Manuel Szapiro, 'Comitologie: rétrospective et prospective après la réforme de 2006' (2006) *Revue du droit de l'Union européenne* 545–86; Gregor Schusterschitz and Sabine Kotz, 'The Comitology Reform of 2006: Increasing the Powers of the European Parliament Without Changing the Treaties' (2007) 3 *European Constitutional Law Review* 68–90; Matthijs van der Plas, 'Rol Europees Parlement fors toegenomen door nieuw Comitologiebesluit' (2006) 54 *Tijdschrift voor Europees en economisch recht* 410–18.

[91] For an earlier argument to this effect, see Merijn Chamon, 'Institutional balance and Community method in the implementation of EU legislation following the Lisbon Treaty' (2016) 53 *Common Market Law Review* 1501–44.

However, as Christiansen and Dobbels correctly noted after the entry into force of the Lisbon Treaty: 'it would be simplistic and ultimately misleading to regard the Parliament as a 'winner' solely on the basis of the new passages in the treaty text. The real 'test' should not be the letter of the law, but the way that this has been put into practice'.[92] With the entry into force of the Lisbon Treaty, the different EU institutions put forward their own reading of the Treaty framework. The sometimes more or less subtle differences between these readings of course reflected the different institutional interests at stake, each institution pushing an interpretation that was more congenial to its own position.[93] Some divergences in interpretation were smoothed over in the practice of decision-making or even formalised through inter-institutional agreements. Noteworthy in this regard are the Common Understandings on Delegated Acts of 2011 and 2016, the 2016 IIA on Better Law-Making and the 2019 non-binding criteria guiding the legislator in its choice between conferring delegated or implementing powers. Other disagreements (first) had to be brought before the Court of Justice before they were resolved, while still others continue to linger on.

Especially where the first option is followed, there is a possibility of constitutional modification by the political institutions. Such a modification entails that the key constitutional assumptions underlying the Lisbon schema are sidelined or even undermined,[94] and gives rise to what in political science has been termed 'interstitial institutional change', which typically occurs after a (new) formal rule that is ambiguous is introduced. Such change is relevant since it happens between two formal rule revisions and will typically inform the (second) revision of the ambiguous formal rules in question.[95] It is more difficult to qualify judicial settlement as informal interstitial institutional change, since adjudication by the Court is highly formalised and because, from a legal perspective, when the Court interprets ambiguous formal rules it is not changing them but rather 'clarifies and defines the meaning and scope of that rule as it ought to have been understood and applied from the time of its coming into force'.[96] From the perspective of the latter *Denkavit* legal fiction, one could argue that the Court cannot engage in constitutional modification either. The present analysis will however depart from that legal fiction: as will be noted, at a number of critical junctures the Court has seemingly ignored a number of key assumptions underlying the

[92] Thomas Christiansen and Mathias Dobbels, 'Comitology and delegated acts after Lisbon: How the European Parliament lost the implementation game' (2012) 16 *European Integration Online Papers* Art 13, 8.

[93] For each of the three political institutions, the following documents are particularly noteworthy: European Commission, COM (2009) 673 final; European Commission, SEC (2011) 855; Resolution of the European Parliament of 5 May 2010 on the power of legislative delegation, [2011] OJ C81E/6 and European Parliament resolution of 25 February 2014 on follow-up on the delegation of legislative powers and control by Member States of the Commission's exercise of implementing powers, OJ [2017] C 285/11; Council Legal Service, Application of Articles 290 (delegated acts) and 291 (implementing acts) TFEU, Council Doc 8970/11.

[94] See Paul Craig, 'Comitology, Rulemaking and the Lisbon Settlement – Tensions and Strains' in Carl Fredrik Bergström and Dominique Ritleng (eds), *Rulemaking by the European Commission – The New System for Delegation of Powers* (Oxford, OUP, 2016) 173.

[95] On this 'anticipative' function, see Marco Urban, 'The Anticipation Function of Interinstitutional Agreements: A Smooth Mechanism to Recalibrate Executive-Legislative Relations' in Diane Fromage and Anna Herranz-Surrallés (eds), *Executive-Legislative (Im)balance in the European Union* (Oxford, Hart Publishing, 2020) 35–49.

[96] Case 61/79, *Denkavit*, ECLI:EU:C:1980:100 [16].

original Lisbon reform. As will be shown below, from the very beginning, the general direction in which the constitutional modifications were heading was the pre-Lisbon status quo.

In the following chapters, different constitutional modifications will be flagged thematically and their impact for the inter-institutional relations and the position of the Parliament will be assessed. This will be done regardless of the origin of the constitutional modification (judicial decision, political compromise or unilateral decisions by one of the political institutions). The multiplication of delimitation problems resulting from the Lisbon Treaty will be taken as a starting point.

4

The Exponential Multiplication of Delimitation Problems

One of the repercussions of the Lisbon reform's doubling of acts (*cf* Figure 2.1) is the exponential growth of delimitation problems, since

$$D = \frac{n(n-1)}{2}$$

where D is the number of delimitation problems and n is the number of different acts. Where there are only two types of acts (pre-Lisbon basic acts and implementing acts), there is only one delimitation problem $\left(1 = \frac{2(2-1)}{2}\right)$. With at least four post-Lisbon types of acts, however, there are at least six potential delimitation problems $\left(6 = \frac{4(4-1)}{2}\right)$. The delimitation problems that are implied in the Lisbon Treaty itself are not the only ones, however. As will be shown, post-Lisbon constitutional modifications have resulted from the discovery, recognition, or even downward creation of *additional* types of acts. This has important knock-on effects for the delimitation problem. For instance, a simple addition of two further acts (eg the EU agencies' acts discussed in section 6.IV.A and the *sui generis* enforcement decisions discussed in section 6.IV.B) to the existing four, would increase the number of delimitation problems from six to fifteen $\left(15 = \frac{6(6-1)}{2}\right)$.

Not all possible delimitation problems will be discussed in full, and some are of less practical relevance than others. However, they are never purely theoretical either as, for instance, even the delimitation problem between an autonomous executive act and a delegated act could potentially arise. In normal circumstances these two acts operate in different and unconnected spheres since the former is non-legislative, while the latter can only exist if there is a legislative 'parent' act. Yet, even if an autonomous executive act can never confer a delegated power on the Commission, a problem might still arise where such an act conflicts or overlaps with the provisions of a delegated act adopted pursuant to a third, legislative, act.[1] In what follows, the main delimitation problems will be discussed in turn. Since these delimitation problems at the same time constitute a first set of limits

[1] A similar case has recently been brought before the Court and is pending at the time of writing. In *Parliament v Council*, the Parliament argues that the Council adopted autonomous executive acts pursuant to Art 43(3) TFEU, regulating issues for which the Commission had been empowered to adopt delegated acts pursuant to a legislative act adopted pursuant to Art 43(2) TFEU. See Action brought on 22 April 2021, Case C-259/21, *Parliament v Council*, OJ [2021] C 320/26.

to the powers in question, the discussion of the further limits to the autonomous executive powers, the delegated power under Article 290 TFEU and the implementing power under Article 291 TFEU will follow that of the delimitation problem.

I. Delimitation of Autonomous Executive Acts against (Delegated) Legislation and Implementation

The following section will discuss how the category of autonomous executive acts relates to the other post-Lisbon acts. Two main issues specifically arise in this regard: (i) how do autonomous executive acts relate to legislative acts; and (ii) given that autonomous executive acts are not legislative and cannot therefore contain empowerments under Article 290 TFEU, how can they be amended?

A. Autonomous Executive Acts vs Legislation

On the delimitation problem between legislative and autonomous executive acts, the Court has already brought some useful clarification in *Slovakia & Hungary v Council*.[2] In these cases the validity of the temporary relocation mechanism,[3] adopted in response to the 2015 migration crisis, was at issue. The mechanism was established through an autonomous executive act adopted pursuant to Article 78(3) TFEU. Through a non-legislative act a de facto exception to the Dublin III Regulation had thus been created,[4] the latter Regulation itself being a legislative act based on Article 78(2) TFEU. Slovakia had inter alia argued that based on its content, the contested decision was a legislative act but that its legal basis (Article 78(3) TFEU) does not allow for the adoption of legislative acts, meaning that 'the form of the contested decision [did] not correspond to its content'.[5] Seemingly linking the functions of delegated and implementing acts under Articles 290 and 291 TFEU with that of autonomous executive acts, Hungary argued that the latter type of acts may only supplement legislative acts or facilitate their implementation.[6]

Both AG Bot and the Court forcefully rejected Slovakia's suggestion that the nature of the contested decision could be derived from its content.[7] However, that did not yet address the question of *which* formal requirement triggered an act's qualification as

[2] Joined Cases C-643/15 and C-647/15, *Slovakia & Hungary v Council*, ECLI:EU:C:2017:631.

[3] Council Decision 2015/1601 establishing provisional measures in the area of international protection for the benefit of Italy and Greece, OJ [2015] L 248/80.

[4] Regulation 604/2013 of the European Parliament and of the Council establishing the criteria and mechanisms for determining the Member State responsible for examining an application for international protection lodged in one of the Member States by a third-country national or a stateless person, OJ [2013] L 180/31.

[5] See Opinion of AG Bot in Joined Cases C-643/15 & C-647/15, *Slovakia & Hungary v Council*, ECLI:EU:C:2017:618 [48].

[6] ibid [52].

[7] ibid [62]–[63]. For the Court this follows implicitly but unambiguously from its purely formal definition of legislative acts, see n 11.

legislative or otherwise. After all, in the *Front Polisario* cases, both AG Wathelet[8] and the General Court[9] had found that a Council act concluding an international agreement constituted a legislative act, since Article 289(3) TFEU inter alia provides that the adoption by the Council of a decision with the participation of the Parliament constitutes a special legislative procedure.[10] Does this formal requirement mean that *any* procedure in which the Council acts with the participation of the Parliament (as in most procedures by which the Council concludes an international agreement on behalf of the Union) constitutes a (special) legislative procedure, even if the legal basis in question does not explicitly provide so? That logical implication of the findings by AG Wathelet and the General Court was rejected by AG Bot and the Court in *Slovakia & Hungary v Council*. Instead, an act can only be qualified as legislative when the legal basis relied on explicitly prescribes that the ordinary or a special legislative procedure is to be followed for the adoption of the act.[11]

On Hungary's argument as to the function of autonomous executive acts (based on Article 78(3) TFEU), both the AG and the Court made it clear that they need not merely supplement or implement legislative acts. Instead, they implicitly made clear that the legal bases conferring autonomous executive powers on the institutions are to be interpreted and applied on their own terms. Since Article 78(3) TFEU provides that the Council may adopt provisional measures to address emergency situations, both the AG and Court stressed that it need simply be determined whether these conditions were met.[12] Since the contested autonomous executive act's material and temporal scope was circumscribed and as result did not replace or permanently amend the legislative act(s) adopted under Article 78(2) TFEU,[13] the Court found that the Council had properly exercised its autonomous executive power.

At first sight the findings of the Court in *Slovakia & Hungary v Council* may seem to clash with its judgment in the *Venezuela fisheries* cases[14] where the question of the proper delimitation between a legislative and a non-legislative legal basis was also at issue. In *Venezuela fisheries*, the legal bases concerned were Article 43(2) and (3) TFEU, whereby the Council had relied on the latter whereas Parliament and Commission were of the opinion that the former, legislative, legal basis ought to have been used. Here the Court ruled that the measures necessary for the pursuit of the objectives of the Common Fisheries Policy (CFP) were policy measures that therefore had to be based on Article 43(2) TFEU whereas measures of a primarily technical nature and taken in order to implement provisions adopted on the basis of Article 43(2) TFEU, should be based on Article 43(3) TFEU.[15]

[8] See Opinion of AG Wathelet in Case C-104/16 P, *Council v Front Polisario*, ECLI:EU:C: 2016:677 [151]–[161].

[9] Case T-512/12, *Front Polisario v Council*, ECLI:EU:T:2015:953 [70]–[71].

[10] This argument would work both ways. Just after the entry into force of the Lisbon Treaty, Türk argued that the acts resulting from special legislative procedures that only foresee a minimal (advisory) role for the Parliament should not be qualified as legislative in nature. See Alexander Türk, 'Lawmaking after Lisbon' in Andrea Biondi, Piet Eeckhout and Stefanie Ripley (eds), *EU Law after Lisbon* (Oxford, OUP, 2012) 69.

[11] See Joined Cases C-643/15 and C-647/15, *Slovakia & Hungary v Council*, ECLI:EU:C:2017:63 [62]–[64]. In actions for annulment, the General Court still treats decisions concluding international agreements as legislative acts for the purposes of checking admissibility. See Case T-279/19, *Front Polisario v Council*, ECLI:EU:T:2021:639 [139].

[12] See Opinion of AG Bot in Joined Cases C-643/15 and C-647/15, *Slovakia & Hungary v Council*, ECLI:EU: C:2017:618 [76]; Joined Cases C-643/15 and C-647/15, *Slovakia & Hungary v Council*, ECLI:EU:C:2017:63 [73].

[13] Joined Cases C-643/15 and C-647/15, *Slovakia & Hungary v Council*, ECLI:EU:C:2017:63 [79].

[14] Joined Cases C-103/12 and C-165/12, *Parliament & Commission v Council*, ECLI:EU:C:2014:2400.

[15] ibid [50].

Did the Court itself thereby not make a link between the function of an implementing act under Article 291 TFEU and the autonomous executive acts (as Hungary had suggested in *Slovakia & Hungary v Council*)?

While the Court's language in this case might suggest so, *Venezuela fisheries* may be argued to be wholly consistent with the subsequent *Slovakia & Hungary v Council* ruling. After all, in both cases the Court was simply guided by the actual terms of the legal bases. When it decided on the scope of the competence conferred by the legal bases, the Court drew the limits to the autonomous executive powers from those clauses themselves,[16] and in light of the *effet utile* principle: where legislative and non-legislative legal bases appear side by side (as in the case of Articles 43 and 78 TFEU) the Court gives useful effect to *both* legal bases without a priori subordinating one to the other. That the Court nonetheless finds a degree of subordination of Article 43(3) TFEU to Article 43(2) TFEU then resulted from the drafting of the former provision, but not as such from its quality as a non-legislative legal basis.[17] The Court progressively set the record straight by first noting, in *Multi-annual cod plan*, that the acts adopted pursuant to Article 43(3) TFEU 'are not simply to be considered the same as those provided for in Article 291(2) TFEU',[18] further clarifying in *Germany v Parliament & Council* that Article 43(3) TFEU 'grants the Council the power to adopt acts going beyond what can be regarded as an 'implementing act' [in the sense of Article 291 TFEU]'.[19] Arguably, then, it results from this case law that autonomous executive acts might even regulate essential elements, just like formal legislative acts.[20]

That there is no a priori subordination between legislative and non-legislative legal bases is further corroborated by the fact that in *Venezuela fisheries* both the AG and the Court applied the standard legal basis test to arrive at the conclusion that in light of the aim and content of the contested measure, Article 43(2) TFEU was the proper legal basis.[21] The test here is entirely similar to the test in those cases where the Court has to identify the proper legal basis between two alternative legislative legal bases. That it is the terms of Article 43(3) TFEU itself that 'relegated' it to a subordinate provision also becomes clear if the two non-legislative legal bases in *Slovakia & Hungary v Council* and *Venezuela fisheries* are compared. Textually, Article 78(3) TFEU is much more open-ended, whereas Article 43(3) TFEU suggests a closed list of the issues on which the Council can decide through autonomous executive act.[22]

[16] Also finding as such, see René Barents, 'De post-Lissabon-rechtspraak over het institutioneel evenwicht' (2019) 67 *Tijdschrift voor Europees en economisch recht* 340.

[17] AG Sharpston was very clear on this; see Opinion of AG Sharpston in Joined Cases C-103/12 and C-165/12, *Parliament & Commission v Council*, ECLI:EU:C:2014:334 [164].

[18] Joined Cases C-124/13 and C-125/13, *Parliament & Commission v Council*, ECLI:EU:C:2015:790 [54].

[19] Case C-113/14, *Germany v Parliament & Council*, ECLI:EU:C:2016:635 [57].

[20] Already foretelling this based on the text of the Constitutional Treaty, see Carl Fredrik Bergström, *Comitology – Delegation of Powers in the European Union and the Committee System* (Oxford, OUP, 2005) 353–54.

[21] Joined Cases C-103/12 and C-165/12, *Parliament & Commission v Council*, ECLI:EU:C:2014:2400 [51]–[73]; Opinion of AG Sharpston in Joined Cases C-103/12 and C-165/12, *Parliament & Commission v Council*, ECLI:EU:C:2014:334 [140]–[154].

[22] It should be noted, however, that the Court did not take position on the question whether the issues in Art 43(3) TFEU constitute a closed list, while AG Sharpston came to the conclusion that Art 43(3) TFEU should be read restrictively without necessarily constituting a closed list. See Opinion of AG Sharpston in Joined Cases C-103/12 and C-165/12, *Parliament & Commission v Council*, ECLI:EU:C:2014:334 [160]ff. Instead, the Court has suggested this might be an open list; see Case C-113/14, *Germany v Parliament & Council*, ECLI:EU:C:2016:635 [60].

Table 4.1 Comparison of Articles 43(3) and 78(3) TFEU

Article 43(3) TFEU	Article 78(3) TFEU
The Council, on a proposal from the Commission, shall adopt measures on fixing prices, levies, aid and quantitative limitations and on the fixing and allocation of fishing opportunities.	In the event of one or more Member States being confronted by an emergency situation characterised by a sudden inflow of nationals of third countries, the Council, on a proposal from the Commission, may adopt provisional measures for the benefit of the Member State(s) concerned. It shall act after consulting the European Parliament.

The Court's interpretation of these autonomous executive powers as not a priori subordinate to the legislative power puts them, hierarchically, at the same level,[23] and ensures the coherence of this category of executive powers.[24] This becomes especially clear if one considers that most autonomous executive powers, differing from those at issue in *Slovakia & Hungary v Council* and *Venezuela fisheries*, are 'self-standing' and do not accompany a legislative legal basis. Had the Court read a subordination of autonomous executive powers to legislative powers in the two cases discussed, this would have resulted in a further distinction between self-standing and 'corollarily' autonomous executive legal bases.

B. Autonomous Executive Acts vs Implementation

Whereas pre-Lisbon, implementing acts could amend, supplement and implement basic acts, the Lisbon split raised the question whether the normative function of amending basic acts could continue to be fulfilled by implementing acts. In section 6.II.B, the possibility for implementing acts to amend legislative acts is discussed. Here the focus is on the possibility for implementing acts to amend autonomous executive acts. Both issues are distinct since, while Article 290 TFEU explicitly foresees the possibility of amending legislative acts through a simplified procedure, no such simplified procedure is foreseen for the amendment of autonomous executive acts. A priori, delegated acts cannot be relied upon to amend autonomous executive acts (given the procedural definition of 'legislation' in Article 289 TFEU). Still, as noted above (section 2.II), the Lisbon Treaty's differentiation as to which acts should be adopted in the form of legislation and which in the form of autonomous executive act itself is at times arbitrary. An example here is the Common Customs Tariff, which is adopted by the Council pursuant to Article 31 TFEU but which is routinely amended by the Commission through implementing acts.[25] Since the current Common Customs Tariff Regulation dates from before the entry into force of the Lisbon Treaty, it raises the question whether post-Lisbon, it is only possible to amend autonomous executive acts by

[23] Also Barents notes that there is no hierarchy between both; see Barents, 'De post-Lissabon-rechtspraak' (2019) 341.

[24] Explicitly rejecting a hierarchy as advocated by the Commission, see Case C-113/14, *Germany v Parliament & Council*, ECLI:EU:C:2016:635 [59].

[25] See, for instance, Commission Implementing Regulation 2020/1369 amending Annex I to Council Regulation 2658/87 on the tariff and statistical nomenclature and on the Common Customs Tariff, OJ [2020] L 319/2.

going through the default (Treaty) procedure? Craig indeed argued that the possibility to amend autonomous executive acts through implementing acts was wrong in principle,[26] and he proposed two solutions. First, the Court could opt for a substantive interpretation of the notion of legislative act (despite the procedural definition in Article 289 TFEU), which would mean autonomous executive acts would in fact be legislative (at least or also for the purposes of Article 290 TEU). Secondly, Craig suggested that the Court could hold that the control regime of Article 290 TFEU be applied *mutatis mutandis*.[27] Evidently, Craig's first suggestion clashes with the formalism in Article 289 TFEU, and has now also been ruled out by the Court's judgment in *Slovakia & Hungary v Council*.

Further, considering the post-Lisbon *Eures Network* case where the Court opted for a transposition of its pre-Lisbon case law on 'implementation' (when the latter still included amendment of basic instruments), it seems more likely that in these cases an amendment through implementing acts is indeed acceptable. Considering the applicable control regimes, this would result in a reinforcement of the Commission and a weakening of the Parliament, but only in those areas where autonomous executive acts may only be adopted with Parliamentary consent.[28]

Remarkably, however, there is hardly any post-Lisbon practice confirming the possibility of amending post-Lisbon autonomous executive acts through implementing acts. The only illustrations are to be found in the Regulations adopted pursuant to Article 215 TFEU imposing restrictive measures. These Regulations may identify the national authorities responsible for enforcing the restrictive measures in an annex and provide that the 'Commission shall be empowered to amend [the annex] on the basis of information supplied by Member States'.[29] While the Regulations do not describe through which procedure or act the Commission may do so,[30] the Commission has relied on an implementing act to amend the annexes.[31] While this is the only clear case of a post-Lisbon autonomous executive act being amended through a post-Lisbon implementing act and while the Court has not unequivocally sanctioned this practice, it would thus seem that the post-Lisbon implementing act has not entirely lost its function of amending basic acts. Of course, one main reason why this function is so rarely relied upon is because the procedure to adopt an autonomous executive act is typically much simpler than the (ordinary) legislative procedure. As a result, there is hardly a need for a simplified amendment procedure and any amendments can (normally) easily be adopted through the default procedure prescribed by the relevant legal basis in the Treaties.

[26] Paul Craig, 'Delegated Acts, Implementing Acts and the New Comitology Regulation' (2011) 36 *European Law Review* 677.

[27] Paul Craig, *The Lisbon Treaty: law, politics and treaty reform* (Oxford, OUP, 2016) 259–60.

[28] As follows from ch 2 n 66, these instances are extremely rare.

[29] See eg Art 7 of Council Regulation 833/2014 concerning restrictive measures in view of Russia's actions destabilising the situation in Ukraine, OJ [2014] L 229/1.

[30] The Council therefore opted to not apply a comitology procedure, but contrary to the practice discussed in section 6.V.B.ii, the Council did not explicitly note that no control should be exercised over the Commission.

[31] See Commission Implementing Regulation 2019/1163 amending and setting out a single list for the Annexes containing contact details of Member States competent authorities and address for notifications to the European Commission to certain Regulations concerning restrictive measures, OJ [2019] L 182/32.

C. Institutional Implications

In institutional terms, the consequence of *Slovakia & Hungary v Council* and *Venezuela fisheries* is a limit to the parliamentarisation and increase of transparency which the Lisbon Treaty potentially harboured. Indeed, while the Court endorsed the more natural reading of the Treaty provisions, it should still be noted that from the perspective of both Parliament and the issues around transparency, it could have taken a bolder stance. Proponents of greater transparency will deplore that the suggestion of AG Wathelet in the *Front Polisario* case was not followed. AG Wathelet had read Article 289 TFEU in such a way that whenever Parliament is involved in a procedure based on a Treaty provision, that procedure was to be qualified as a (special) legislative procedure, with the result that higher transparency requirements apply (see section 2.II). Proponents of greater parliamentarisation will equally deplore that the Court did not follow the Parliament's (and the Commission's) suggestion in *Multi-annual cod plan* to read autonomous executive legal bases restrictively (in favour of a default application of a legislative legal basis). However, as this section has set out, the Court's rulings on this issue do not amount to a constitutional modification and instead result from the fact that the simplification and parliamentarisation of the EU have remained a work in progress under the Lisbon Treaty.

II. Delimitation of Legislation and Delegation

That Article 290 TFEU prescribes the essentiality requirement as a strict limit to any delegation begs the question what the essential elements of legislation are and how they can be identified. While it may be tempting to look to the principle of democracy as the normative foundation for the essentiality requirement,[32] it should be noted that this rationale does not flow explicitly from the Treaties and neither has it been confirmed by the Court. The potential pitfall of doing so should indeed be clear: as noted above (section 4.I.A) the Treaties take a purely formal view on the notion of legislation. No differentiation is made in terms of democratic pedigree even though one could argue that the ordinary legislative procedure is democratically superior over a special legislative procedure where the Parliament is only consulted. As also noted above (section 2.II) the procedure followed to adopt an autonomous executive act may be identical to a special legislative procedure, resulting in an almost similar democratic pedigree, even if one act will be qualified as non-legislative and the other as legislative.[33] As a result, since the formal designation of an act as a legislative act is not conclusive for its democratic pedigree, and because the essentiality requirement is formally only linked to the formal qualification of an act, the normative foundation of this requirement cannot be retraced to a democratic principle. Unless and until the EU fully

[32] Jonathan Bauerschmidt, 'Verordnung (EU) Nr. 596/2014 – Artikel 35 Ausübung der Befugnisübertragung' in Christoph Seibt, Petra Buck-Heeb and Rafael Harnos (eds), *BeckOK Wertpapierhandelsrecht*, 3rd edn (2022) § 24.

[33] In terms of input-legitimacy, both acts would be as democratically legitimate. One could, however, counterargue that the greater transparency in the special legislative procedure would still result in higher throughput and democratic legitimacy of the legislative act.

evolves into a parliamentary system, the normative foundation of the essentiality requirement simply is the (self-referential) principle of institutional balance: essential elements are to be laid down by the institutions that have been conferred the competence to do so under the Treaties.

Leaving the question of the normative foundation of the requirement aside, how can these essential elements be identified? In the *Schengen Borders Code* (*SBC*) case, the Commission and Council argued that it was up to the legislator itself to determine what it thought was (non-)essential.[34] This issue would, as a result, not be justiciable. The Court however, borrowed from its standard legal basis test,[35] and found that 'which elements of a matter must be categorised as essential … must be based on objective factors amenable to judicial review'.[36] While this statement itself is clear enough, its application in concrete cases is less straightforward also because the Court does not clearly identify the 'objective factors' and further informs us that 'the characteristics and particularities of the domain concerned'[37] must be taken into account. The essential elements test is therefore fundamentally different from the choice of legal basis test which it seemingly recalls. The latter is genuinely horizontal (since it does not depend on the domain concerned) and does identify the objective factors clearly as being the content, aim and context of the measure to be adopted, even if the test itself may still turn out rather subjective.[38]

Determining the essential elements thus risks becoming unpredictable. Indeed, the Court in the *SBC* case simply arrives at the tautological conclusion that 'provisions which, in order to be adopted, require political choices falling within the responsibilities of the European Union legislature cannot be delegated'.[39] Put differently, what is essential is political and what is political is essential. *In casu* the Court ruled that the non-legislative measure of the Council[40] touched on essential elements given that it interfered with fundamental rights and the sovereign rights of third countries.[41] That would mean that essential elements are at least those elements which require the balancing of multiple conflicting interests, or which permit significant encroachments on fundamental rights.[42]

This does not mean, however, that whenever a measure interferes with fundamental rights, recourse should be had to formal legislation. As Article 52(1) of the Charter makes clear, limitations of fundamental rights should be provided for *by law*. Should this be considered to refer to laws in a formal sense, ie legislative acts, or merely law in a substantive sense,

[34] Case C-355/10, *Parliament v Council*, ECLI:EU:C:2012:516 [45]–[46].

[35] Bradley rightly points out that I had overlooked this in an earlier comment on *SBC*, see Kieran Bradley, 'Legislating in the European Union' in Catherine Barnard and Steve Peers (eds), *European Union Law* (Oxford, OUP, 2020) 143. On the Court's legal basis test, see eg Opinion 2/00 re *the Cartagena Protocol*, ECLI:EU:C:2001:664 [22]. Less consistently, in its proportionality review the Court also emphasises 'objective criteria' which need to inform policy choices lest the measures in question are found to be disproportionate. See eg Case C-127/07, *Société Arcelor Atlantique et Lorraine ea*, ECLI:EU:C:2008:728 [58].

[36] Case C-355/10, *Parliament v Council*, ECLI:EU:C:2012:516 [67].

[37] ibid [68].

[38] See eg Opinion 1/19 re *the Istanbul Convention*, ECLI:EU:C:2021:832 [284].

[39] ibid [65].

[40] While this was a post-Lisbon case, the contested act *in casu* had been adopted following the PRAC, which is still applied in some areas and which may still result in the Council adopting measures which, under the post-Lisbon framework, would normally be delegated acts. See section 4.III.C.

[41] Case C-355/10, *Parliament v Council*, ECLI:EU:C:2012:516 [76].

[42] Bauerschmidt, 'Verordnung (EU) Nr. 596/2014' (2022) § 29.

ie norms of general application? AG Mengozzi in his Opinion on the EU–Canada PNR Agreement opted for the latter reading, referring to the *Volker and Markus Schecke*[43] and *Schwarz*[44] cases.[45] However, both cases related to the pre-Lisbon constitutional framework in which there was no notion of formal legislation. In its Opinion the Court approached the problem differently and first noted that while international agreements are no formal legislative acts, they are the external equivalent to legislative acts and can therefore be considered as meeting the requirement of Article 52(1) of the Charter.[46] It furthermore added that

> it has not in any way been argued in the present procedure that the envisaged agreement may not meet the requirements as to accessibility and predictability required for the interferences which it entails to be regarded as being laid down by law within the meaning of … Article 52(1) of the Charter.[47]

This indeed implies that limitations on fundamental rights can be introduced through delegated (or autonomous executive, and even implementing) acts, since these can as easily meet the accessibility and predictability requirements as formal legislative acts.[48]

The Court also confirmed this in the *Europol* case. The question in that case was whether the list of third countries with which Europol can set up cooperation should be defined by the legislator or not. The Parliament stressed the implications on fundamental rights of drawing up the list (transfers of data being made possible between Europol and the third countries concerned). However, the Court accepted that the Council could draw up the list in its executive capacity, given that the legislator had sufficiently framed the power to draw up the list.[49] This means that *SBC*'s emphasis on the limitation of fundamental rights requiring legislative intervention becomes more problematic. Under Article 52(1) of the Charter, executive acts may limit fundamental rights as long as they meet the accessibility and predictability requirements. Following *Europol*, executive acts may do so as long as the limitation is sufficiently foreseen by the basic legislative act, but so far the Court has not developed this 'sufficiently foreseen' test. Also, in further jurisprudence on the essentiality requirement, the Court focuses on the 'political choices' limb of essentiality rather than the 'human rights' limb introduced in *SBC*.[50] The fundamental rights focus in *SBC* might then be an isolated case, perhaps resulting from the national background of the juge-rapporteur. Indeed, without referring to the *SBC* case,[51] the Court in *Multi-annual cod plan* recalibrated its focus and noted that 'measures which entail a policy choice [are] reserved to the EU legislature because the measures are necessary for the pursuit of the objectives of the common policies [at issue]'.[52] What is essential therefore corresponds to what is political,

[43] Joined Cases C-92/09 and C-93/09, *Volker and Markus Schecke*, ECLI:EU:C:2010:662 [66].
[44] Case C-291/12, *Schwarze*, ECLI:EU:C:2013:670 [35].
[45] Opinion of AG Mengozzi in Opinion procedure 1/15 re *the EU-Canada PNR Agreement*, ECLI:EU:C:2016:656 [191].
[46] Opinion 1/15 re *the EU-Canada PNR Agreement*, ECLI:EU:C:2017:592 [146].
[47] ibid.
[48] Also suggesting this, see Case C-130/10, *Parliament v Council*, ECLI:EU:C:2012:472 [83]–[85].
[49] See Case C-363/14, *Parliament v Council*, ECLI:EU:C:2015:579 [50]–[51].
[50] See also Bauerschmidt (n 32) § 29.
[51] That the Court did not refer to *SBC* could be because it was asked to draw the dividing line between a legal basis conferring a legislative power and one conferring an autonomous executive power, rather than between a legislative act and a non-legislative act adopted pursuant to an empowerment in the legislative act.
[52] Joined Cases C-124/13 and C-125/13, *Parliament & Commission v Council*, ECLI:EU:C:2015:790 [50].

which is what is necessary to define a policy. This might give the impression that essentiality may be determined through a 'top-down approach', but as will be noted in section 5.III, ultimately a bottom-up approach will often be required.[53]

The question of how to test this rather self-evident principle of essential elements remains confusing[54] and has already resulted in several decisions in the EU Courts. The underlying cases are typically first brought before the General Court (when a party challenges a Commission decision) and are often appealed before the Court of Justice which, on several occasions, has quashed and corrected the General Court's findings on the essentiality requirement of Article 290 TFEU. Constraints of space do not permit a fully fledged analysis of these cases,[55] but the main recurring threads will be highlighted in the discussion in section 5.III on testing the specificity requirement in practice, since the case law shows that the latter is often confused with the essentiality requirement.

III. Delimitation of Delegated and Implementing Acts

A third delimitation problem is that of distinguishing between the acts foreseen in Articles 290 and 291 TFEU. It is this delimitation problem which has been perceived by practitioners and commentators as the most acute, since the differences in preferences between the Parliament and Council are the starkest while (typically) both institutions will need to find an agreement on which power is conferred. In a nutshell, the Parliament wants to see delegated acts rather than implementing acts since it can veto delegated acts, but not implementing acts. The Council, in contrast, prefers implementing acts because it gives the Member States more control. To block a delegated act, a reinforced qualified majority voting (QMV) is needed (see section 5.IV.B), whereas depending on the precise comitology procedure (see section 6.V), a mere blocking minority is sufficient to prevent the Commission from (immediately) adopting implementing measures, creating room for further deliberation with national experts (and further influence over the draft measure). However, simply focusing on the control regime applicable would be to commit the 'control fallacy' (see further).

More fundamentally, the different control regimes reflect the different constitutional logics underpinning Articles 290 and 291 TFEU. The first provides for a completely voluntary and horizontal delegation relationship, while the former provides for a compulsory and vertical delegation relationship.[56] Schütze thereby argues that 'to avoid a functional

[53] Bauerschmidt refers to an 'induktiver Prüfvorgang'; see Bauerschmidt (n 32) § 27.1.

[54] Brandsma and Blom-Hansen note in this regard that '[g]enerally speaking, annexes to legislative acts can be considered non-essential elements, and they can be amended through delegated acts'. See Gijs Jan Brandsma and Jens Blom-Hansen, *Controlling the EU executive? The politics of delegation in the European Union* (Oxford, OUP, 2017) 15. This, however, puts things upside down. Annexes are not in themselves non-essential. Instead, the legislator typically puts a coherent set of non-essential provisions in an annex.

[55] For an analysis of some of these cases, see Merijn Chamon, 'Limits to Delegation under Art 290 TFEU – The Specificity and Essentiality Requirements Put to the Test' (2018) 25 *Maastricht Journal of European and Comparative Law* 231–45.

[56] Robert Schütze, '"Delegated" Legislation in the (new) European Union: A Constitutional Analysis' (2011) 74 *MLR* 690.

overlap between Article 290 and Article 291, both provisions must be seen from different constitutional perspectives. The former is designed directly to protect democratic values, while the latter is primarily designed to protect federal values'.[57] As noted by Bradley, a problematic functional overlap flows from the TFEU itself.[58] As pointed out above (see section 2.III), Article 290 TFEU qualifies the delegated act both functionally and materially, whereas the definition of the implementing act is purely defined in terms of its function. A priori, however, laying down uniform conditions for implementing legally binding Union acts (Article 291 TFEU) may very well be done through non-legislative acts of general application (Article 290 TFEU).

Since both provisions would allow for the adoption of non-legislative acts of general application, the crux of the matter would reside in whether such acts are of an implementing or a supplementing/amending nature. This is also why, of the different problems for the proper delimitation of delegated and implementing acts, Craig identified the 'language problem' as the most fundamental: since all derived measures involve some 'addition' to the basic or primary act, the question boils down to the semantic difference in meaning between implementation and supplementation.[59]

According to Craig, this language problem results in a second, temporal, problem since it is only in light of a derived measure's content, ie only after it is adopted, that one could determine whether the addition amounts to implementation or supplementation.[60] That, however, would appear to be a false problem: the delegation or conferral of power restricts the Commission (or exceptionally the Council) as to which measures it can adopt both in a formal and substantive sense. Which formal power is conferred (ie delegated or implementing), is clear from the outset and thus determines *ex ante* the possible content of the acts to be adopted. Articles 290(3) and 291(4) TFEU thereby also require the nature of the act to be formally spelled out in its title.[61] Secondly, the content of a derived measure as ultimately adopted does not ex post determine the nature of the act.[62] Instead, and in case there is a misalignment between the two, it will merely result in the invalidity of the derived measure. Still, the language problem, which Craig rightly predicted would give rise to inter-institutional disputes,[63] is real, although not entirely novel with the Lisbon Treaty reform.

[57] ibid 691. Given the unclear normative foundation of the essentiality requirement (see above), it arguably goes too far to reduce the logic underpinning Art 290 TFEU purely to the value of democracy.

[58] Kieran Bradley, 'Delegation of Powers in the European Union – Political Problems, Legal Solutions?' in Carl Fredrik Bergström and Dominique Ritleng (eds), *Rulemaking by the European Commission – The New System for Delegation of Powers* (Oxford, OUP, 2016) 77.

[59] Paul Craig, 'Delegated Acts, Implementing Acts' (2011) 672–74. Further on the language problem, see also Atilla Vincze, 'Delegation versus Implementation: a deconstruction of the promise of the Lisbon Treaty' in Eljalill Tauschinsky and Wolfgang Weiß (eds), *The Legislative Choice Between Delegated and Implementing Acts in EU Law* (Cheltenham, Edward Elgar, 2018) 25–28.

[60] Craig (ibid) 674–75.

[61] According to AG Kokott in *Esso Italiana*, not qualifying them as such constitutes a procedural irregularity. At the same time AG Kokott found that such an irregularity does not warrant the invalidation of a contested decision if its implementing nature is clear from its content and the context in which it was adopted. Opinion of AG Kokott in Joined Cases C-191/14 and C-192/14, Case C-295/14 and Joined Cases C-389/14, C-391/14 to C-393/14, *Esso Italiana*, ECLI:EU:C:2015:754 [177].

[62] For a possible suggestion to the contrary, see Opinion of AG Kokott in Case C-723/17, *Craeynest*, ECLI:EU:C:2019:168 [70].

[63] Craig (n 26) 673.

Arguably it was introduced in the sphere of comitology in the 1990s by the Commission's original proposal for a second comitology decision. In its proposal the Commission wanted to reserve the regulatory procedure to the adoption of 'measures of general scope designed to apply, update or adapt essential provisions of basic instruments'.[64] The scope of the regulatory procedure thus proposed would therefore combine the function of the current delegated act with part of the function performed by the current implementing act. While it would not create the delimitation problem currently discussed,[65] since it amalgamated rather than distinguished the current notions of implementation and supplementation, it did explicitly recognise the functions of applying, updating and adapting as being distinct. As is clear from the second comitology decision, the Council did not follow the Commission on this point. Under the second comitology decision, the regulatory procedure could instead only be used to *apply* essential provisions whereas only the non-essential provisions could be *adapted or updated*.[66]

Further, in its very essence and outside the realm of comitology, Craig's language problem is as old as the EU legal order itself. As was noted (see section 2.III.B) the latter always had executive federalism as one of its fundamental characteristics. When Article 189 EEC then prescribed that the Regulation was directly applicable, ie that its creation in the EU legal order automatically and immediately resulted in its existence in the national legal order,[67] Craig's language problem was created since the direct applicability of a regulation did not mean it was automatically directly effective or did not need to be complemented by further measures in order to be effective.[68] Indeed, Member States were required to implement such regulations (as if they were national statutes),[69] but they could evidently not alter or modify such regulations while doing so. An interesting parallel may thus be found in the Court's early case law on the legal effects of regulations.[70] According to the Court in *Krohn*, since a regulation is directly applicable, Member States cannot, 'for the purpose of ensuring the application of [a] regulation, take measures the purpose of which is to amend its scope or to add to its provisions'.[71] Even when EU regulations refer back to national law, such a reference cannot be understood as somehow delegating a power to complete

[64] See Art 2(2) of European Commission, COM (1998) 380 final.

[65] As Kortenberg noted, the delimitation problems would be to distinguish essential from non-essential provisions, since only the former would come under the regulatory procedure. See Helmut Kortenberg, 'Comitologie: le retour' (1998) 34 *Revue trimestrielle de droit européen* 324–25.

[66] See Art 2(b) of Council Decision 1999/468, OJ [1999] L 184/23. This after the Parliament in its opinion even proposed to simply make it impossible to modify basic instruments. See the new recital 4a in the European Parliament's Resolution on the Exercise of implementing powers conferred on the Commission, OJ [1999] C 249/404.

[67] See Case 34/73, *Variola*, ECLI:EU:C:1973:101 [10].

[68] On this, see Robert Kovar, 'Le règlement est directement applicable dans tout État membre: certes mais encore' in Nathalie De Grove-Valdeyron and Marc Blanquet (eds), *Mélanges en l'honneur du Professeur Joël Molinier* (Paris, LGDJ, 2012) 355–72. Seemingly equating direct applicability and direct effect, see Paul Craig, 'The Role of the European Parliament under the Lisbon Treaty' in Stefan Griller and Jacques Ziller (eds), *The Lisbon Treaty* (Wien, Springer, 2008) 120–21.

[69] On this already, Jean-Victor Louis, *Les règlements de la Communauté économique européenne* (Bruxelles, Presses Universitaires de Bruxelles, 1969) 329–32.

[70] See on this, Richard Lauwaars, 'Implementation of Regulations by National Measures' (1983) 10 *Legal Issues of Economic Integration* 41–52.

[71] Case 74/69, *Krohn*, ECLI:EU:C:1970:58 [4]. In *Bollmann*, the Court even referred to a prohibition to *supplement* a regulation's provisions (the Court uses the same language as that of Art 290 TFEU also in the German and French versions of the ruling). See Case 40/69, *Bollmann*, ECLI:EU:C:1970:12 [4].

EU regulations, but merely allowing the Member States to define 'the technical and procedural rules designed to ensure compliance with [the Regulation]'.[72] Member States are thus allowed, and even required,[73] to enforce, apply and implement[74] a regulation, but cannot amend or supplement it. AGs Jacobs and Capotorti, in *Commission v Germany* and *Amsterdam Bulb* respectively, deduced from this case law that (only) those national measures which presuppose the content of the Regulation[75] and merely see to its enforcement are entirely permissible: 'by taking steps under national law to enforce an obligation arising under a regulation, the national authorities are not altering the scope of that Regulation or supplementing its provisions; they are merely giving effect to it'.[76]

While this issue may have been settled decades ago in the Court's early case law, it still sporadically results in litigation before the Court in modern times. In a recent infringement action brought by the Commission against Denmark, the Court confirmed that since the relevant EU regulation did not define the key concept of 'cabotage' with sufficient precision, every Member State could adopt implementing measures clarifying what cabotage meant for the application of the regulation in that Member State (even if *in casu* the resulting Danish application differed from those in other Member States).[77] It may be questioned, however, whether by leaving the precise definition of such a crucial concept in the hands of the Member States, the legislator failed to properly define the Regulation's scope (in contravention of *Krohn*, *cf* above) and thus an essential element. Alternatively, one could argue that this is still covered by 'ensuring compliance' with the Regulation. In order to ensure such compliance, different AGs in the past have noted that Member States may have a broad discretion in 'giving effect' to regulations,[78] and can even adopt additional rules of administrative or procedural character that are *reasonably necessary* for giving effect to a regulation.[79] From this perspective, implementation under Article 291 TFEU would encompass the adoption of all additional rules as reasonably necessary to give effect to binding EU acts. Anything going beyond that and adding rules to legislative acts that change the act's content and/or scope, would qualify as supplementation under Article 290 TFEU.

In light of the above, the actual post-Lisbon developments can now be assessed. Before doing so, one important observation needs to be made: despite the Court and the institutions now accepting that the scope of Articles 290 and 291 TFEU overlap, this overlap is only *partial*, and delegated and implementing acts are not fully interchangeable. This is also the premise of the present enquiry (and one which is held by the EU institutions, including the Court) despite some radical proposals being made, notably by Zdobnõh,[80] to consider that

[72] Case 131/73, *Grosoli*, ECLI:EU:C:1973:158 [8].
[73] See Case 30/70, *Scheer*, ECLI:EU:C:1970:117 [10].
[74] See Case C-403/98, *Azienda Agricola Monte Arcosu*, ECLI:EU:C:2001:6 [26].
[75] See Opinion of AG Capotorti in Case 50/76, *Amsterdam Bulb*, ECLI:EU:C:1976:183 [4].
[76] Opinion of AG Jacobs in Case C-217/88, *Commission v Germany*, ECLI:EU:C:1990:201 [16].
[77] Case C-541/16, *Commission v Denmark*, ECLI:EU:C:2018:251. It should be noted, however, that while the English version of the judgment refers to implementing measures (adopted by Denmark), the French version refers to *mesures d'application* (thus not using the same language as Art 291 TFEU).
[78] Opinion of AG Van Gerven in Case C-326/88, *Hansen & Soen*, ECLI:EU:C:1989:609 [8].
[79] Opinion of AG Gordon Slynn in Joined Cases 123 and 330/87, *Jeunehomme*, ECLI:EU:C:1988:274, 4534. Explicitly referring to the administrative or procedural character of such additional rules, see Opinion of AG Warner in Case 94/77, *Fratelli Zerbone*, ECLI:EU:C:1977:206, 126.
[80] Dmitri Zdobnõh, 'Competition between articles 290 and 291 TFEU: what are these two articles about' in Tauschinsky and Weiß, *The Legislative Choice* (2018) 42–64.

delegated and implementing powers are indeed interchangeable and that they merely differ in the control regime applicable to them.[81] While this is an entirely legitimate suggestion for Treaty reform (which would result in merging Articles 290 and 291 TFEU again and giving discretion to the legislator to determine the control regime applicable) it would reverse the logic of the current Treaties. Under the latter, the nature of the empowerment determines the control regime applicable and not the other way around. While it is politically tempting (for the institutions) to reverse the Treaties' logic, they would be committing what may be termed the 'control fallacy'. That fallacy will pop up throughout the subsequent sections.

A. Judicial Clarifications in *Biocides*, *Eures Network* and *Visa Reciprocity*

As noted further in section 6.II, the Court did not opt to transpose the case law on Member States' powers to implement (but not supplement) regulations, and instead reconfirmed its pre-Lisbon understanding of implementation (under Articles 155 and 145 EEC). This is important, since while the distinction between delegated and implementing acts was generally supported in legal doctrine,[82] there was disagreement whether a possible overlap between the two would have to be tolerated, or whether the Court should enforce the distinction between the two acts strictly.[83] At the time of the Convention, Jacqué noted that a material criterion ought to be found to distinguish supplementation from implementation.[84] Subsequently, some suggested that the degree of discretion left to the Commission could function as such a material criterion.[85] Türk, in contrast, suggested transposing the distinction between the regulatory and management procedures, under the second comitology decision, to distinguish delegated from implementing acts.[86] Of course, this would only have eased the adaptation of existing (pre-Lisbon) basic acts to the post-Lisbon framework, and would not have helped much in deciding between granting delegated or implementing powers in legislative acts adopted *after* the entry into force of the Lisbon Treaty. In addition,

[81] See also Vihar Georgiev, 'Too much executive power? Delegated law-making and comitology in perspective' (2013) 20 *Journal of European Public Policy* 537.

[82] Very critically however, see Ellen Vos, 'Editorial: White and Black Smoke Coming from the Justus Lipsius Building' (2004) 11 *Maastricht Journal of European and Comparative Law* 228–30; Carl Fredrik Bergström, *Comitology – Delegation of Powers in the European Union and the Committee System* (Oxford, OUP, 2005) 351–63.

[83] Bast and Bianchi did not find the overlap problematic. See Jürgen Bast, 'New categories of acts after the Lisbon reform: Dynamics of parliamentarization in EU law (2012) 49 *Common Market Law Review* 920–21; Daniele Bianchi, 'La comitologie est morte! Vive la comitologie!' (2012) 48 *Revue trimestrielle de droit européen* 93. For authors that argued for a (more) strict separation, see inter alia Paolo Stancanelli, 'Le système décisionnel de l'Union' in Giuliano Amato, Herve Bribosia and Bruno de Witte (eds), *Genèse et destinée de la constitution européenne: commentaire du traité établissant une Constitution pour l'Europe à la lumière des travaux préparatoires et perspectives d'avenir* (Bruxelles, Bruylant, 2007) 524; "Robert Schütze, '"Delegated" Legislation in the (new) European Union: A Constitutional Analysis' (2011) 74 *MLR* 5 690; Thomas Kröll, 'Delegierte Rechtsetzung und Durchführungsrechtsetzung und das institutionelle Gleichgewicht der Europäischen Union' (2011) 66 *Zeitschrift für öffentliches Recht* 267.

[84] Jean-Paul Jacqué, 'L'étemel retour – Réflexion sur la comitologie' in Georges Vandersanden (ed), *Mélanges en hommage à Jean-Victor Louis*) Bruxelles, Editions de l'Université de Bruxelles, 2003) 220–21. Jacqué therein rightly noted that a much simpler solution would have been to confine the function of the delegated act to the amendment of legislative acts.

[85] See below, n 106.

[86] Türk, 'Lawmaking after Lisbon' (2012) 75.

Türk also refers to the *Forest Focus* case, where the Court juxtaposed the normative activity of 'developing a specific scheme' on the one hand, and that of 'implementing aspects already clearly defined' on the other. That distinction goes back to Article 2 of the second comitology decision, which distinguished between 'management measures' on the one hand and 'measures of general scope designed to apply essential provisions of basic instruments' on the other, but these notions were not reproduced in Articles 290 and 291 TFEU.[87]

As noted, the different institutions had each adopted their own viewpoint on how to give effect to the new Treaty framework[88] but *Biocides*[89] presented the first case for the Court to clarify the demarcation line. At issue was the validity of the legislator's mandate to the Commission to fix the fees payable to the European Chemicals Agency (ECHA) under the Biocides Regulation[90] through implementing acts. According to the Commission, it ought to have been granted a delegated instead of an implementing power since it was effectively being asked to supplement rather than implement the Regulation, the legislator merely having defined general principles which could not be readily implemented.

The Court set out its decision by identifying the functions of the two acts, finding that a delegated act is used 'to achieve the adoption of rules coming within the regulatory framework as defined by the basic legislative act',[91] while an implementing act would allow the Commission 'to *provide further detail* in relation to the content of a legislative act, in order to ensure that it is implemented under uniform conditions in all Member States'.[92] The English language version of the Court's ruling departs on this point from the original French version and from other language versions which do not allude to 'providing further detail', but which instead refer to the notion of 'specifying', or *préciser, präzisieren, precisare, nader bepalen*, etc. The latter notion is therefore to be preferred to qualify the normative activity of *implementing* binding EU acts. Crucially, the Court further confirmed that the legislator has a discretion in choosing between implementation and delegation and that, as a result, it would only intervene if the legislator has manifestly erred when granting the one or the other power to the Commission. Evidently, this meant that the Court rejected the Commission's argument on Articles 290 and 291 TFEU constituting two mutually exclusive realms.[93] The Court then concluded that the legislator could reasonably have taken the view that its framework applicable to the fees was complete and therefore merely required further implementation, instead of supplementation, by the Commission.

In *Eures Network*, a Commission implementing decision was challenged by the Parliament claiming that the Commission had overstepped its mandate and had supplemented, and on some points even amended,[94] the legislative parent act. While this constellation is different from *Biocides* and *Visa reciprocity* (see below) where the validity of the enabling clause in the parent act was challenged, *Eures Network* also turned on the distinction between Articles 290 and 291 TFEU and presented an opportunity to the Court to clarify the

[87] See Case C-122/04, *Commission v Parliament & Council*, ECLI:EU:C:2006:134 [44].
[88] See above ch 3 n 93.
[89] Case C-427/12, *Commission v Parliament and Council*, ECLI:EU:C:2014:170.
[90] Opinion of AG Cruz Villalón in Case C-65/13, *Parliament v Commission*, ECLI:EU:C:2014: 2071 [77].
[91] Case C-427/12, *Commission v Parliament and Council*, ECLI:EU:C:2014:170 [38].
[92] ibid [39] (emphasis added).
[93] ibid [23].
[94] See Case C-65/13, *Parliament v Commission*, ECLI:EU:C:2014:2289 [68]–[70].

difference between supplementation and implementation. While this case is discussed more in depth in section 6.II.B, given its relevance for the question of implementation, it is useful to highlight here that the Parliament advanced a very narrow conceptualisation of implementation. According to the Parliament 'an implementing measure under Article 291 TFEU is only supposed to give effect to the [*already*] existing rules in the act on which it is based'.[95] As a result, for those provisions of the implementing act that developed the rules on promoting or facilitating the free movement of workers which did not originate in the parent act or which it believed were not specific or purely technical in nature, the Parliament argued they constituted supplementation.[96] The Court reaffirmed its definition of implementation put forward in the *Biocides* case,[97] but also applied its pre-Lisbon case law on the limits to the Commission's implementing power (see section 6.II.B). As a result, 'implementation' was not interpreted by the Court in the restrictive way advanced by the Parliament or even in the case law on the implementation of regulations (see section 4.III). Instead, the Court seemed to proceed based on a narrow conceptualisation of supplementation.

'Seemed' is important here since the Court did not clarify further on when the Commission would go 'beyond' implementation. Instead, it relied on a *petitio principii* when it found that implementation encompasses adopting those measures useful or necessary to *implement* a parent act. Where the AG still suggested that one of the provisions of the implementing act left too much discretion,[98] the Court did not pick up on this suggested criterion for distinguishing Articles 290 and 291 TFEU and confirmed explicitly in *Visa reciprocity* that the degree of discretion left to the Commission is not a useful criterion to distinguish implementation from supplementation.[99]

In that case, the Commission again challenged a legislative mandate, but this time it had received a delegated power, arguing that it ought to have been conferred an implementing power. The Court in *Visa reciprocity* confirmed its previous ruling in *Biocides* and also addressed a number of ambiguities that had persisted following *Biocides*.[100] The mechanism created by the legislative act in *Visa reciprocity* followed several stages: in a first stage, a visa exemption granted to the nationals of a third country may be suspended through an implementing act; in a second stage, the suspension is effectuated through a delegated act whereby a footnote is also added next to the third country concerned in the annex to the basic legislative regulation; and finally, in a third stage, the Commission may submit a legislative proposal to the ordinary legislature with a view of amending the basic legislative regulation.

The Commission argued that in the second stage, just like in the first, it would simply be implementing the rules of the basic regulation and that adding a footnote next to an entry in

[95] Case C-65/13, *Parliament v Commission*, ECLI:EU:C:2014:2289 [25]. The adverb 'already' was added to this citation because it transpires from the Parliament's subsequent arguments that it believed that implementing measures cannot add anything to the parent act that is not *already* foreseen in that act.

[96] Case C-65/13, *Parliament v Commission*, ECLI:EU:C:2014:2289 [29], [32]–[33].

[97] ibid [43]. Again, in the English language version, the notion of 'providing further detail' is also carried over from *Biocides*.

[98] Opinion of AG Cruz Villalón in Case C-65/13, *Parliament v Commission*, ECLI:EU:C:2014: 2071 [77].

[99] See below n 104.

[100] See Dominique Ritleng, 'The dividing line between delegated and implementing acts: The Court of Justice sidesteps the difficulty in *Commission v Parliament and Council (Biocides)*' (2015) 52 *Common Market Law Review* 250–57.

an annex to the basic legislative act could not be qualified as an amendment in the sense of Article 290 TFEU.[101] As to the legal effects of the addition of such a footnote, the Commission argued that it was 'a mere technical tool used abusively in order to disguise the implementing act as a delegated act'.[102] In its decision, the Court confirmed again that the legislator has a large discretion when choosing between Article 290 or 291 TFEU, something which was still debated following *Biocides*.[103] Also in line with *Biocides*, the Court refused to elaborate the Treaty framework by identifying further criteria. Crucially, it thereby unambiguously noted that 'neither the existence nor the extent of the discretion conferred on it by the legislative act is relevant for determining whether the act to be adopted by the Commission comes under Article 290 TFEU or Article 291 TFEU'.[104] By doing so, it did not follow up on the suggestion of AG Mengozzi,[105] or that of AG Cruz Villalón in *Eures Network* (see above), the General Court in *Czechia v Commission*, as well as the Commission and Parliament themselves and a number of commentators, that had advanced the 'degree of discretion' left to the Commission as a useful distinguishing criterion.[106] In contrast to *Biocides*, however, the Court no longer connected the two Treaty provisions. In *Biocides* it still noted that 'the concept of an implementing act within the meaning of Article 291 TFEU must be assessed in relation to the concept of a delegated act, as derived from Article 290 TFEU',[107] but in *Visa reciprocity* the Court found that it only needed to be ascertained whether the conditions of Article 290 TFEU were met, ie whether the Commission had been empowered to adopt acts of general application amending (or supplementing) the non-essential elements of the basic legislative act.[108] The Court found that this was indeed the case and dismissed the Commission's action. It thereby noted that the three stages of the mechanism are 'characterised by measures of increasing gravity and political sensitivity, to which instruments of different kinds correspond'.

[101] Case C-88/14, *Commission v Parliament and Council*, ECLI:EU:C:2015:499 [20].

[102] ibid [21].

[103] See Ritleng, 'The dividing line between delegated and implementing acts' (2015) 254; Merijn Chamon, 'Clarifying the Divide between Delegated and Implementing Acts?' (2015) 42 *Legal Issues of Economic Integration* 184–88; Camilla Buchanan, 'The Conferral of Power to the Commission Put to the Test' (2014) 5 *European Journal of Risk Regulation* 2271.

[104] Case C-88/14, *Commission v Parliament and Council*, ECLI:EU:C:2015:499 [32]. This part of *Visa reciprocity* overruled the General Court's finding in Joined Cases T-659/13 and T-660/13, *Czechia v Commission*, ECLI:EU:T:2015:771 [47].

[105] Opinion of AG Mengozzi in Case C-88/14, *Commission v Parliament and Council*, ECLI:EU:C:2015:304 [45].

[106] The margin of discretion left to the Commission had also been suggested in doctrine as a criterion to distinguish Arts 290 and 291 TFEU. See Jean-Paul Jacqué, 'Introduction: Pouvoir législatif et exécutif dans l'UE' in Jean-Bernard Auby and Jacqueline Dutheil de la Rochère (eds), *Droit Administratif Européen* (Bruxelles, Bruylant, 2007) 47; Kröll, 'Delegierte Rechtsetzung und Durchführungsrechtsetzung' (2011) 284; Dominque Ritleng, 'La délégation du pouvoir législatif de l'Union européenne' in Gérard Cohen-Jonathan, Vlad Constantinesco, Valérie Michel, Jean-Claude Piris and Patrick Wachsmans (eds), *Chemins d'Europe: Mélanges en l'honneur de Jean Paul Jacqué* (Paris, Dalloz, 20100 575. Earlier the Commission had also noted that its powers under Art 291 TFEU are 'purely executive' whereas those under Art 290 TFEU are 'always discretionary'. See European Commission, COM (2009) 673 final 3. 'Purely executive' implementing powers much resembles the Court's language in *Meroni*, making it highly fortunate that the Court did not pick up on this suggestion (see also ch 3 n 29). In its 2014 resolution, the Parliament also found that the Commission has considerable discretion under Art 290 TFEU, but only limited discretion under Art 291 TFEU. See point 1 of European Parliament resolution of 25 February 2014 on follow-up on the delegation of legislative powers and control by Member States of the Commission's exercise of implementing powers, OJ [2017] C 285/11. Explicitly arguing against discretion as a criterion to distinguish Arts 290 and 291 TFEU, see Vincze, 'Delegation versus Implementation' (2018) 28–30.

[107] Case C-427/12, *Commission v Parliament & Council*, ECLI:EU:C:2014:170.

[108] Case C-88/14, *Commission v Parliament & Council*, ECLI:EU:C:2015:499 [32].

Finally, as to the question whether the basic legislative act would be *amended* by the Commission's delegated acts, the Court noted that they would have 'the *effect* of amending, if only temporarily, the normative content of the legislative act in question'.[109] In this regard, the importance of the footnote was relativised by the Court and taken to demonstrate 'the intention of the EU legislature to insert the act adopted on the basis of [the contested] provision in the actual body of [the legislative regulation], as amended'.[110] In *Visa reciprocity*, then, the Court seems to accept that a legislative act may *effectively* be amended without an actual change to the text of that act.[111]

To conclude, the take-home message of these three cases suggests that the distinction between Articles 290 and 291 TFEU in the Lisbon Treaty only makes sense if a sufficiently clear (if not mutually exclusive) distinction can be made between delegated and implementing acts. Such a distinction could have been operationalised by the Court requiring the legislator's choice between the one or the other to be informed by 'objective factors amenable to judicial review'.[112] This would have fitted nicely with the Court's well-established choice of legal basis test,[113] with its essential elements test[114] and even with the proportionality test.[115] However, the Court did not follow this path[116] and instead has left the choice to grant either implementing or delegated powers firmly in the hands of the legislator, de facto undoing much of the distinction between Articles 290 and 291 TFEU and arguably resulting in a constitutional modification. As is also apparent from the lack of further cases brought by the Commission, the confirmation of the legislator's discretion means that it has become almost completely pointless for the Commission to challenge the legislator's choice.

B. Amendments as Implementation

As the previous section discussed, the Court did not step in to uphold the Lisbon Treaty's distinction between delegated and implementing powers. However, it must be noted that in addition to the inherent difficulty of conceptually distinguishing supplementation from implementation, the political institutions did not make the Court's job easier, and instead contributed to muddying the waters, as the next two sections will show. First, the problematic overlap in function between delegated and implementing acts is illustrated by the comitology regulation's automatic alignment of the comitology procedures (see section 6.V.B.ii).

[109] ibid [42] (emphasis added). Pre-*Visa reciprocity*, Kröll had already argued that the notion of amendment could also cover such a situation. See Kröll (n 83) 267.

[110] Case C-88/14, *Commission v Parliament & Council*, ECLI:EU:C:2015:499 [43].

[111] However, in *Connecting Europe Facility* (see section 5.II.B) the Court again opted for understanding 'amending' in a formal sense.

[112] As also advocated by Annalisa Volpato, *Delegation of Powers in the EU Legal System* (London, Routledge, 2022) 65.

[113] See eg Opinion 2/00 re *the Cartagena Protocol*, ECLI:EU:C:2001:664 [22].

[114] Case C-355/10, *Parliament v Council*, ECLI:EU:C:2012:516 [67].

[115] Referring to objective factors in the proportionality assessment, see Case C-58/08, *Vodafone*, ECLI:EU:C:2010:321 [53].

[116] Türk also notes that the Court thereby deviated from its 'traditional approach'. See Alexander Türk, 'Legislative, delegated acts, comitology and interinstitutional conundrum in EU law – configuring EU normative spaces' (2020) 26 *European Law Journal* 421.

Under the second comitology decision, the regulatory procedure was to be used 'to adapt or update non-essential provisions of a basic instrument'.[117] From 2006 onwards, the PRAC (regulatory procedure with scrutiny) was introduced to fulfil this function in so far as basic instruments adopted through the co-decision procedure had to be updated or adapted. In contrast, under the Lisbon scheme, amending (or supplementing) *any* legislative act is a function which *only* a delegated act can fulfil.[118] Yet the Comitology Regulation automatically aligned the regulatory procedure to the examination procedure (see section 6.V.B.ii). As a result, all the references in pre-Lisbon 'legislation' prescribing the regulatory procedure to amend or supplement basic instruments, resulted in a post-Lisbon empowerment to adopt implementing acts that actually fulfil the function of a delegated act. A concrete example of this can be found in Council Directive 1999/105 on the marketing of forest reproductive material.[119] This pre-Lisbon 'basic instrument' was not adopted through the ordinary legislative procedure (and therefore did not come within the scope of application of the PRAC). At the time of writing, Article 23 of the Directive still allows the Commission to amend the annexes of the Directive 'in the light of the development of scientific or technical knowledge' and this pursuant to the regulatory procedure (to be read as the examination procedure following the entry into force of the Comitology Regulation). Another example can be found in Council Directive 2009/158 on animal health conditions governing intra-Community trade in, and imports from third countries of, poultry and hatching eggs.[120] This pre-Lisbon basic instrument was adopted under the advisory procedure and could therefore not prescribe the PRAC where its Annexes needed to be updated. Instead, the regulatory procedure is prescribed to adapt the Annexes to changes in diagnostic methods and to variations in the economic importance of particular diseases. The reference to the regulatory procedure must, following the entry into force of the Comitology Regulation, be read as a reference to the examination procedure, and that procedure, rather than a delegated act, has been used to amend the 'legislative' directive.[121] While these cases do not pose particular problems, because of the automatic alignment prescribed by the Comitology Regulation, it is different for those existing pre-Lisbon basic acts that still contain clauses referring to the PRAC.

C. The PRAC, a Zombie in EU Law

As noted in the previous section, the exception to the automatic alignment of comitology procedures between the regulation and the decision was the PRAC. In most cases the

[117] See Art 2(b) of Council Decision 1999/468 laying down the procedures for the exercise of implementing powers conferred on the Commission, OJ [1999] L 184/23.

[118] Subject of course to the possibility for a subsequent legislative act to amend or supplement an earlier legislative act.

[119] See Council Directive 1999/105 on the marketing of forest reproductive material, OJ [2000] L 11/17.

[120] See OJ [2009] L 343/74.

[121] See Commission Implementing Decision 2011/879 amending Annexes II and IV to Council Directive 2009/158/EC on animal health conditions governing intra-Community trade in, and imports from third countries of, poultry and hatching eggs, OJ [2011] L 343/105.

references (in basic instruments) to the PRAC should not be replaced with a reference to a comitology procedure (of the Comitology Regulation), but with a reference to the delegated act under Article 290 TFEU, for which there is no horizontal instrument.[122] Updating these legislative acts to the new legal reality of the Lisbon Treaty would thus require an amendment of every single one of these basic instruments, a process which the Commission originally had wanted to conclude before the end of the seventh parliamentary term in 2014.[123] Because of Member States' resistance in Council, the overhaul has proven much more difficult than expected. The Council did not agree to the Commission's proposal for an automatic alignment of most of the references to the PRAC into references to delegated acts.[124] This because of the Council's general preference for implementing acts rather than delegated acts (see section 4.III), but also because legally, Article 290 TFEU is no perfect transplant of the PRAC.[125] Article 290 TFEU prescribes both an essentiality and specificity requirement (see section 2.III.A) whereas the PRAC only prescribed an essentiality requirement. In replacing a PRAC empowerment with a delegated empowerment, one can assume that the essentiality requirement will be respected, but this cannot be assumed for the specificity requirement.[126] On a political note, one reason for the Council to cling on to the PRAC was that at the time of the Commission's original proposals there was not yet agreement between the institutions on the systematic consultation of national experts in the drafting of delegated acts (which dates only from 2016; see section 5.IV.A.i).[127]

Given the Council's objections, and despite the Parliament's broad agreement,[128] the new Juncker Commission decided to withdraw the 2013 proposals, indicating that the issue would be addressed in the new inter-institutional agreement on Better Law-Making.[129] The IIA provides that the Commission would propose a new alignment by the end of 2016.[130] As developed in section 5.IV.A.i, a Common Understanding on

[122] See Birgit Daiber, 'EU-Durchführungsrechtsetzung nach Inkrafttreten der neuen Komitologie-Verordnung' (2012) 47 *Europarecht* 241; Daniele Bianchi, 'La comitologie est morte! vive la comitologie! – Premières réflexions sur l'exécution du droit de l'Union après le Traité de Lisbonne – L'exemple de la Politique agricole commune' (2012) 48 *Revue trimestrielle de droit européen* 96.

[123] See the statements by the Commission annexed to the comitology regulation, OJ [2011] L 55/19.

[124] See Liesbeth A Campo, 'Delegated versus implementing acts: how to make the right choice?' (2021) 22 *ERA Forum* 197.

[125] See also Craig (n 26) 675–77.

[126] For a specific illustration, see A Campo, 'Delegated versus implementing acts' (2021) 199.

[127] In terms of drafting, the three measures proposed in the 2013 package would also have been 'standalone' regulations that technically would not have amended the roughly 220 remaining acts that referred to the PRAC but that would have to be read together with those remaining acts. See COM (2013) 451 final, COM (2013) 452 final and COM (2013) 751 final. COM (2013) 451 final listed the acts for which PRAC references would have to be read as references to the delegated procedure. COM (2013) 452 final related to measures in the area of Justice of Home Affairs to which Protocols No 21 and 22 applied and which therefore could not be included in the other proposal to which all EU Member States participated. Finally, COM (2013) 751 final combined a mixed bag with some references to the PRAC to be read as references to the delegated procedure whereas other references were to be read as referring to the procedures under the comitology regulation.

[128] See the three legislative resolutions adopted on 25 February 2014, OJ [2017] C 285/169-190-194.

[129] See Annex II to the Commission Work Programme of 2015, 11–12.

[130] See point 27 of the Interinstitutional Agreement between the European Parliament, the Council of the European Union and the European Commission on Better Law-Making, OJ [2016] L 123/1.

Delegated Acts was annexed to the IIA, which foresees a compulsory consultation of national experts for the adoption of delegated acts. At the end of 2016 the Commission proposed a new alignment which, in contrast to the 2013 package, consisted of genuine amending regulations.[131] Despite the Member States now being guaranteed their experts would be involved in the drafting of all delegated acts (see section 5.IV.A.i), the 2016 package has only been slightly more successful than the 2013 package however, since at the end of the eighth parliamentary term in 2019, only a partial alignment had been agreed to.[132] The hardest cases (around two-thirds of the 171 acts covered by the Commission's proposals) were thus left for a new Parliament to agree on together with the Council.[133] Whether a full alignment will be achieved in the short term remains doubtful.[134] The COVID pandemic halted ongoing discussions on the alignment,[135] and these were only kickstarted again by the French presidency in 2022. Unlike in 'normal' legislative negotiations, where there are different negotiating positions that can be traded off against each other (see section 7.I), no such trade-offs are possible in the alignment of the PRAC. References to the PRAC will therefore remain part of EU law for a long time to come and will only incrementally disappear as the pre-Lisbon acts are revised progressively ad hoc. Until then, the Member States in Council can and will combine the best features of the delegated and implementing act in one procedure, which is enough reason for them to refuse to properly 'Lisbonise' EU secondary law in a horizontal manner.[136] In a way, the PRAC therefore is a zombie of EU law: it should long be dead, but it stays alive nonetheless.

Although no new references to the PRAC can be introduced in the body of (formal) EU legislation since the entry into force of the Lisbon Treaty, the 'legislation' currently in force still contains ample references to the procedure. Decisions adopted pursuant to the PRAC thus continue to be adopted (see Figure 4.1). These measures are not qualified (by the Commission or Council) as implementing or delegated acts, pursuant to Articles 290(3) or 291(4) TFEU and might therefore look (based on their title) like autonomous executive acts.

[131] See n 127. See COM (2016) 798 final, COM (2016) 799 final. As explained in the latter proposal, the proposed alignment did not cover all remaining acts with a reference to the PRAC since a set of eight acts in the area of pesticides and food was left out; see COM (2016) 799 final 3.

[132] See Regulation 2019/1243 of the European Parliament and of the Council adapting a number of legal acts providing for the use of the regulatory procedure with scrutiny to Arts 290 and 291 of the Treaty on the Functioning of the European Union, OJ [2019] L 198/241.

[133] See Jean-Paul Jacqué, 'Actes délégués et mesures d'exécution' (2020) *Revue trimestrielle de droit européen* 671.

[134] On the problematic pace of the alignment, see also A Campo (n 124) 210.

[135] See Council of the European Union, Implementation of the Interinstitutional Agreement on Better Law-Making – State of play, Council Doc 14699/21, point 5.

[136] The Member States are also quite candid about this. When it comes to the REACH Regulation, one of the Presidency's Progress Reports on the 2016 alignment even decided to 'remove it from the RPS Adaptation Exercise given the difficulties expressed by Member States with these empowerments [in the REACH Regulation]. This file will need to be dealt with individually, and not as part of the adaptation exercise'. See Council of the European Union, Presidency Progress Report, Council Doc 10170/17, 21.

Figure 4.1 Number of PRAC measures adopted

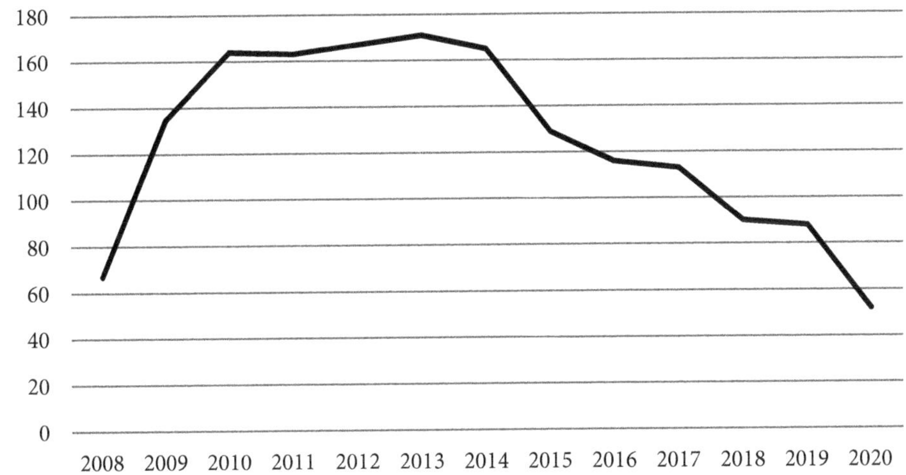

The EU institutions (not to say the Council) clinging on to the PRAC post-Lisbon, instead of simply finalising the alignment of the PRAC legal bases to the Lisbon Treaty, now in force for over a decade, is nothing but an anomalous absurdity. In addition, one may only wonder whether, with the benefit of hindsight, the Parliament does not regret its insistence on updating the second comitology decision to introduce a proto-delegated act after the failed ratification of the Constitutional Treaty. As Figure 4.1 above shows, PRAC measures only started to be adopted as of 2008, two years before the Lisbon Treaty entered into force. The price of these two years of additional parliamentary scrutiny powers is still being paid more than 10 years after the entry into force of the Lisbon Treaty.

D. The 2019 Inter-Institutional Agreement

As already noted, the three political institutions agreed in the 2016 IIA on Better Law-Making to agree on certain non-binding criteria guiding the legislator in its choice between conferring delegated or implementing powers. While the institutions could very well commit to binding criteria pursuant to Article 296 TFEU, the explicit choice for non-binding criteria was already contained in the 2016 IIA. The non-binding criteria adopted in 2019 (the 2019 IIA) consists of three main parts: (i) general principles; (ii) the criteria themselves; and (iii) the monitoring of the application and the review of the criteria. The 2019 IIA has been received sceptically, since it is indeed doubtful that it will genuinely facilitate future legislative negotiations.[137] In quite stark terms, Jacqué doubted the criteria's usefulness since they are a mere 'compendium of self-evident consequences' resulting from the Court's

[137] Bauerschmidt (n 32) § 17.

jurisprudence.[138] The cautious terms in which MEP Corbett, co-rapporteur and negotiator on behalf of the European Parliament, reported back to the committee seem to confirm that. He noted that the IIA

> somewhat clarifies the delineation criteria for when we should use delegated acts and when we should use implementing acts and this may help trilogue negotiations to more easily reach agreement on this sort of issues which frequently cause difficulties in our legislative procedures … Not a great deal of extra clarity … but a little bit of extra clarity … Progress I must confess is only partial … it is still a little bit of progress … It's not a revolution, it's scarcely an evolution but it is at least a few little steps forward.[139]

In what follows, the principles and criteria of the 2019 IIA are presented and assessed.

i. Principles

While the IIA sets out the 'general principles' in seven separate paragraphs, they can be classified into four different categories: the nature and purpose of the IIA; (superfluous) restatements from what already follows from the Treaties; codifications of the Court's post-Lisbon jurisprudence; and genuinely new principles introduced by the IIA.

Firstly, the IIA makes clear that the criteria listed are not exhaustive and that their aim is to guide the legislator.[140] In the second category we find principles prescribing that the power to adopt delegated acts may only be conferred on the Commission[141] and that the essential elements must be determined in the legislative act.[142] In the third category, the institutions reconfirmed that the legislator has discretion in choosing between conferring a delegated or implementing power on the Commission,[143] that policy choices are to be made by the legislator,[144] and that the essential elements are to be respected when the Commission adopts both delegated and implementing acts.[145] As noted above, it is the fourth set of principles which arguably contain new clarifications by advancing a specific reading of Articles 290–291 TFEU.

Among these are, first, that the nature of the envisaged act (delegated or implementing) must be determined by taking into account the objectives, content and context of the act as well as those of the legislative act itself;[146] that the legislator's discretion extends to the question *whether* uniform conditions for implementing a legislative act are required;[147] that the legislator has full discretion in providing (or not) for annexes to legislative acts or to prescribe that delegated acts should rather be adopted as separate acts;[148] and that the essentiality requirement means, for example, that the Commission cannot be conferred a power

[138] See Jacqué, 'Actes délégués et mesures d'exécution' (2020) 671. See also A Campo (n 124) 202.
[139] Intervention by MEP Corbett in the AFCO Committee of 7 March 2019.
[140] Non-Binding Criteria for the application of Arts 290 and 291 of the Treaty on the Functioning of the European Union – 18 June 2019, OJ [2019] C 223/1 (hereafter: 2019 IIA), points 1 and 7.
[141] 2019 IIA, point 6.
[142] ibid, point 5.
[143] ibid, point 3. Thus codifying *Biocides* and *Visa reciprocity*.
[144] ibid, point 5. Thus codifying *Multi-annual cod plan*.
[145] ibid, point 5. Thus codifying *Eures Network*.
[146] ibid, point 2.
[147] ibid, point 3. On this, see section 6.I below.
[148] ibid, point 4.

to 'weigh up conflicting interests on the basis of a number of assessments'.[149] This last principle is remarkable since it is presented as a codification of *SBC*, *Czechia v Commission* and *Dyson v Commission* (see below section 5.III). While the Court indeed referred to the weighing of conflicting interests based on a number of assessments, it only did so in the first two cases, and it is problematic to take this out of its context and present it as a general principle. Put differently, if this principle is understood as implying that whenever the Commission weighs up different interests based on a number of assessments it would be making political choices reserved to the legislator, the IIA would actually be departing from the case law cited. Under that case law, the Court merely noted that some political choices may consist of the weighing-up of different interests (without implying that every such action results in a political choice). In addition, in those cases the Court also clearly noted that some political choices may consist of an interference with fundamental rights (again without implying that every fundamental rights interference results in a political choice).[150]

ii. Criteria

Like the principles of the IIA, the criteria to a large extent either simply reproduce what already flows unequivocally from the Treaties or codify the Court's jurisprudence and therefore cannot as such provide *further* guidance to the legislators. As Table 4.2 shows, even the new guidance is a mixed bag of criteria. One notable clarification (A3) relates to the notion of general application. Since Article 290 TFEU provides that delegated acts are of general application, the question arises when an act may be said to be of general application.[151] This question is not new in EU law, since under Article 173 EEC, an action for annulment brought by non-privileged applicants could not, in principle, be directed against measures of general application.[152] Also, today this question is still relevant since the Court has defined a regulatory act in the sense of Article 263 TFEU as an act of general application.[153] The EU institutions have now transposed this case law to also determine the meaning of 'general application' in Article 290 TFEU.

Other criteria listed in part II of the IIA are arguably less useful since they reflect the general principle of part I of the IIA that the nature of an act must reflect its objectives, content and context. The criteria (E1, F, G) thus confirm that measures prescribing procedures, information obligations or which grant authorisations may be adopted either as legislative, delegated or implementing acts, depending on the case. This is different for methodologies or methods for which the institutions only foresee delegated or implementing acts (E2) suggesting *a contrario* that rules laying down such methods or methodologies can never be essential elements of legislation. Still, for these criteria (E to G) the circular reasoning is glaring and hardly helpful: to recall, the general principle (2) in part I prescribes that the *nature* of the act must be determined by its objectives, content and context, but the more specific criteria prescribe that the *nature* of an act can be legislative, delegated or implementing, depending on its '*nature*, objectives, content and context'. The nature of an

[149] ibid, point 5.

[150] Case C-355/10, *Parliament v Council*, ECLI:EU:C:2012:516 [77]; Case C-696/15 P, *Czechia v Commission*, ECLI:EU:C:2017:595 [78]; see also section 4.II.

[151] On this see also Campo (n 124) 203.

[152] See eg Case 101/76, *Koninklijke Scholten Honig v Council & Commission*, ECLI:EU:C:1977:70 [5]–[9].

[153] Case C-583/11 P, *Inuit Tapiriit Kanatami ea v Parliament & Council*, ECLI:EU:C:2013:625 [60].

act is thus determined by its nature (but also its objectives, content and context). How this may contribute to facilitating negotiations in trilogue is rather unclear.

Table 4.2 Breakdown of the 2019 non-binding criteria

Restatement of the Treaty provisions	Codification	New guidance
• Delegated acts are of general, not individual, application (A1) • Implementing acts may be of general or individual application (A2) • Amendments of legislative acts may only be done through DAs (B1) • Amendments may include the modification, repeal, insertion, addition, deletion or replacement of provisions (B2)	• Definition of supplementation (C) • Definition of implementation (D)	• Definition of general application borrowed from Art 263 TFEU jurisprudence (A3) • Example of supplementation: fleshing out legislative act by affecting its substance (C) • Example of implementation: not affecting the substance of the legislative act, merely giving effect (D) • Rules laying down a procedure may be prescribed in a legislative, delegated or implementing act depending on the nature, objectives, content and context (E1) • Rules laying down a methodology may be prescribed in a delegated or implementing act depending on the nature, objectives, content and context (E2) • Measures imposing an information obligation may be laid down in a legislative, delegated or implementing act depending on nature, objectives, content and context (F) • If these measures affect the substance of the information obligation, a delegated act must be prescribed; if they affect the format in which information must be provided, an implementing act must be prescribed (F) • Measures granting an authorisation may be laid down in a legislative, delegated or implementing act depending on nature, objectives, content and context (G) • Authorisations of general application that go beyond merely applying the criteria laid down in the legislative act should be adopted through delegated acts (G)

Fortunately, the institutions in the IIA give some useful examples to clarify what these objectives, content and context are that we need to look for. Thus, criteria C and D suggest that in terms of content we need to look for substantive prescriptions: if a legislative act's substantive obligations or prescriptions are added to, a delegated act will have to be relied on, otherwise an implementing act can be used. Similarly, in relation to information obligations (F), additional rules further clarifying the scope or substance of the information to be provided will have to be laid down in delegated acts, while rules on *how* the information must be provided must be laid down in implementing acts.[154] Finally, criterion G settles a contentious issue by making clear that authorisations, even if they result in an entitlement to sell goods or services to the public at large, may still be of individual scope and are therefore not (necessarily) measures of general application.[155]

iii. Assessment

The picture presented by the 2019 IIA may be hopelessly ambiguous, but this also means that every institution may profess its own reading of it and it also leaves scope for the present enquiry to propose a way forward in terms of delineating implementation from supplementation that is both in line with the Treaty framework and the codified post-Lisbon institutional practice. The first point may be illustrated by comparing the text of the 2019 IIA with the Parliament's 2014 resolution where it set out its own non-exhaustive list of delimitation criteria. Most of the criteria put forward by the Parliament have returned in the 2019 IIA, including the vague statement that some provisions may be of an implementing, delegated or even legislative nature 'depending on their nature, objectives, content and context'. The only criterion of the Parliament that did not make it to the 2019 IIA is its insistence on the degree of discretion being determinative for distinguishing implementing from delegated powers.[156]

In addition, the way forward proposed here builds on two strands of case law from the Court of Justice in other areas of EU law: the Court's jurisprudence on the powers of Member States when implementing regulations, recalled in section 4.III; and the Court's findings on institutional and procedural provisions of international agreements.

The two key complementing notions in this way forward are those of normative density and ancillarity. As follows from Article 290 TFEU and *Eures Network* (see section 6.II.B), the

[154] Jacqué links this to the degree of discretion left to the Commission when he notes that if the legislative act 'laisse une large marge d'appréciation quant au contenu des mesures à prendre, le recours aux actes délégués s'impose, les actes d'exécution étant utilisés dans le cas contraire'. See Jacqué (n 133) 671. However, this is not provided as such by the criteria and it would furthermore have meant a reversal of the Court's findings in *Visa reciprocity* where it ruled that the degree of discretion left to the Commission is immaterial for the distinction between delegated and implementing acts.

[155] See Jacqué (n 133) 671.

[156] In its resolution, it still noted that '[implementing] powers given to the Commission should not leave any significant margin of discretion', that 'delegated acts should be used where the basic act leaves a considerable margin of discretion to the Commission', that 'Only for elements that do not reflect any further political or policy orientation the legislator may decide to allow for their adoption through implementing acts' and that '[m]easures leading to a choice of priorities, objectives or expected results should be adopted by means of delegated acts'. See point 1 of European Parliament resolution of 25 February 2014 on follow-up on the delegation of legislative powers and control by Member States of the Commission's exercise of implementing powers, OJ [2017] C 285/11.

essential normative prescriptions need to be settled in formal legislation.[157] If the legislator follows a minimalistic approach, it simply establishes a framework that leaves a lot to flesh out, ie the framework has limited normative density and requires supplementation through delegated acts. Once the body of rules (composed of legislative and delegated acts) acquires a sufficient normative density that only requires the adoption of ancillary measures, this is to be done through implementing acts. As to which measures are ancillary, inspiration can be taken from the field of external relations and the jurisprudence of the Court when it looks at institutional and procedural provisions of international agreements that aim to ensure the effective application of the substantive provisions of those agreements. In the Court's case law provisions that are (merely) aimed at ensuring effective application are ancillary to the substantive provisions and therefore do not require a specific competence of the EU to be shown.[158]

While the institutions have not confirmed this as such, the more generally philosophy which can be induced from the 2019 non-binding criteria, or one which is at least compatible with it, is that provisions which are aimed at ensuring the effectiveness of the substantive prescriptions or obligations may be adopted through implementing acts. That aligns with, but is more restrictive than, the scope left to Member States to implement EU regulations, defined above as encompassing the adoption of all additional rules as reasonably necessary to give effect to binding EU acts (see section 4.III).

This more restrictive notion results from the EU's set up of executive federalism (see section 2.III.B), which requires that specific attention is paid to two dimensions to the implementation of EU law at EU level. A first raises the question *how* implementation is realised and puts the focus on the requirement in Article 291(2) TFEU that EU actors will only exceptionally implement when Member States' authorities cannot ensure sufficient *uniformity*. Assuming such uniformity is secured (or that sufficient uniformity is unproblematic to begin with) a second type of question boils down to *what* implementation should be, ie what is the end result that should be achieved when a legislative act is being applied.

Looking at the 2019 non-binding criteria from the perspective of the first dimension indeed reveals a similar logic: where information obligations or rules on procedures are further built upon, ie substantively added to and increasing normative density, delegated acts are prescribed. When the rules putting into effect an information obligation merely concern the ancillary issues of the format or technical means, an implementing act is prescribed. Of course, many types of rules and requirements are to be situated in between these extremes of imposing substantive obligations and defining a format to present certain information, and also the Court's test (in the area of external relations) of when a provision is ancillary is not without its ambiguities.[159] However, conceiving the exercise of an implementing power as adopting those *necessary* ancillary measures to make the substance of

[157] Abstraction made of the possibility to regulate essential elements through autonomous executive acts; see section 4.I.A.

[158] See eg Opinion 2/15 re *the EU–Singapore Free Trade Agreement*, ECLI:EU:C:2017:376 [276] and [282]; Case C-137/12, *Commission v Council*, ECLI:EU:C:2013:675 [70]; Opinion of AG Sharpston in Opinion 2/15 re *the EU–Singapore Free Trade Agreement*, ECLI:EU:C:2016:992 [509].

[159] Criticising the lack of a clear methodology and commenting on that relied on by AG Sharpston in her Opinion on the Singapore FTA, see David Kleimann, 'Reading Opinion 2/15: Standards of Analysis, the Court's Discretion, and the Legal View of the Advocate General', EUI Working Paper RSCAS 2017/23, 13–19.

regulation operative in a sufficient uniform manner would seem to capture the first dimension of the implementation of EU law at EU level.

Outside of the peculiar context of executive federalism there is of course the more colloquial understanding of implementation (which is also reflected in Article 291 TFEU) where implementation is understood in the sense of 'putting into effect'. The 2019 IIA partially reflects this idea too; for instance, authorisations can be granted through implementing acts unless authorisations do not simply depend on applying the criteria of the legislative act. Whether implementing acts can be used thus depends on the normative density of the existing body of rules. Again, in light of the EU's executive federalism however, the legislator should always reflect carefully on why this type of implementing power should be exercised at EU level rather than at national level. While the threshold may be lower for allowing EU actors to further specify *how* EU law is to be implemented (procedures, formats, methodology, etc), it should arguably be higher where an EU actor is empowered to substantively determine *what* the implementation of EU law should be. Put differently, the threshold for an EU actor to prescribe the *how* of implementation could be set at whether EU intervention is necessary, in the sense of useful, whereas the threshold for an EU actor to prescribe the *what* of implementation would be set at whether EU intervention is necessary in the sense of indispensable.[160]

E. Legislative Practice in Light of the 2019 IIA

Before the adoption of the 2019 IIA, one insider noted that 'in many cases more time is spent discussing whether or not certain issues should be the subject of a delegated act than the substantive content of the actual legislation'.[161] The question thus is whether the 2019 IIA brought any improvement in this regard. On some issues, the institutions could not agree on non-binding criteria,[162] meaning legislative negotiations (on these issues) may in any event remain lengthy. One such issue is the binding nature of delegated and implementing acts. According to the Commission, even though the 2019 IIA is silent on this, 'It is generally agreed between the three institutions that only legally binding acts may be adopted by means of delegated acts under Article 290 [TFEU]'.[163] In contrast, the Parliament and Council do not believe the same goes for implementing acts,[164] suggesting that for them

[160] This again links with the Court's external relations jurisprudence. Art 3(2) TFEU provides the EU is exclusively competent to conclude international agreements where this conclusion is necessary to enable the Union to exercise its internal competence. Similarly, Art 216(1) TFEU provides that the EU is competent to conclude international agreements where this is necessary in order to achieve one of the objectives of the Treaties. However, in its Opinion 2/15 the Court clearly distinguished both provisions, setting a lower threshold for necessity in the sense of Art 216(1) TFEU compared to that for necessity in the sense of Art 3(2) TFEU. See Opinion 2/15 re *the EU-Singapore FTA*, ECLI:EU:C:2017:376 [237]–[242].

[161] See María José Martínez Iglesias, 'The European Parliament and the Better Law-Making Agenda' in Sacha Garben and Inge Govaere (eds), *The EU Better Regulation Agenda – A Critical Assessment* (Oxford, Hart Publishing, 2018) 111.

[162] Liesbeth A Campo explicitly mentions the adoption of annual and multiannual work programmes implementing financial instruments. See Campo (n 124) 206.

[163] European Commission, Delegated and Implementing Acts – Guidelines for the Services of the Commission, SEC(2020) 361 11.

[164] ibid.

this could also be a criterion distinguishing delegated from implementing acts. If the Commission had agreed with the Parliament and Council on the latter point that could have been a further delineation criterion. It is, however, worth reflecting on the apparent consensus that delegated acts must be binding. Although this might seem obvious, Article 290 TFEU does not explicitly state so. Evidently, a delegated act *amending* a legislative act must be binding, otherwise it could not amend a legislative act.[165] It is not entirely clear, however, why a legislative act might not be *supplemented* by non-binding measures. While institutional practice is not decisive in itself, it is at least interesting to first note that pre-Lisbon the PRAC (the delegated act's precursor; see section 4.III.C) has been prescribed to adopt soft law.[166] Secondly, there are indeed post-Lisbon instances of a *supplementing* delegated empowerment foreseeing the adoption of non-binding measures.[167] In the same vein, the Commission's claim with regard to Article 291 TFEU that 'the only way to ensure a uniform implementation of legally binding Union act[s] is indeed to adopt binding measures'[168] may seem to reflect the natural state of affairs, but it cannot be a cast iron rule – if only because the Court in *ENISA* already accepted that 'in order to facilitate the uniform implementation and application of acts based on [Article 114 TFEU], the adoption of non-binding supporting and framework measures seems appropriate'.[169] While the Commission is rightfully wary of being conferred implementing powers to adopt non-binding measures, and while soft law comes with evident drawbacks, the possibility to implement binding EU legal acts through soft law cannot therefore be dismissed. This possibility is also relied upon in practice,[170] and as chapter seven shows, this broadens the options available to the legislator.

Returning to the IIA laying down the non-binding criteria and those topics actually covered by it, it is as of yet it unclear whether the 2019 IIA has now facilitated legislative decision-making, by reducing the time spent during trilogues on negotiating the form empowerments will take.[171] Shortly after the 2019 IIA was concluded and the new Parliament started its term, the COVID pandemic hit, which also had repercussions for legislative negotiations and trilogues as these had to be organised online. As we all know by now, online meetings have a completely different dynamic and, compared to in-person meetings, do not readily allow for tactical breaks for informal consultations. The impact of the 2019 IIA therefore cannot be assessed yet. Given its rather underwhelming content, its main added value may be expected to simply lie in providing negotiators with a common vocabulary and frame of reference through and within which to exchange arguments and to fall back on to reach compromises.

[165] This since legislative acts are a priori binding; see Art 289 *iuncto* Art 288 TFEU.

[166] See eg Art 36(10) of Directive 2009/73 of the European Parliament and of the Council concerning common rules for the internal market in natural gas, OJ [2009] L 211/94.

[167] See Art 61(3) of Regulation 2019/943 of the European Parliament and of the Council on the internal market for electricity, OJ [2019] L 158/54.

[168] European Commission, Delegated and Implementing Acts – Guidelines for the Services of the Commission, SEC(2020) 361 11.

[169] See Case C-217/04, *UK v Parliament & Council*, ECLI:EU:C:2006:279 [44].

[170] See eg Art 9 of Directive 2010/40 of the European Parliament and of the Council on the framework for the deployment of Intelligent Transport Systems in the field of road transport and for interfaces with other modes of transport, OJ [2010] L 207/1.

[171] One insider notes that while the non-binding criteria 'are supposed to take repetitive issues off the negotiating table, practice shows that the choices made often still reflect general institutional preferences with regard to the applicable procedures'. See A Campo (n 124) 201.

The underwhelming content of the 2019 IIA has a further repercussion in the sense that we should not expect a change in the Parliament's Legal Affairs Committee's recourse to Rules 41(3) or 41(4) of the Rules of Procedure. As Voermans, Hartmann and Kaeding point out,[172] these rules were introduced inter alia to guard the delimitation between Articles 290 and 291 TFEU and they allow the Committee to adopt an opinion (at its own initiative or at the request of the lead committee in a legislative file), similar to the opinions which it adopted pursuant to Rule 40 in which it checks whether the legal bases identified by the Commission in its legislative proposals are correct. Unlike under Rule 40, however, pursuant to which the Legal Affairs Committee regularly adopts opinions, it does not make use of Rules 41(3) and (4). Since the entry into force of the Lisbon Treaty, it adopted only three opinions relating to Commission proposals to confer either delegated or implementing powers, and all three date from before the Court's ruling in *Biocides*.[173] This is not that surprising given that unlike for the choice of the legal basis test, there are no objective factors for delegated and implementing acts to check (apart from the essential elements test; see section 4.II), and the 2019 IIA has not made much of a contribution in this regard.

A final question is whether the criteria, while non-binding, are legally relevant. At least the Commission thinks they are.[174] In any event, the view could be taken that the status of the non-binding criteria of the 2019 IIA are similar to those for the choice between different comitology procedures (see section 6.V.A). According to AG Sharpston in *Czechia v Parliament and Council*,[175] where the institutions do not follow up on a non-binding prescription of the 2016 IIA on Better Law-Making, they have a duty to set out why the prescription was not followed.[176] This essentially comes down to a duty to motivate why certain non-binding criteria (or principles) are diverted from, similarly to the duty resulting from the *LIFE* judgment (see section 6.V.A).[177] There should be no doubt, however, that the threshold for diverting from the 2019 criteria would still remain very low. Unlike the prescriptions in the IIA on Better Law-Making and the criteria for the choice of comitology

[172] Wim Voermans, Josephine Hartmann and Michael Kaeding, 'The Quest for Legitimacy in EU Secondary Legislation' (2014) 2 *The Theory and Practice of Legislation* 25. Christiansen and Lange helpfully note that this rule was originally found in Rule 37a, renumbered to Rule 40 (in 2016) before its current numbering in 2019. See Thomas Christiansen and Sabina Lange, 'Executive-Legislative Relations and Delegated Powers in the European Union' in Diane Fromage and Anna Herranz-Surrallés (eds), *Executive-Legislative (Im)balance in the European Union* (Oxford, Hart Publishing, 2020) 78.

[173] See Opinion of the Committee on Legal Affairs on the Use of Delegated Acts in the proposal for a directive of the European Parliament and of the Council amending Directive 2006/66/EC on batteries and accumulators and waste batteries and accumulators as regards the placing on the market of portable batteries and accumulators containing cadmium intended for use in cordless power tools, 26 February 2013, PE506.019v02-00; Opinion of the Committee on Legal Affairs on the Use of Delegated Acts in the proposal for a directive of the European Parliament and of the Council on the approximation of the laws, regulations and administrative provisions of the Member States concerning the manufacture, presentation and sale of tobacco and related products, 10 July 2013, PE516.597v01-00; Opinion of the Committee on Legal Affairs on the Use of Delegated Acts in the proposal for a regulation of the European Parliament and of the Council amending Council Regulation (EC) No 207/2009 on the Community trade mark, 16 October 2013, PE521.700v01-00.

[174] In its internal guidance, the Commission stresses that 'The institutions *should follow* these criteria in negotiations' and that 'there are no *legal* obstacles to the Commission accepting [a modification of its proposal by the legislators] where it follows the guidance in the delineation criteria and where deemed appropriate'. See European Commission, Delegated and Implementing Acts – Guidelines for the Services of the Commission, SEC(2020) 361 8 (emphasis added).

[175] Opinion of AG Sharpston in Case C-482/17, *Czechia v Parliament & Council*, ECLI:EU:C:2019:321.

[176] ibid [99]–[100].

[177] See Case C-378/00, *Commission v Parliament & Council*, ECLI:EU:C:2003:42 [50]–[51].

procedures, the non-binding criteria of the 2019 IIA are at times so vague that is not even possible to know whether the legislator is deviating from them. Still, that should not detract from the principled possibility of a (privileged) party bringing a case before the Court, contesting the validity of an empowerment because the legislator did not properly indicate why, in its choice on the nature of the empowerment, it deviated from the 2019 criteria.

5

Delegated Power: Further Limits and Procedure

The delegated power under Article 290 TFEU comes with personal, substantive and procedural limits. Indeed, it follows from the provision's clear wording that there is only one actor that may delegate powers under Article 290 TFEU, ie the legislator, and that there is only one actor that can be the recipient of this power, ie the Commission. The first substantive limit, then, is the essentiality requirement, already discussed. This must be distinguished from the specificity requirement which prescribes that the objectives, content, scope and duration of the delegation of power should be explicitly defined.[1] After presenting some basic statistics, the section devoted to delegation under Article 290 TFEU will first analyse whether the Commission is indeed effectively the only actor that may be empowered to adopt delegated acts. Subsequently, the post-Lisbon case law on the specificity requirement will be assessed before the procedural limits to delegated powers are analysed. Since the Common Understanding (CU) on Delegated Acts annexed to the 2016 IIA on Better Law-Making is entirely devoted to the procedure for adopting delegated acts (and not to their possible content or scope), it will also be discussed together with the procedural limits.

Figure 2.2 in section 2.III showed the overall numbers of legislative acts adopted by the Parliament and/or Council. Here it should be pointed out that while only legislative acts can delegate powers under Article 290 TFEU, not every legislative act does so. As is clear from Figure 5.1, a distinction in this regard should be made between legislative acts adopted pursuant to the ordinary legislative procedure and those adopted pursuant to a special legislative procedure.

That in institutional practice powers under Article 290 TFEU are almost exclusively granted by OLP-legislative acts need not surprise. The purpose of the delegated act under Article 290 TFEU is to allow changes to legislative acts without having to go through a cumbersome legislative procedure. Yet the special legislative procedures provided for in the Treaties are very effective and not at all as cumbersome as the ordinary legislative procedure, obviating much of the need to delegate powers under Article 290 TFEU. In total, only some 8.5 per cent of all acts adopted pursuant to a special legislative procedure (over the period 2010–2021) also delegates powers. Yet, even for OLP-legislative acts it is (only) a minority that delegates powers. In total (over the period 2010–21) just under half contains delegated enabling clauses. One single legislative act may of course contain multiple delegated empowerments.

[1] Contra, see Herwig Hofmann, 'Legislation, Delegation and Implementation under the Treaty of Lisbon: Typology Meets Reality' (2009) 15 *European Law Journal* 488–89.

Figure 5.1 Legislative acts containing delegated enabling clauses[2]

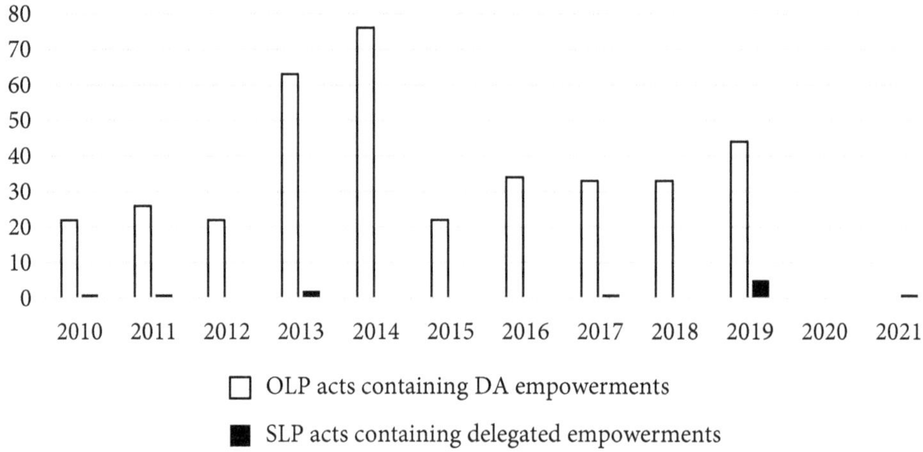

On average, every OLP-legislative act that delegates powers, contains 5.4 delegated enabling clauses compared to 1.5 enabling clauses for the average SLP-act that delegates powers.

I. The Passive Personal Scope of Article 290 TFEU

A reading of Article 290 TFEU that would permit the legislator to grant a delegated power to a body other than the Commission at first sight would seem to go against the clear will of the Treaty authors. Still, the suggestion to do so is not too far-fetched. This, in light of the agencification of the EU administration and the Court's ruling in *Short-selling* where it held that EU agencies can engage in executive rulemaking without upsetting the legal framework established by Articles 290–291 TFEU. Since the power at issue in *Short-selling* was arguably an implementing power under Article 291 TFEU the case will be discussed more elaborately in section 6.IV.A. Suffice to point out here that the Court in *Short-selling* did not qualify the contested power in that case itself and did not make a distinction, in its ruling, between Articles 290 and 291 TFEU. One reading of *Short-selling* then is that the Court did not only sanction a non-exhaustive reading of Article 291 TFEU but also of Article 290 TFEU, resulting in a possibility for the EU legislator to empower EU agencies (or still other bodies) to amend or supplement formal EU legislation. Just as is more elaborately discussed in relation to Article 291 TFEU, the institutional balance implications of this would be profound for both the Commission and the Parliament, the one seeing its executive rule-making prerogative affected, the other its democratic control function.

[2] Figures based on a combination of data from Eur-Lex (for the SLP acts) and European Parliament, Overview of delegated and implementing acts in the Parliament, October 2020, 2 (on file with the author) (for the OLP acts).

In light of *Short-selling*, different suggestions have been made to the effect that notwithstanding the Court's general statement of Articles 290 and 291 TFEU constituting an open system, that statement in fact only applies to Article 291 TFEU. The power to adopt delegated acts would then constitute the exclusive *domaine réservé* of the Commission. According to the Commission in the *Short-selling* case itself, the contested power in that case was permissible because

> unlike the delegation of quasi-legislative powers, which is expressly governed by Article 290 TFEU, there is no mention in the Treaties as to whether or to what extent executive powers may be delegated. As regards executive powers, Articles 17 TFEU and 291 TFEU do not rule out the possibility that the EU legislature or the Commission may, in principle, delegate such powers to a non-institutional body.[3]

This argument itself is of course unconvincing, since it rests on the notion of 'quasi-legislative powers' being distinguished from executive powers. But this distinction is not provided for by the Treaties since there is no notion of 'quasi-legislative powers' either. Still, in essence, the Commission proposed that the Court allow the ESMA to adopt an Article 291-type act but that the delegated act of Article 290 TFEU would remain exclusive to the Commission.

Advocate General Jääskinen followed the Commission's suggestion, although only in terms of its outcome, and observed that agencies such as ESMA could never be empowered to adopt delegated acts 'because the exercise of such powers changes the normative content of legislative acts'.[4] The principle of democracy then requires that such changes are effected 'by an EU institution that is democratically accountable, in other words by the Commission, which is ultimately accountable to the European Parliament'.[5] The Court did not take over this limitation, but even if it had, this limit would not protect the Commission's prerogatives under Article 290 TFEU. After all, the Commission is not *inherently* more democratically accountable than the EU decentralised agencies. Indeed, (in theory) nothing prevents the legislator from establishing EU agencies that are more democratically accountable to the Parliament than the Commission, in which case the outcome of the AG's reasoning would even be reversed and the legislator might be required to empower the (more democratically accountable) agency rather than the Commission.

Lenaerts relies on different arguments to reserve the power under Article 290 TFEU exclusively to the Commission. Firstly, he draws attention to the wording of Article 290 TFEU which expressly reserves this power to the Commission. Secondly, and more importantly (since Article 291(2) TFEU also explicitly reserves implementing powers to the Commission and Council), Lenaerts argues that it follows from the principle of the hierarchy of norms that the power to amend or supplement legislation requires the intervention by an authority grounded in the Treaties. Lastly, Lenaerts argues that delegated acts are of quasi-legislative nature which would ipso facto mean that they cannot be adopted pursuant to

[3] Case C-270/12 *UK v Parliament & Council*, ECLI:EU:C:2014:18 [76].

[4] Opinion of AG Jääskinen in Case C-270/12 *UK v Parliament & Council*, ECLI:EU:C:2013:562 [85].

[5] ibid. Weiß also rules out the possibility to entrust Art 290 TFEU powers to EU agencies because their current independence results in a lower democratic legitimacy. See Wolfgang Weiß, 'Dezentrale Agenturen in der EU-rechtsetzung' (2016) 51 *Europarecht* 651.

'clearly defined executive powers' as required by *Meroni*.[6] This third argument is again more problematic, since it begs the question in what way delegated acts are 'quasi-legislative'.[7] If it is because they are acts of general application then a lot of implementing acts under Article 291 TFEU (and arguably acts adopted by ESMA pursuant to the power contested in *Short-selling*)[8] may also qualify as quasi-legislative.[9] Does quasi-legislative then refer to the substance of the delegated act, being 'almost legislative'? This is doubtful as well, because the distinction between legislative and delegated acts (in theory) is binary: the essential elements, those that are the subject of political decisions, are reserved to the legislator.[10] 'Quasi-legislative' in this sense would mean that there are also 'quasi-essential elements' (possibly) determined by quasi-political decisions. This reasoning would thus seem to lead to a dead end.[11] In any event, it does not result from the *Meroni* doctrine that agencies would be barred from adopting delegated acts. After all, it is (perfectly) conceivable for a legislative act to mandate the amendment of one of its annexes if certain conditions (provided for in the legislative act itself) are met. Unless the view is taken that for such amendments a delegated act could not be used (since no discretion is exercised),[12] in such a scenario, the authority amending the legislative act would surely exercise a precisely delineated power.[13]

As a result, the most convincing argument is the second reason indicated by Lenaerts: from a constitutional perspective, the amendment or supplementation of a formal legislative act is of such importance that it can only be entrusted to one of the main institutions of the Union.[14] Without explicitly using these terms, Lenaerts thereby effectively makes

[6] Koen Lenaerts, 'EMU and the EU's constitutional framework' (2014) 39 *European Law Review* 762.

[7] See also Paul Craig, 'Delegated Acts, Implementing Acts and the New Comitology Regulation' (2011) 36 *European Law Review* 674.

[8] The ESMA exercised its power (contested by the UK in *Short-selling*) for the first time during the COVID pandemic and indeed adopted a 'quasi-legislative' measure requiring all natural or legal persons that have short positions equalling 0.1% of the share capital of a company to notify the national competent authorities thereof. See ESMA Decision 2020/525 of 16 March 2020, OJ [2020] L 116/5. Thus lowering the default threshold of 0.2% set by the Short-Selling Regulation. See Art 5 of Regulation 236/2012 of the European Parliament and of the Council on short selling and certain aspects of credit default swaps, OJ [2012] L 86/1.

[9] Making the same point, see Weiß, 'Dezentrale Agenturen' (2016) 655.

[10] However, suggesting that essentiality may be a matter of degree, see Liesbeth A Campo, 'Delegated versus implementing acts: how to make the right choice?' (2021) 22 *ERA Forum* 201.

[11] Similarly, Michel notes that quasi-legislative acts could not be adopted by the agencies but that this does not mean that agencies could not adopt normative acts (*Rechtsakten mit normativem Charakter*). See Katja Michel, *Institutionelles Gleichgewicht und EU-Agenturen – Eine Analyse unter besonderer Berücksichtigung der European Banking Authority* (Berlin, Duncker & Humblot, 2015) 115.

[12] This view was expressed by AG Mengozzi in *Visa reciprocity*, but in that case the Court confirmed that the degree of discretion is no useful criterion to distinguish delegated from implementing powers (thus implying that a delegated power entailing no discretionary power is indeed possible).

[13] See for instance Art 9d of Directive 1999/62/EC of the European Parliament and of the Council of 17 June 1999 on the charging of heavy goods vehicles for the use of certain infrastructures [1999] OJ L187/42. This provision allows the Commission to adapt, by way of delegated acts, Annex 0 of the Directive to the Union acquis. Adapting an annex of a legislative act so that it remains in line with other EU legislation appears to leave no discretion to the Commission. Note however that the Commission's guidelines on delegated acts, followed in this by AG Mengozzi in *Visa reciprocity*, originally opined that where the Commission would have no discretion at all, the updating of an annex should not be effectuated by delegated acts. See Opinion of AG Mengozzi in Case C-88/14 *Commission v Parliament and Council* ECLI:EU:C:2015:304 [49]; European Commission, Guidelines on delegated acts, SEC (2011) 855 [37].

[14] It should be noted that the threshold suggested in the present enquiry is higher than the one indicated by Lenaerts, since he speaks of an authority grounded in the Treaties rather than one of EU institutions. All EU

an institutional balance argument: the Treaty authors would have given the Commission the exclusive power of delegated law-making precisely because this normative activity is so important. An institutional balance test of the Court's findings in *Short-selling* is developed in section 6.IV.A.ii. It suffices to note here that such a test, drawing on a teleological reading of Article 291 TFEU, indeed reveals scope for the power under that provision to be entrusted to EU agencies and this because in some situations, the uniform implementation of EU law requires very specific technical or scientific expertise which the Commission lacks. A similar argument for Article 290 TFEU is, however, much more difficult to make: the purpose of the power foreseen in Article 290 TFEU is to unburden the legislator. One would thus have to argue that there are non-essential issues that in principle the legislator would be able to regulate in legislative acts and which it can outsource but for which it would be ineffective to outsource them to the Commission. Since under no reading of Article 290 TFEU (for the systemic and historical readings of Article 290 TFEU, see section 5.IV.A.iii) there would be scope for empowering EU agencies, doing so would go against the institutional balance.

Before moving on to the specificity requirement, two important caveats need to be flagged that both relate to the premise of the previous paragraph's argument that amendment and supplementation of formal legislation is constitutionally more significant than implementation. Firstly, as discussed above (see section 2.II), one could rightly argue that the designation of formal legislative power in the EU's constitutional charter at times appears arbitrary. That arbitrariness of course trickles down when the constitutional significance of amending or supplementing such formal legislation is raised. Concretely: why would the amendment of the non-legislative Common Customs Tariff be less constitutionally significant than the amendment of a legislative act such as the Directive on road infrastructure safety management? However, this is a distinction which flows from the EU Treaties, and should as such be accepted. That is different for the second caveat: qualifying amendment and supplementation as constitutionally more significant is only tenable if one then accepts that the distinction between (notably) supplementation and implementation should not be left to the discretion of the political institutions. Yet, a recognition of such a discretion results precisely from the Court's jurisprudence in *Biocides* and *Visa reciprocity* (see section 4.III.A). If the latter two judgments are considered 'good law', insisting that implementation (in the sense of Article 291 TFEU) can be entrusted to EU agencies but that delegation would be off limits actually becomes a moot point. The rather cynical conclusion, then, is that if no Article 290 TFEU powers have been entrusted to bodies like EU agencies this is simply because there is no political agreement for doing so, rather than this being seen as legally impossible.

II. Breaking Down the Specificity Requirement

Just like essentiality, specificity is a double-edged sword: it first of all imposes a requirement on the EU legislator to define objectives, content, scope and duration of the delegation,[15]

institutions are authorities grounded in the Treaties, but not all authorities grounded in the Treaties are EU institutions. See above ch 1 n 41.

[15] Contra, see Sylvain Thiery, *Les actes délégués en droit de l'Union européenne* (Bruxelles, Bruylant, 2020) 135.

but at the same time it imposes a requirement on the Commission to act in accordance with those objectives and content, scope and duration when exercising the delegated power. Put differently, where the essentiality requirements deals with the issue of *whether* a certain power may be delegated, the specificity requirement turns on the question *how* the powers that can be delegated must be framed.[16] It is important in this regard to stress that what foremost needs to be specific is not the delegated power as such but the delegation of power. This becomes clearer when an attempt is made to break down the four components of the specificity requirement, as should arguably be done when the Court is asked to review the Commission's adherence to the specificity requirement (see section 5.III).[17]

A. Duration and Objectives

As far as the specificity requirement's components go, those pertaining to objectives and duration are quite straightforward. The former requires the legislator to define for which purpose or to which end a delegation has been granted. The legislator typically does so in the recitals of the legislative act. The duration component requires the legislator to explicitly define for how long the power is delegated, even if this period may be of unlimited duration.[18] Duration may thereby also include provisions prescribing that the Commission is to exercise a certain delegated power by a specific date.[19]

The CU provides for two main options in terms of duration, as a power can be delegated to the Commission for an indeterminate or fixed period. The former evidently is preferred by the Commission.[20] In the latter case, the legislator can prescribe that the delegation is tacitly renewed before its expiry. Of the around 400 legislative acts adopted until 2021 that delegated powers to the Commission pursuant to Article 290 TFEU, around a fifth did so for an indeterminate period. In the other 80 per cent a predetermined duration is prescribed. This may be done in a number of ways: the start and end date may be explicitly defined (*from … until* clauses),[21] the end date may be specifically defined (*until* clauses),[22] but most of the time a specific duration is defined ranging from one to eight years (*for x years* clauses).

[16] Cosima Haselmann, *Delegation und Durchführung gemäß Art 290 und 291 AEUV* (Berlin, Duncker & Humblot, 2012) 110–11.

[17] In this regard it is interesting to see that when the Council Legal Service is asked to verify whether a Commission draft delegated act respects the specificity requirement, it does not always distinguish between objectives, content and scope but instead tests them together. See eg Council Legal Service, Council Doc 10357/19.

[18] See also Haselmann, *Delegation und Durchführung* (2012) 111–12.

[19] For an illustration of how the courts can review Commission (in)action in the light of the legislative mandate, see Case T-521/14, *Sweden v Commission*, ECLI:EU:T:2015:976. In a currently pending case, the Parliament also reproaches the Commission of not having exercised a delegated power to retaliate against the United States' decision to impose a visa requirement for nationals of Cyprus, Croatia, Bulgaria and Romania. For the Parliament's position, see European Parliament resolution of 22 October 2020 on obligations of the Commission in the field of visa reciprocity in accordance with Art 7 of Regulation (EU) 2018/1806, OJ [2021] C 404/157. For the Commission's position, see European Commission, COM(2020) 851 final. For the case lodged before the Court, see Action brought on 4 March 2021, Case C-137/21, *Parliament v Commission*, OJ [2021] C 147/12.

[20] See European Commission, Delegated and Implementing Acts – Guidelines for the Services of the Commission, SEC(2020) 361, 22.

[21] In this case, the duration typically comes down to seven years, these are also included in Figure 5.2.

[22] This technique is effectively also used when the duration of the delegation is framed in terms of the validity of the legislative act concerned or when the duration is linked to the period in which a specific EU programme runs.

When the latter option is relied on, and while there are always special cases,[23] the overwhelming majority of acts limits the delegation to five years. As is clear from Figure 5.2,[24] the second most prescribed period is seven years, which needs to be understood in light of the typical length of the EU's multi-annual financial frameworks. Where the delegation is not granted for an indeterminate period of time, in 80 per cent of the cases the legislative act still prescribes that the delegation is tacitly extended upon expiry.[25]

Figure 5.2 Duration of delegated empowerment

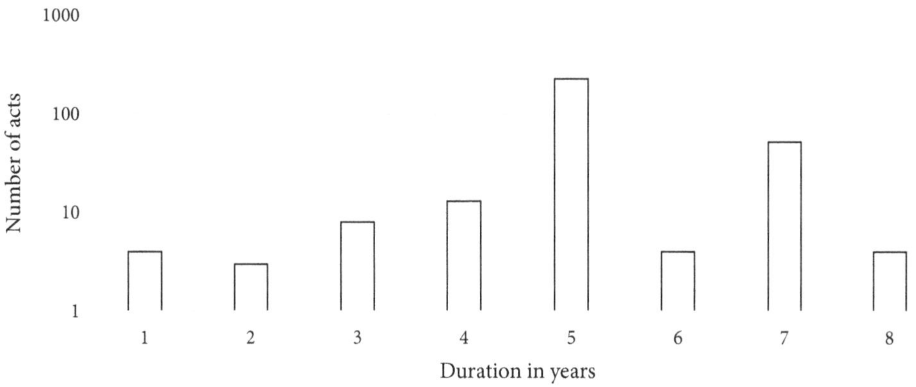

B. Content and Scope

The more elusive components coming under the specificity requirement are those related to the content and scope of the delegation, especially if these two components are to be given an independent meaning.[26] Haselmann, however, treats them together,[27] and Kollmeyer also notes that it is unclear how scope could be distinct from content if

[23] One and a half years in Art 269 of Regulation 2018/1046 on the financial rules applicable to the general budget of the Union, OJ [2018] L 193/1; six and a half years in Art 9 of Decision 573/2014/EU on enhanced cooperation between Public Employment Services, OJ [2014] L 159/32; five months in Art 2 of Directive 2020/700 amending Directives (EU) 2016/797 and (EU) 2016/798, as regards the extension of their transposition periods, OJ [2020] L 165/20; two months in Art 7 of Regulation 549/2013 on the European system of national and regional accounts in the European Union, OJ [2013] L 174/1; three and a half years in Art 17 of Regulation 2017/825 on the establishment of the Structural Reform Support Programme for the period 2017 to 2020, OJ [2017] L 129/1; one year and three months in Art 1(13) of Regulation 671/2012 amending Council Regulation (EC) No 73/2009 as regards the application of direct payments to farmers in respect of the year 2013, OJ [2012] L 204/11, 8 years in Art 12 of Decision 529/2013 on accounting rules on greenhouse gas emissions and removals resulting from activities relating to land use, land-use change and forestry and on information concerning actions relating to those activities, OJ [2013] L 165/80.

[24] Note that given the outlier for the delegation for a period of five years, the graph uses a logarithmic scale on the y axis.

[25] For an example of where this is not the case, see Art 147(3) of Regulation 2019/6 of the European Parliament and of the Council on veterinary medicinal products, OJ [2019] L 4/43.

[26] This is also clear from the Commission's internal guidelines on delegated acts which contain one subsection which treats the components of 'objectives, content and scope' indistinguishably. See European Commission, SEC(2011) 855, 15–16; European Commission, SEC(2020) 361 21–22.

[27] See Haselmann (n 16) 111.

content is understood as determining in which situations the delegated power may be exercised and which type of measures may be adopted.[28] To ensure that both components have an independent meaning,[29] scope may be conceived broadly as encompassing the material, personal and territorial scope of the power that is being delegated. This evidently encompasses the usual meaning of 'content' but to ensure that concept's independent meaning, it may be conceived narrowly in terms of what type of power is being delegated.[30] Article 290(1) TFEU itself makes clear this can be either the power to amend or to supplement legislation. In *Connecting Europe Facility* the Court also ruled that these are the only types possible. In that case the Parliament challenged a delegated act of the Commission[31] because the delegated act amended its basic legislative act while the latter only allowed the Commission to specify certain funding priorities ('detailing' them).[32] In this case, the Commission had suggested that there might be other categories of delegated act next to the delegated acts that amend and supplement,[33] but this was firmly rejected by the Court. In addition, the Court found a fundamental difference between the two types of delegated act and found support for this in the Lisbon Treaty's *travaux préparatoires* and in the Commission's own internal guidelines relating to Article 290 TFEU. In both, 'amending' is juxtaposed to 'fleshing out the detail'. In light of this the Court found that if the legislator allows the Commission to 'detail' certain funding priorities, this should be understood as allowing the Commission to supplement the legislative act but not to amend it.[34] The Court's rather dogmatic turn could be seen as surprising,[35] especially since the legal effects of a delegated act and the control exercised over the Commission are the same regardless whether it is of the supplementing or amending type.[36] The Court, however, read a certain hierarchy in the types of delegated power since it observed that a supplementing delegated act must conform to the whole legislative act and can only add new rules on which the legislator had not expressed itself,[37] whereas in adopting an amending delegated act the Commission is not bound by those parts of the legislative acts which it intends to amend.[38] To be clear, the Court itself does not

[28] Daniel Kollmeyer, *Delegierte Rechtsetzung in der EU – Eine Analyse der Art. 290 und 291 AEUV* (Baden-Baden, Nomos, 2015) 267–68.

[29] Thus following the traditional rules of interpretation whereby different concepts should have different meaning. See Case C-465/17, *Falck Rettungsdienste*, ECLI:EU:C:2019:234 [32]; Opinion of AG Bobek in Case C-529/15, *Folk*, ECLI:EU:C:2017:1 [78].

[30] See also Haselmann (n 16) 111.

[31] Commission Delegated Regulation (EU) 275/2014, OJ [2014] L 80/1.

[32] See Art 21(3) of Regulation 1316/2013, OJ [2013] L 348/129.

[33] See Case C-286/14, *Parliament v Commission*, ECLI:EU:C:2016:183 [33].

[34] Case C-286/14, *Parliament v Commission*, ECLI:EU:C:2016:183 [47]–[50].

[35] Merijn Chamon, 'Institutional balance and Community method in the implementation of EU legislation following the Lisbon Treaty' (2016) 53 *Common Market Law Review* 1519.

[36] As was also noted by AG Jääskinen, see Opinion of AG Jääskinen in Case C-286/14, *Parliament v Commission*, ECLI:EU:C:2015:645 [62]. Because of this AG Jääskinen concluded that if the legislator uses ambiguous terms then the Commission is left the choice of how the delegated act will affect the basic legislative act. See also Anne Pieter Van der Mei, 'Delegation of Rulemaking Powers to the European Commission post-Lisbon' (2016) 12 *European Constitutional Law Review* 547. In this regard, the Court follows a rather circular reasoning: where the Commission is (only) empowered to supplement legislation, it should not amend that legislation since this would create confusion because the Commission was not empowered to amend the act. See Case C-286/14, *Parliament v Commission*, ECLI:EU:C:2016:183 [53].

[37] Case C-286/14, *Parliament v Commission*, ECLI:EU:C:2016:183 [41].

[38] ibid [42].

explicitly link this distinction to the content-component of the specificity requirement but conceptualising it as such allows that component to have a meaning independent from the scope-component and *Connecting Europe Facility* would show that this is also reviewable by the EU courts.

This notwithstanding, *Connecting Europe Facility* remains an odd case.[39] After all, if a delegated power may be either of the amending or supplementing type, and if the distinction between both is so important that the Commission must not be left the choice between the two,[40] did the legislator not violate Article 290 TFEU by not explicitly prescribing the content of the delegation of powers? Should the legislator not have been explicit on the amending or supplementing nature of the delegated power rather than referring to a delegated power to *detail* certain provisions?[41] Regardless, the take-home message from the case is that amendment and supplementation are normatively different and that the Commission cannot be presumed to have been empowered to amend a legislative act. If such a power is not explicitly granted, the power delegated must be presumed to be a power to supplement the legislative act.

As noted by Van der Mei, in the *Connecting Europe Facility* case, the Court thereby also clarified that the notion of amendment has to be understood in the sense of a textual amendment.[42] When the Commission is empowered to add, modify or delete an element that is an integral part of the legislative act, it is amending that act,[43] and this regardless how significant the resulting amendment is. In *Visa reciprocity*, AG Mengozzi had suggested that textually amending a legislative act in a way that does not entail any exercise of discretion on the part of the Commission, would not constitute an amendment in the sense of Article 290 TFEU (and hence would not require recourse to a delegated act). Yet after the Court rejected the degree of discretion left to the Commission as a useful criterion to distinguish delegated from implementing acts (see section 4.III.A), the suggestion of

[39] This is also linked to a rather esoteric disagreement between the Parliament and Commission on the execution of the EU budget. The Commission has taken the view that when it implements the EU's budget, this should be done directly pursuant to the relevant legislative acts (*in casu* the regulation on the Connecting Europe Facility). The Parliament, on the other hand, long argued that there could be an additional normative layer between budget implementation and the legislative acts setting up budgetary programmes. The reason behind these different positions need not surprise: the legislator will have a hard time drafting a (sufficiently) detailed legislative act and if no additional normative layer is allowed for, the Parliament loses control against the Commission which can directly implement (vague) legislative provisions through budgetary measures. The Commission thus consciously chose to adopt an amending delegated act since if it had adopted a supplementing delegated act, it would act against its view that no additional normative layer (between formal legislation and implementation) is possible. Although *in casu* the degree of control for the Parliament was the same, it still brought the case pre-emptively to have the Court confirm its view and reject that of the Commission.

[40] Case C-286/14, *Parliament v Commission*, ECLI:EU:C:2016:183 [46].

[41] Dero-Bugny indeed notes that its follows from *Connecting Europe Facility* that the Court imposes a precise duty on the legislator to clearly indicate which type of power it has delegated to the Commission. See Delphine Dero-Bugny, 'Cour de justice, 5e ch., 17 mars 2016, Parlement européen c/ Commission, aff. C-286/14' in Fabrice Picod (ed), *Jurisprudence de la CJUE 2016* (Bruxelles, Bruylant, 2017) 27. Similarly, Spasova notes this requirement and stresses that (only) in the first years after the entry into force of the Lisbon Treaty did the legislator not explicitly identify the nature (amending or supplementing) of the delegated power. See Rumyana Spasova, 'Powers of the European Commission – delegated and implementing acts in practical terms' (2021) 22 *ERA Forum* 512.

[42] Van der Mei, 'Delegation of Rulemaking' (2016) 548. Vincze agrees that this understanding is beneficial in terms of clarity and transparency but still rejects it, see Atilla Vincze, 'Delegation versus Implementation: a deconstruction of the promise of the Lisbon Treaty' in Eljalill Tauschinsky and Wolfgang Weiß (eds), *The Legislative Choice Between Delegated and Implementing Acts in EU Law* (Cheltenham, Edward Elgar, 2018) 26.

[43] Case C-286/14, *Parliament v Commission*, ECLI:EU:C:2016:183 [55].

AG Mengozzi could not be followed either, resulting in the formalistic reading of the notion of amendment in *Connecting Europe Facility*.

III. Testing Specificity in Practice

While it seems straightforward enough that the legislator is to define the objectives, content, scope and duration of a delegation, and for the Commission to adhere to that mandate, the fact that the Commission in its guidance has found it difficult to spell out precisely how the different components of the specificity requirement interrelate,[44] suggests that applying the requirement in practice may be more cumbersome. Here as well the procrastination at aligning the PRAC to the post-Lisbon framework comes into play (see section 4.III.C). Since the second comitology decision only explicitly sets out the essentiality requirement, but not the specificity requirement, for the PRAC, it is not straightforward to use the specificity standard of Article 290 TFEU to test the legality of Commission acts adopted pursuant to the PRAC. In their post-Lisbon jurisprudence, the EU courts have indeed struggled in coming to grips with the specificity requirement and seem inclined to (re)phrase challenges invoking specificity in terms of essentiality.[45] At other post-Lisbon occasions, the Court of Justice has been firm on treating both requirements as distinct (see further). As with so many legal questions posed by the Lisbon Treaty's redefinition of the framework for executive rule-making, this issue predates the Treaty of Lisbon's entry into force. A case in point here is the 2005 *Alliance for Natural Health* case in which the Court set strict limits to the Commission's power to amend legislative acts. One would assume that in this case of pre-Lisbon comitology the Court would simply have applied its traditional *Köster* test. The Court indeed did so but also imposed further limitations:

> [W]hen the Community legislature wishes to delegate its power to amend aspects of the legislative act at issue, it must ensure that that power is clearly defined and that the exercise of the power is subject to strict review in the light of objective criteria (see, to that effect, Meroni v High Authority) …
>
> In this instance … the recitals to Directive 2002/46 … limit the Commission's power to modify the lists through their reference to objective criteria connected exclusively with public health. They show that in this instance the Community legislature laid down the essential criteria to be applied in the matter when the powers thus delegated are exercised (see, to that effect, Case 25/70 Köster).[46]

This case has not been picked up again post-Lisbon, which is remarkable on two accounts. As Kollmeyer notes, in post-Lisbon terms, it appears to amalgamate essentiality and specificity.[47] Secondly, the Court seemed to merge its case law on legislative conferrals to

[44] See above, n 26.

[45] Also noticing a convergence of both requirements in the courts' case law, see René Barents, 'De post-Lissabon-rechtspraak over het institutioneel evenwicht' (2019) 67 *Tijdschrift voor Europees en economisch recht* 338. For a case in point where the General Court held that a Commission PRAC act exceeded the scope (ie specificity in the sense of Art 290 TFEU) of its empowerment and linking this to essentiality, see Joined Cases T-684/19 and T-704/19, *MEKH & FGSZ v ACER*, ECLI:EU:T:2022:138 [136]–[142].

[46] Joined cases C-154/04 and C-155/04, *Alliance for Natural Health*, ECLI:EU:C:2005:449 [90]–[92].

[47] Kollmeyer, *Delegierte Rechtsetzung in der EU* (2015) 264–65.

the Commission (*Köster*) with Commission delegations to the private bodies (*Meroni*).[48] Yet even under the pre-Lisbon framework, delegations from the legislator to the Commission should not be treated the same as executive delegations from the Commission (or even High Authority) to private law bodies. If one were to conceptualise *Alliance for Natural Health* as anticipatively operationalising the specificity requirement under Article 290 TFEU, the scope left for the Commission to adopt any delegated acts would be extremely limited since it would be barred from exercising any discretionary powers.[49] As noted, this case has not resurfaced yet in the Court's jurisprudence on Article 290 TFEU. In *Czechia v Commission*, the Court did refer to it, but not to apply the high standard set by the *Meroni* doctrine.[50] Still, such a transposition of *Alliance for Natural Health* to the post-Lisbon setting cannot a priori be excluded either, and *Alliance for Natural Health* in any case shows how the existing non-delegation requirements (essentiality and specificity) may be malleable or how further implied non-delegation elements could even be read into Article 290 TFEU (or Article 291 TFEU for that matter).

As noted, distinguishing the essentiality and specificity requirement has not been evident. In *Czechia v Commission*, for instance, the General Court merged the two requirements, finding that the Commission had not modified an essential element of the legislation at issue *because* it had respected the specificity requirement.[51] On appeal, the Court corrected the General Court on this point and clearly distinguished the two.[52] To determine whether the essentiality requirement was respected, the Court engaged in a bottom-up, rather than top-down (cf section 4.II) approach: Czechia had argued that the Commission had modified essential elements of the Intelligent Transport Services Directive because the Commission had required Member States to establish independent monitoring bodies. The Court assessed the merits of Czechia's plea by first looking at the type of powers which the Commission required the monitoring bodies to have (rather than to look at what qualifies as 'defining a policy' in this area) and concluded that since the bodies only had monitoring (and no real enforcement powers),[53] no essential elements were in play. Squaring the circle, this meant that no political choices which require 'the conflicting interests at issue to be weighed up on the basis of a number of assessments'[54] were in play either.

[48] Case 9/56, *Meroni & C. v High Authority*, ECLI:EU:C:1958:7. In a recent case before it, the General Court also rebuked the attempt of Germany to apply the original *Meroni* doctrine to an EU agency: 'That case-law cannot … apply directly in the present case. Firstly, the powers of the ECHA and of its Board of Appeal which are at issue in the present case were not granted to them by way of a delegation by the Commission. They are powers granted by the EU legislature in the context of Regulation No 1907/2006. Secondly, the ECHA is not a body governed by private law, but a body of the Union created by that legislature'. See Case T-755/17, *Germany v ECHA*, ECLI:EU:T:2019:647 [138].

[49] Several authors seem to miss this point when they suggest that the Commission's power under Art 290 (or 291) TFEU could be tested under the *Meroni* doctrine. See Nieto Garrido and Martín Delgado, *European administrative law in the Constitutional Treaty* (Oxford, Hart Publishing, 2007) 13; Wim Voermans, Josephine Hartmann and Michael Kaeding, 'The Quest for Legitimacy in EU Secondary Legislation' (2014) 2 *The Theory and Practice of Legislation* 17–18.

[50] Case C-696/15 P, *Czechia v Commission*, ECLI:EU:C:2017:595 [49]. See also Opinion of AG Campos Sánchez-Bordona in Case C-255/18, *State Street Bank International*, ECLI:EU:C:2019:539 [108].

[51] See Joined Cases T-659/13 and T-660/13, *Czechia v Commission*, ECLI:EU:T:2015:771 [72]–[73].

[52] Case C-696/15 P, *Czechia v Commission*, ECLI:EU:C:2017:595 [79]–[80].

[53] ibid [86].

[54] ibid [78].

The difficulty in distinguishing essentiality and specificity is also clear from the arguments presented by parties and the *ratio decidendi* in some of the other decisions of the courts. Indeed, it seems that both parties and the courts are more comfortable with framing question of delegation in terms of essentiality rather than in terms of specificity. Some cases in point that can be mentioned here are *Dyson v Commission*,[55] *DK Recycling und Roheisen v Commission*,[56] and *Paris/Bruxelles/Madrid v Commission*.[57] In the first case, the legislator had adopted a directive requiring electrical appliances to bear energy labels that reflect their actual energy consumption and had left the Commission the power to adopt delegated acts setting out the methodology to determine the correct energy label for each appliance.[58] When it comes to vacuum cleaners, however, the Commission required the electric consumption of vacuum cleaners to be calculated while operating with empty receptacles. Dyson argued that the delegated act was unlawful since it resulted in incorrect energy labels (as vacuum cleaners are typically not used with empty receptacles). In *DK Recycling und Roheisen v Commission* the applicant had requested to be granted additional free carbon dioxide allowances by invoking a hardship clause in the German law that implemented a Commission PRAC act. Because the Commission's act did not foresee free 'hardship'-allowances, the Commission had refused to give Germany permission to grant such allowances to the applicant. In *Paris/Bruxelles/Madrid v Commission* the Commission, following the *Dieselgate* scandal, had adapted, pursuant to the PRAC, the methodology to determine whether certain cars complied with the relevant Euro emission standards. In its new methodology, however, the Commission had included a multiplier which effectively increased the acceptable levels resulting in a nominal standard that was *higher* than the one laid down in legislation. Again, the applicants argued that the Commission had therefore acted unlawfully.

Without dwelling too much on the details of these rather technical cases, it is interesting to point out that the Court of Justice, in *Dyson v Commission*, and the General Court, in *Paris/Bruxelles/Madrid v Commission*, ruled that the Commission had breached the essentiality requirement. In *Dyson v Commission*, the Court found that 'the requirement [that the information supplied to consumers must reflect energy consumption while the machine is in use] is an essential element of the directive'.[59] In *Paris/Bruxelles/Madrid v Commission*, the General Court held that the exhaust limits constitute essential elements which the Commission could therefore not de facto amend.[60] In *DK Recycling und Roheisen v Commission* the Court of Justice held that the applicant's reasoning could not be followed since it would have required the Commission to breach the essential elements of the Directive: the Directive had been adopted with the express objective to lower carbon dioxide emissions while maintaining competitive conditions in the internal market.[61]

[55] Case C-44/16 P, *Dyson v Commission*, ECLI:EU:C:2017:357.

[56] Case C-540/14 P, *DK Recycling und Roheisen v Commission*, ECLI:EU:C:2016:469.

[57] Joined Cases T-339/16, T-352/16 and T-391/16, *Paris, Brussels & Madrid v Commission*, ECLI:EU:T:2018:927.

[58] See Art 10(4)(b) of Directive 2010/30 of the European Parliament and of the Council on the indication by labelling and standard product information of the consumption of energy and other resources by energy-related products, OJ [2010] L 153/1.

[59] Case C-44/16 P, *Dyson v Commission*, ECLI:EU:C:2017:357 [60].

[60] Joined Cases T-339/16, T-352/16 and T-391/16, *Paris, Brussels & Madrid v Commission*, ECLI:EU:T:2018:927 [118] and [128].

[61] Case C-540/14 P, *DK Recycling und Roheisen v Commission*, ECLI:EU:C:2016:469 [49]–[50].

If the Commission were to supplement the Directive with a measure that allows handing out free allowances for reasons of hardship, that objective and essential element would have been undermined.

The courts' findings in these cases are remarkable since the legal problem in all three does not actually concern the essentiality requirement but, instead, seems to turn on the Commission (not) respecting the objectives of the delegation (and thus the specificity requirement). Were the Commission in its decision at issue in *DK Recycling und Roheisen v Commission* to have included a hardship clause allowing for free allowances, would the Commission have redefined the greenhouse gas emissions policy of the EU? This is what the Court implies by invoking the essentiality requirement. Yet, what really would seem to be the issue is that the transitional free allowances were introduced by the legislator to ease the transition to a low-carbon economy without distorting competition.[62] The Commission had then been delegated the power to work out the harmonised allocation of the allowances to achieve this purpose, but, at least according to the Court, basing free allowances on a hardship clause would go against the objective of defining a harmonised system with minimal distortions of competition.[63]

Similarly, the purpose of the delegation from the legislator to the Commission in *Dyson v Commission* and *Paris/Bruxelles/Madrid v Commission* was to ensure that certain technical characteristics of the goods in question would be properly and accurately quantified: how much electricity does a household appliance typically consume? How much nitrogen oxide (and other hydrocarbons) does a car emit while it is operating in normal conditions? By devising methodologies that result in information that does not reflect normal use, the Commission breached the objectives for which a power was delegated to it, and thus the specificity requirement, but it did not redefine the EU's policy on energy efficiency or its air quality policy, and thus the essentiality requirement. Ascertaining the reasons why the courts seem inclined to requalify specificity problems into essentiality problems falls outside the scope of the present enquiry, but it could have to do with the fact that in *Paris/Bruxelles/Madrid v Commission* and *DK Recycling und Roheisen v Commission* the contested measures were PRAC measures and not delegated acts as such. As noted above, the second comitology decision only explicitly prescribes essentiality as a limit, rather than specificity. In addition, there is the binary appearance of essentiality which may give the impression of allowing for clear cut decisions: something is essential, or it is not. In contrast, especially the purpose component of specificity is much more a matter of degree.

This leaves one important question to be addressed: other than for reasons of legal tidiness, why should we care about this shift from specificity to essentiality, and more specifically, does this shift have any institutional balance repercussions?

In terms of institutional balance, there might be repercussions if specificity is neglected in favour of essentiality. First, and as the Court also explicitly and rightly noted in *Dyson*, the Commission only enjoys discretion within the limits of the mandate granted to it by the legislator but should not be afforded any discretion (and the courts should not exercise a marginal review) on the question of what the limits are that have been set by

[62] See Directive 2009/29 amending Directive 2003/87/EC so as to improve and extend the greenhouse gas emission allowance trading scheme of the Community, OJ [2009] L 140/63.

[63] Case C-540/14 P, *DK Recycling und Roheisen v Commission*, ECLI:EU:C:2016:469 [53]–[54].

the legislator.[64] While this applies to both essentiality and specificity, it will be clear that the idea of full judicial review will typically and necessarily only apply to essentiality. The Court may remain on relatively firm ground when it identifies the essential elements of legislation, and the same goes for the duration and content under specificity. However, when it has to rule on whether the Commission, by adopting a specific delegated act, has respected the objectives and scope of its mandate, it risks having to take the place of the Commission. In doing so, the Court would itself breach the institutional balance.[65] In addition, essentiality is a binary concept and the elements genuinely defining a policy are limited. Arguably, many provisions in formal legislation are not essential and could have been delegated to the Commission to be adopted through delegated acts. In contrast, it is through the components of objectives and scope that the legislator defines the mandate given to the Commission, and thus sets further useful limits to control the exercise of the delegated power. Where specificity allows for a deferential but fine-tuned control, essentiality only foresees a fully objective but a limited and binary control.[66] Inflating the latter at the expense of the former would thus risk both demanding too much and too little of the Court as well leaving too much discretion to the Commission.

Also, from the perspective of procedural law, distinguishing specificity and essentiality is not a mere legal nicety. This is arguably demonstrated by the General Court's ruling in *Paris/Bruxelles/Madrid v Commission*: because the Commission had de facto amended an essential element, the General Court ruled that the Commission had acted ultra vires. Under Article 263 TFEU this corresponds to the ground for annulment of lack of competence which is of public order and which the judge must assess of its own motion.[67] A breach of the specificity requirement may, in contrast, be conceptualised as a breach of a higher-ranking rule, which goes to the internal legality of an act and which the Union judge must not verify of its own motion.[68] Indeed, the repercussion of the General Court's *ultra vires* finding and the inflation of the essentiality requirement would be that the EU judges would have to consistently check the internal (or substantive) legality of all Commission delegated (and implementing, cf above) acts that are challenged before them.[69]

IV. Procedural Limits to the Exercise of Delegated Powers

Article 290 TFEU is silent on the procedure to adopt delegated acts, other than foreseeing that the legislator can provide for a right to object. The Commission originally seized this silence to claim that the Lisbon Treaty had excised comitology from the process of

[64] Case C-44/16 P, *Dyson v Commission*, ECLI:EU:C:2017:357 [52]–[53].

[65] By analogy, see Case 415/85, *Commission v Ireland*, ECLI:EU:C:1988:320 [9].

[66] This if essentiality is genuinely understood as only those measures entailing policy choices that are necessary for the pursuit of the objectives of the common policy in question. See Joined Cases C-124/13 and C-125/13, *Parliament & Commission v Council*, ECLI:EU:C:2015:790 [50].

[67] See Case C-210/98 P, *Salzgitter v Commission*, ECLI:EU:C:2000:397 [56] and further jurisprudence cited by AG Mengozzi in his Opinion in Case C-443/05 P, *Common Market Fertilizers SA v Commission*, ECLI:EU:C:2007:127 [103] fn 56.

[68] See Case C-467/15 P, *Commission v Italy*, ECLI:EU:C:2017:799 [15].

[69] The General Court's ruling was quashed by the Court of Justice, but on an unrelated point. According to the Court, the three cities concerned did not have standing to challenge the Commission's decision to begin with, preventing the General Court (and the Court of Justice) from looking into the merits of the case. See Joined Cases C-177/19 P to C-179/19 P, *Germany, Hungary and Commission v Paris, Brussels & Madrid*, ECLI:EU:C:2022:10.

adopting delegated acts,[70] and to emphasise that it could thus draft delegated acts autonomously. At the same time, it signalled that it would systematically consult national experts unless the drafting of a delegated act did not require new expertise.[71] The Parliament's position was twofold: evidently it did not wish that the new instrument of the delegated act would result in a diminution of its position which it had gradually built up in pre-Lisbon comitology. This meant that it stressed the need to have full and proactive information on the drafting and preparation of delegated acts.[72] Secondly, it insisted on the formal equality under Article 290 TFEU between itself and the Council.[73] The Council for its part seemed to have been caught off guard by the Commission's unsurprising reading of Article 290 TFEU and the reaction of the Member States in Council was twofold: firstly, the Council has succeeded in reintroducing Member State scrutiny in the procedure for adopting delegated acts (see section 5.IV.A.i). Secondly, the Council has resisted completely aligning the pre-Lisbon basic instruments granting implementing powers to the Commission to the Lisbon legal framework. By dragging out the alignment of the PRAC to the Lisbon framework (see section 4.III.C), the Member States retain a tighter grip over executive rulemaking than they would otherwise have. For the Parliament, however, it results in a reduced say. This not because of any zero-sum game considerations, but because its scrutiny powers in the PRAC are still inferior to its scrutiny powers under Article 290 TFEU (see section 5.IV.B.i).

Before focusing on the actual control exercised, it is useful to recall the extent of executive rulemaking through delegated acts. Figure 5.3 essentially reproduces the information already presented in Figure 2.2, but focuses solely on the delegated acts.

The clear upward trend should of course be nuanced. Immediately after the entry into force of the Lisbon Treaty there was no legislation in place that contained delegated enabling clauses and therefore no delegated acts could be adopted. Since the delegated acts are largely the functional equivalent to the PRAC, a more accurate picture is presented by combining the total number of delegated and PRAC acts adopted each year, as shown in Figure 5.4.

The picture thus presented is much less impressive from a parliamentary perspective. Reliance on the instrument(s) which give(s) the Parliament the greatest control over the normative activity of the Commission has remained constant and the Lisbon Treaty therefore would not prove to be a watershed moment for parliamentary control. The only nuance here is that in relative terms, the number of implementing acts adopted by the Commission has fallen (see Figure 6.3), meaning the relative share of PRAC and delegated measures (within the whole of executive measures) has still increased.

Given this study's focus on the *inter*-institutional relations and the legal framework, the internal organisational arrangements of the different institutions are not discussed in detail. However, it still must be pointed out that in order for it to practically make use of its (additional or newly) acquired control prerogatives, the European Parliament

[70] See the Guidelines for the services of the Commission on Delegated Acts, SEC(2011)855 [86].

[71] European Commission, COM(2009)673 final, 6–7.

[72] See Resolution of the European Parliament of 5 May 2010 on the power of legislative delegation, OJ [2011] C 81E/6, points 11–12.

[73] ibid, point F.

Figure 5.3 Number of delegated acts adopted

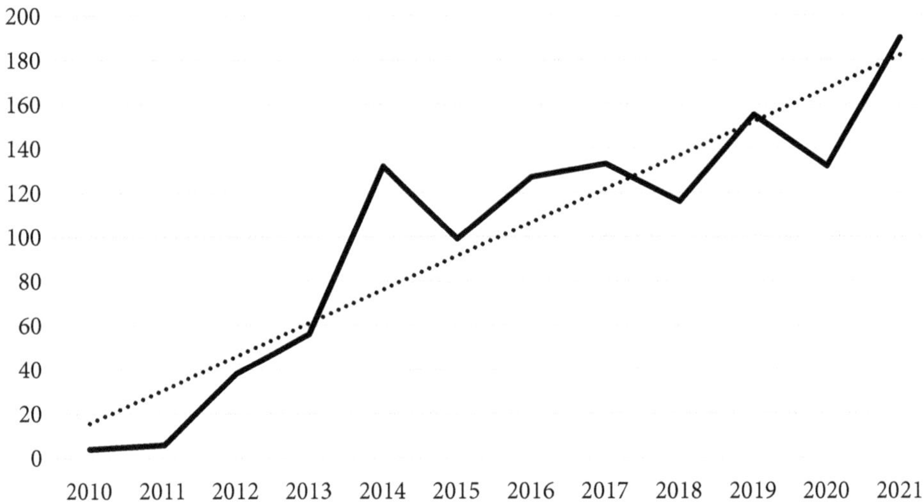

Figure 5.4 Number of delegated acts and PRAC measures adopted[74]

undertook some internal reforms, discussed more extensively by Marissen and Christiansen and Lange.[75]

[74] The number of PRAC measures were drawn from the Commission's annual comitology reports; the number of delegated acts from a search on Eur-Lex.

[75] See Vicky Marissen, 'The European Parliament and EU Secondary Legislation: Improved Scrutiny Practices and Upstream Involvement for Delegated Acts and Implementing Acts' in Olivier Costa (ed), *The European Parliament in Times of EU Crisis – Dynamics and Transformations* (Springer, 2019) 150–51, available

A. The Drafting of Delegated Acts

As noted above in section 2.III.A, the control regime foreseen in the Treaties for delegated acts is essentially composed of two limbs: *ex ante* and ex post control, without any real ongoing control. One of the constitutional modifications in executive rule-making post-Lisbon consists of the addition of *mandatory* ongoing control during the drafting of the delegated acts. As will be discussed below, it is perfectly possible for the Commission to consult widely and to ask and receive input when it is drafting delegated acts. The Commission has institutionalised such practices through its Better Regulation agenda. However, when these voluntary institutionalised consultations are turned into a general rule imposed by the legislator of requiring the consultation of a specific group of experts, the institutional balance is affected, even if the Commission itself has agreed to this requirement (see section 5.IV.A).

As Lafarge notes, the Better Regulation agenda goes back to the beginning of the 2000s.[76] Although reliance on impact assessments (IAs) was originally only foreseen for genuine policy or legislative proposals,[77] its potential scope was widened to executive rulemaking. This also because of the growing realisation that some of the decisions taken by the Commission under pre-Lisbon comitology were not necessarily apolitical.[78] The Parliament also put pressure to generalise IAs for executive rulemaking as part of its historical struggle to seize greater control over comitology.[79] Under the 2015 Better Regulation agenda launched by the Juncker Commission it was fully recognised that delegated or implementing acts may be so significant that they warrant an impact assessment of their own (separate from the basic act pursuant to which they are adopted).[80] As Table 5.1 shows, this practice of course remains rare. In addition, under the Better Regulation agenda, the Commission has also imposed a requirement on itself to publish most draft delegated and implementing acts and open them to the public for feedback during a four week period.[81] As noted by Smulders and Paquet, this in itself 'represents a quantum leap in terms of

at doi.org/10.1007/978-3-319-97391-3. Thomas Christiansen and Sabina Lange, 'Executive-Legislative Relations and Delegated Powers in the European Union' in Diane Fromage and Anna Herranz-Surrallés (eds), *Executive-Legislative (Im)balance in the European Union* (Oxford, Hart Publishing, 2020) 75–79.

[76] François Lafarge, 'The Legislative Choice Between Delegated and Implementing Acts in EU Law' in Eljalill Tauschinsky and Wolfgang Weiß (eds), *The Legislative Choice Between Delegated and Implementing Acts in EU Law* (Cheltenham, Edward Elgar, 2018) 65.

[77] Alberto Alemanno and Anne Meuwese, 'Impact Assessment of EU Non-Legislative Rulemaking: The Missing Link in 'New Comitology'' (2013) 19 *European Law Journal* 78.

[78] ibid 80.

[79] ibid. See also point 15 of European Parliament resolution on Better law making 2004: application of the principle of subsidiarity – 12th annual report, OJ [2006] C 297E/128. Where the Parliament in 2006 still seemed to call for a general requirement to have impact assessments for tertiary law, in 2011 it only called for impact assessments 'where appropriate'. See point 13 of European Parliament resolution Guaranteeing independent impact assessments European Parliament resolution of 8 June 2011 on guaranteeing independent impact assessments, OJ [2012] C 380E/31.

[80] European Commission, Better Regulation Toolbox 2021 – Tool #42 Delegated and implementing acts.

[81] European Commission, Better Regulation Toolbox 2021 – Tool #51 Consulting stakeholders. These drafts are available at ec.europa.eu/info/law/better-regulation/have-your-say. Just as the Commission has a discretion in opting for an impact assessment (see n 84) it has also claimed it need not have a public and stakeholders' consultation for every delegated act. See the Answer given by Ms McGuinness to Parliamentary Question E-001103/2022, 2 June 2022.

transparency in what has traditionally been seen as a complex and opaque process'.[82] As a result, while it may be left open whether Georgiev was right in 2012 to note that 'The lack of transparent procedures for collecting input from stakeholders is a serious impediment to the social legitimacy of the delegated acts',[83] it seems that his critique can no longer be upheld. In terms of transparency and participation in the drafting of delegated legislation, the EU sets a global benchmark.

However, the potential which the technical Better Regulation agenda harboured to ensure greater or more effective political control over the Commission does not seem to have fully materialised. As Lafarge notes, whether or not impact assessments will be conducted for executive rulemaking is still within the discretion of the Commission.[84]

Table 5.1 Impact assessments per type of act[85]

	IA	DA	PRAC	Legislation	Other	Total
2012	0	3	2	53	18	76
2013	1	0	1	67	20	89
2014	1	3	4	22	16	46
2015	0	2	2	10	1	15
2016	1	2	3	49	2	57
2017	2	1	2	44	4	53
2018	0	0	1	70	2	73
2019	0	3	12	3	0	18
2020	0	0	0	17	2	19
2021	0	2	0	54	3	59

i. The Reintroduction of Comitology?

As noted above, Article 290(2) TFEU appears to lay down an open list of control mechanisms since it provides that the conditions to which the delegation is subject *may* consist of the objection and/or revocation mechanism. Clearly, then, Article 290 TFEU does not explicitly foresee the control of Member States (through committees), but as Bergström predicted, the Member States would insist on having some ongoing control over the drafting of delegated acts rather than limiting their control to the (ex post) objection phase.[86]

[82] Ben Smulders and Jean-Eric Paquet, 'The European Commission and its Better Regulation Agenda' in Sacha Garben and Inge Govaere (eds), *The EU Better Regulation Agenda – A Critical Assessment* (Oxford, Hart Publishing, 2018) 90.

[83] Vihar Georgiev, 'Too much executive power? Delegated law-making and comitology in perspective' (2013) 20 *Journal of European Public Policy* 545.

[84] Lafarge, 'The Legislative Choice' (2018) 85–86. In addition, the Regulatory Scrutiny Board (evidently) does not review the impact assessments of all delegated and implementing acts. See RSB, Annual Report 2016, 18.

[85] Figures obtained by searching on the Register of Commission Documents (see ec.europa.eu/transparency/documents-register) for documents classified as 'impact assessment' under 'document type'.

[86] Carl Fredrik Bergström, *Comitology – Delegation of Powers in the European Union and the Committee System* (Oxford, OUP, 2005) 358.

In light of this, it has been argued that the reintroduction of comitology was realised through the CU on delegated acts of 2016.[87] The CU of 2016 replaces that of 2011, and updated the latter at the request of the Council,[88] which felt that Member States had insufficient oversight over the drafting process of delegated acts.[89] The CU aims to facilitate legislative drafting, and while a large part of the 2016 CU takes over the content of the 2011 CU, the alleged reintroduction of comitology in part II of the CU was a genuine novelty. The original CU had one paragraph dedicated to the consultations during the drafting of delegated acts, while the 2016 CU expanded this to nine paragraphs.[90]

The relevant paragraphs provide that as a rule, the Commission will consult national experts when it drafts delegated acts, and that Member States decide who they will be represented by.[91] Mirroring Article 3 of the standard rules of procedure of comitology committees,[92] the CU prescribes that 'Member States' experts shall be provided with the draft delegated acts, the draft agenda and any other relevant documents in sufficient time to prepare'. Unlike in comitology procedures, the expert groups do not adopt a formal opinion by voting.[93] Yet the CU does prescribe that the Commission should communicate how it will take into consideration the feedback provided by the national experts,[94] and that it should reconsult them if it changes the draft.[95] That the Member States' experts are not granted the same procedural prerogatives as members of the comitology committees

[87] Carlo Tovo, 'Delegation of Legislative Powers in the EU: How EU Institutions Have Eluded the Lisbon Reform' (2017) 42 *European Law Review* 677–705; Merijn Chamon, 'The legal framework for delegated and implementing powers ten years after the entry into force of the Lisbon Treaty' (2021) 22 *ERA Forum* 21–38. Also, Ritleng referred to a return to comitology but based on the original proposal of the Council, which went (much) further than the final compromise in the 2016 IIA (see n 105); see Dominique Ritleng, 'La nouvelle typologie des actes de l'Union' (2015) 51 *Revue trimestrielle de droit européen* 7–20.

[88] See Council of the EU, Initiative to complement the Common Understanding on delegated acts as regards the consultation of experts, Council Doc 6774/14.

[89] A Campo, 'Delegated versus implementing acts' (2021) 198.

[90] The 2011 CU was silent on the fact that *Member State* experts needed to be consulted as the relevant para [4] read as follows: 'The Commission, when preparing and drawing up delegated acts, will ensure a simultaneous, timely and appropriate transmission of relevant documents to the European Parliament and the Council and carry out appropriate and transparent consultations well in advance, including at expert level. The European Parliament and the Council shall indicate to the Commission their respective functional mailboxes to be used for the transmission of documents relating to these consultations'.

[91] See Common Understanding between the European Parliament, the Council and the Commission on Delegated Acts, OJ [2016] L 123/10 (hereafter '2016 CU'), point 4.

[92] See OJ [2011] C 206/11.

[93] Stressing this fundamental difference between comitology light and genuine comitology, see Lafarge (n 76) 82. Further, the Commission's 2016 Horizontal rules on expert groups provides generally that expert groups act by consensus (in contrast to simply majority under the comitology advisory procedure or QMV under the examination procedure), but as Lafarge notes, this consensus-requirement is not prescribed by the 2016 CU on Delegated Acts, see ibid 83

[94] 2016 CU, point 5.

[95] 2016 CU, point 7. See also European Commission, Delegated and Implementing Acts – Guidelines for the Services of the Commission, SEC(2020) 361, 28. The General Court has, however, ruled that not consulting the expert group again does not per se amount to a violation of an essential procedural requirement since a(n) (privileged) applicant still has to show how the resulting contested decision's substance could have been different. See Case T-626/17, *Slovenia v Commission*, ECLI:EU:T:2020:402 [249].

thereby appears to be a clear red line of the Parliament.[96] Mirroring Article 10(4) of the comitology regulation, the CU provides that all documents will be transmitted in a timely manner to the Parliament, Council and experts,[97] and that the first two institutions may attend the meetings.[98] Tovo notes that the combined effect of these provisions is that a comitology light procedure has effectively been reintroduced under Article 290 TFEU.[99] Furthermore, this comitology light procedure does not appear to be a mere default procedure since the requirements are prescribed in mandatory language and no exceptions are foreseen. As a result, whenever a delegated power is granted to the Commission the comitology light procedure will *always* apply. Subsequent institutional practice indeed confirms this as even in the cases of the Brexit contingency measures, where both the objection and revocation mechanisms were dispensed with (see section 5.IV.B), comitology light was prescribed.[100]

Before looking at the legality of this (additional) requirement, it is important to highlight that it constituted a considerable win for the Member States in Council, which raises the question why the Commission and Parliament agreed to it. According to Lafarge, the Commission agreed to this as part of a trade-off for the agreement, in point 14 of the IIA on Better Law-Making, by the Parliament and Council to take full account of the Commission's impact assessments, thus protecting the Commission's drafts (informed by its impact assessments) from being freely amended by Council and Parliament.[101] What is more, Lafarge suggests that the Commission will be able to elude the new control mechanism resulting from the introduction of the Member States' scrutiny over delegated acts by shifting the phase in which policy is decided: where the critical phase in the past has been the discussion in expert groups, the Commission could instrumentalise the Better Regulation agenda by presenting the Member States' representatives in the expert groups with a *fait accompli* protected by the Commission's impact assessment.[102] For the Parliament, the creation of this new imbalance (between itself and the Council)[103] was palatable because its own role was also upgraded and because it could be considered a strategic concession, informed by the hope that by agreeing to the systemic consultation of national experts, the

[96] See point 49 of European Parliament resolution of 30 May 2018 on the interpretation and implementation of the Interinstitutional Agreement on Better Law-Making, OJ [2020] C76/54.

[97] 2016 CU, point 10.

[98] 2016 CU, point 11. For the latter, the Parliament was a significant improvement over the concession it acquired in the 2010 Parliament-Commission Framework Agreement, since the latter only prescribed that 'If so requested by Parliament, the Commission may also invite Parliament's experts to attend those meetings'. See Framework Agreement on relations between the European Parliament and the European Commission, OJ [2010] L 304/47, point 15. Typically, the Parliament sends administrators of the Secretariat who are in charge of delegated and implementing acts in the relevant Committees to these expert groups. See European Commission, Delegated and Implementing Acts – Guidelines for the Services of the Commission, SEC(2020) 361, 28; Marissen, 'The European Parliament and EU Secondary Legislation' (2019) 153.

[99] Thiery notes that even after the 2016 CU the differences between the procedures for the adoption of delegated and implementing acts remain fundamental, but this is only so if one compares with the examination (rather than the advisory) procedure. See Thiery, *Les actes délégués* (2020) 91.

[100] See the acts cited in n 167.

[101] See Lafarge (n 76) 79.

[102] ibid 85.

[103] See Marissen (n 75) 152.

Council would give up its protracted resistance to include delegated enabling clauses in legislation.[104]

While legal puritans might argue that qualifying the expert groups as comitology light committees is incorrect, given that they do not adopt any opinion on draft acts and because there never is a formal vote,[105] but merely consultation,[106] the question remains whether section II of the 2016 CU on delegated acts constitutes an instance of constitutional modification altering the institutional balance. Judging from the text of Article 290 TFEU, there is indeed scope for an institutional balance test since the Treaty provision does not explicitly prescribe or exclude the ongoing control institutionalised by the 2016 CU. That Article 290 TFEU provides that the conditions (for control) must be laid down in the legislative act and *may* consist of the objection and revocation procedure can be read in two ways. The *may* either implies that other control mechanisms are possible or that there is a possible choice between objection and revocation. Since Article 290(2) TFEU provides that 'Legislative acts shall explicitly lay down the conditions to which the delegation is subject', dispensing altogether with both objection and revocation would not be possible. The question thus is whether the three institutions could agree (in the 2016 CU) to prescribe Member States' experts ongoing control in the drafting of delegated acts and whether the legislator can include provisions to that effect in legislative acts that grant a delegated power to the Commission. At the outset it should be clear that the fact that the Commission has contributed to the muddling of the legal framework,[107] and that it entered the negotiations on the 2016 CU by noting that 'a mandatory consultation procedure essentially similar to the [comitology] advisory procedure … would not be compatible with the Treaty'[108] but ultimately agreed to the 2016 CU, is as such not decisive. After all, an institution cannot relinquish its own prerogatives. Before pursuing a legal assessment of this issue, it is useful to have a closer look at the phenomenon of expert groups.

[104] See María José Martínez Iglesias, 'The European Parliament and the Better Law-Making Agenda' in Sacha Garben and Inge Govaere (eds), *The EU Better Regulation Agenda – A Critical Assessment* (Oxford, Hart Publishing, 2018) 111.

[105] The fact that there is no formal opinion and vote in the expert group is apparently decisive for the Commission. In its initial reply to the initiative of the Council (see below n 108), it objected to the proposal by the Council, arguing it boiled down to a reintroduction of comitology under Art 290 TFEU. However, comparing the final CU with the original proposal of the Council (see above n 88), the (only) fundamental difference is that the Council had proposed to have the expert groups adopt formal opinions as far as possible through consensus or if a vote is taken by simple majority. Research suggests that the fact that there is no vote indeed fundamentally changes the dynamics in expert groups compared to comitology committees. See Katrijn Siderius and Gijs Jan Brandsma, 'The Effect of Removing Voting Rules: Consultation Practices in the Commission's Delegated Act Expert Groups and Comitology Committees' (2016) 54 *Journal of Common Market Studies* 1265–79.

[106] These are also elements which Bianchi, in 2012, invoked to distinguish the experts groups from comitology but at that time he could also still add that '*La consultation reste une faculté et non une obligation.*' See Daniele Bianchi, 'La comitologie est morte! vive la comitologie!' (2012) 48 *RTDE* 92.

[107] Specifically regarding the role of expert groups, the Commission itself contributed to conflating delegated and implementing act by involving its expert groups in the preparation of implementing acts. Under the 2010 Horizontal rules, this task was not envisaged, yet it was added in the 2016 Horizontal rules. Compare specifically Rule 3 of the 2010 Horizontal rules with Art 3(1)(d) of the 2016 Horizontal rules.

[108] See reply of Mr Maroš Šefčovič regarding the Council's Initiative to complement the Common Understanding on delegated acts as regards the consultation of experts, Council Doc 7792/14.

ii. Expert Groups

Since the expert groups on which the Commission relies have acquired an accrued importance, the stakes in terms of who sits at the table and how these groups function have been raised. As Article 3 of the Commission's horizontal rules on expert groups reveals, there is quite some variety in these bodies,[109] even if they are typically all chaired by the Commission (like comitology committees).[110] Their tasks may consist of: (i) the preparation of legislative proposals and policy initiatives; (ii) the preparation of delegated acts; (iii) the implementation of Union legislation, programmes and policies, as well as coordination and cooperation with Member States and stakeholders in that regard; and (iv) the early preparation of implementing acts, before submission to the committee in accordance with the comitology regulation. Some expert groups are set up for only one of these tasks, while others combine all of them. Evidently, the focus in the present enquiry is on those groups fulfilling either the second or fourth task. According to the Register of Commission Expert Groups,[111] of the 724 currently active expert groups,[112] there are 155 that help prepare delegated acts and 123 that help prepare implementing acts, whereby 65 of those fulfil both functions. Controversially, the Council has also proposed to formally establish expert groups (assisting the Commission with the preparation of delegated acts) as comitology committees under Regulation 182/2011.[113]

This in itself is a remarkable development which may seem problematic at least in transparency terms, since it contributes to muddying the different control regimes in place for (what ought to be) different normative functions (amendment and supplementation vs implementation). The Court, however, has implicitly sanctioned this practice in *Commission v Denmark* when it had to rule on the legal value of a Q&A adopted by the Commission following discussions in a comitology committee (but outside of a formal comitology procedure). The committee had thus acted as an expert group, giving input to the Commission's preparation of a soft law measure. On this the Court noted that the committee's rules of procedure made a distinction between agenda items discussed for the purpose of obtaining formal opinions and agenda items limited to an exchange of views, such as the Q&A *in casu*.[114] On balance, this indeed appears to be the proper way forward since insisting on an absolute separation of comitology committees and expert groups would be quite artificial, as it would not in any event do away with the (unavoidable) personal overlap between both.[115] Instead, their dual function might as well be embraced as long as sufficient safeguards for transparency and the Parliament's prerogatives are put in place.[116] In terms of the

[109] See Commission Decision establishing horizontal rules on the creation and operation of Commission expert groups, C(2016) 3301 final.

[110] See Art 12 of Commission Decision C(2016) 3301 final.

[111] See ec.europa.eu/transparency/regexpert.

[112] This in itself is already a reduction compared to historic levels, see Jarle Trondal, *An Emergent European Executive Order* (Oxford, OUP, 2010) 44.

[113] See Art 16b(4) as proposed by the Council in the four-column document NEGO_CT(2018)0178(2019-10-23)_XL 197 at line 387. This suggestion did not make it to the final legislative act, however. See Art 24 of Regulation 2020/852 of the European Parliament and of the Council of 18 June 2020 on the establishment of a framework to facilitate sustainable investment, OJ [2020] L 198/13.

[114] Case C-541/16, *Commission v Denmark*, ECLI:EU:C:2018:251 [47].

[115] See also Bianchi, 'La comitologie est morte!' (2012) 92.

[116] See in this sense also the internal Commission guidance which stresses that 'Under no circumstances may a comitology committee be consulted on a draft delegated act or asked to prepare it', but which at the same time

former, it should be clearly indicated (in agendas, minutes, etc) in which capacity a body is seized and, resulting from that, any combination of tasks should not go at the expense of the prerogatives which the Parliament has (to be fully informed of comitology proceedings and to be invited to attend expert meetings).[117]

Returning to expert groups in general, it may be noted that these have a varied composition,[118] but those that advise the Commission on delegated and implementing acts will (always) have Member States representatives sitting on them. That said, they need not be exclusively composed of Member States representatives, which distinguishes them from formal comitology committees.[119] When it comes to advising on the drafting of delegated acts, this varied composition may become problematic from a Member State perspective. The purpose of the mandatory consultation of expert groups (prescribed by the 2016 CU) is to allow Member State control, but if the expert groups are not exclusively made up of national representatives, stakeholder are effectively given a privileged role in the drafting of delegated acts. This is why when the preparation of delegated acts was added to the tasks of the Caracal expert group (Competent Authorities for the REACH and CLP Regulations), a discussion unfolded whereby Member States tried to simply exclude non-Member State representatives' participation for that activity of the expert group.[120]

Of course, the Commission's need for external policy expertise did not result from the Lisbon Treaty and neither did it provide the first impetus for their reform,[121] but Lisbon did change the legal and political context in which the Commission relies on these expert groups. Where pre-Lisbon expert groups mainly assisted the Commission in exercising its power of legislative initiative, the Lisbon Treaty resulted in the Commission also requiring the expert groups' input for the preparation of delegated acts, since comitology no longer applied here.[122] This is significant, too, from a political perspective since Trondal found that, pre-Lisbon, national civil servants sitting in expert groups identified themselves more as (independent) professionals assisting the Commission than as representatives of their Member States as they did when they sat on comitology committees or Council

recognises that one and the same group of people may convene on the same day, first as a comitology committee and then as an expert group as long as the two meetings are differentiated. European Commission, Delegated and Implementing Acts – Guidelines for the Services of the Commission, SEC(2020) 361, 27.

[117] For the Parliament insisting on these issues, see eg Statement of the European Parliament annexed to Directive 2014/30 of the European Parliament and of the Council on the harmonisation of the laws of the Member States relating to electromagnetic compatibility, OJ [2014] L 96/79.

[118] See Art 7 of Commission Decision establishing horizontal rules on the creation and operation of Commission expert groups, C(2016) 3301 final.

[119] Stressing this fundamental difference between comitology light and genuine comitology, see Lafarge (n 76) 82.

[120] As reported in the Comitology Newsletter, September 2019, 3. In the end, Caracal meetings on delegated acts are not specifically reserved to the Member States representatives since Art 11 of the Rules of Procedure already provided that at the request of one-third of the members a meeting can be restricted to representatives of the Member States, the Commission and ECHA. See European Commission, Revised Rules of Procedure for CARACAL, Doc CA/64/2019. On this possibility in general, see European Commission, Delegated and Implementing Acts – Guidelines for the Services of the Commission, SEC(2020) 361, 28.

[121] The first reform of Commission expert groups was implemented in 2005 when the Commission defined a new institutional framework replacing the annual authorisation system introduced in the 1980s. See European Commission, Framework for Commission's Expert Groups: Horizontal Rules and Public Register, C(2005) 2817.

[122] See European Commission, Framework for Commission's Expert Groups: Horizontal Rules and Public Register, C(2010) 7649 final. Compare specifically Rule 3(2) of the 2010 Horizontal rules with point 3.1(b) of the 2005 Horizontal rules.

working groups.[123] Now that the expert groups are (partially) recuperated as comitology light committees, there may be reason to believe that this dynamic has changed as well.

Because of the expert groups' accrued importance, they have also caught the European Parliament's attention. Just like the Parliament had used its budgetary powers in the 1990s as leverage in its fight over comitology (see section 3.III.B), it used its budgetary powers when the expert groups were being turned into comitology light committees post-Lisbon. For the budget of 2012, the Parliament put the part of the budget committed to ensure the expert groups' functioning in reserve, attaching conditions to the release of these funds. The Parliament thus required the Commission to amend its horizontal rules on expert groups to the effect that: (i) gender balance would be attained in the expert groups; (ii) representatives of single-interest groups would not constitute a majority of the non-governmental and non-EU parties in expert groups; (ii) lobbyists would be banned from sitting in personal capacity in expert groups; (iii) the different Commission DGs would apply common criteria for selecting members of expert groups; and (iv) more information on the expert groups' functioning would be made publicly accessible.[124] While the Council was ready to release these appropriations in April 2012, the Parliament refused since it felt its conditions were still not met by the Commission.[125] After assurances by the Commission,[126] the reserve was lifted[127] but changes to the horizontal rules remained forthcoming. As a result, the Parliament again tried to put part of the budget in reserve in 2014.[128] It thereby attached much the same conditions as in 2011 to the funds' release and also tied this to the outcome of the Ombudsman's ongoing strategic enquiry. The latter had been opened by the Ombudsman in 2014 and resulted in a recommendation accepted by the Commission in 2016.[129] Based on the recommendation, the Commission then finally reviewed its horizontal rules and adopted the 2016 ones currently in force.

iii. An Institutional Balance Assessment

Assuming an 'open' control regime (see section 5.IV.B), we can now return to the institutional balance assessment of the mandatory ongoing control through expert groups composed of Member States' representatives. Looking at the requirement of mandatory consultation from the perspective of a historical and systemic interpretation of Article 290

[123] Trondal, *An Emergent European Executive Order* (2010) 182–83.

[124] See Compromise Amendment 1297 of Amendments to the draft general budget of the European Union for the financial year 2012 adopted at the sitting of 26 October 2011, PE 473.473, 245–46.

[125] See Council Doc 13295/12.

[126] See the supporting documents annexed to the Commission's proposal for a transfer of appropriations No DEC 24/2012, Council Doc 12929/12.

[127] See point 21 of the Minutes of the Committee on Budgets, meeting of 19 September 2012.

[128] The justification given for the amendment was that 'In clear contradiction with the principles agreed on between the Parliament and the Commission in 2012, the practice of expert groups continues to violate the standards of balanced composition and transparency'. See amendment 1096 of the amendments adopted by the Committee on Budgets to the 2015 budget. While the plenary of the Parliament first approved this amendment, it did not survive the conciliation procedure, see point 1.7 of the Annex to the Parliament's Resolution of 17 December 2014 on the Council position on the new draft general budget of the European Union for the financial year 2015, OJ [2016] C 294/88.

[129] See Strategic inquiry OI/6/2014/NF concerning the composition and transparency of European Commission expert groups.

TFEU, an ongoing control of Member States appears out of place. An ongoing control was a defining feature of the (pre-Lisbon) comitology system, but the Lisbon Treaty carved the delegated act (and Article 290 TFEU) out of Article 202 EC. Since the Lisbon Treaty retained Article 202 EC (rewriting and recasting it as Article 291 TFEU), also systemically an ongoing control for delegated acts appears out of place. Article 291 TFEU expressly refers to Member States' control which *a contrario* underscores the absence of such a reference in Article 290 TFEU. The notion of ongoing control by the Member States is thus foreign to Article 290 TFEU. In a second and final step, we must then assess how such control would impact on the prerogatives of the institutions concerned. Starting with the prerogatives of the Council and Parliament which should be able to control the Commission when it exercises a delegated power, it may be noted that these are not directly negatively affected by any ongoing control by the Member States. At the same time, their control prerogatives are also not necessarily supported or facilitated: the Member States are a foreign control body under Article 290 TFEU, which may potentially but not necessarily improve or facilitate the control exercised by the Parliament and Council.[130] The most pressing issue, then, is that the mandatory ongoing control by the Member States may affect the Commission's prerogatives. While the Commission remains the only body empowered to adopt delegated acts, it no longer determines the drafting process of its own delegated acts. Whereas the legislators can (and must) define the objectives, content, scope and duration of the delegation, the drafting process of an act itself arguably comes under the autonomy of the institution empowered to adopt that act,[131] and the conduct of its proceedings should therefore to be decided by the Commission (within the limit of the Treaties' prescriptions).[132] In this regard, two features of the mandatory involvement of Member States' experts need to be reiterated: the involvement is prescribed as a rule without exceptions and therefore the input (or control) is detached from an actual need for Member States' expertise; and the involvement is detached from the logic of Article 290 TFEU, which only provides for control by the delegating authority. It is a condition to which the delegation is subject in the sense of Article 290(2) TFEU, but one which does not fit the logic underlying the expressly mentioned objection and revocation options.

In sum, because the requirement is imposed on the Commission, preventing it from organising its internal drafting process as it sees fit, as a general rule without exception and because it results in the involvement of an actor (the Member States) that are as such alien to the logic of Article 290 TFEU, the 'comitology light' procedure for delegated acts should be qualified as a constitutional modification undermining the institutional balance, even if the three institutions have acquiesced in it.

[130] This for instance in contrast to a requirement to keep the Council and Parliament fully informed whenever expert committees discuss draft delegated acts, see also below at n 142.

[131] Noting that 'the principle of institutional balance … entails autonomy of the institutions', see Opinion of AG Jääskinen in Case C-409/13, *Council v Commission*, ECLI:EU:C:2014:2470 [111].

[132] See Opinion of AG Mengozzi in Case C-28/12, *Commission v Council*, ECLI:EU:C:2015:43 [56]. Emphasising that under the institutional balance, 'Each institution should enjoy a sufficient independence in order to exercise its powers', see Koen Lenaerts and Amaryllis Verhoeven, 'Institutional Balance as a Guarantee for Democracy in EU Governance' in Christian Joerges and Renaud Dehousse (eds), *Good Governance in Europe's Integrated Market* (Oxford, OUP, 2002) 44.

B. The Control Exercised by the Legislator: Objection and Revocation

Given the CU's predominant focus on the procedural issues underlying the delegation of powers, it is especially relevant to assess the institutional practice and the procedural limits to the exercise of delegated powers that can be induced therefrom. Here it should be stressed that the CU is mainly phrased in mandatory terms. In its annex, the CU lists a number of standard clauses to be used by the legislator when establishing its control mechanisms in legislative acts and provides that 'the institutions] undertake to refer as far as possible to the standard clauses'. While the verb 'undertake' generally suggests a binding commitment,[133] it is clear that deviations from the standard clauses are allowed since they should (only) be followed 'as far as possible'. Still, regardless of whether the default rule of relying on the standard clauses is binding or not, it may be argued that in line with the *LIFE* judgment a binding duty to properly motivate any deviation from the standard clauses would in any event apply.[134]

The relevant procedural prescriptions under Article 290 TFEU aim to ensure that the legislators retain control over the Commission when the latter amends or supplements legislation. According to Article 290 TFEU conditions (for control) *must* be laid down by the legislator and that control *may* exist in two forms: (i) both Parliament and Council may, independently from each other, block any draft delegated act by the Commission; or (ii) they may, independently from each other, revoke a delegation granted to the Commission. While no other control mechanisms are being included in legislative acts in practice, an open question is whether the legislator, when delegating powers, may prescribe further control elements other than the revocation and objection. At least the text of Article 290 TFEU itself seems to suggest that further mechanisms are indeed possible,[135] and while the *travaux préparatoires* are not conclusive, they also point in this direction. In a first draft, the relevant provision prescribed that the control mechanisms 'shall consist of one or more of the following possibilities', whereby the objection and revocation were mentioned together with a third control mechanism in the form of a sunset clause for the validity of delegated acts.[136] Two key changes were subsequently made to the draft: the option of the sunset clause was considered to potentially result in legal uncertainty and was therefore scrapped but at the same time, the 'shall consist' was changed into 'may involve' to give expression to the idea that this choice should fall to the legislator and that control mechanisms are not

[133] This is at least so in international law. The Inter-American Juridical Committee (CJI) of the Organization of American States recently concluded a study on the proliferation of non-binding agreements in international law. In its adopted guidelines, the CJI concludes that verbs like 'shall', 'agree', 'must' and 'undertake' denote binding commitments. See CJI, Guidelines on binding and non-binding agreements, CJI/RES 259 (XCVII–O/20), para 3.4. See also the Award on Jurisdiction in *Philippines v China*, PCA Case No 2013-19, 29 October 2015 [216].

[134] See Case C-378/00, *Commission v Parliament & Council*, ECLI:EU:C:2003:42 [50]–[51].

[135] This is also the position of the Parliament, see Resolution of 5 May 2010 on the power of legislative delegation, OJ [2011] C 81E/6, point 3. Contra, see the Council Legal Service Opinion on the Application of Arts 290 (delegated acts) and 291 (implementing acts) TFEU, Council Doc 8970/11, point 20. See also Bergström, *Comitology* (2005) 362.

[136] See the Presidency's 'Projet d'articles 24 à 33 du Traité constitutionnel', 26/02/2003, CONV 571/03, 7.

a compulsory feature of legislative acts that delegate powers to the Commission.[137] As a result, it arguably results from the *travaux préparatoires* that Article 290(2) TFEU constitutes an open list, since the sunset clause mechanism was only deleted for reasons of legal certainty and the Convention members were well aware of the possibility of other potential control mechanisms, but did not opt for restrictive language when explicitly envisaging the objection and revocation mechanisms.

Still, Thiery argues that the introduction of control mechanisms not expressly foreseen by Article 290 TFEU might result in a power grab of the Parliament and Council which could go counter to the institutional balance.[138] However, this objection seems to treat the institutional balance as a shorthand for the (express) provisions of the Treaties, whereas its function precisely is to determine the legality of institutional (in)action on which the Treaties are silent (see section 1.I). If we read the control regime as the mechanism through which the legislator may protect its prerogative (to define EU policy and to ensure the Commission does not tread on the essential elements of legislation), the principle of institutional balance would allow for other control mechanisms, next to the objection and revocation, that fulfil this role.[139] This fits the overall logic of Article 290 TFEU, which, it should be stressed, *never* requires the legislator to delegate powers and only creates an entitlement for the Commission in the sense that *if* powers are delegated (according to Article 290 TFEU) they can only be delegated to the Commission.[140] Of course, as also assessed in the previous section, additional control mechanisms should still fit with the logic of Article 290 TFEU and may not interfere with the prerogatives of the Commission.

In terms of ex post control, an endorsement mechanism requiring the approval of the Parliament and Council before a delegated act may enter into force would thus be possible. A valid critique here would be that this would make delegation under Article 290 TFEU less efficient while it is precisely the purpose of Article 290 TFEU to allow for more efficient rulemaking than is possible under the legislative procedure. While undeniably so, this does not detract from the more fundamental point that delegation under Article 290 TFEU (unlike implementation under Article 291(2) TFEU) is always optional. If tomorrow the legislator would forego at empowering the Commission altogether pursuant to Article 290 TFEU this would foremost be politically, but not legally,[141] problematic. In terms of ongoing control, it has been noted above that introducing a mandatory consultation of the Member States goes beyond what the institutional balance arguably permits.

[137] See Note for the Praesidium, 'Articles 24 to 33 "Exercise of Union competence"' 26/05/2003, 14–15 (on file with the author – I would like to express my thanks to the former member of the European Convention who sent me this document). As noted above, however, the view taken here is that at least some control must be foreseen, 'no control' not being an option.

[138] Thiery (n 15) 133.

[139] Ultimately, Thiery also finds that other control mechanisms would be possible but without testing this against the institutional balance. See Thiery (n 15) 158.

[140] While *Romano* has arguably been overruled by *Short-selling* (see also section 6.IV.A.i), the same logic as presented here permeated that ruling. See Case 98/80, *Romano*, ECLI:EU:C:1981:104 [20].

[141] The only situation in which such a refusal would be legally problematic is where the proper development of EU policies depends on the possibility for the Commission to adopt delegated acts; ie, in those cases where delegated acts are indispensable because it is simply impossible for the legislator to deal with every issue itself in a sufficiently timely manner. If in such situations the legislator still refuses to delegate powers to the Commission, it would arguably be in breach of the principle of sincere cooperation under Art 13(2) TFEU in so far as the refusal of the legislator prevents the EU from realising its objectives.

However, other options are available. For instance, a requirement to invite Parliament and Council to any expert meetings organised by the Commission would seem entirely feasible, just as it would be permissible for the Council and Parliament to prescribe that the Commission is to periodically report back to Parliament and Council when it is preparing and drafting specific delegated acts.[142]

i. Objection

As is already clear from Article 290 TFEU, where a draft delegated act is based on a legislative act adopted pursuant to the ordinary legislative procedure, the co-legislators can exercise their right of objection independently from each other. According to the General Court, the time period available for the co-legislators to object is an integral part of the procedure for adopting delegated acts,[143] with the consequence that delegated acts which have been adopted by the Commission but which are still scrutinised are not definitive yet and cannot be challenged in an action for annulment.[144]

For the Council, the drafts are scrutinised by the relevant Council Working Groups where delegations can signal disagreement with the drafts. The internal rules for the Parliament to express objections are naturally more complex. Here the relevant committee of the Parliament is in the driving seat: it receives all relevant draft delegated acts and may assign a rapporteur. Any objections are then first decided on in the committee and subsequently put to the Plenary. If the committee itself does not propose to object to a draft delegated act 10 days prior to the last Plenary session before the deadline to object ends, a political group or 36 MEPs may propose to the Plenary to express an objection.[145] As Thiery rightly notes, the effect of these procedural rules is that the Parliamentary control over the Commission's (delegated) output essentially depends on the competent committee since it is highly impractical for a political group or 36 MEPs to organise on such short notice.[146]

As the Court effectively confirmed in *SBC*, the fact that the Parliament (or for that matter the Council) did not object to a delegated act does not deprive it of the possibility of subsequently challenging that act before the Court pursuant to Article 263 TFEU.[147]

[142] A parallel may be drawn here with the procedure for negotiating international agreements. Under Art 218 TFEU, this is not necessarily (but still typically) a task entrusted by the Council to the Commission, whereby Art 218(4) TFEU explicitly provides that the Council may issue negotiation directives and may establish 'a special committee in consultation with which the negotiations must be conducted'. By contrast, Art 290 TFEU explicitly identifies the Commission as the delegate authority and does not mention any consultative committee. On Art 218(4) TFEU, the Court in the *Australia ETS* case ruled that the Council could impose requirements on the Commission to keep it informed of the progress of negotiations but could not empower the special committee to adopt specific additional negotiation positions that were binding on the Commission. See Case C-425/13, *Commission v Council*, ECLI:EU:C:2015:483.

[143] Case T-885/19, *Aquind ea v Commission*, ECLI:EU:T:2021:118 [29].

[144] ibid [32]. An appeal case against the General Court's order is pending at the moment of writing, see Appeal brought on 17 May 2021, Case C-310/21 P, *Aquind ea v Commission*, OJ [2021] C 320/26.

[145] See Rule 111 of the Parliament's Rules of Procedure. The same Rule makes clear that the committee also decides on extensions of the deadline to object.

[146] Thiery (n 15) 167. This is in line with the general political economy of legislative vetos, see Kevin Stack, 'The Irony of Oversight: Delegated Acts and the Political Economy of the European Union's Legislative Veto Under the Treaty of Lisbon' (2014) 2 *The Theory and Practice of Legislation* 69–72.

[147] Case C-355/10, *Parliament v Council*, ECLI:EU:C:2012:516 [37]–[40].

In terms of majority to be attained, it is easier to bring such cases before the Court,[148] but of course the Parliament and Council will have to show an incompatibility or irregularity vitiating the legality of the delegated act while an objection may be based on a purely political disagreement. This also raises the question whether an objection must be motivated by a statement of reasons pursuant to Article 296 TFEU.[149] In practice, we see that the Parliament in its objections also sets out the reasons for objecting,[150] but for the Council this is not (always) the case.[151] In this regard it should first be noted that the question whether the reasons given are correct is distinct from the question whether reasons are given.[152] It would seem that the former is in any event unreviewable by the Court; also because, unlike what applies under the PRAC, the reasons for which the Parliament and Council can object are not predefined.[153] On the requirement to state reasons as such, the Court's established case law provides that the statement

> must be appropriate to the measure at issue and must disclose in a clear and unequivocal fashion the reasoning followed by the institution that adopted that measure in such a way as to enable the persons concerned to ascertain the reasons for it and to enable the Union judicature to exercise its power of review. It is not necessary for the reasoning to go into all the relevant facts and points of law, since the question whether the statement of reasons for a measure meets the requirements of the second paragraph of Article 296 TFEU must be assessed with regard not only to its wording but also to its context and to all the legal rules governing the matter in question.'[154]

Applied to the specific context and nature of an objection under Article 290 TFEU, this suggests that an unmotivated objection would in fact, still be valid. The legislator is never obliged to delegate powers (see section 5.IV.B) and, once given, there are no predetermined reasons when a delegated power can be taken away again. Even if an objection is a legal act, the context in which it is adopted militates against the view that it ought to be motivated under Article 296 TFEU. It is this context that also distinguishes the objection against a Commission delegated act from a Commission decision to withdraw a legislative proposal. With regard to the latter, the Court in *MFA* has confirmed such a decision needs

[148] See Rule 149 of the EP's Rules of Procedure. In essence, the Parliament can go to Court based on a decision with the Legal Affairs Committee, whereas a plenary vote is needed to object. For the Council, the decision to bring an action for annulment before the Court is considered a procedural matter in the sense of Art 240(3) TFEU (merely requiring a simple majority).

[149] Spasova argues that an objection is an act with legal effects and thus must be motivated. See Spasova, 'Powers of the European Commission' (2021) 510. This is also the view of the Commission, see European Commission, Delegated and Implementing Acts – Guidelines for the Services of the Commission, SEC(2020) 361, 35.

[150] See eg European Parliament resolution of 20 January 2022 objecting to the Commission delegated regulation of 29 September 2021 supplementing Regulation 2019/918, in which the Parliament notes that the Commission had been empowered to lay down procedures to determine in which cases identity data can be considered the same or similar but that instead the Commission in its delegated act simply subdelegated the power to determine these procedures.

[151] See its objection to the Commission's delegated regulation of 13 March 2019 supplementing Directive 2010/40 in Council Doc 10471/19.

[152] See eg Case C-17/99, *France v Commission*, ECLI:EU:C:2001:178 [35].

[153] Under Art 5a(3)(b) of the second comitology decision 'the European Parliament, acting by a majority of its component members, or the Council, acting by a qualified majority, may oppose the adoption of the said draft by the Commission, justifying their opposition by indicating that the draft measures proposed by the Commission exceed the implementing powers provided for in the basic instrument or that the draft is not compatible with the aim or the content of the basic instrument or does not respect the principles of subsidiarity or proportionality'.

[154] Case C-611/17, *Italy v Commission*, ECLI:EU:C:2019:332 [40].

to be motivated pursuant to Article 296 TFEU.[155] This difference in context precludes a transposition of *MFA* since in that case the Court stressed that the Commission should not have a veto in the legislative process and *therefore* must give reasons for (exceptionally) withdrawing its proposals. Yet it is precisely one of the defining features of the power of objection that Parliament and Council *do* have a veto power. Also, even where an objection does not indicate its legal basis, this would not be a violation of the duty to state reasons.[156] It would then appear that the only way to require Parliament and Council to give (substantive) reasons for their objections is to base such a requirement on Article 13(2) TEU and the duty to practice mutual sincere cooperation: if Parliament and Council do not set out why they object, this may unduly complicate the task of the Commission when it goes back to the drawing board.

The threshold for objecting to a delegated act required in the Plenary is a majority of the Parliament's component members. To cope with the extra workload and to usefully scrutinise the Commission's draft delegated acts, the Parliament had to build up internal expertise. As Christiansen and Lange note, it inter alia did so by establishing a permanent European Parliamentary Research Service and by increasing the political groups' support staff.[157] This, however, is an ongoing process, as the Parliament noted in 2019 when it adopted a resolution calling on itself 'to reinforce its capacity for scrutinizing the preparation and implementation of delegated and implementing acts' that it still lacked sufficient resources.[158] For the Council a reinforced qualified majority is required to object to a delegated act (or revoke a delegation), since the Council would not be acting on a proposal from the Commission (the Commission submits a draft delegated act, but this is not a proposal and the Commission obviously does not propose to the Council to object to its delegated act). As a result, a qualified majority would require 72 per cent of the Member States representing 65 per cent of the population, in accordance with Article 238(3)(b) TFEU, despite some Member States still arguing that a normal qualified majority is enough.[159]

In the CU the institutions agreed that as a default, the period to object should be two months (extendable by either or both the Parliament and Council by two months).[160] In practice, some 80 per cent of the delegations in legislative acts indeed foresee in an objection period of two (plus two) months. The remaining 20 per cent mostly provides for an objection period of three (plus three) months, yet exceptionally four (plus two) months may also be prescribed.[161] *Against* the prescriptions of the CU, in very exceptional cases objection

[155] See Case C-409/13, *Council v Commission*, ECLI:EU:C:2015:217 [75]–[81].

[156] Under the Court's established case law, the failure to indicate a legal basis does not amount to a breach of the duty to state reasons if the legal basis clearly (albeit implicitly) transpires from other elements of the contested measure. See eg Case C-370/07, *Commission v Council*, ECLI:EU:C:2009:590 [56]. For an objection that condition is always met, since the legal basis is provided by the very same provisions (in the legislative act) from which the Commission derives its power to adopt the delegated act in question.

[157] Christiansen and Lange, 'Executive-Legislative Relations' (2020) 76.

[158] European Parliament resolution of 12 February 2019 on the implementation of the Treaty provisions on Parliament's power of political control over the Commission, OJ [2020] C449/22, point 30.

[159] This issue is as of yet unsettled. In the cases where the Council objected to a delegated act and where the difference between the two thresholds was close, the Member States agreed to reach a reinforced qualified majority to ensure the highest threshold was also met.

[160] 2016 CU, point 18. The period for expressing objections starts when the draft has been made available in all official language versions, see 2016 CU, point 15.

[161] See Art 23(6) of Regulation 2020/852 on the establishment of a framework to facilitate sustainable investment, OJ [2020] L 198/13.

periods of one (plus one) month,[162] or even three (plus three) weeks are foreseen.[163] While arguably any deviation from the prescriptions of the CU ought to be motivated, only in the case of the three (plus three) weeks objection period did the EU legislator include an explicit justification as to why the default rule of two (plus two) months was deviated from.

In exceptional cases, the legislator may empower the Commission to adopt immediately applicable delegated acts pursuant to an urgency procedure (analogous to the immediately applicable implementing acts under Article 8 of the Comitology regulation), for which a right of objection may be exercised subsequent to, rather than prior to, adoption. This delegation remains exceptional as only around 10 per cent of the legislative acts that delegate powers to the Commission pursuant to Article 290 TFEU also contain an urgency procedure clause. Since it complicates the control exercised over the Commission, the CU prescribes that such urgency procedures 'should be reserved for exceptional cases, such as security and safety matters, the protection of health and safety, or external relations, including humanitarian crises'.[164] Where an urgency procedure is prescribed, the CU further prescribes that the 'European Parliament and the Council should justify the choice of an urgency procedure in the basic act'.[165] However, here again, the duty to motivate why an urgency procedure is necessary is not always respected.[166]

Furthermore, in 2019 the impending Brexit required the EU to adopt contingency measures, one of which included delegations to the Commission. Remarkably enough, the Commission was thereby given a power to adopt delegated acts without the Parliament and Council reserving to themselves a power to object (or to revoke, cf below).[167] This clearly goes against the prescriptions of the CU, since it amounts to the introduction of an urgency procedure but without the possibility of a *post factum* objection.[168] In addition, this practice arguably also goes against the Treaties themselves. Even if it is assumed that Article 290 TFEU gives the legislator some discretion to decide which control mechanisms are appropriate, not providing for any control mechanism would manifestly exceed the limits to this discretion. Here it must be remembered that Article 290(2) TFEU provides that conditions

[162] See Art 33(6) of Regulation 2021/241 establishing the Recovery and Resilience Facility, OJ [2021] L 57/17; Art 23(4) of Regulation 2015/1017 on the European Fund for Strategic Investments, the European Investment Advisory Hub and the European Investment Project Portal, OJ [2015] L 169/1.

[163] See Art 23(5) of Regulation 2015/1017 on the European Fund for Strategic Investments, the European Investment Advisory Hub and the European Investment Project Portal, OJ [2015] L 169/1.

[164] See 2016 CU, point 20.

[165] See 2016 CU, point 20.

[166] See eg Directive 2014/23 on the award of concession contracts, OJ [2014] L 94/1. While this legislative act predates the 2016 CU, it should be noted that the 2011 CU laid down the same justification requirement; see 2011 Common Understanding on Delegated Acts, Council Doc 8753/1/11 [12].

[167] See Art 11 of Regulation 2019/501 on common rules ensuring basic road freight and road passenger connectivity with regard to the withdrawal of the United Kingdom of Great Britain and Northern Ireland from the Union, [OJ] L 85I/39; Art 11 of Regulation 2020/2224 on common rules ensuring basic road freight and road passenger connectivity following the end of the transition period provided for in the Agreement on the withdrawal of the United Kingdom of Great Britain and Northern Ireland from the European Union and the European Atomic Energy Community, OJ [2020] L 437/74.

[168] In addition, while the preamble to those Regulations (setting out contingency measures) emphasise the exceptional character of these measures, they do not include a specific motivation justifying the absence of a right of objection (or revocation). This lack of justification for an urgency + procedure stands in contrast to the CU's emphasis on the need for the Parliament and Council to 'justify the choice of an [ordinary] urgency procedure in the basic act'. See 2016 CU, point 20.

to which the delegation is subject *shall* be laid down in the legislative act and *may* consist of objection and/or revocation.[169]

Given the prevalent reliance on the ordinary legislative procedure in the legislative process, the right to object to draft delegated acts will usually be granted to both the Parliament and the Council, but ultimately the right to object is a function of the actors' involvement in the legislative process rather than who is the author of the legislative act. Indeed, when the legislative act is adopted by the Council pursuant to a special legislative procedure, the Parliament will still have a right to object if the special legislative procedure required the consent of the Parliament.[170] Conversely, where the special legislative procedure only prescribes that the Parliament can issue an opinion, the latter will not be granted the right to object to delegated acts. Still, in those cases a right of information on the adoption of delegated acts is provided for in the legislative act. As a minimum, the latter will provide that the Parliament is informed when a delegated act is adopted. Some such legislative acts go further and provide that the Parliament receives this information simultaneously with the Council[171] and/or that the Parliament is also informed when the Council objects to a draft delegated act or revokes the delegation.[172] Notably, these information requirements do not extend to the phase in which delegated acts are prepared. Yet, in light of the principle of institutional balance it could be argued that there exists a requirement for the Commission to keep the 'European Parliament immediately and fully informed at all stages of the procedure to adopt a delegated act'. Readers familiar with the law of EU external relations will recognise the requirement which Article 218(10) TFEU explicitly lays down for international agreements. In institutional balance terms, it could be argued that the same requirement applies in the internal sphere of executive rulemaking. Under the institutional balance it is a necessary corollary to the Parliament's power of opinion in the legislative procedure: whenever that legislative act is subsequently amended or supplemented, Parliament should be informed, just as it is informed of the process of the negotiation and conclusion of international agreements, even where it is not even formally involved in the conclusion of that agreement.[173]

[169] Bergström, however, seems to suggest that the use of 'may' could also allow the legislature not to provide for control. See Bergström (n 86) 349.

[170] See eg Art 7(6) of Council Regulation 2019/1197 on measures concerning the implementation and financing of the general budget of the Union in 2019 in relation to the withdrawal of the United Kingdom from the Union, OJ [2019] L 189/1; Art 115 of Council Regulation 2017/1939 implementing enhanced cooperation on the establishment of the European Public Prosecutor's Office, OJ [2017] L 283/1; Art 7 of Council Regulation 2019/1197 on measures concerning the implementation and financing of the general budget of the Union in 2019 in relation to the withdrawal of the United Kingdom from the Union, OJ [2019] L 189/1.

[171] See Art 51(5) of Directive 2020/262 laying down the general arrangements for excise duty, OJ [2019] L 58/4.

[172] See Art 7 of Regulation 1386/2011 temporarily suspending autonomous Common Customs Tariff duties on imports of certain industrial products into the Canary Islands, OJ [2013] L 345/1; Art 93(7) of Regulation 2019/1111 on jurisdiction, the recognition and enforcement of decisions in matrimonial matters and the matters of parental responsibility, and on international child abduction, OJ [2019] L 178/1.

[173] See Case C-658/11, *Parliament v Council*, ECLI:EU:C:2014:2025; Case C-263/14, *Parliament v Council*, ECLI:EU:C:2016:435. The reasons invoked by the Court in the context of external action in the CFSP can be applied mutatis mutandis: to enable the Parliament to exercise democratic scrutiny and to allow Parliament to exercise its own powers with full knowledge of the EU's action as a whole. See Case C-263/14, *Parliament v Council*, ECLI:EU:C:2016:435 [71].

Finally, what then of the actual use of the power of objection since the entry into force of the Lisbon Treaty?[174] Up until early 2022 19 objections had been made to delegated acts, whereby the Council had raised an objection seven times and the Parliament 12 times.[175] Given the number of delegated acts adopted (and therefore not objected to), this is a very modest number. In relative terms, it is completely in line with the number of objections raised in the PRAC (see section 4.III.C) as for both it fluctuates around 1.5 per cent of the total number of delegated/PRAC measures adopted.[176]

Figure 5.5 Number of objections to delegated acts

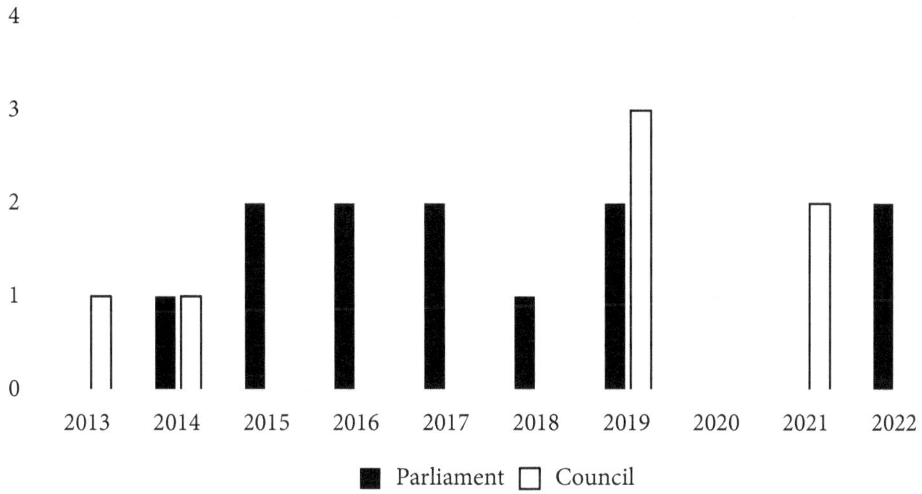

These figures suggest that the bar for the (co-)legislator(s) to object to draft delegated acts has not been particularly affected by the Lisbon reform. According to Marissen, the technical nature, workload and the requirement of an absolute majority explain the low number of Parliamentary objections, together with the overall increased involvement of the Parliament in the preparation of delegated acts.[177] As noted by Kaeding, the limited number of vetoes does not mean that the Commission normative activity largely goes unchecked. Instead, there is always the 'shadow of the veto' where the Commission will strategically adapt its behaviour (and its draft delegated acts) in a context of latent oversight by Parliament and Council.[178] Still, the Commission has come under criticism for frustrating the objection control mechanism through its practice of the bundling of delegated acts.

[174] This question may have relevance beyond the simple consequence of a delegated act entering into force when it is not objected to. In the action for damages following the *Dyson* cases, the General Court suggested that while the Commission's delegated regulation was vitiated by an illegality, it was still excusable because Parliament and Council could have objected to the delegated act but had not. See Case T-127/19, *Dyson v Commission*, ECLI:EU:T:2021:870 [96].

[175] See the inter-institutional database on delegated and implementing acts at webgate.ec.europa.eu/regdel.

[176] Based on the Commission's annual comitology reports (2008–20), 24 objections against a total of 1615 PRAC measures is in line with the 19 objections against a total of 1188 adopted delegated acts.

[177] Marissen (n 75) 148.

[178] Michael Kaeding, 'Out of Balance? Practical Experience in the European Union with QuasiLegislative Acts' in Olivier Costa (ed), *The European Parliament in Times of EU Crisis – Dynamics and Transformations* (Springer, 2019) 173, available at doi.org/10.1007/978-3-319-97391-3.

The Practice of Bundling and the Possibility of Partial Objections

The 'bundling' of delegated acts is possible when a legislative act contains several delegated empowerments. When the Commission subsequently 'bundles' delegated acts, it will adopt one single draft delegated act in which it exercises multiple different empowerments, even if the issues covered by these empowerments are not strictly connected.[179] This may arguably frustrate the scrutiny of the (co-)legislator(s) since it raises the bar for objecting to draft delegated acts: if the Commission bundles five delegated acts into one and the Parliament or Council take issue with only one of them, do they have to object to all five (and therefore also prevent the four delegated acts which they support from entering into force)? This led the Parliament, in the negotiations on the 2016 PRAC reform package (see section 4.III.C) to propose that it be recognised that

> bundling and presenting empowerments that are not closely linked with each other within a single delegated act of the Commission impedes the exercise of Parliament's right of scrutiny, as it is forced to simply accept or refuse the entire delegated act, which leaves no room to express an opinion on each empowerment individually.[180]

However, the final legislative act ultimately adopted cross-references to the compromise provision reached between the institutions in the of the 2016 IIA on Better Law-Making which provides that 'On condition that the Commission provides objective justifications based on the substantive link between two or more empowerments contained in a single legislative act, and unless the legislative act provides otherwise, empowerments may be bundled'.[181] This provision in itself adds to the framework set out in Article 290 TFEU and could be said to interfere with the Commission's autonomy in drafting delegated acts, begging the question whether it amounts to a constitutional modification or whether, instead, it is institutional balance compliant.

To answer that question, first the practice of bundling, which is neither explicitly allowed nor precluded by Article 290 TFEU, needs to be assessed. Applying the institutional balance test to this issue is not straightforward given the silence of Article 290 TFEU and the lack of useful reference points in applying a historic or systemic reading of Article 290 TFEU. From a teleological perspective, the benefits and risks of bundling become clearer: the purpose of the inclusion of a second paragraph in Article 290 TFEU, and thus the co-legislators' prerogative of objecting to draft delegated acts (or revoking a delegation altogether), is to ensure that the essentiality and specificity requirements are upheld. Bundling may then facilitate this scrutiny in so far as it brings together delegated acts that are substantively linked, and which need to be read together in order for their impact on the parent legislative act to become clear. In its report on the Animal Health Law the Commission went as far as noting that 'bundling [is] necessary in the interest of simplicity, transparency, to facilitate the effective application of the rules and to avoid duplication'.[182]

A ban on bundling may then frustrate the co-legislators in their scrutiny if it artificially breaks up what constitutes a normative whole, obfuscating the normative implications of the separate delegated acts. Conversely, bundling delegated acts that are not normatively linked

[179] See, eg, Commission Delegated Regulation 480/2014 supplementing Regulation 1303/2013, OJ [2014] L 138/5.
[180] See proposed recital 8a in the four-column table NEGO_CT(2016)0400B(2018-05-25)_XL, 6–7.
[181] See 2016 CU, point 31.
[182] See COM(2021) 425 final, 2. For an example of a requirement to bundle, see Art 19(5) of Regulation 2020/852.

may frustrate effective scrutiny because the implications of specific delegated acts may get drowned out. Allowing the Commission to bundle 'unconnected' delegated acts would thus undermine the institutional balance since it obstructs the Parliament and Council in exercising their prerogatives. This would even be so taking into account the solution proposed by the Council Legal Service (CLS) in 2014. Commenting on the practice of bundling, it proposed that where a draft delegated act bundles 'unconnected' acts, it should be possible for Parliament and Council to object only to part of a delegated act by effectively treating that part as a separate delegated act.[183] However, it should be clear that such a solution would not address the increased difficulty in scrutinising draft acts for which, it should be remembered, strict deadlines apply.

In addition, it is unclear whether the CLS's proposed solution itself is in line with the institutional balance. Under Article 290 TFEU it is arguably a prerogative of the Commission to draft and present delegated acts. The Parliament and Council would be stepping on this function of the Commission if they were to requalify one single draft delegated act as in fact separate draft delegated acts. Instead, the sounder solution would be to object to part of a delegated act (as proposed by the CLS) insofar as the contested part is severable from the other parts of the delegated act, much like in the case law of the Court on the possible partial annulment of acts.[184] The objective criterion of whether a part is severable from the other parts (of a draft delegated act) thereby also prevents Parliament and Council from determining at will whether a draft delegated act falls apart in different delegated acts. Conversely, while it is settled case law that severability is not linked to the political intention of the authority which adopted the (contested) measure,[185] the Commission could always withdraw its draft delegated act in the face of a (threat of a) partial objection by the Parliament or Council if it feels that the objection would negatively impact the balance struck in its draft act.

The compromise struck in the IIA on the issue of bundling then is largely in line with the above and does not as such constitute a constitutional modification. The IIA explicitly allows for bundling, but only where the Commission can objectively show that the bundled parts of the delegated act substantively belong together.[186] It should be equally clear, however, that the IIA does not fully settle the issue: it does not spell out a general possibility for Parliament and Council to partially object to a delegated act, and it does not lay down a duty for the Commission to bundle in objectively determined cases.

As the IIA explicitly foresees, legislative acts may also rule out the practice of bundling. One way for the legislator to do so is to set different deadlines for the Commission to adopt different delegated acts, which frustrates the practice of bundling.[187] Other legislative acts go even further and include anti-bundling clauses. For instance, Article 116 of the Medical Devices Regulation prescribes that 'The Commission shall adopt a separate delegated act in respect of each power delegated to it pursuant to this Regulation'.[188] While an outright ban

[183] See Council Doc 8574/14 [12].

[184] See eg Case C-29/99, *Commission v Council*, ECLI:EU:C:2002:734 [45]–[46].

[185] Case C-504/09 P, *Commission v Poland*, ECLI:EU:C:2012:178 [108].

[186] For examples, see recital 8 of the preamble to Commission Delegated Regulation 2021/630, OJ [2021] L 132/17; recital 1 of the preamble to Commission Delegated Regulation 2016/2072, OJ [2016] L 320/5.

[187] See eg Art 153 of Regulation 2019/6 of the European Parliament and of the Council on veterinary medicinal products, OJ [2019] L 4/43.

[188] See Art 116 of Regulation 2017/745 of the European Parliament and of the Council on medical devices, OJ [2017] L 117/1.

on bundling would not seem permissible, since bundling connected delegated acts should be possible,[189] the legislator can indeed limit undue bundling by defining the delegation restrictively through the specificity requirement. In any event, following the 2016 CU, the issue of bundling which originally resulted in some frictions between the institutions has now been largely pacified with the institutions finding a *modus vivendi*.

ii. Revocation

The CU also prescribes a standard clause on revocation that provides:

> The delegation of power referred to in Article(s) … may be revoked at any time by the European Parliament or by the Council. A decision to revoke shall put an end to the delegation of the power specified in that decision. It shall take effect the day following the publication of the decision in the Official Journal of the European Union or at a later date specified therein. It shall not affect the validity of any delegated acts already in force.

While such a revocation clause is included in the vast majority of legislative acts granting delegated powers, there are some exceptions where the only control provided for is the objection mechanism. Sometimes this may be explained because of the limited period of time for which a delegated power is granted.[190] The contingency measures adopted in the context of Brexit may be recalled here. Adopted for a duration of less than a year, the legislator did not include a revocation clause.[191] Still in an exceptional case, one legislative act has foreseen in a delegation for an indeterminate period of time without the option of revocation and without giving any justification for doing so.[192] The legislator, of course, has discretion in only opting for the control mechanism of the objection when delegating powers to the Commission, especially if its legislative act in any event has a fixed duration in time, but prescribing no control mechanism at all goes against the letter of Article 290(2) TFEU and raises the question how the co-legislators might be able to dispense their obligation to ensure control of the exercise of delegated powers. From this perspective, there would at least be a duty to motivate the absence of control mechanisms.

So far, neither the Council nor the Parliament has ever revoked a delegation or refused the tacit extension of a delegation.

[189] In the same vein, see European Commission, Delegated and Implementing Acts – Guidelines for the Services of the Commission, SEC(2020) 361 31.

[190] See Art 1(4) of Regulation (EU) 662/2014 amending Regulation No 525/2013 as regards the technical implementation of the Kyoto Protocol to the United Nations Framework Convention on Climate Change, OJ [2014] L 189/155.

[191] See the acts above in n 167.

[192] See Art 62 of Regulation 223/2014 on the Fund for European Aid to the Most Deprived, OJ [2014] L 71/1.

6

Implementing Power: Triggering Factors, Nature, Extent and Procedure

As noted in section 2.III.B, Article 291 TFEU continues to provide the legal basis for the comitology system post-Lisbon. That continuity must of course be qualified on two accounts. In that section the key differences between Article 291 TFEU and its predecessor Article 202 EC were flagged. These differences may, and arguably should, be reflected in the post-Lisbon institutional practice. Further, the scope of Article 291 TFEU has been fundamentally altered given that the pre-Lisbon notion of implementation has been restricted through the carve-out of delegated acts from Article 202 EC. Again, the question poses itself whether the spirit of the Lisbon reform has been adhered to in post-Lisbon institutional practice and jurisprudence and how the political institutions' prerogatives have been definitely settled as a result.

This chapter will return to the key issues flagged in section 2.III.B. In turn, it will analyse the triggering threshold for conferring implementing powers, the nature and extent of an implementing power under Article 291(2) TFEU, the exceptional implementing powers reserved to the Council, the closed list of implementing actors under Article 291(2) TFEU and the procedure for the adoption of implementing acts by the Commission. Before doing so, however, it is useful to have a quick glance at the extent to which the legislator confers implementing powers on the Commission. Figure 6.1 below is the 'twin' of Figure 5.1, but contains an extra bar since non-legislative acts can also confer implementing powers on the Commission.

The ordinary legislative procedure (OLP) acts conferring implementing powers on the Commission represent around half of all the OLP acts adopted. In contrast, and differently from what was noted in relation to the grant of delegated powers (see Figure 5.1), around 23 per cent of all special legislative procedure (SLP) acts confer implementing powers on the Commission. Finally for the autonomous executive acts this is around 7.5 per cent. The lower percentage for autonomous executive acts indeed suggests that these are typically rather concrete executive measure of an implementing kind, requiring much less 'follow up' implementing measures than legislative acts. The higher percentage found for SLP acts (compared to the 8.5 per cent found in chapter five) also suggests the different function of delegated and implementing acts: the delegated act's function is to bypass a cumbersome legislative procedure where this is not necessary (ie when no decisions on essential elements are made) but the SLPs are typically not that cumbersome to begin with. This is different for implementing acts which only see to the uniform implementation of EU acts, which may also be at issue for SLP acts. That there still is a significant difference between the number of OLP acts and SLP acts conferring implementing powers can then be explained by the more concrete measures typically contained in SLP acts (for which the challenge of uniform

Figure 6.1 Acts conferring implementing powers on the Commission[1]

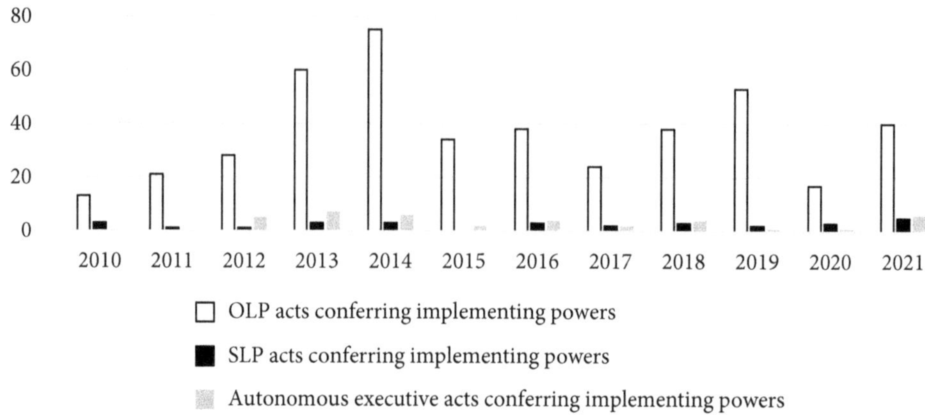

implementation is less acute). This coincidentally also suggests that despite their fundamentally different nature (as prescribed by the Treaties) autonomous executive acts and SLP acts may be very similar, giving further ammunition to the critique developed above on the seemingly arbitrary qualification in the EU Treaties of some powers as executive and other as legislative (see section 2.II).

I. The Notion of Uniform Conditions

Where Article 290 TFEU foresees in an option to delegate powers, Article 291(2) TFEU *requires* implementing powers to be conferred when uniform conditions in implementation are required. In this regard, Article 291 TFEU has objectified the cases in which implementing powers are to be exercised at EU level.[2] Although the Commission's original proposal for a Comitology Regulation followed this logic, it was deviated from in the final regulation, the second recital of which provides that 'It is for the legislator, fully respecting the criteria

[1] The data in Figure 6.1 were drawn from Eur-Lex. Some important caveats are to be noted: the acts conferring implementing powers were identified by searching for (basic) acts that confer implementing powers to the Commission in accordance with the Comitology Regulation. The resulting picture therefore underestimates the actual extent of the conferral of implementing powers since it does not include those that fall outside the scope of the Comitology Regulation. This includes the implementation of the EU's competition policy (see section 6.V.B.ii), implementation by the Council (see section 6.III), implementation by EU agencies (see section 6.IV.A), and implementation by the Commission for which the legislator decided not to prescribe comitology (see section 6.V.B.ii).

[2] Stressing this objectivisation, see Opinion of AG Cruz Villalón in Case C-427/12, *Commission v Parliament & Council*, ECLI:EU:C:2013:871 [50]. See also Thomas Kröll, 'Delegierte Rechtsetzung und Durchführungsrechtsetzung und das institutionelle Gleichgewicht der Europäischen Union' (2011) 66 *Zeitschrift für öffentliches Recht* 283; Claude Blumann, 'Un nouveau départ pour la Comitologie. Le règlement n° 182/2011 du 16 février 2011' (2011) 47 *Cahiers de droit européen* 26; Merijn Chamon, 'Institutional balance and Community method in the implementation of EU legislation following the Lisbon Treaty' (2016) 53 *Common Market Law Review* 1508; Jakob Greiner, *Die Reform der Komitologie durch den Vertrag von Lissabon: Delegierte Rechtsetzung und Durchführungsrechtsetzung nach Art. 290 und Art. 291 AEUV* (Tübingen, Mohr Siebeck, 2018) 147.

laid down in the Treaty on the Functioning of the European Union ("TFEU"), to decide in respect of each basic act whether to confer implementing powers on the Commission in accordance with Article 291(2) of that Treaty'. The recital was added in the trilogues by the Council[3] and is marvelously confusing the Treaty's logic without as such going against its text, since it explicitly refers to the criteria in Article 291(2) TFEU (see below). As noted in section 4.III.D.i, the institutions went even further in the 2019 IIA where they agreed that the legislator's discretion extends to the question *whether* uniform conditions for implementing a legislative act are required.[4]

Still, relying on this uniformity requirement as a condition before implementing powers may be exercised at EU level seems problematic at first sight. It has been a tenet in the Court's jurisprudence that EU law loses its raison d'être if it is not applied in a uniform and consistent manner.[5] How, then, could EU law be implemented other than under uniform conditions? Dougan's pertinent question in 2003 when commenting on the Draft Constitutional Treaty therefore still stands: 'Just *how* uniform would 'uniform' have to be, before implementation could take place through the Commission rather than the Member States?'.[6]

On this, Haselmann suggested that the Court's general limits to the procedural autonomy of Member States may be taken as inspiration.[7] She noted that the Court in *Deutsche Milchkontor* observed that Member States are to ensure that the rules and procedures which they apply in the implementation of EU law must be equivalent (to those applied in the implementation of national law) and effective. If disparities in the rules and procedures of the Member States would distort or impair the implementation of EU law, the EU institutions ought to step in and adopt the necessary provisions.[8] As Haselmann notes, however, the threshold at which uniform conditions would be required would still remain vague but cannot in any event be lower under Article 291(2) TFEU compared to the threshold for finding that EU action is necessary under the general subsidiarity principle.[9] Indeed, Kröll puts the bar at the same level as the subsidiarity principle, finding the requirement to be met when it is shown that the EU institutions would do a better job at the uniform implementation of EU law.[10] Vincze is more demanding, arguing that if Article 291(1) TFEU and the subsidiarity principle are taken into account, the threshold is only met if implementation by the Member States would be so diverging as to become intolerable.[11]

Following on from the question when uniform conditions are required is the question whether the legislator should motivate its decision to entrust the implementation to the

[3] See the new recital 1a in the four-column table NEGO_CT(2010)0051 of 17 November 2010.

[4] 2019 IIA, point 3.

[5] Starting from Case 6/64, Costa, ECLI:EU:C:1964:66, 593–94.

[6] Michael Dougan, 'The Convention's draft Constitutional Treaty: bringing Europe closer to its lawyers?' (2003) 28 *European Law Review* 786 (emphasis in original).

[7] Cosima Haselmann, *Delegation und Durchführung gemäß Art. 290 und 291 AEUV* (Berlin, Duncker & Humblot, 2012) 206–07. See also Greiner, *Die Reform der Komitologie durch den Vertrag von Lissabon* (2018) 147–48.

[8] See Joined Cases 205 to 215/82, *Deutsche Milchkontor*, ECLI:EU:C:1983:233 [17]–[24].

[9] Haselmann, *Delegation und Durchführung* (2012) 208.

[10] Kröll, 'Delegierte Rechtsetzung und Durchführungsrechtsetzung' (2011) 282. Similarly, Greiner (n 2) 148.

[11] Atilla Vincze, 'Delegation versus Implementation: a deconstruction of the promise of the Lisbon Treaty' in Eljalill Tauschinsky and Wolfgang Weiß (eds), *The Legislative Choice Between Delegated and Implementing Acts in EU Law* (Cheltenham, Edward Elgar, 2018) 27. Further on Vincze refers to 'extravagant differences', see ibid 39.

Commission or Council and whether that is a decision reviewable by the Court of Justice.[12] On the latter, Kröll suggests that the objective factors test should apply, which would exclude a discretion on the part of the legislator.[13] In contrast, and downplaying the objective standard set by Article 291(2) TFEU, Dubos argues that it would be up to the legislator to justify why implementation at EU level is necessary, but that the Court could apply its manifest error test on this issue.[14] In any event, the institutions' view in the 2019 IIA that the legislator has discretion on whether uniform conditions are required conflicts with the objective standard of Article 291 TFEU.

Here it should be noted that the lack of discretion arguably only concerns the vertical dimension of the implementation question: once uniform conditions are required it is clear that Member States cannot be entrusted with the implementation of EU law on their own anymore. Horizontally, however, the legislator still has a discretion to identify the most appropriate actor at EU level to uniformly implement EU legislation.[15] This could be the Commission, Council (see section 6.III) or, following *Short-selling* (see section 6.IV.A) an EU agency or still some other body. This is also the only way in which the above-mentioned second recital to the Comitology Regulation can be read consistently with Article 291 TFEU.

The above demonstrates that even a provision as innocuous as 'uniform conditions' gives rise to fundamentally differing interpretations. Unfortunately, as will be shown below, these differences have not been settled yet since the question of 'uniform conditions' has either not been put to the Court or the Court has sidestepped the issue. Still, the view advanced here is that given the change of language from Article 202 EC to Article 291 TFEU, the requirement of implementation under uniform conditions is an objective one and the legislator's choice should therefore be informed by objective factors that are amenable to judicial review. As a result, that review cannot be a manifest error review. Those objective factors must still show why implementation at EU level is necessary. The crux of the matter, then, is how that necessity requirement is to be operationalised. Without dismissing the relevance of the subsidiarity principle for this question, it should be noted that pursuing a simple subsidiarity-style test would be problematic. An interesting parallel may be drawn here between harmonisation pursuant to Article 114 TFEU and the question of uniform conditions for the implementation of EU law. In a nutshell, scrutinising Article 114 TFEU harmonisation measures from the perspective of the subsidiarity principle has shown to be largely futile: when the conditions for triggering Article 114 TFEU are already met (ie when divergences in national legislation are such to obstruct the fundamental freedoms, thus

[12] Kollmeyer finds that the decision is in any event not reviewable by the Court. See Daniel Kollmeyer, *Delegierte Rechtsetzung in der EU – Eine Analyse der Art. 290 und 291 AEUV* (Baden-Baden, Nomos, 2015) 193.

[13] Kröll (n 2) 283.

[14] Olivier Dubos, 'Objectif d'efficacité de l'exécution du droit de l'union européenne: la tectonique des compétences' in Eleftheria Neframi (ed), *Objectifs et compétences dans l'Union européenne* (Bruxelles, Bruylant, 2012) 297.

[15] Similarly, Haselmann notes that this requirement does not result in a *domain réservé* of the Commission. In addition she notes that the legislator also has discretion to be as exhaustive in its legislation as it wishes, pre-empting any need for further implementation. See Haselmann (n 7) 210. On this Kollmeyer notes that it is difficult to square this latter (supposed) discretion with Haselmann's insistence on the relevance of the subsidiarity principle in applying the uniform conditions requirement. See Kollmeyer, *Delegierte Rechtsetzung in der EU* (2015) 190.

having a direct impact on the functioning of the internal market) then a fortiori the EU is the level best placed to achieve those aims.[16]

Analogously, when EU legislative acts are adopted and the question of implementation is raised, a fortiori the EU level is better placed to implement that legislation if the aim is to do so under uniform conditions. Any test to determine whether 'uniform conditions' are required should therefore take this into account. As a result, to ensure that the ethos of subsidiarity underlying Article 291 TFEU is respected, the first of the two tests enshrined in Article 5(3) TEU[17] needs to be put at the forefront: rather than looking at the comparative efficiency test (cf 'the objectives of the proposed action … can rather … be better achieved at Union level'), emphasis should lie on the national insufficiency test (cf 'the objectives of the proposed action cannot be sufficiently achieved by the Member States').[18] The onus is then on the EU legislator to justify, relying on objective factors, why the national insufficiency test is met and why action at EU level is necessary.[19] If this is indeed the relevant standard, the legislator hardly meets it in its legislative decision-making. Its standard justification in the recitals of its legislative acts is that 'in order to ensure uniform conditions for the implementation of this Regulation, implementing powers should be conferred on the Commission' or simply to state (but not show) that 'the implementation of [this legislative act] requires uniform conditions'. Only seldomly does the legislator provide a proper reasoning.[20]

The caveat here has already been noted above: The Court itself has not yet been given (or seized) the opportunity to clarify the uniform conditions requirement. The only thing that is clear from the Court's case law is that the EU legislator does not have to show that implementation by the Member States is simply impossible. After all, in *Spain v Council* (see section 6.IV.B) it found that whatever the EU institutions do under Article 291(2) TFEU should be something that in principle the Member States could also do but which *in casu* cannot be left to them if this 'would clearly result in a risk of divergence, a risk that is inherent in the coexistence, within the legal order of the European Union, of potentially

[16] See eg Case C-358/14, *Poland v Parliament & Council*, ECLI:EU:C:2016:323 [111]–[127]. See further, Allan Rosas and Lorna Armati, *EU Constitutional Law* (Oxford, Hart Publishing, 2018) 30–31; Merijn Chamon, 'Het verbod op mentholsigaretten in de interne markt – Zaak C-358/14, Polen/Europees Parlement en Raad' (2016) *Tijdschrift voor Europees en economisch recht* 362–63.

[17] See Robert Schütze, *From Dual to Cooperative Federalism: the Changing Structure of European Law* (Oxford, OUP, 2009 250.

[18] These two tests were a novelty introduced by the Treaty of Lisbon, since they were earlier linked by the words 'and can therefore' instead of by 'but can rather'. Pre-Lisbon, national insufficiency therefore automatically resulted in (greater) comparative efficiency, whereas today a proposed action should cumulatively pass the two tests before the Union may act.

[19] A critique could be raised here arguing that this necessity criterion is equally elusive. While that is undoubtedly true, it should be stressed that it foremost figures as a backdrop against which the legislator needs to motivate its decision. The Court of Justice itself seems well-positioned to scrutinise this, as its case law on Arts 3(2) and 216(1) TFEU shows. Necessity under Art 291(2) TFEU could then be conceived as somewhere in between necessary as suitable under Art 216(1) TFEU and necessary as absolutely indispensable under Art 3(2) TFEU. See Case C-600/14, *Germany v Council*, ECLI:EU:C:2017:935 [58]–[60]. In [87] of its judgment, the Court explicitly states that the necessity criterion is different under both provisions.

[20] An illustration of this can be found in Regulation 2019/1010 on the alignment of reporting obligations in the field of legislation related to the environment, OJ [2019] L 170/115. In its recital 11 it provides that the Commission should adopt implementing acts to ensure the coherence in reporting information (setting the type, format and frequency of information to be reported); in its recital 12 it refers to a need for consistency and to allow proper monitoring to justify the Commission's implementing powers.

divergent national implementing measures'.[21] One could argue that it results from *Spain v Council* that the trigger must be 'a *clear* risk of divergence', but in that case the Court was not asked to test an empowerment of either the Member States or EU institutions (and therefore did not devise a standard to the test the uniform conditions requirement), and, if this would indeed constitute the relevant threshold, it would set the bar too low. After all, the EU legislator would simply have to show that national implementing measures could *potentially* diverge. As Mendes noted, there would be 'reasons to be sceptical about the relevance of this condition in limiting the power of the Union to adopt implementing acts'.[22]

In other cases before the Court, further opportunities to clarify the notion were missed. In *Visa Reciprocity*, when the Commission argued it should have received an implementing rather than a delegated power, it did not make an argument that the contested power (allowing it to suspend or retract visa waivers) would require it to ensure the Regulation was implemented under uniform conditions. However, in *Spain v Parliament and Council*,[23] one of the cases in the saga on the Unitary Patent Package, this was different. In that case, Spain had challenged the validity of Regulation 1257/2012 inter alia citing a violation of Article 291(2) TFEU since the Regulation instructed the Member States to set up a committee within the European Patent Office (EPO) (and therefore outside the EU) entrusting it with the task of deciding on the renewal fees for unitary patents. In doing so, the EPO committee had to respect the principles set out in Articles 12 and 13 of the Regulation, similarly to the decision on the fees payable to ECHA at issue in *Biocides*. Just like in *Biocides*, the Court concluded that this qualified as implementation. Crucially, however, the Court qualified this as implementation under Article 291(1) TFEU. Unfortunately, the Court's reasoning fails to convince since it argued that the Regulation instructs the Member States to give the EPO committee these tasks,[24] and that the EU Regulation is a special agreement within the meaning of Article 142 of the European Patent Convention (EPC).[25] While the latter may be true for the purposes of the EPC, this is not the case from an EU perspective. An act of secondary EU legislation cannot derogate from primary law and as a result, a regulation cannot deviate from Article 291 TFEU even if it qualifies as a special agreement under the EPC. The Court tried to take the sting out of the problem by finding that the level and distribution of the renewal fees in any event did not necessarily need to be implemented under uniform conditions,[26] but this fails to convince completely: to renew a patent with unitary effect the fee payable is necessarily uniform. The negotiations within the EPO committee on the renewal fees are testimony to this, since the president of the EPO had to work out different proposals before a compromise could be reached,[27] but in all

[21] See Case C-521/15, *Spain v Council*, ECLI:EU:C:2017:982 [47].

[22] Joana Mendes, 'The Making of Delegated and Implementing Acts', Carl Fredrik Bergström and Dominique Ritleng (eds), *Rulemaking by the European Commission – The New System for Delegation of Powers* (Oxford, OUP, 2016) 237 fn 24.

[23] Case C-146/13, *Spain v Parliament and Council*, ECLI:EU:C:2015:298.

[24] ibid [72].

[25] ibid [82].

[26] ibid [81]. AG Bot dealt with this issue equally unconvincingly by finding that the principles set by the legislature did not leave any discretion to the Member States (which has been disproven by the difficult negotiations within the committee). See Opinion of AG Bot in Case C-146/13, *Spain v Parliament and Council*, ECLI:EU:C:2014:2380 [125]–[126].

[27] See Decision of the Select Committee of the Administrative Council of 15 December 2015 adopting the Rules relating to Fees for Unitary Patent Protection, SC/D 2/15.

the proposals the fees were set uniformly and there was not even mention of the possibility to set them other than in a uniform manner.[28] While the very specific context in which this case was ruled should be recognised, the Court's shying away of interpreting the requirement of uniform conditions arguably opened the door to a constitutional modification.

II. Reconceptualising Implementing Powers Post-Lisbon

Because of the different wording of Articles 202 EC and 291 TFEU, and given that delegated acts have been carved out of Article 291 TFEU, the notion of implementation under Article 291 TFEU itself must necessarily have changed and it must necessarily be more narrowly construed than the pre-Lisbon notion of implementation. While evident in theory, it has been difficult to give effect to this in practice. In the following section, a number of issues related to the narrowed notion of implementation will be discussed. First the question whether the Commission can grant an implementing power to itself in delegated acts will be addressed (section 6.II.A). Next the nature and extent of implementing powers under Article 291 TFEU will be explored (section 6.II.B), and the standard set by the Court in *Eures network* will be analysed (section 6.II.C). Finally, the extent of the constitutional modification through interstitial change will be determined (section 6.II.D).

A. May Implementing Acts Implement Delegated Acts?

One important textual difference between Articles 290 and 291 TFEU is that the latter defines the enabling act differently and more broadly as any legally binding Union act (and not just legislative acts). In principle, any binding EU act is therefore open to implementation by the Commission (or Council). While the issue of an implementing act implementing another implementing is moot,[29] a literal reading of Article 291(2) TFEU allows for the possibility of a delegated act (or an autonomous executive act, see section 2.II) to be uniformly implemented. However, Greiner notes that doing so would undermine the control exercised by the legislator.[30]

How this would be precisely so is hard to see: since both the empowerment to adopt implementing acts and the procedure through which it will be adopted must be foreseen in the draft delegated act, the legislator(s) can object to the draft on those grounds.[31]

[28] See President of the EPO, Proposals for the level of renewal fees for European patents with unitary effect, 6 March 2015, SC/4/15; President of the EPO, Adjusted proposals for the level of renewal fees for European patents with unitary effect, 7 May 2015, SC/18/15.

[29] There is no purpose and no need for which the Commission would have to confer such implementing powers to itself. If the Commission were to notice that one of its implementing acts results in divergent practices in the Member States, it could simply adopt a new, more detailed, implementing act based on the same original empowerment. While Spasova does not refer to the Court's case law on secondary legal bases, she suggests that allowing the Commission to do otherwise would result in a breach of the institutional balance. See Rumyana Spasova, 'Powers of the European Commission – delegated and implementing acts in practical terms' (2021) 22 *ERA Forum* 509. For the Court's case law on (prohibited) secondary legal bases, see Joined Cases C-317/13 and C-679/13, *Parliament v Council*, ECLI:EU:C:2015:223. See also above, n 40.

[30] Greiner (n 2) 144–45.

[31] Volpato notes that more legal problems would arise from the revocation of a delegated power which the Commission has already exercised to confer implementing powers on itself. See Annalisa Volpato, *Delegation of*

Different, but equally unconvincing objections have been raised by the Council Legal Service, according to which only the formal legislator can decide to confer implementing powers. The Council Legal Service first argues that this transpires from the Convention's *travaux preparatoires*. As noted in the introduction, when determining the institutional balance, historic or genetic arguments are indeed relevant and the Court itself has already referred to the Working Group on Simplification's deliberations (see section 5.II.B) in the *Connecting Europe Facility* case.[32] However, the Council Legal Service's *a contrario* argument would seem to read too much in one statement of the Working Group which arguably simply reflects the typical situation of a legislative act conferring implementing powers.[33] The question before us here is not whether typically, implementing powers are conferred by the legislator but whether they may only be conferred by the legislator. As also noted in the introduction, different methods of interpretation should be pursued but the Council Legal Service's *a contrario* argument based on an inconspicuous remark cannot in itself outweigh the actual wording [illegible] Article 291(2) TFEU and the systemic combined reading together with Article 290(1) TFEU.

The Council Legal Service also argues that the nature of the power delegated to the Commission would be [illegible]d. However, it is difficult to see the pertinence of this objection: the test fo[illegible] [illegible] implementing power simply is whether uniform con[illegible]s for imple[illegible] [illegible]. If this objective test is met, there is a duty to con[illegible] implementing [illegible] Commission (or Council) (see section 6.I). Lastly, the Council Legal Service advances that it would allow the Commission to auto-delegate allowing it to itself choose the control mechanism which will apply to the exercise of the powers conferred [illegible][34] Here the Council Legal Service seems to have fallen victim to the control fallacy [illegible] possibility of the Commission 'auto-delegating' cannot be determined based on [illegible] control regime that would apply, just like the choice between two alternative legal bases cannot be determined based on the procedure which they prescribe.[35]

In sum, the legal case against allowing the Commission to confer implementing powers on itself through delegated acts seems slim. That the Commission itself is wary of this possibility should therefore be seen in light of the questionable political (but not legal) expediency of auto-empowerments.[36] In any event, that the Commission could auto-empower

Powers in the EU Legal System (London, Routledge, 2022) 124. Yet, a revoked delegated power leaves intact the delegated acts adopted pursuant to that power and therefore the implementing power which the Commission conferred on itself would also remain valid.

[32] Case C-286/14, *Parliament v Commission*, ECLI: EU: C: 2016: 183 [44].

[33] The statement in question is the following: 'it would be for *the legislator to determine whether and to what extent* it was necessary to adopt at Union level acts implementing legislative acts and/or *delegated acts, and, where appropriate, the committee procedure mechanism* (Art 202 TEC) which should accompany the adoption of such acts' (emphasis as added by the Council Legal Service). See Council Legal Service, Council Doc 10357/19 17. For the original document, see Secretariat of the European Convention, Final report of Working Group IX on Simplification, CONV 424/02, 9.

[34] While past practice, even if well-established, cannot be relied upon to show the validity of a certain practice, it may be noted that the Commission already does 'auto-delegate' and this has already come before the Court, see inter alia Case C-433/05 P, *Common Market Fertilizers SA v Commission*, ECLI:EU:C:2007:511; Joined Cases T-261/13 and T-86/14, *Netherlands v Commission*, ECLI:EU:T:2015:671.

[35] See Case C-130/10, *Parliament v Council*, ECLI:EU:C:2012:472 [80].

[36] In its internal guidance, the Commission does not rule out the possibility of doing so but urges its services to ensure that the empowerment is already foreseen in the original legislative act, pursuant to which a delegated will be adopted. See European Commission, Delegated and Implementing Acts – Guidelines for the Services of the Commission, SEC(2020) 361, 9.

itself was already recognised by the Court in the *Common Market Fertilizers* case. While this was a pre-Lisbon case, the Lisbon reform has not affected the Court's reasoning, which may still be applied post-Lisbon. The Court thus confirmed that the Commission could confer implementing powers on itself without prescribing recourse to a comitology committee, in a measure implementing a basic act, in so far as the basic act did not provide otherwise. The Court thereby explicitly noted that the legislator could circumscribe the Commission's power to do so, but since it had stayed silent on the issue it had left the choice to the Commission.[37] Concretely then for the post-Lisbon framework: when the legislator delegates a power to the Commission under Article 290 TFEU it, in any event, has the option to explicitly rule out that the delegation may be used to confer implementing powers or it could prescribe that any delegated acts that confer further implementing powers must thereby also prescribe a comitology procedure for the adoption of the implementing acts. Whether, conversely, the Court's finding in *Common Market Fertilizers* that the Commission is free not to prescribe comitology when the legislator stayed silent is a different question, which should be answered in the same way as the question whether the legislator, when conferring implementing powers on the Commission, can dispense with comitology, addressed in section [illegible]V.B.ii.

St[illegible] the post-Lisbon judgment by the General Court i[illegible] *[illegible] Commission* seems [illegible] point in the same direction as the Council Legal Service [illegible] case, the General Court held that a Commission decision adopted pursuant [illegible]C, which confers an implementing power on the Commission should again prescribe the PRAC. The General Court noted that

> the rules regarding the manner in which the EU institutions arrive at their decision[illegible] down in the Treaty and are not at the disposal of the Member States or of the instituti[illegible]mselves. To acknowledge that an institution can establish secondary legal bases, whether for the purpose of strengthening or easing the detailed rules for the adoption of an act, is tantamount to according that institution a legislative power which exceeds that provided for by the Treaty. It is also tantamount to enabling the institution concerned to undermine the principle of institutional balance which requires that each of the institutions must exercise its powers with due regard for the powers of the other institutions.[38]

However, the General Court, differently from the Court in *Common Market Fertilizers*,[39] came to its finding without checking whether the measures implementing the act adopted through the PRAC themselves still came within the scope of the PRAC. That the further implementing measures adopted by the Commission did not come within this scope also undermines the General Court's further finding linked to the general prohibition to create secondary legal bases. That case law is only relevant when the procedure prescribed by a secondary legal basis conflicts with that prescribed by the Treaties (or by an act of organic

[37] Case C-433/05 P, *Common Market Fertilizers SA v Commission*, ECLI:EU:C:2007:511 [128] and [134].

[38] Joined Cases T-261/13 and T-86/14, *Netherlands v Commission*, ECLI:EU:T:2015:671 [49].

[39] Noteworthy in this regard is the applicant in *Common Market Fertilizers* had argued that the Commission ought to have prescribed the regulatory procedure when it auto-empowered itself in its implementing measure. The Court noted, however, that the applicant challenged an individual decision and that individual measures fall outside the scope of the regulatory procedure. See Case C-433/05 P, *Common Market Fertilizers SA v Commission*, ECLI:EU:C:2007:511 [120]–[128].

law),[40] the point *in casu* being that the PRAC could not be prescribed to begin with (since the contested measures did not come within its scope of application).

In contrast, in *Esso Italiana*, AG Kokott followed the approach suggested here when she concluded that the Commission, in an act adopted pursuant to the PRAC, could empower itself to adopt implementing measures without recourse to the PRAC.[41] The AG arrived at this conclusion by finding that the further measures adopted pursuant to the PRAC measure came within the Court's definition of implementation in *Biocides*.[42] Since the PRAC is only applicable for amending or supplementing measures and because the further measure did not amend or supplement the legislative directive or the PRAC measure (adopted pursuant to the legislative directive), the AG held that the Commission could auto-empower itself.[43]

Returning to the Council Legal Service, its conclusion that

> the conferral of implementing powers on the Commission through a delegated act is only possible where the basic legislative act which has empowered the Commission to adopt such delegated acts makes clear provision for such implementing acts [since][p]roviding for the conferral of such powers in the legislative act would also allow the legislator to consider the appropriate committee procedure to be applied (if necessary) on the basis of the general nature of those implementing powers and the area concerned[44]

cannot therefore convince and should actually be inverted, as suggested above: the legislator has the option of limiting the freedom of the Commission, but if it remains silent, the choice is left to the Commission. That choice is not unfettered, of course. The Commission must continue to respect the constitutional framework governing delegated legislation. The real concern of the Council (Legal Service) might then be that if it is (politically) accepted that the Council (and Parliament) take a loose approach to that framework, the latter also loses its constraining force when (exceptionally) the Commission acts both as delegating and as delegate authority.

[40] In *Minimum common lists*, the Council had created a secondary legal basis for the adoption of basic acts. The Court first checked whether it could reclassify the to be adopted measures as implementing measures (under the current Art 291(2) TFEU, in which case the Council could have reserved the implementing power to itself and the secondary legal basis would not have been problematic). Since a reclassification was not possible, the Court was compelled to find that the Council illegitimately had created a secondary legal basis. See Case C-133/06, *Parliament v Council*, ECLI:EU:C:2008:257 [44]–[51]. Similarly, in *Visa Information System*, the Court held that the prohibition of secondary legal bases 'must also be applied to the legal bases provided for in secondary legislation which make it possible to adopt measures for the implementation of that legislation'. See Joined Cases C-317/13 and C-679/13, *Parliament v Council*, ECLI:EU:C:2015:223 [43]. However, this was only so because (at the relevant point in time) the EU Treaties not only prescribed the procedure for adopting basic acts in the Area of Freedom Security and Justice, but also the procedure for the implementation of those basic acts. Had the relevant Treaty provision not prescribed the Parliament's consultation for the adoption of implementing measures by the Council, the latter would have been free to adopt implementing measures itself under the default system (see section 6.III) and therefore without consulting the Parliament.

[41] The Court invalidated the measure in question on another ground and therefore did not deal with this issue.

[42] Opinion of AG Kokott in Joined Cases C-191/14 and C-192/14, Case C-295/14 and Joined Cases C-389/14, C-391/14 to C-393/14, *Esso Italiana*, ECLI:EU:C:2015:754 [179]–[182].

[43] ibid [187]. Since the Court invalidated the Commission's decision on other grounds, it did not rule on this point. See Joined Cases C-191/14, C-192/14, C-295/14, C-389/14 and C-391/14 to C-393/14, *Esso Italiana*, ECLI:EU:C:2016:311.

[44] See Council Legal Service, Council Doc 10357/19, 18.

While Greiner notes that in any event the option of a delegated act conferring implementing powers has not been used post-Lisbon and Bradley even ruled this out,[45] exceptionally this option has indeed been relied upon. The Commission has not only done so in acts adopted pursuant to the PRAC.[46] Through an *amending* delegated act, it has also expanded the legislative provision setting out the information requirements on which the Commission can adopt implementing acts.[47] Even more pointedly, the Commission has also granted itself (without prescribing comitology) in a *supplementing* delegated act setting out a milk production reduction scheme, the power to adopt acts ensuring the implementation of the scheme.[48] Differently from when the parent act is an amending delegated act, it is therefore not the legislative act that will be implemented and instead the binding act to be uniformly implemented is genuinely a self-standing delegated act. A further example may be found in the follow up to the *Esso Italiana* case (see above). After the revision of the (legislative) Directive 2003/87, whereby the reference to the PRAC was updated with a reference to a delegated act to determine the transitional rules for the free allocation of emission allowances, the Commission replaced its PRAC act with Delegated Regulation 2019/331. Like the PRAC act, that Regulation confers an implementing power to determine the precise correction factor for allocating free allowances.[49] However, the empowerment in the Delegated Regulation is not couched in the terms of an implementing power (and neither does it prescribe a comitology procedure for the adoption of the correction factor). The act subsequently adopted by the Commission still is designated as an implementing act in the title (unlike the act at issue in *Esso Italiana*).[50] While perhaps exceptional, these cases show that also delegated acts might require uniform conditions for their implementation, in which case they can legitimately confer implementing powers on the Commission (or Council). When the Commission adopts a delegated act, the duties typically imposed on the legislator apply to it *mutatis mutandis*. As a result, if uniform

[45] Kieran Bradley, 'Delegation of Powers in the European Union – Political Problems, Legal Solutions?' in Carl Fredrik Bergström and Dominique Ritleng (eds), *Rulemaking by the European Commission – The New System for Delegation of Powers* (Oxford, OUP, 2016) 63. Bradley noted that this possibility is an institutional chimera since it would presuppose that the Commission imposes comitology on itself (or that the Parliament and Council require the Commission to grant implementing powers to itself in the legislative delegation). Yet the example cited in n 48 shows that in these cases, the Commission simply confers an implementing power to itself without recourse to comitology. On the latter possibility, see section 6.V.B.ii.

[46] See Commission Regulation 282/2008 on recycled plastic materials and articles intended to come into contact with foods as amended by Commission Regulation 2015/1906, OJ [2015] L 278/11.

[47] See Greiner (n 2) 145. See Commission Delegated Regulation 1155/2013 amending Regulation (EU) No 1169/2011 of the European Parliament and of the Council on the provision of food information to consumers as regards information on the absence or reduced presence of gluten in food, OJ [2013] L 306/7. The Commission also exercised this (new) implementing power. See Commission Implementing Regulation 828/2014 on the requirements for the provision of information to consumers on the absence or reduced presence of gluten in food, OJ [2014] L 228/5.

[48] See Art 4(2) of Commission Delegated Regulation 2016/1612 providing aid for milk production reduction, OJ [2016] L 242/4. The Commission has also exercised this power, see Commission Implementing Regulation 2016/1845, fixing the allocation coefficient to be applied to applications for aid for milk production reduction pursuant to Delegated Regulation (EU) 2016/1612, OJ [2016] L 282/42.

[49] See Art 14(6) of Commission Delegated Regulation 2019/331 determining transitional Union-wide rules for free allocation of emission allowances, OJ [2019] L 59/8.

[50] Commission Implementing Decision 2021/927 determining the uniform cross-sectoral correction factor for the adjustment of free allocations of emission allowances for the period 2021 to 2025, OJ [2021] L 203/14.

conditions are required for the implementation of the delegated act, the Commission must confer implementing powers on itself (or on the Council). If it is accepted that Parliament and Council, in the more typical situations, can forego at prescribing control by comitology committees (see section 6.V.B.ii), so should the Commission under the same conditions. Unlike what the General Court in *Netherlands v Commission* suggested, that would not allow the Commission to undermine the institutional balance, since as noted earlier, the legislator, if it wished could clarify already in the legislative act that implementation of the legislative act and any delegated act should be subject to comitology and because Parliament and Council can object to any draft delegated act.[51]

B. The Nature and Extent of Implementing Powers under Article 291 TFEU

If the Commission under Article 290 TFEU exercises a 'legislative' power, what is the nature of the power under Article 291(2) TFEU? The straightforward answer would be that that power is an executive power to apply, implement or give effect to the parent act. However, in light of the language problem noted by Craig (see section 4.III) this difference could be merely semantical. Indeed also Bast finds that 'the new functional definition [of the implementing act in Article 291(2) TFEU] is broad enough to cover the whole range of implementing acts adopted under the previous [ie pre-Lisbon] regime'.[52] That of course would be problematic: recalling Figure 2.1, if the post-Lisbon implementing act is conceptualised in such a broad manner that it encompasses the pre-Lisbon implementing act, there is no scope left for the delegated act to exist, unless a complete overlap is accepted in which the case the whole point of the Lisbon split is nullified.

It follows that to uphold the Lisbon reform, the political institutions and the Court were required to narrow down the conceptualisation of the notion of implementing act. In terms of content (or the type of power, see section 5.II.B) this has been partially realised since implementing acts will not be used anymore to formally amend legislative acts (see section 4.III.B). This also follows from a combined reading of *Biocides* and *Spain v Council*: under *Biocides*, exercising the power under Article 291(2) TFEU allows the Commission (or Council) to specify the content of a legislative act in a way which, according to *Spain v Council*, Member States in principle could also do were it not for the requirement of uniform conditions. This arguably works both ways. As a result, since Member States cannot amend the scope or content of EU acts (see section 4.III), this should also be ruled out for implementing acts in the sense of Article 291(2) TFEU.

While the amendment of legislative acts has been definitively taken outside of the potential range of post-Lisbon implementing acts, the political institutions and the Courts

[51] See also Opinion of AG Campos Sánchez-Bordona in Joined Cases C-313/15 and C-530/15, *Eco-Emballages*, ECLI:EU:C:2016:551 [70].

[52] Jürgen Bast, 'Is There a Hierarchy of Legislative, Delegated, and Implementing Acts?' in Carl Fredrik Bergström and Dominique Ritleng (eds), *Rulemaking by the European Commission – The New System for Delegation of Powers* (Oxford, OUP, 2016) 161.

have not further pushed through the reconceptualisation of the implementing act. For the political institutions this is most clearly illustrated by the 2019 IIA (see section 4.III.D). For the Court, this is exemplified by the *Eures network* case,[53] the first post-Lisbon case where the Parliament asked the Court to annul a Commission implementing act, arguing that the Commission had overstepped its mandate and had supplemented rather than implemented the parent act. The specific point addressed in this section was also explicitly made by the Parliament before the Court. While the relevant provisions of the post-Lisbon parent and implementing acts were identical to the corresponding provisions of the pre-Lisbon parent and implementing acts, a reconceptualisation of what the Commission was allowed to do pursuant to an implementing power was necessary, simply because the constitutional framework (of Articles 290–291 TFEU) had been altered.[54]

To make this clear, it is useful to compare the relevant provisions of the pre- and post-Lisbon parent and implementing acts. As Table 6.1 shows, these provisions are virtually identical (the only textual differences being emphasised):

Table 6.1 Comparison of the pre- and post-Lisbon framework governing the EURES Coordination Office

Pre-Lisbon	**Post-Lisbon**
Parent act (Regulation 1612/68)[55]	**Parent act (Regulation 492/2011)**[56]
Article 21	*Article 18*
The European Office for Co-ordinating the Clearance of Vacancies and Applications for Employment …, shall have the general task of promoting vacancy clearance at *Community* level. It shall be responsible in particular for all the technical duties in this field which, under the provisions of this Regulation, are assigned to the Commission, and especially for assisting the national employment services.	The European Office for Coordinating the Clearance of Vacancies and Applications for Employment …, shall have the general task of promoting vacancy clearance at *Union* level. It shall be responsible in particular for all the technical duties in this field which, under the provisions of this Regulation, are assigned to the Commission, and especially for assisting the national employment services.
Article 44	*Article 38*
The Commission shall adopt measures pursuant to this Regulation for its implementation. To this end it shall act in close cooperation with the central public authorities of the Member States.	The Commission shall adopt measures pursuant to this Regulation for its implementation. To this end it shall act in close cooperation with the central public authorities of the Member States.

(continued)

[53] Case C-65/13, *Parliament v Commission*, ECLI:EU:C:2014:2289.

[54] See Opinion of AG Cruz Villalón in Case C-65/13, *Parliament v Commission*, ECLI:EU:C:2014:2071 [15].

[55] Council Regulation 1612/68 on freedom of movement for workers within the Community, OJ [1968] L 257/2.

[56] Regulation 492/2011 of the European Parliament and of the Council on freedom of movement for workers within the Union, OJ [2011] L 141/1.

Table 6.1 ***(Continued)***

Pre-Lisbon	**Post-Lisbon**
Implementing act (Decision 2003/8)[57]	**Implementing act (Decision 2012/733)**[58]
Article 4	*Article 4*
[the EURES Coordination Office] shall, in particular, undertake: ... the analysis of geographic and occupational mobility and the development of a general approach to mobility in accordance with the European Employment Strategy;	[the EURES Coordination Office] shall, in particular, undertake: ... (b) the analysis of geographic and occupational mobility, *in the light of the achievement of a balance between supply and demand*, and the development of a general approach to mobility in accordance with the European Employment Strategy

While the Parliament challenged the legality of more than one provision of the Commission's Implementing Decision, only point (b) of Article 4(3) is reproduced here since this is the provision on which the AG agreed with the Parliament that the Commission had gone beyond its mandate. From the overview, however, it is immediately clear that: (i) the mandate of the Coordination Office as defined by the legislator had not been altered under post-Lisbon legislation; (ii) the mandate granted to the Commission had not textually changed; and (iii) the relevant task entrusted to the Office by the Commission had not been altered either.

The crux of the matter thus was whether the task to 'develop a general approach to mobility in accordance with the European Employment Strategy' which (presumably) came under the pre-Lisbon notion of implementation pursuant to Article 202 EC could still qualify as implementation in the sense of Article 291 TFEU. On this the AG found that it amounted 'to a qualitative leap in terms of the tasks assigned to the Office'.[59] This because even if the broad outline of the general approach to be adopted by the Office would already follow from the European Employment Strategy, defined by the Council when it coordinates the economic policies of the Member States, there would still be too much discretion afforded to the Office meaning that it could not be said to be merely specifying the normative content of the legislative (parent) act as allowed by *Biocides*.[60] The AG here relied on the degree of discretion to distinguish implementation from supplementation since this case preceded *Visa reciprocity* in which the Court categorically rejected that criterion (see section 4.III.A). In addition, the AG suggested that the Office could only support the policy-makers with the information they needed but could not 'become an architect of or active participant in the creation of those policies'.[61] The AG therefore also ultimately disagreed with the Parliament which had argued that the Commission had '"supplemented certain non-essential elements" of the Regulation, for which purpose it

[57] Commission Decision 2003/8, OJ [2003] L 5/16.
[58] Commission Implementing Decision 2012/733, OJ [2012] L 328/21.
[59] Opinion of AG Cruz Villalón in Case C-65/13, *Parliament v Commission*, ECLI:EU:C:2014:2071 [77].
[60] ibid.
[61] ibid [78].

lacked the necessary authorisation under Article 290 TFEU'. This implies that, according to the Parliament, the legislator could have delegated this power under Article 290 TFEU. In contrast the AG held that the Office would be defining a policy, which the Court in *SBC* defined as a prerogative of the legislator which cannot be delegated under Article 290 TFEU (see section 4.II).

The Court itself, like the AG, recalled the function of an implementing act as defined in *Biocides*,[62] but crucially also recalled its pre-Lisbon jurisprudence on the limits to the Commission's implementing powers. The latter effectively killed the Parliament's attempt at reconceptualising the Commission's implementing powers, since the Court simply carried over the standard which it applied to the Commission's (broad) pre-Lisbon implementing power to the (narrower) post-Lisbon implementing power. According to the Court, also post-Lisbon

> it is settled case-law that, within the framework of the Commission's implementing power, the limits of which must be determined by reference amongst other things to the essential general aims of the legislative act in question, the Commission is authorised to adopt all the measures which are necessary or appropriate for the implementation of that act, provided that they are not contrary to it.[63]

The Court only qualified this pre-Lisbon case law on two accounts. First, it added that the Commission could not amend or supplement the basic legislative act even as to its non-essential elements.[64] This is not so much the Court extending the essentiality requirement to Article 291 TFEU, but rather a simple restatement of the different functions of the delegated and implementing act: the delegated act cannot amend or supplement legislation on its essential elements whereas the implementing act cannot amend or supplement legislation in any event (not even on the non-essential elements).[65] The latter reading thus still leaves unscathed the possibility for the Commission to implement the essential elements of legislation through implementing acts.[66] Secondly, the Court in *Eures network* was also careful to avoid referring to the Commission's powers as 'wide', as it had done in the pre-Lisbon case law which it cited.

Given the ramifications of the Court copy-pasting its pre-Lisbon test, it is useful to briefly recall the pre-Lisbon 'settled case law' on which the Court in *Eures network* explicitly relied: in *Parliament & Denmark v Commission*,[67] the contested implementing act that was quashed was a decision of the Commission[68] *amending* an annex of an act adopted pursuant to the co-decision procedure,[69] a normative activity which now squarely falls within Article 290 TFEU. In *Parliament v Commission*,[70] the Court struck down a decision of the

[62] Case C-65/13, *Parliament v Commission*, ECLI:EU:C:2014:2289 [43].

[63] ibid [44].

[64] ibid [45].

[65] See also Spasova, 'Powers of the European Commission' (2021) 510.

[66] Claude Blumann, 'Le système normatif de l'Union européenne vingt ans après le traité de Maastricht' (2012) *Revue des affaires européennes* 254.

[67] See Joined Cases C-14/06 and C-295/06, *Parliament & Denmark v Commission*, ECLI:EU:C:2008:176.

[68] Commission Decision 2005/717 amending for the purposes of adapting to technical progress the Annex to Directive 2002/95/EC of the European Parliament and of the Council on the restriction of the use of certain hazardous substances in electrical and electronic equipment, OJ [2005] L 271/48.

[69] Directive 2002/95 of the European Parliament and of the Council on the restriction of the use of certain hazardous substances in electrical and electronic equipment, OJ [2003] L 37/19.

[70] Case C-403/05, *Parliament v Commission*, ECLI:EU:C:2007:624.

Commission whereby the latter had exercised an implementing power to change the scope of the basic act, effectively amending the essential elements of that act.[71] In *The Netherlands v Commission*, the latter had acted pursuant to an enabling clause that allowed it to adopt detailed rules on a non-exhaustive list of issues.[72] The Court held that by adopting further rules on issues not explicitly listed in the parent act, the Commission had not exceeded its implementing powers.[73] Finally, in *Portugal v Commission*, the Council had empowered the Commission to increase the import quotas for textile from China 'in particular circumstances', but the Court held that the circumstances invoked by the Commission to increase the allowed quantities were not 'particular'.[74] These four cases related to different normative activities, and fully represent the broad pre-Lisbon notion of implementation showing how the Court applied one and the same standard to those different normative activities.

Returning to the *Eures network* case, after confirming the continued validity of its pre-Lisbon test, the Court subsequently applied it, scrutinising the provisions flagged by the Parliament. It first did so by identifying the essential general aim of the legislative basic act as 'putting workers in a position to take up concrete offers of employment from other regions of the Union by ensuring in a general way a clearer picture of the labour market'.[75] From that, it found that the objective of the contested decision, viz promoting transparency and exchange of information on European labour markets through Eures, to be consistent with the essential general aim of the legislative basic act.[76] Focusing specifically on the one provision which the AG had found to go beyond the Commission's implementing power, the Court noted in relation to Article 4(3)(b) of the Commission's Implementing Decision that allowing the Office to develop a general approach to labour mobility was intended to allow the network to realise its full potential, which is in line with promoting transparency and exchange of information on European labour markets (itself in line with the essential general aims of the legislative act).[77] Finding that the contested provision did not go against the objectives set by the legislator, the Court moved on to the question whether it was necessary or appropriate for the implementation of the legislative act and whether it did not supplement or amend that act.[78] Focusing here again only on Article 4(3)(b) of the implementing act, the Court applied constitutional avoidance and found that the general approach to labour mobility which the Office was mandated to draw up 'may be directed merely at preparing for the adoption of the controlling measures [by the Member States]'.[79] Devising a general approach was then necessary or appropriate according to the Court and as long as the Office's role (as defined in the implementing decision) was limited to

[71] Notably the AG was explicit on this, see Opinion of AG Kokott in Case C-403/05, *Parliament v Commission*, ECLI:EU:C:2007:290 [77]–[78].

[72] See Art 20 of Council Regulation 404/93 on the common organization of the market in bananas, OJ [1993] L 47/1.

[73] See Case C-478/93, *The Netherlands v Commission*, ECLI:EU:C:1995:324 [32].

[74] Case C-159/96, *Portugal v Commissi on*, E CLI:E U:C:1998:550 [48].

[75] Case C-65/13, *Parliament v Commission*, ECLI:EU:C:2014:2289 [50].

[76] ibid [52].

[77] ibid [55]–[56].

[78] ibid [61].

[79] Case C-65/13, *Parliament v Commission*, ECLI:EU:C:2014:2289 [71]. These controlling measures consist of binding decisions which the Member States may adopt to ensure a balance between labour supply and demand and non-binding reports which the Commission presents to the Council and Parliament.

preparing controlling measures, the Court held that the Commission had remained faithful to the Office's role as originally defined by the legislator.[80]

The importance of *Eures network* cannot be underestimated. As AG Bot stressed in *Pesce*, it means that both before and after the Lisbon Treaty 'the Commission's implementing power is characterized by the significant discretion allowed to that institution which is free to determine … what is necessary and appropriate in the light of the objectives pursued by the basic [act]'.[81] As will be noted in section 6.II.D below, this broad understanding contributed to a constitutional modification and contributed to the problematic delimitation between delegated and implementing acts.

C. The *Eures Network* Standard as the Single Standard for Implementation

Does it matter in which policy field an implementing power is exercised to determine the extent of that power? A number of commentators has interpreted the pre-Lisbon case law in that way, suggesting that the Commission's implementing powers are notably broader in the Common Agricultural Policy (CAP) compared to other policy areas.[82] It is unclear, however, whether this was truly the case, even in pre-Lisbon times. While it is true that the Court has ruled that 'Since only the Commission is in a position to keep track of agricultural market trends and to act quickly when necessary, the Council may confer on it wide powers *in that sphere*',[83] it does not necessarily and *a contrario*[84] follow from that case law that this is not the case for other policy fields. Indeed, the Court has made the same observations in the relation to the Common Commercial Policy, noting that 'Since only the Commission is in a position to watch closely and constantly international market trends and to act quickly when necessary, the Council may confer on it wide powers in this sphere'.[85] The apparent emphasis in the courts' case law on the peculiarity of the CAP may then also simply be the result of the CAP being the traditional testing ground for comitology (see section 3.I). The cases referred to by Hofmann, Rowe and Türk, which seem to suggest a more strict approach of the Court outside the CAP, can also be understood as the Court stepping in when the Commission (or Council) adopts measures that go against the aims and objectives of the parent act.[86]

[80] Case C-65/13, *Parliament v Commission*, ECLI:EU:C:2014:2289 [78].

[81] Opinion of AG Bot in Joined Cases C-78/16 and C-79/16, *Pesce*, ECLI:EU:C:2016:340 [86].

[82] Alexander Türk, *The concept of legislation in European community law: a comparative perspective* (Den Haag, Kluwer Law International, 2006) 229; Herwig Hofmann, 'Legislation, Delegation and Implementation under the Treaty of Lisbon: Typology Meets Reality' (2009) 15 *European Law Journal* 490–91.

[83] This is a statement (emphasis added) that the Court repeats in numerous CAP cases, see inter alia Case C-478/93, *The Netherlands v Commission*, ECLI:EU:C:1995:324 [30]; Case C-239/01, *Germany v Commission*, ECLI:EU:C:2003:514 [54]; Case 265/85, *Van den Bergh v Commission*, ECLI:EU:C:1987:121 [14].

[84] In some cases the Courts indeed seem to hint at an *a contrario* reasoning. The General Court has for instance noted: 'Thus, the Court has held that, in matters relating to agriculture, the Commission is authorised to adopt all the implementing measures which are necessary or appropriate for the implementation of the basic legislation, provided that they are not contrary to such legislation or to the implementing legislation adopted by the Council'. See Joined Cases T-64/01 and T-65/01, *Afrikanische Frucht-Compagnie v Council & Commission*, ECLI:EU:T:2004:37 [118]. See also Case C-478/93, *The Netherlands v Commission*, ECLI:EU:C:1995:324 [31].

[85] See Case C-159/96, *Portugal v Commissi on*, E CLI:E U:C:1998:550 [41].

[86] Herwig Hofmann, Gerard Rowe and Alexander Türk, *Administrative law and policy of the European Union* (Oxford, OUP, 2011) 233–35. In particular, they refer to Case C-314/99, *The Netherlands v Commission*, ECLI:EU:C:2002:378;

In any event, it is remarkable that post-Lisbon the Court has not yet ruled a case on the Commission's (or Council's) implementing powers in which it recalled its standard pre-Lisbon phraseology suggesting broader implementing powers in the CAP. Instead, the pre-Lisbon standard which the Court in *Eures network* transferred to the post-Lisbon legal framework is partially built on the Court's pre-Lisbon case law relating to implementing measures in the CAP. This would further suggest that when it comes to implementation there is only one standard that applies across different policy areas. One pending case to look out for in this regard is the second case in which the Parliament challenged the legality of a Commission implementing act, this time implementing the REACH Regulation.[87]

D. The Institutions' Constitutional Modification of Article 291(2) TFEU

To conclude, it follows from the political institutions' practice and the jurisprudence of the Court that the post-Lisbon implementing power under Article 291 TFEU has not been reconceptualised compared to the pre-Lisbon implementing power. The only exception here is that legislative acts cannot be amended through implementing acts. This lack of reconceptualisation constitutes a constitutional modification that undermines the institutional balance.

An institutional balance test can indeed be applied here since the notion of implementation is clearly provided for in Article 291 TFEU, but what that notion concretely means is left open. Historically, implementation has been construed broadly by the Court, but a systemic interpretation of Article 291 TFEU requires the notion to be redefined more narrowly given the carve out of Article 290 TFEU. The Court also recognises this since it notes that the Commission cannot amend or supplement legislative acts under Article 291 TFEU. However, given that the test itself is otherwise not altered, the Court appears to merely pay lip service to the reformed Treaty framework. This becomes clear if one considers that this constitutional modification is intimately tied with, and cannot be dissociated from, that related to the delimitation of delegated and implementing acts discussed in sections 4.III.A and 4.III.D. When the EU institutions fail to properly disentangle and differentiate supplementation from implementation, it is also impossible to come to a proper redefinition of implementation, and vice versa: since the pre-Lisbon notion of implementation encompasses 'supplementation', confirming the pre-Lisbon notion of implementation makes it impossible to identify a separate notion of supplementation.

Joined Cases C-14/06 and 295/06, *Parliament and Denmark v Commission*, ECLI:EU:C:2008:176; Case C-403/05, *Parliament v Commission*, ECLI:EU:C:2007:624. Further, two cases traditionally cited to show the courts' more restrictive take on implementation outside the CAP in fact also concerned the Commission's powers to implement the CAP. See Case 291/86, *Central-Import Münster*, ECLI:EU:C:1988:361; Case 22/88, *Vreugdenhil*, ECLI:EU:C:1989:277. A genuine non-CAP case where the Court took a restrictive turn is *Alliance for Natural Health*, see Joined Cases C-154/04 and C-155/04, *Alliance for Natural Health*, ECLI:EU:C:2005:449. As was noted above, however, (see section 5.III), trying to generalise that case would be problematic since it would imply that (outside the CAP) the Commission's (pre-Lisbon) implementing powers were governed by the *Meroni* doctrine, which would be an untenable finding.

[87] See Action brought on 5 March 2021, Case C-144/21, *Parliament v Commission*, OJ [2021] C 163/22.

Zooming in on the *Eures network* test, its most problematic aspect is the requirement that the Commission needs to respect 'the essential general aims' of the basic act when implementing the latter. After all, that an implementing act (in the post-Lisbon sense) must do so is inherent in the notion of implementation as 'giving effect' and its inclusion only makes sense if one starts from the pre-Lisbon notion of implementation (which encompassed supplementation and amendment). The Court's findings thereby ultimately negatively affect the prerogatives of the Parliament since it may result in an implementation notion that is too broad (at the expense of the supplementation notion) which negatively affects the possibility for the Parliament to control executive rule-making in delegated legislation.

III. Exceptional Implementation by the Council

Pre-Lisbon, Article 202 EC provided that the Council could reserve implementing powers to itself in specific cases, but Article 291(2) TFEU provides that this is only exceptionally so and in duly specified cases. Article 291(2) TFEU further added a second scenario where the Council will implement binding acts, namely 'in the cases provided for in Articles 24 and 26 of the Treaty on European Union'. This second scenario concerns the implementation of the acts adopted under the common foreign and security policy (CFSP). In institutional balance terms, the stakes at play here for the Parliament seem evident. Generally, the Parliament has no active role to play in the CFSP. The broader the CFSP and, crucially here, its implementation are conceived, the more Parliament's scrutiny over the implementation of EU law will be reduced.[88] A similar logic applies to the first scenario: where the Parliament has a general control function over the Commission and the Comitology Regulation provides in a specific *droit de regard* for the Parliament (see section 6.V.D), such accountability relationships are not in place between the Parliament and the Council. Where an implementing power is not entrusted to the Commission, but instead is exceptionally entrusted to the Council, the Parliament's control role is nullified.

Without necessarily linking this to the Parliament's reduced role, a number of commentators have indeed argued that the possibility to entrust the implementation of EU law to the Council pursuant to Article 291(2) TFEU was an anomaly under the Lisbon Treaty.[89] One very bold reading of the reference to implementation by the Council in Article 291(2) TFEU was advanced by Kollmeyer who argued that it was superfluous, or purely declaratory, since it simply reaffirmed that the Commission's implementing function under that Article is without prejudice to the Council's autonomous executive powers conferred by specific Treaty provisions.[90] However, given the origins of this provision and the consequence of this proposed reading (it not being possible for secondary legislation to entrust the Council with

[88] Noting this as a general feature resulting from Art 40 TEU, see Andreas von Arnauld, 'Das System der Europäischen Außenbeziehungen' in Andreas von Arnauld (ed), *Europäische Außenbeziehungen* (Baden-Baden, Nomos, 2013) 72.

[89] Robert Schütze, '"Delegated" Legislation in the (new) European Union: A Constitutional Analysis' (2011) 74 *MLR* 693; Koen Lenaerts and Marlies Desomer, 'Towards a Hierarchy of Legal Acts in the European Union? Simplification of Legal Instruments and Procedures' (2005) 11 *European Law Journal* 756. But see Kröll, who argued that the exception in Art 291(2) TFEU allowing the Council to exercise executive powers should be interpreted in light of the pre-Lisbon case law that sanctioned this practice. See Kröll (n 2) 287.

[90] Kollmeyer (n 12) 348–49.

its implementation) that reading cannot be supported. Kollmeyer's linking of the Council's implementing power under Article 291(2) TFEU with its autonomous executive powers of course does raise the question how both compare in terms of their scope. As noted in section 4.I.A, in *Germany v Parliament & Council*, the Court confirmed that the Council enjoys less far-reaching powers under Article 291(2) TFEU. While the Court has not yet confirmed this explicitly,[91] for reasons of internal consistency of Article 291(2) TFEU, the Council's implementing powers under this provision should be the same as those of the Commission, meaning the *Eures network* test would also be applicable. The Court will have a first opportunity to clarify this in the (pending at the time of writing) *Fenix International* case.[92] In this preliminary reference case, the validity of a Council implementing regulation (adopted pursuant to a VAT directive) is challenged because it allegedly *supplements* the directive instead of *implementing* it. The premise of the reference seems to be that the contested provision may only be saved if the Court confirms that the Council has greater power under Article 291(2) TFEU than the Commission, but that premise seems incorrect: as noted in section 6.II.B, *Eures network* is a permissive standard and the Court may well confirm both that it applies to the Council and at the same time uphold the contested provision.

Before looking into the exceptional implementation of non-CFSP EU law by the Council, first the second scenario, introduced by the Lisbon Treaty, will be explored.

A. CFSP Implementation by the Council

The question when the Council implements a CFSP act seems straightforward enough but has still resulted in litigation. In *National Iranian Oil Company*, the legality of a Council implementing act adopted pursuant to a regulation adopted on the basis of Article 215 TFEU was challenged. Article 215 TFEU is the legal basis that provides a link between formal CFSP decisions and the economic sanctions which the EU might impose on third countries or natural and legal persons. In these cases in which no formal CFSP act is being implemented, which of the two scenarios foreseen in Article 291(2) TFEU applies? According to the General Court, while the basic regulation did not refer to Article 291 TFEU, the conferral concerned a specific case that was duly justified,[93] bringing it under the first scenario envisaged in Article 291(2) TFEU. However, AG Cruz Villalón found that even if a measure

[91] At the time this manuscript was finalised, the Court ruled on the rule of law conditionality regulation cases. It is to be expected that when the first measures are adopted pursuant to the Regulation, they will be challenged in Court. If and when this happens, the first thorny issue will be to determine which court has jurisdiction. The Council measures adopted under the Regulation are arguably measures which the Member States cannot adopt themselves, similarly to the measures at issue in *Spain v Council* (see section 6.IV.B). They would therefore not be implementing measures in the sense of Art 291 TFEU and the Court of Justice (rather than the General Court) would be competent to review them. However, as noted in section 6.III.B, the Court of Justice has already accepted that the Council's power at issue is an Art 291(2) TFEU power. Depending on how the power is qualified, these cases could thus offer a further opportunity to the Court of Justice to clarify if and how the *sui generis* implementing power differs from the implementing power in Art 291(2) TFEU.

[92] See Case C-695/20, Reference for a preliminary ruling from First-tier Tribunal (Tax Chamber) (United Kingdom) made on 22 December 2020 – Fenix International Limited v Commissioners for Her Majesty's Revenue and Customs, OJ [2021] C 110/17.

[93] See Case T-578/12, *National Iranian Oil Company v Council*, ECLI:EU:T:2014:678 [57]–[83].

is adopted based on Article 215 TFEU, it is still adopted in the sphere of the CFSP (even if not pursuant to a CFSP legal basis) and that therefore the conferral of the implementing powers to the Council (rather than the Commission) did not have to be motivated since the Council is the default actor for the implementation of the CFSP.[94] Interestingly, and agreeing with the General Court, the AG did note that the Council being the default actor did not prevent the conferral of CFSP implementing powers on the Commission, in specific duly justified cases.[95] Differently from its AG, the Court applied the 'duly justified in specific cases test' of the first scenario.[96] The Court thus seems inclined to restrict the scope of CFSP-implementation as much as possible, something which, more generally, is in line with its external relations case law and its expansive interpretation of its own jurisdiction over the CFSP.[97] Significantly, however, despite the stricter language of Article 291(2) TFEU compared to Article 202 EC, the Court also applied its pre-Lisbon test (see section 6.III.B) to determine whether the Council could be exceptionally empowered. While the Court could have seized this opportunity to align its test to the new (stricter) wording of Article 291(2) TFEU, it must be noted that in any event applying a higher standard would not have made a difference here. While Article 215 TFEU is not a CFSP legal basis, the acts adopted pursuant to it are intimately linked with the CFSP in which the Council *is* the default actor. That in itself is arguably sufficient to exceptionally empower the Council.

B. Duly Justified Specific Cases of Implementation by the Council

Turning to the first scenario where the Council may exceptionally be empowered to adopt implementing measures, it should be noted that pre-Lisbon, the Court has been permissive in testing the relevant standard. In *Visa policy*, the Commission had challenged the legality of the Council's decision, in a basic act, to reserve implementing powers only to itself. When the Court set out to determine whether this was a specific case and whether the Council had 'properly explain[ed], by reference to the nature and content of the basic instrument to be implemented or amended, why exception is being made to the rule that … it is the Commission which, in the normal course of events, is responsible for exercising that power',[98] it subsequently accepted the Council's justifications although qualifying them as 'both general and laconic'.[99] While the Court did not rely on a manifest error test in this regard, that it did put the bar this low probably explains why the Commission or Parliament have since not seized it to contest a decision by the Council to reserve implementing powers to itself. Both institutions have so far also refrained from doing so after the entry into force of the Lisbon Treaty when it may be argued that the threshold to empower the Council has been raised, given the stricter language of Article 291(2) TFEU.

[94] Opinion of AG Cruz Villalón in Case C-440/14 P, *National Iranian Oil Company v Council*, ECLI:EU:C:2015:545 [114].

[95] ibid [115].

[96] Case C-440/14 P, *National Iranian Oil Company v Council*, ECLI:EU:C:2016:128 [49]–[55].

[97] See Graham Butler, *Constitutional Law of the EU's Common Foreign and Security Policy* (Oxford, Hart Publishing, 2019) 145–222.

[98] See Case C-257/01, *Commission v Council*, ECLI:EU:C:2005:25 [51].

[99] ibid [53].

Alternatively, the reformulated provision in Article 291(2) TFEU could be read as simply codifying *Visa policy*,[100] and this also seems to flow from *National Iranian Oil Company* where the Court linked Article 291(2) TFEU with Article 145 EEC and Article 202 EC without noting the former's stricter language.[101] The case on the conditionality regulation further points in this direction.[102] This would mean that the pre- and post-Lisbon standard would be one and the same. Nevertheless, it is remarkable that even this minimal standard is not always respected in the post-Lisbon era, when the Council reserves implementing powers to itself (see further). Before looking into these cases it is important to note that the Comitology Regulation, governing the Commission's exercise of implementing powers (see section 6.V.B), recalls in the fourteenth recital of its preamble that:

> When considering the adoption of … implementing acts concerning particularly sensitive sectors, notably taxation, consumer health, food safety and protection of the environment, the Commission, in order to find a balanced solution, will, as far as possible, act in such a way as to avoid going against any predominant position which might emerge within the appeal committee against the appropriateness of an implementing act.

It should be stressed here that a similar provision was lacking in the (second) comitology decision. Arguably, under the pre-Lisbon framework such a provision was not necessary since there was the option to refer a file to the Council both under the management and regulatory procedures. That option does not exist anymore under the post-Lisbon advisory and examination procedures (see section 6.V.B.ii) While logical from this perspective, the fourteenth recital of the Comitology Regulation is still remarkable since it must *a contrario* mean that a basic act justifying the conferral of implementing powers to the Council by reason of the (particularly) sensitive nature of the sector for which implementing measures have to adopted would be insufficient. The main caveat here is that the secondary legislator cannot override or alter the Treaty framework, but assuming that the Regulation's fourteenth recital reflects the spirit of Article 291(2) TFEU, the Commission may exercise implementing measures in '*particularly sensitive* sectors', which in itself cannot therefore be a sufficient reason to have recourse to exceptional Council implementation.

i. Recourse to Exceptional Council Implementation

In quantitative terms, the exceptional implementing function of the Council is becoming more important as now there are six important policy areas where the Council has been exceptionally empowered under Article 291(2) TFEU. The first two date from the pre-Lisbon era. A first relates to the implementation of the common VAT rules under Directive 2006/112,[103] while the second relates to psychoactive substances pursuant to a

[100] Advancing this reading, see René Barents, 'De post-Lissabon-rechtspraak over het institutioneel evenwicht' (2019) 67 *Tijdschrift voor Europees en economisch recht* 339.

[101] Case C-440/14 P, *National Iranian Oil Company v Council*, ECLI:EU:C:2016:128 [49]–[50].

[102] Case C-156/21, *Hungary v Parliament & Council*, ECLI:EU:C:2022:97. See below n 134.

[103] See Council Directive 2006/112 on the common system of value added tax, OJ [2006] L 347/1. Until recently, only the Council could uniformly implement the Directive, as provided for by Art 397 of the Directive. The Commission in 2020 also proposed a further amendment that would transfer some of these implementing powers from the Council to the Commission. See European Commission, COM(2020) 749 final.

pre-Lisbon third pillar legal basis.[104] More recently and interestingly, four existential crises for the EU have seen implementing powers being conferred on the Council. Politically this will not be surprising, since these crises concerned policy areas that go to the core of Member States' sovereignty. EU integration has been allowed to further proceed in these areas precisely because Member States have secured greater control over the implementation of the new EU rules in this area.

Following the migration crisis which hit the EU in 2015, the Council has been more involved in the implementation of the Schengen acquis. For instance, while the Schengen Borders Code (SBC) Regulation had conferred implementing powers to the Council already before the migration crisis, the latter still triggered a first application of these powers, when the Council adopted a recommendation on prolonging internal border controls.[105] Remarkably, while Article 29 of the SBC Regulation refers to a recommendation to be adopted by the Council, the Council adopted an 'Implementing Decision setting out a Recommendation'. The Council has also reserved significant implementing powers to itself when the Frontex Regulation was reviewed in 2016. Among the many revisions, a possibility for the Frontex agency to essentially take over the border control of a Member State in case a 'situation at the external border requires urgent action' was introduced. In its original proposal the Commission had foreseen that declaring such a situation (and therefore triggering Frontex's exceptional intervention powers) would be done by the Commission through immediately applicable implementing acts.[106] The final Regulation, however, leaves it to the Council to determine whether there is such a situation.[107] A similar dynamic is visible in another policy area that has been subject to significant agencification. The three European Supervisory Authorities (ESAs) in the financial sectors were established in 2010 following the financial crisis. The ESAs are a further development of the Level 3 committees, bringing together national supervisors, of the Lamfalussy process established in 2001.[108] In its original proposal, the Commission envisaged that it could declare the existence of an emergency situation, which would allow the ESAs to issue binding decisions to the national supervisors.[109] In the regulations ultimately adopted, this mechanism is retained, but it is left to the Council to declare the existence of such emergency situations (although the ESA Regulations do not explicitly prescribe this is to be done through implementing acts).[110]

[104] Following a challenge by the European Parliament, the Court upheld the legality of this implementing power in light of Protocol 36 to the Lisbon Treaty (on transitional provisions). See Joined cases C-317/13 and C-679/13, *Parliament v Council*, ECLI:EU:C:2015:223 [51]–[59]. See also Chamon, 'Institutional balance and Community method' (2016) 1535ff.

[105] See eg Council Implementing Decision (EU) 2017/246 of 7 February 2017 setting out a Recommendation for prolonging temporary internal border control in exceptional circumstances putting the overall functioning of the Schengen area at risk, OJ [2017] L35/59.

[106] See Art 18 in European Commission, Proposal for a Regulation of the European Parliament and of the Council on the European Border and Coast Guard, COM (2015) 671 final.

[107] See Art 19 of Regulation (EU) 2016/1624 of the European Parliament and of the Council of 14 September 2016 on the European Border and Coast Guard, OJ [2016] L 251/1. The same provision was taken over in the Frontex Regulation of 2019 which applies presently.

[108] See Carl Fredrik Bergström, 'EU Rulemaking in the Internal Market after the Financial Crisis' in Carl Fredrik Bergström and Magnus Strand (eds), *Legal Accountability in EU Markets for Financial Instruments: The Dual Role of Investment Firms* (Oxford, OUP, 2021) 10–17.

[109] See Art 10 in European Commission, Proposal for a Regulation of the European Parliament and of the Council establishing a European Securities and Markets Authority, COM (2009) 499 final.

[110] See Art 18 of Regulation 1095/2010 establishing a European Supervisory Authority, OJ [2010] L 331/84.

Following the eurocrisis and the pandemic, Member States also compensated further integration in the broader area of Economic and Monetary Union (EMU) by activating the Council's exceptional implementing function under Article 291(2) TFEU. The non-legislative European Financial Stabilisation Mechanism (EFSM) Regulation provided a first occasion to grant an exceptional implementing function to the Council.[111] In line with the proposal of the Commission,[112] the Regulation indeed provides that the decision on granting a loan to a Eurozone Member State is taken by the Council.[113] A second important example is the Council's power under the (legislative) two-pack framework to adopt macroeconomic adjustment programmes for those Eurozone countries that have requested financial assistance from the European Stability Mechanism (ESM).[114] These programmes will then replace the economic partnership programmes which the Member States concerned will have adopted under the excessive deficit procedure that would normally already have been initiated against those states.[115] A third implementing power has been granted to the Council in the Single Supervisory Mechanism (SSM) Regulation, since the Chair and Vice-Chair of the Supervisory Board are formally appointed by the Council pursuant to implementing acts.[116] A fourth implementing power may be found in the Single Resolution Mechanism (SRM) Regulation, notably on the determination of the *ex ante* contributions payable by Eurozone banks to feed the Single Resolution Fund. In the original proposal of the Commission, these would be calculated based on a methodology worked out by the Commission in delegated acts.[117] In the final SRM Regulation, however, this methodology is prescribed in Council implementing acts.[118] The Council also exercised this power when it adopted Implementing Regulation 2015/81.[119]

[111] See Council Regulation 407/2010 of 11 May 2010 establishing a European filisation mechanism (Council Regulation 407/2010). Thus, here again the Council relied on a primary law executive power to confer implementing powers to itself.

[112] See Art 4 of European Commission, Communication from the Commission EUROPE 2020: A strategy for smart, sustainable and inclusive growth, COM (2010) 2010 final.

[113] See Art 3 of the European Financial Stabilisation Mechanism (EFSM) Regulation.

[114] See Art 7 of Regulation 472/2013 of the European Parliament and of the Council of 21 May 2013 on the strengthening of economic and budgetary surveillance of Member States in the euro area experiencing or threatened with serious difficulties with respect to their financial stability (Regulation 472/2013). The Commission also proposed this implementing power in European Commission, Proposal for a Regulation of the European Parliament and of the Council on the strengthening of economic and budgetary surveillance of Member States experiencing or threatened with serious difficulties with respect to their financial stability in the euro area, COM (2011) 819 final.

[115] See Art 9 of Regulation 473/2013.

[116] See Art 26(3) of Regulation 1024/2013. In the Commission's original proposal (see European Commission, Proposal for a Regulation of the European Parliament and of the Council on the strengthening of economic and budgetary surveillance of Member States experiencing or threatened with serious difficulties with respect to their financial stability in the euro area, COM (2012) 511 final), the Chair and Vice Chair were elected by the ECB Governing Council, from the members of the Executive Board and the Governing Council respectively.

[117] See Art 66 of European Commission, Proposal for a Regulation of the European Parliament and of the Council establishing uniform rules and a uniform procedure for the resolution of credit institutions and certain investment firms in the framework of a Single Resolution Mechanism and a Single Bank Resolution Fund and amending Regulation 1093/2010 of the European Parliament and of the Council, COM (2013) 520 final.

[118] See Art 70(7) of Regulation 806/2014 of the European Parliament and of the Council of 15 July 2014 establishing uniform rules and a uniform procedure for the resolution of credit institutions and certain investment firms in the framework of a Single Resolution Mechanism and a Single Resolution Fund and amending Regulation (EU) No 1093/2010 (Regulation 806/2014).

[119] See OJ 2015 L 15/1.

In response to the Covid pandemic, the Council has been granted further implementing powers. Under the SURE Regulation, in line with the original proposal of the Commission,[120] loans are granted to Member States through implementing acts adopted by the Council on a proposal from the Commission.[121] Under the Recovery and Resilience Facility, the Council, through implementing acts, approves the national plans based on the Commission's assessment and the Council may suspend payments and commitments to ensure coherence with economic governance under the Stability and Growth Pact.[122] In the Commission's original proposal the suspension was already foreseen to be decided upon by the Council, but the approval of the national plans would have been decided upon by the Commission.[123]

Finally, in the context of the rule of law crisis, the Conditionality Mechanism Regulation was adopted through which the Council, on proposal of the Commission, may adopt measures protecting the EU budget. An example of such a measure is the suspension of payments to a Member State that breaches the rule of law.[124] Also in its proposal the Commission foresaw that this power would be exercised by the Council, albeit that it had proposed that the Council would take its decision pursuant to a reverse qualified majority (the proposal being deemed adopted, unless a QMV in the Council votes against).[125]

As the following section makes clear, the justifications given by the legislator are shallow at best and hardly informative as to why the Council rather than the Commission is empowered. Taking a step back, these cases are interesting in that they reveal the political limits to the Lisbon Treaty's reform of comitology. After the Council had been excised from comitology (both in Article 291(3) TFEU and in the Comitology Regulation) (see section 6.V.B), the above cases suggest that the Member States (in Council) are discontent with the degree of control possible through the comitology procedures and will therefore make more ample use of the exceptional possibility to confer implementing powers on the Council. Although this is guesswork, some of the implementing powers flagged above might not have been conferred on the Council if the legislator could still prescribe the pre-Lisbon regulatory procedure which allowed a referral the Council in the case of a lack of positive opinion in the committee. Still, for some of the cases highlighted above there are strong indications of this: the Council acts declaring an emergency situation at the external borders under the Frontex Regulation; approving loans under the SURE; imposing measures under the conditionality mechanism; approving the national plans and possible suspension of commitments under the RRF Regulation; and establishing the methodology for *ex ante* contributions under the SRM Regulation are all drafted and prepared by the Commission.

[120] See Art 6 of the Commission proposal, COM (2020) 139 final.

[121] See Art 6 of Council Regulation 2020/672 on the establishment of a European instrument for temporary support to mitigate unemployment risks in an emergency (SURE) following the COVID-19 outbreak, OJ [2020] L 159/1.

[122] See Arts 20(1) and 10(3) of Regulation 2021/241 of the European Parliament and of the Council of 12 February 2021 establishing the Recovery and Resilience Facility ('Regulation 2021/241').

[123] See Arts 9 and 17 of the Proposal for a Regulation of the European Parliament and of the Council establishing a Recovery and Resilience Facility, COM (2020) 408 final.

[124] See Art 6 of Regulation 2020/2092 on a general regime of conditionality for the protection of the Union budget, OJ [2020] L 433I/1.

[125] See Art 5 of the Proposal for a Regulation of the European Parliament and of the Council on the protection of the Union's budget in generalised deficiencies as regards the rule of law in the Member States, COM(2018) 324 final.

It is only the actual adoption of these measures that is reserved to the Council. In the case of the suspension of commitments under the RRF Regulation, this decision is even taken by the Council under the rule of reverse qualified majority. Clearly, the point here is that while the Commission is drafting these decisions, the Member States (in Council) insist on having the final say and control over them.

ii. Justifications Given and Assessment

The Council's implementing power to determine whether an exceptional situation exists at the Schengenzone's external border was justified as follows in the 2016 Frontex Regulation: 'The implementing power to adopt such a decision should be conferred on the Council because of the potentially politically sensitive nature of the measures to be decided, which are likely to touch on national executive and enforcement powers'.[126] In contrast, the Council's power to declare emergency situations in the financial markets is simply justified by noting that 'The power to determine the existence of an emergency situation should be conferred on the Council, following a request by any of the ESAs, the Commission or the ESRB'.[127] On the Council deciding on granting EFSM loans, the EFSM Regulation provides: 'Given their particular financial implications, the decisions to grant Union financial assistance pursuant to this Regulation require the exercise of implementing powers, which should be conferred on the Council'. In relation to the MAPs, Regulation 472/2013 provides that the power to adopt them should be conferred on the Council since it is 'of particular relevance to the policy of economic coordination of Member States, which, pursuant to Article 121 TFEU, is to take place within the Council'.[128] On the Council's power to define the methodology for *ex ante* contributions, the SRM Regulation provides that:

> The Council should, within the framework of the delegated acts adopted under Directive 2014/59/EU, adopt implementing acts to specify the application of the methodology for the calculation of individual contributions to the Fund, as well as the technical modalities for computing the flat contribution and the risk-adjusted contribution.[129]

In the SURE Regulation, the fact that the Council decides on the grant of loans is justified by noting the particular financial implications which these decisions have.[130] Similarly, under the Conditionality Regulation, this choice is justified by noting 'the importance of the financial effects of measures [adopted pursuant to the Regulation]'.[131] Finally, when it comes to the approval of the Member States' recovery and resilience plans and the possible suspension of commitments to ensure coherence with sound economic governance, Regulation 2021/241 on the Recovery and Resilience Facility respectively provides that

> The Council should approve the assessment of the recovery and resilience plans by means of an implementing decision'[132] and that 'in view of the importance of the financial effects of

[126] See recital 28 of Regulation 2016/1624.
[127] See recital 30 of Regulation 1095/2010.
[128] See recital 18 of the Regulation's preamble.
[129] See recital 114 of the SRM Regulation.
[130] See recital 13 of Regulation 2020/672.
[131] See recital 20 of Regulation 2020/2092.
[132] See recital 45 of Regulation 2021/241.

> the measures imposed [ie the suspension of commitments], implementing powers should be conferred on the Council.[133]

Undoubtedly all these 'justifications' may be qualified as rather 'general and laconic', but this does not exclude that, read in their context, they may amount to duly justified substantiations in the sense of Article 291(2) TFEU. Taking the most conservative stance possible, whereby the threshold to reserve implementing powers to the Council under Lisbon rules is the same (or, at least, not lower) than the threshold pre-Lisbon, the justifications given in the Frontex, EFSM, SURE and two-pack Regulations would indeed seem sufficient. When Frontex (partially) takes over border control from a Member State, it is quite the understatement to note that this is politically sensitive and will affect a Member State's police and enforcement powers. Given the possible impact on the EU budget and the Council's role in establishing the budget, a role for that institution in the decision on granting EFSM loans indeed seems appropriate or at least does not seem manifestly ill-considered. Again, given the role of the Council in the coordination of the Member States' economic policies, it is not manifestly inappropriate to grant the Council an implementing power to adopt MAPs. Even if a higher threshold is applied, because for instance the Comitology Regulation makes clear that the Commission may also be empowered to adopt implementing measures in 'particularly sensitive sectors' it seems doubtful that the Council manifestly erred in reserving to itself an implementing power, since in the legislator's justification there is no reference to the sensitivity of the area concerned, but only (implicitly) to the traditional dominant role of the Council in budgetary and economic coordination affairs. The same may finally be said regarding the suspension of commitments under the Recovery and Resilience Facility Regulation and the sanctions under the Conditionality Regulation. Regarding the latter, the Court also confirmed as such in *Hungary v Parliament and Council*,[134] which further suggests, like the *National Iranian Oil Company* case that the Lisbon Treaty has not changed the standard for exceptionally empowering the Council rather than the Commission.

The situation is different, however, for the Council's implementing power to declare emergency situations in the financial sector, to determine the methodology for the calculation of *ex ante* contributions under the SRM Regulation and for the approval of national plans under Recovery and Resilience Facility. The only relevant recitals in those Regulations simply postulate that the Council should have the power to declare such emergency situations, establish the methodology and that it should approve the plans but without justifying why this ought to be so. The complete absence of justification then arguably amounts to a violation of the duty to provide a statement of reasons under Article 296 TFEU.

It is important to recall here that these are not just cases of insufficient motivation. The relevant acts conferring implementing powers on the Council were all adopted pursuant to the ordinary legislative procedure (apart from the EFSM Regulation) and if implementing powers had been conferred on the Commission, the exercise thereof would be fully subject to the requirements in place to safeguard the Parliament's prerogatives (see infra section 6.V.B). Here no institutional balance test is in fact necessary to see how the institutional balance

[133] See recital 29 of Regulation 2021/241.

[134] See Case C-156/21, *Hungary v Parliament & Council*, ECLI:EU:C:2022:97 [188].

is undermined.[135] If it is accepted that the motivation for conferring powers on the Council does not meet the standard set by Article 291(2) TFEU, these powers have invalidly been reserved and the institutional prerogatives of the Commission are violated, but also those of the Parliament since it cannot control the exercise of implementing powers by the Council to the same extent as the exercise of implementing powers by the Commission. While the prospects for this seem slim, given the recent judicial pronouncements of the Court, it therefore still seems advisable to subject the choice to exceptionally empower the Council with the implementation of EU law under Article 291(2) TFEU to an objective factors test. By requiring (typically) the legislator to adduce objective factors amenable to judicial review that show why exceptionally the Council must be empowered, the institutional prerogatives of the Commission and Parliament would be better safeguarded.

The only caveat here is the possibility that these Council implementing powers are not implementing powers in the sense of Article 291 TFEU. In *Spain v Council* (see section 6.IV.B), the Court confirmed the existence of such implementing powers. Arguably then, such '*sui generis*' implementing powers might be granted to the Council without requiring any special justification at all, since there would be no default actor to exercise them to begin with. Whether that holds up will be returned to at the end of section 6.IV.B.

C. Implementation by the European Council

At first sight, the suggestion that the European Council may be entrusted a role in the implementation of EU law should be dismissed out of hand. As Article 15(1) TEU provides, 'the European Council provides the necessary impetus for [the EU's] development and shall define the general political directions and priorities thereof. It shall not exercise legislative functions'. If the European Council's role is to give general impetus to the integration project and if the Treaties explicitly rule out a role in the more concrete process of legislative decision-making, it would be out of place for the European Council to get into the minute detail of the implementation of EU legislation. Yet a formal role for the European Council in the implementation of the rule of law conditionality mechanism and the recovery and resilience facility is exactly what the legislator has prescribed. It needs no explaining that this role was not envisaged in the Commission's original proposals and that it was included in the recitals of the Regulations at the request of (some of) the Member States. Just like the increasingly frequent exceptional recourse to the Council under Article 291(2) TFEU it suggests that Member States want to retain greater control over the implementation of EU legislation, but the involvement of the European Council is completely anathema to the letter and spirit of Articles 291 TFEU and Article 15 TEU.

How does the referral to the European Council foreseen in the rule of law Conditionality Regulation and in the regulation on the recovery and resilience facility work? As noted above, the first entrusts the adoption (but also the lifting) of sanctions to the Council, but

[135] Volpato also notes this risk but finds that it is the absence of a specific procedure for the exercise of Council implementing powers that is controversial from an institutional balance perspective. See Volpato (2022) 188–89. That it is arguably only indirectly so. The lack of a specific procedure in itself logically flows from Art 291(2) TFEU and is therefore an intrinsic part of the institutional balance. The view taken here is that the institutional balance is only effectively endangered when implementation by the Council ceases to be exceptional and/or when recourse to the Council is insufficiently motivated.

it equally provides in its recitals that the Member State concerned may refer its case to the European Council and that for as long as the European Council has not discussed the matter, the Council cannot adopt any decision.[136] Similarly, it was noted above that Member States' recovery and resilience plans are adopted by the Council. After the Council approves these plans through implementing acts, Member States may start to request the disbursement of the relevant financial contributions or loans. Article 24 of the Regulation provides that the Commission decides on this after it is satisfied that the conditions (laid down by the Council in its implementing acts) are met, but again in the recitals it is provided that Member States (this time *other* than the Member State concerned) may refer a file to the European Council if they have doubts on whether the Member State concerned meets the targets or requirements laid down in the Council implementing acts.[137]

These two examples form part of a broader trend whereby the European Council's role is generally expanded beyond what the Treaties allow,[138] but the inscription of a referral mechanism in these regulations is still nothing less than legally absurd and suggests a context of pervasive distrust. There is distrust between the Member States and vis-à-vis the president of the European Council if they feel that those recitals are necessary to get something on the agenda of the European Council. Clearly however also the Commission is not trusted to act in the general interest and to faithfully check the requirements and conditions laid down in the Council implementing acts approving recovery and resilience plans.[139]

Fortunately, the Court has clearly hit back at this sly technique of introducing a role for the European Council through the recitals of legislative acts in the case on the rule of law conditionality mechanism. In *Hungary v Parliament & Council*, it held that there not being a formal role for the European Council in the procedure as set out by Article 6 of the Regulation is consistent with Article 15(1) TEU and that the referral to the European Council foreseen in the recitals is not taken over in Article 6. As a result, 'recital 26 cannot be relied on as a ground for derogating from the actual provisions of the contested regulation or for interpreting those provisions in a manner that is contrary to their wording'.[140] This should serve as a stern warning to the legislator to refrain from this type of provisions in future legislation. Undoubtedly the decisions to be taken are very sensitive, but it is

[136] See recital 26 of the preamble to Regulation 2020/2092 on a general regime of conditionality for the protection of the Union budget, OJ [2020] L 433I/1. The recital does prescribe that the referral to the European Council should be finished within three months after the Commission presented its proposal for the implementing decision to the Council.

[137] See recital 52 of the preamble to Regulation 2021/241establishing the Recovery and Resilience Facility, OJ [2021] L 57/17. Again, a time limit of three months is prescribed for the European Council to discuss the issue.

[138] On the thin line between giving impetus and encroaching on the Commission's prerogative of legislative proposal see Marieke Eckhardt and Wolfgang Wessels, 'The European Commission – Agent, Principal and Partner to the European Council?' in Jörn Ege, Michael Bauer and Stefan Becker (eds), *The European Commission in Turbulent Times: Assessing Organizational Change and Policy Impact* (Baden-Baden, Nomos, 2018) 31–50. The Court has pushed back against attempts of the Member States to give legal force to the European Council's conclusions, see Joined Cases C-643/15 and C-647/15, *Slovakia & Hungary v Council*, ECLI:EU:C:2017:631 [143–149; Case C-5/16, *Poland v Parliament & Council*, ECLI:EU:C:2018:483 [76]–[86].

[139] This is all the more remarkable given that the request to include the recitals apparently came from The Netherlands and the typical justification of the 'community method' prescribing an important role to the Commission is precisely to protect the interests of smaller Member States like the Netherlands. See Merijn Chamon, 'De conditionaliteitsverordening: een (beperkte) uitbreiding van het rechtsstaat-arsenaal van de EU' (2022) 70 *Tijdschrift voor Europees en economisch recht* 7–8.

[140] Case C-156/21, *Hungary v Parliament & Council*, ECLI:EU:C:2022:97 [191].

precisely for these cases that Article 291(2) TFEU allows that the Council may be exceptionally empowered.

IV. The (not so) Closed List of Implementing Actors and Implementing Acts

When Article 291 TFEU sets out who is to implement EU law, it only identifies three actors. As noted, the default rule is laid down in the first paragraph, prescribing that the Member States normally implement EU law. Exceptionally, implementation is done at the EU level and the default actor here is the Commission, with the Council only exceptionally implementing EU law. As noted in sections 6.I and 6.III, policing the lines between the default actors to implement EU law (Member States, Commission) and the exceptions (Commission, Council) may be fuzzy, but a subsequent question is whether Article 291 TFEU is to be read as *exhaustively* settling who can implement EU law.

Put differently, are there actors other than the Member States, Commission or Council that can be conferred an implementing power under EU secondary legislation? This question arises especially in light of the ongoing agencification of the EU administration. Just as for the exceptional implementation of EU law by the Council, the stakes for the Parliament in institutional balance terms are evident. Especially when a further exception to the default of Commission implementation (at EU level) is created, the question arises whether the Parliament's control function is not undermined or diluted. This risk becomes real when the control mechanisms in place for those 'other actors' are not equivalent to the Parliament's control mechanisms over Commission implementation. However here the Parliament arguably has more leverage compared to the situation in which the Council exceptionally implements EU law. After all, both the empowerment of and possible parliamentary control over EU agencies are determined by the EU legislator itself and since the turn of the century EU agencies are, as a rule, established pursuant to legal bases prescribing the ordinary legislative procedure. This contrasts with the situation where the Council is empowered since the Council is an EU institution on equal footing with the Parliament, whereby the latter cannot establish any control regime over the former in secondary legislation.

A. EU Agencies

The ongoing agencification of the EU administration[141] means that EU decentralised agencies are increasingly empowered to adopt binding acts, rather than just drafts or non-binding opinions or recommendations. What if these binding acts uniformly implement

[141] On the phenomenon, see Merijn Chamon, *EU Agencies: Legal and Political Limits to the Transformation of the EU Administration* (Oxford, OUP, 2016); Carlo Tovo, *Le agenzie decentrate dell'Unione europea* (Napoli, Editoriale Scientifica, 2016); Andreas Orator, *Möglichkeiten und Grenzen der Einrichtung von Unionsagenturen* (Tübingen, Mohr Siebeck, 2017); Steffen Augsberg, 'Agencification der Kommissionsverwaltung' (2016) *Europarecht* 119–42; Merijn Chamon, 'Les agences de l'union européenne: Origines, état des lieux et défis' (2015) 51 *Cahiers de droit européen* 293–318.

binding Union law in the sense of Article 291(2) TFEU? Should the EU legislator not be restricted in its choice to entrust binding executive powers to EU agencies rather than to the Commission (or Council)? After all, the silence of the EU Treaties on the possibility to empower EU agencies can hardly be qualified as an oversight. The importance of EU agencies in the EU administration was already well understood at the time of the Convention on the Future of Europe (in 2004) and the 2007 IGC.[142] Of course, it would be excessively dogmatic to infer from the Treaties' silence that EU agencies cannot adopt any binding acts, especially since numerous Treaty provisions related to the direct actions before the EU courts implicitly foresee that EU agencies may adopt acts producing legal effects vis-à-vis third parties. In addition, the proper implementation of EU law in a lot of areas today stands or falls with the involvement of EU agencies. However, that still does not solve the constitutional question of how EU agencies fit in the framework established by Articles 290 and 291 TFEU.[143]

The argument developed here starts from the premise that the constitutional framework applicable to EU agencies should not be self-standing, but should instead be fully integrated or linked with the framework established by Articles 290 and 291 TFEU. This as a precondition to uphold the latter's coherence and reflecting the idea of a single institutional balance governing the question of executive rule-making pursuant to secondary legislation. This assumption safeguards the Commission's Treaty-enshrined prerogatives from an encroachment and thereby indirectly also safeguards the Parliament's control prerogatives. Simply put, if the Parliament and Council (acting as legislators) would be left the freedom to decide when and how to empower EU agencies, the Commission's position and the democratic control exercised by the Parliament pursuant to Articles 290 and 291 TFEU would be undermined. The only way to uphold the latter is to accept that the choice of empowering an agency is governed by an institutional balance and a framework that is the same or coherent with the institutional balance and framework transpiring from Articles 290 and 291 TFEU.

i. The Short-Selling *Case*

The relevant case, and constitutional modification, of the Court here is *Short-selling.*[144] In this case, the UK challenged the EU legislator's decision to confer an executive power on an EU decentralised agency, the European Securities and Markets Authority (ESMA). One of the pleas invoked by the UK was that by granting such a power to the ESMA in Article 28 of Regulation 236/2012, the legislator violated Articles 290 and 291 TFEU. The UK's argument properly construed was that the decisions which the ESMA had been empowered to adopt would meet all the characteristics of an implementing act under Article 291(2) TFEU except that it would not be adopted by (either) the Commission

[142] Ellen Vos, 'E ditorial: White and Black Smoke Coming from the Justus Lipsius Building' (2004) 11 *Maastricht Journal of European and Comparitive Law* 230; Koen Lenaerts and Marlies Desomer, 'La recherche d'un équilibre pour l'Union' in Olivier De Schutter and Paul Nihoul (eds), *Une Constitution pour l'Europe – Réflexions sur les transformations du droit de l'Union européenne* (Bruxelles, Larcier, 2004) 78; Hofmann, Rowe and Türk, *Administrative law and policy* (2011) 914.

[143] The analysis here is partially based on Merijn Chamon, 'Beyond delegated and implementing acts: where do EU agencies fit in the Arts 290 and 291 TFEU scheme?' in Eljalill Tauschinsky and Wolfgang Weiß (eds), *The Legislative Choice Between Delegated and Implementing Acts in EU Law* (Cheltenham, Edward Elgar, 2018) 174–99.

[144] Case C-270/12 *UK v Parliament and Council* ECLI:EU:C:2014:18.

(or the Council), meaning that the legislator had undermined the Commission's prerogatives and had violated Article 291 TFEU. Of course, this is not exactly how the UK had argued its plea before the Court, since the UK's objective was to safeguard its own national autonomy in the implementation of EU financial services legislation. In reality, the UK did not want any EU authority (regardless of whether this was an EU agency or the Commission), to (exceptionally) perform tasks which would otherwise be performed by its own national financial supervisor.

The Court itself identified the fundamental issue with clear-cut precision, observing that it was

> called upon to adjudicate on whether the authors of the FEU Treaty intended to establish, in Articles 290 TFEU and 291 TFEU, a single legal framework under which certain delegated and executive powers may be attributed solely to the Commission or whether other systems for the delegation of such powers to Union bodies, offices or agencies may be contemplated by the Union legislature.[145]

Since the Court explicitly referred to the intention of the Treaty authors, one would expect it to look into to the (Convention) origins of Articles 290 and 291 TFEU, as it has done in a number of other cases concerning new provisions in in the Lisbon Treaty.[146] Instead, however, the Court confirmed that the EU legislator could contemplate such 'other systems'. It based this conclusion on two findings: since the entry into force of the Lisbon Treaty it was possible to challenge binding acts adopted by agencies before the EU Courts; and the type of power conferred on ESMA was qualitatively different from the powers envisaged in Articles 290 and 291 TFEU. Both findings necessitate a closer look at the case.

While some commentators have been more sympathetic to the open reading of Articles 290 and 291 TFEU in light of the references to agencies in Articles 263 and 277 TFEU,[147] on balance it is a rather weak argument.[148] To recall, under the pre-Lisbon framework, Article 230 EC (current Article 263 TFEU) did not explicitly mention 'bodies, offices and agencies' of the EU as having passive *locus standi*. This was one of the reasons which led AG Warner in *Romano* to dismiss the possibility for such a body to adopt binding measures:

> The idea that there may be set up for the Community an administrative body empowered to make binding decisions, but whose decisions are, in themselves, incapable of review by this Court seems to me incompatible with the scheme of the Treaty.

As the agencification of the EU administration nonetheless proceeded, the courts were ultimately faced with the question of the justiciability of agency acts. In order to uphold the right to an effective remedy, the General Court in *Sogelma* therefore applied a *Les Verts* reasoning in order to find an action for annulment against an agency act admissible.

[145] ibid [78].
[146] See Case C-583/11 P, *Inuit Tapiriit Kanatami e.a. v Parliament & Council*, ECLI:EU:C:2013:625 [59] and [70]; Case C-286/14, *Parliament v Commission*, ECLI:EU:C:2016:183 [44]; Joined Cases C-622/16 P to C-624/16 P, *Scuola Elementare Maria Montessori Srl v Commission*, ECLI:EU:C:2018:873 [26]; Case C-543/17, *Commission v Belgium*, ECLI:EU:C:2019:573 [34] and [52].
[147] See Wolfgang Weiß, 'Dezentrale Agenturen in der EU-rechtsetzung' (2016) 51 *Europarecht* 647–48.
[148] Finding the Court's reasoning labourious, see Barents, 'De post-Lissabon-rechtspraak' (2019) 342.

Without discussing the issue in depth,[149] it should be clear that this was no ideal solution, not in the least because EU agencies, unlike the Parliament in *Les Verts*, are not created by the Treaties, let alone that they would qualify as EU institutions. This undermines much of the analogy between their pre-Lisbon position and the Parliament's pre-Maastricht position. The solution offered by the Lisbon Treaty, of explicitly bringing EU agencies within the scope of Article 263 TFEU is therefore to be preferred. Yet the point of explicitly mentioning the EU agencies in that provision was simply to ensure that there were no gaps in the EU's system of judicial protection, not to confirm in some way that agencies are constitutionally entitled to exercise binding powers. As Ruffert notes, 'it is highly questionable to infer a power to issue certain acts from powers to call into question such acts by means of judicial review'.[150]

Turning to the Court's second finding, it held that the conferral to ESMA did 'not correspond to any of the situations defined in Articles 290 TFEU and 291 TFEU'.[151] Again, here there are commentators sympathetic to the Court's finding,[152] but again the Court's reasoning is not fully convincing. After all, it seems difficult to view the power conferred on ESMA as anything other than a power to implement EU law under uniform conditions. Indeed, the Regulation conferring the contested power on the ESMA had been adopted by the legislator precisely because during the financial crisis different national authorities had taken divergent decisions implementing EU law.[153] If the Regulation was adopted to create a common regulatory framework to deal with short selling and if exceptionally the ESMA was empowered to adopt a single decision for the entire internal market, prohibiting or restricting short-selling, did the legislator not confer a power on the ESMA which belongs to the Commission pursuant to Article 291(2) TFEU? Also Bertrand notes in this regard that 'Il est … difficile d'affirmer, comme le fait la Cour, que l'attribution de pouvoirs aux agences ne relève pas de l'article 291 TFUE'.[154]

According to the Court, this really was not the case since the contested

> provision must be perceived as forming part of a series of rules designed to endow the competent national authorities and ESMA with powers of intervention to cope with adverse developments which threaten financial stability within the Union and market confidence. To that end, *those authorities must be in a position to impose temporary restrictions on the short selling of certain*

[149] See on this Chamon, *EU Agencies* (2016) 328–30.

[150] See Matthias Ruffert, 'The many faces of rule-making in the EU' in Elaine Fahey (ed), *The Actors of Postnational rule*-making (London, Routledge, 2016) 60.

[151] Case C-270/12 *UK v Parliament and Council* ECLI:EU:C:2014:18 [83].

[152] Paul Craig, 'Comitology, Rulemaking and the Lisbon Settlement – Tensions and Strains' in Carl Fredrik Bergström and Dominique Ritleng (eds), *Rulemaking by the European Commission – The New System for Delegation of Powers* (Oxford, OUP, 2016) 194–95.

[153] Recital 1 of the Regulation's preamble provides: 'At the height of the financial crisis in September 2008, competent authorities in several Member States … adopted emergency measures to restrict or ban short selling in some or all securities …. The measures adopted by Member States were divergent as the Union lacks a specific common regulatory framework for dealing with short selling issues'. The latter does not mean that national authorities were not implementing EU law, only that that EU law was not tailored to the issue of short-selling. After all, national authorities already had intervention powers under the 2003 Market Abuse Directive. See Directive 2003/6 of the European Parliament and of the Council on insider dealing and market manipulation (market abuse), OJ [2003] L96/16.

[154] See Brunessen Bertrand, 'La compétence des agences pour prendre des actes n ormatifs; le dualisme des pouvoirs d'exécution' (2015) *RTDE* 28.

> *stocks*, credit default swaps or other transactions in order to prevent an uncontrolled fall in the price of those instruments.[155]

The Court's circular reasoning here is glaring.[156] If the premise was that the ESMA must be in a position to impose restrictions on short-selling, the contested provision was bound to be upheld. The Court continued by observing that the ESMA and the national authorities 'have a high degree of professional expertise and work closely together in the pursuit of the objective of financial stability within the Union',[157] leading to the conclusion that ESMA's contested power 'cannot be regarded as undermining the rules governing the delegation of powers laid down in Articles 290 TFEU and 291 TFEU'.[158] The Court came to this conclusion without comparing the object and purpose of the power granted to ESMA with the object and purpose of the typical delegated or implementing power granted to the Commission.[159]

Yet, that the ESMA is indeed implementing EU law in the sense of Article 291(2) TFEU is further corroborated by its decision of 16 March 2020 where it exercised, for the very first time, the power which the UK had contested in *Short-selling*. The ESMA exercised its power against the backdrop of the pandemic and restricted (rather than prohibited) short-selling.[160] In its decision which requires persons with certain net short positions to notify these positions to the national supervisors, the ESMA sets out why it believes the conditions of its exceptional intervention power under Article 28 of Regulation 236/2012 were met. In this regard it inter alia noted that the threat to market integrity (resulting from the pandemic), 'have a pan-EU character' since the financial markets of all EU Member States are affected;[161] that different national supervisors had adopted diverging but insufficient measures based on Article 23 of the Regulation and that a *single measure applicable across the EU* would help the national supervisors and itself to better monitor the situation;[162] and that an EU-wide measure would be more effective than sectorial national measures.[163] In plain terms it would seem that Member States could no longer ensure the proper implementation of the EU rules governing short-selling under Article 23 of the Regulation and that in the context of an exceptional pandemic, with exceptional knock-on

[155] Case C-270/12 *UK v Parliament and Council* ECLI:EU:C:2014:18 [85].

[156] See also Chamon (n 141) 294–95; Laure Clément-Wilz, 'Les agences de l'Union européenne dans l'entre-deux constitutionnel' (2015) *RTDE* 346.

[157] Case C-270/12 *UK v Parliament and Council* ECLI:EU:C:2014:18 [85].

[158] ibid [86].

[159] In contrast, in the case on the rule of law conditionality regulation, the Court properly addressed Hungary's and Poland's argument that the mechanism established by the Regulation circumvented the mechanism of Art 7 TEU. The Court distinguished the purpose of both mechanisms (safeguarding the EU budget against rule of law deficiences vs safeguarding the EU's values) and their object (imposition budgetary sanctions vs suspension of any rights under the Treaties) to conclude that the conditionality regulation did not circumvent or undermine Art 7 TEU. See C-156/21, *Hungary v Parliament & Council*, ECLI:EU:C:2022:97 [167]–[179].

[160] ESMA Decision 2020/525 to require natural or legal persons who have net short positions to temporarily lower the notification thresholds of net short positions in relation to the issued shares capital of companies whose shares are admitted to trading on a regulated market above a certain threshold to notify the competent authorities in accordance with point (a) of Art 28(1) of Regulation (EU) No 236/2012 of the European Parliament and of the Council, OJ [2020] L 116/5.

[161] ESMA Decision 2020/525, point 13.

[162] ibid, point 22.

[163] ibid, point 47.

effects on the real and financial economy, the requirement of a uniform implementation by the ESMA pursuant to Article 28 imposed itself.

Alternatively, it could also be claimed that the ESMA Decision 2020/525 is a delegated act in disguise. After all, in its decision, ESMA temporarily lowered the default transparency threshold which Article 5(2) of the (legislative) Short-selling Regulation sets at 0.2 per cent of the issued share capital of the company concerned and each 0.1 per cent above that. Article 5(4) thereby grants a delegated power to the Commission to set different thresholds 'taking into account the developments in financial markets'. From this perspective, ESMA might be said to have de facto amended Article 5(2) of the Regulation, de facto exercising the power which is vested in the Commission pursuant to Article 5(4), albeit by adopting a measure that is only temporary. For reasons of constitutional avoidance, such a reading is discarded here. In section 5.I above it was noted that EU agencies should not be empowered to adopt delegated acts. Conceptualising the power in Article 28 of the Short-selling Regulation as such would go against this and would also breach the Court's case law on the role of the Member States in the *implementation* (but not modification) of regulations (see section 4.III), since the ESMA only intervenes when Member State action proves to be ineffective. Finally, the Court already (implicitly) accepted the possibility for implementing acts to (temporarily) suspend the application of a legislative act.[164]

ii. Assessing Short-Selling through an Institutional Balance Test

The view taken here is thus to recognise that the EU agencies are partaking in the implementation function and that the Court should thus embrace the implications of its ruling rather than bluntly claim that ESMA's powers (or those of EU agencies in general) 'do not undermine the rules on delegation laid down in Article 291 TFEU'. Linked to this blunt statement is the fact that the Court did not explicitly set any clear conditions to when the legislator may empower EU agencies. As noted by Ohler, the paradoxical result of this is that following *Short-selling*, it has arguably become easier for the legislator to delegate powers to bodies not provided for in the EU Treaties than to delegate powers to a formal EU institution.[165] If the Court would recognise that EU agencies are indeed exercising an implementing function in the sense of Article 291 TFEU, this would also require the Court to establish some clear limits to ensure that the core of Article 291(2) TFEU is maintained. This not simply for dogmatic reasons or for the sake of legal elegance but because of the profound impact which opening up Article 291 TFEU has for the prerogatives of both the Commission, Council and, indirectly, the Parliament.

An institutional balance test shows how this is the case: by not referring to EU agencies, Articles 290 and 291 TFEU textually seem to exclude that agencies may be conferred a delegated or implementing power. At the same time, there are no sufficient textual clues to definitively conclude that Articles 290 and 291 TFEU constitute a closed system. Under a systemic reading of the Treaties, however, no convincing clues that we are dealing with an open system can be found. EU agencies are not mentioned in Title III of the TEU

[164] See Case C-88/14, *Commission v Parliament and Council*, ECLI:EU:C:2015:499, discussed in section 4.III.A.

[165] Christophe Ohler, 'Rechtsetzungsbefugnisse der Europäischen Wertpapier- und Marktaufsichtsbehörde (ESMA)' (2014) 69 *Juristenzeitung* 5 251.

(provisions on the institutions) or Title I of Part Six of the TFEU (institutional provisions), apart from the provisions on judicial protection. As noted above, the latter can hardly be considered an adequate clue to conclude that agencies can be integrated in the Treaty framework on executive rule-making that is itself completely silent on agencies. Historically, the more convincing argument even goes against recognising Articles 290 and 291 TFEU as an open system. The accrued importance of EU agencies was known to the drafters of the Constitution (and the Lisbon Treaty), but they opted not to include the possibility to grant them delegated or implementing powers, even if suggestions to this end had been made during the Convention and during the IGC leading to the Nice Treaty.[166] Only from a teleological perspective can a good argument be made that Articles 290 and 291 TFEU should constitute an open system. The ultimate purpose of these provisions is to unburden the legislator and to ensure the proper implementation of EU law, respectively. Both indicate the Commission as the only/default actor (at EU level) to do so. Meanwhile, from a teleological perspective, it was argued that it is unlikely that an agency would be better placed (than the Commission) to unburden the legislator (see section 5.I), but it is indeed conceivable that there are instances in which the Commission is not the best placed actor to ensure proper implementation. There could therefore be some scope in granting EU entities other than the Commission (or Council) with a power coming under Article 291 TFEU.

The final step in an institutional balance test then is to ascertain how accepting this possibility (of empowering EU entities other than the Commission or Council) would affect the prerogatives of the Commission, Council and Parliament. For the Commission, any such empowerment would go at the expense of its prerogative to be the default delegate authority at EU level under Article 291 TFEU. For the Council, it is the same since Article 291(2) TFEU indicates that institution as the appropriate EU implementing authority in exceptional cases. For the Parliament, depending on whether the control regime in place over the EU agency mimics the control regime under Article 291 TFEU, empowering the latter might mean fewer (or no) means of control over executive rule-making. In sum, under the institutional balance, recognising Article 291 TFEU as an open system would require concomitant safeguards for the institutions' prerogatives to be put in place.

Put differently, how might the legislator's freedom in choosing between empowering either the Commission or an agency be constrained? For this it is useful to first look for some clues in the Court's jurisprudence. In *Biocides*, the Court identified the function of the implementing act, finding that 'on the basis of Article 291(2) TFEU, the Commission is called on to [specificy] the content of a legislative act, in order to ensure that it is implemented under uniform conditions in all Member States'.[167] To distinguish the Commission's power under Article 291(2) TFEU from the power(s) conferrable on agencies two options then exist. Either a separate function for the agency implementing act is identified or one accepts that the agency implementing act fulfils the same function as the Commission implementing act albeit that further requirements have to be met.

[166] For a discussion, see Chamon (n 141) 373–76.

[167] Case C-427/12 *Commission v Parliament and Council* ECLI:EU:C:2014:170 [39]. As noted in section 4.III.A the French version of this ruling was wrongly translated in English. The more correct term has therefore been employed here.

From an institutional balance perspective the soundest option would be to identify a separate function, since this would optimally safeguard the Commission's prerogatives: the power conferred on an EU agency fulfils a function that is simply different from the function of an implementing act. This would be akin to how the Court ruled in *Spain v Council* (see section 6.IV.B).[168] It would also fit well with the Court's reasoning in *Short-selling* where the Court seems to imply that the acts to be adopted by the ESMA simply would never be implementing acts in the first place. In the preceding paragraphs, however, it was precisely this reasoning that was found to be unconvincing. It seems necessary therefore to acknowledge that an agency implementing act essentially fulfils the same function as a Commission implementing act.[169] In order to safeguard the Commission's prerogatives under Article 291 TFEU, then, further requirements would have to be met before an agency,[170] rather than the Commission, could be empowered. What could these requirements be?

In *Short-selling* the Court, when addressing the plea related to Articles 290 and 291 TFEU, emphasised 'the high degree of professional expertise' of the ESMA and the national authorities and the need for these bodies to 'work closely together'.[171] When dealing with the plea related to the *Meroni* doctrine, the Court also stressed that the ESMA is tasked to carry out technical factual assessments[172] and again noted that ESMA will have to work closely with the national authorities when taking decisions.[173] The Court thus seemed to imply that because of the nature of its task, the EU authority taking decisions on short-selling should be linked to the national authorities and should house very specific technical and professional expertise, a condition met for the ESMA but not for the Commission. This may indeed be linked to the ethos in Article 291(2) TFEU which sees to the *effective* implementation of EU law. It is the (risk of) insufficiently uniform (and therefore ineffective) implementation that triggers the Commission's exceptional implementing power under Article 291(2) TFEU. Conversely, the possibility to grant an implementing power to an agency would be 'unlocked' if it is shown that a high degree of technical, scientific and/or professional expertise and/or capacity, lacking within the 'generalist' Commission, is required in order to uniformly implement common rules.[174] Because of the agency's institutional set-up, they can tap the expertise available in their national counterparts more easily than (a DG or unit of) the Commission which has to rely on less institutionalised expert groups (see section 5.IV.A.ii). Of course, drawing the line between the Commission's 'general' expertise and an EU agency's 'specific technical/professional' expertise will not be straightforward in practice. Hence, the EU legislator will inevitably have some leeway

[168] Case C-521/15, *Spain v Council*, ECLI:EU:C:2017:982.

[169] As a result, just like a Commission implementing act, an agency implementing act could not change the essential elements of legislation. After all, the purpose of any implementing act is merely to facilitate the *mise en oeuvre* of legislation. See Blumann, 'Un nouveau départ pour la Comitologie' (2011) 27. Ritleng essentially comes to the same conclusion, following a different approach. See Dominique Ritleng, 'The Reserved Domain of the Legislature – The Notion of "Essential Elments of an Area"' in Carl Fredrik Bergström and Dominique Ritleng (eds), *Rulemaking by the European Commission – The New System for Delegation of Powers* (Oxford, OUP, 2016) 148.

[170] Similarly, see Weiß, 'Dezentrale Agenturen' (2016) 656.

[171] Case C-270/12 *UK v Parliament and Council* ECLI:EU:C:2014:18 [85].

[172] ibid [52].

[173] ibid [50].

[174] According to Bertrand, the Court in *Short-selling* also emphasised that a special *intervention* power had been conferred on the ESMA. See Bertrand, 'La compétence des agences' (2015) 27. However, this is an element specific to the *Short-selling* case and it would seem ill-advised to qualify it as one of the conditions that have to be met before powers may be conferred on an EU agency.

in choosing between empowering the Commission and empowering an agency. The first requirement would therefore put the onus on the EU legislator to state the objective factors (in the preamble to its legislative act) which require it to grant an implementing power to an agency rather than to the Commission. Subjecting this choice to an objective factors test appears necessary to uphold the institutional balance, but of course the prospect of such a test would be slim if such an objective factors test does not apply (or is not accepted) for the issue of *whether* uniform conditions in implementation are required in the sense of Article 291(2) TFEU (see section 6.I) and for the question when exceptional recourse to Council implementation is possible (see section 6.III).

A second element distinguishing the Commission implementing act from an agency implementing act is the fact that the former, unlike the latter, is not constrained by the *Meroni* doctrine. Following *Short-selling*, *Meroni* requires that only precisely delineated powers are being conferred on EU agencies. This is different from the limits to the Commission's powers under Article 291 TFEU as clarified in the *Eures network* case discussed in section 6.II.C. Unlike an agency, the Commission can exercise a discretionary power when adopting implementing acts. Commission implementing acts must merely be appropriate for the implementation of a legislative act, comply with the latter's essential general aims, should not be contrary to the legislative act and cannot supplement or amend the legislative act. In two judgments rendered in 2021 the Court developed its *Short-selling* doctrine, providing further building blocks to differentiate a Commission (and Council) implementing power under Article 291 TFEU from an agency implementing power. To recall, in the original *Short-selling* ruling, the Court mellowed the *Meroni* doctrine by simply requiring that a power be 'precisely delineated and amenable to judicial review in the light of the objectives established by the delegating authority'.[175] In *FBF* and *Commission v Germany*,[176] the Court reintroduced an element of the original *Meroni* doctrine by requiring that 'precise delineation' of the delegated powers to be based on objective criteria (rather than simply objectives) set by the legislator and on which the Court exercises 'stringent judicial review in the light of those objective criteria'.[177] At least semantically, the resulting test is thus quite different from the one in *Eures network*.

As a result, the two building blocks would demarcate the area open for agency implementing act in the following way: The exceptional implementation of EU law at EU level (Article 291(2) TFEU) is by default done by the Commission. However, under specific circumstances the EU legislator may choose to empower the Council or the EU agencies rather than the Commission. The agencies may thereby: (i) only be granted an implementing power precisely delineated by objective criteria (*Short-selling*); and (ii) the authority conferring the implementing power should adduce objective factors amenable to judicial review that show that the conferral to the agency is necessary in light of the very specific expertise required to effectively implement the basic (legislative) act. Setting these limits would correct the Court's disregard in *Short-selling* for the institutional balance (and its implicit constitutional modification).

[175] Case C-270/12 *UK v Parliament & Council*, ECLI:EU:C:2014:18 [53].

[176] Case C-911/19, *FBF*, ECLI:EU:C:2021:599 [67]; Case C-718/18, *Commission v Germany*, ECLI:EU:C:2021:662 [131].

[177] Case C-911/19, *FBF*, ECLI:EU:C:2021:599 [67].

B. Sui Generis Implementing Acts

The Court's ruling in *Short-selling*, effectively declaring Articles 290 and 291 TFEU an 'open system', was followed a few years later by its ruling in *Spain v Council*, which was as remarkable but received much less attention. Crucially, however, and while the ruling does result in the recognition of a new type of implementing acts not explicitly foreseen in the Lisbon Treaty, the Court's judgment should not necessarily be qualified as an instance of constitutional modification. In this case, the Council had made use of its new powers under the reformed SGP and had imposed a fine on Spain pursuant to Article 8 of Regulation 1173/2011 for misrepresenting its deficit and debt statistics. In order to determine which of the EU courts had jurisdiction to hear the case lodged by Spain, the Court of Justice first had to qualify the nature of the Council's decision. It had been adopted as an Implementing Decision,[178] presumably to be in line with Article 291(4) TFEU. But if it really was an implementing act in the sense of Article 291(2) TFEU, the Court of Justice would have had to decline jurisdiction pursuant to Article 51 of the CJEU Statute.

The Court, pointing to the autonomous executive powers of the Council and to its own *Short-selling* ruling, noted that the issue of implementing powers is not exhaustively regulated in Article 291(2) TFEU.[179] The Court therefore proceeded by verifying whether the implementing power *in casu* was an implementing power in the sense of Article 291(2) TFEU.[180] For this the Court noted that Article 291 TFEU as a whole needed to be taken into account.[181] In doing so, it found that the Council's function under Article 291(2) TFEU is essentially the same as that of the Member States under Article 291(1) TFEU – the difference being that under Article 291(2) TFEU *uniform* conditions in implementation are required.[182] Linking this to the contested decision, the Court found that the act to impose a fine on a Member State is conceptually different from the types of acts which Member States could adopt under Article 291(1) TFEU.[183] The Court thereby added that Regulation 1173/2011 does not refer to Article 291 TFEU[184] and that the purpose of the power under Article 8 of Regulation 1173/2011 is not the uniform implementation of EU law, but the deterrence of Member States from misrepresenting budgetary statistics.[185]

The broader ramifications of the Court's decision are that it endangers the Commission's political claim to being the primary executive at EU level and further complicates the attempt at simplification pursued by the Lisbon Treaty. This because whenever an implementing power is to be exercised at EU level, the Commission cannot simply be assumed anymore, despite Article 291(2) TFEU, to be the default actor to confer the implementing power on. This not just because Article 291 TFEU does not exhaustively list the possible implementing actors (*Short-selling*) but because the notion of implementation itself is

[178] Council Decision 2015/1289 imposing a fine on Spain for the manipulation of deficit data in the Autonomous Community of Valencia, OJ [2015] L 198/19, requalified as an Implementing Decision in OJ [2015] L 291/10.
[179] Case C-521/15, *Spain v Council*, ECLI:EU:C:2017:982 [43].
[180] ibid [44].
[181] ibid [45].
[182] ibid [47]–[48].
[183] ibid [49].
[184] ibid [52].
[185] ibid [53].

not exhaustively covered by Article 291 TFEU (*Spain v Council*).[186] *Spain v Council* thus requires the EU legislator to first determine what type of implementing power it wishes to confer. Is it an implementing power in the sense of Article 291 TFEU? Or is it an implementing power that cannot be exercised by the Member States? In the latter case the rules of Article 291 TFEU would not apply, and the Council may be empowered, and this seemingly without any justification. The Court's decision thus goes in the opposite direction of the course advocated by some commentators who argued that the possibility to entrust the implementation of EU law to the Council pursuant to Article 291(2) TFEU was an anomaly under the new Treaty (see section 6.III).[187] This is not to say that *Spain v Council* amounts to a constitutional modification upsetting the institutional balance. While the wording and position of Article 291 TFEU in the Treaties suggest that its scope is comprehensive and all-encompassing,[188] the Court's systemic reading of the two first paragraphs of Article 291 TFEU also carries force and is in fact more convincing than the teleological argument of the Court in *Short-selling*. Alternatively, however, an argument whereby the Court would find that precisely *because* Member States cannot sanction themselves, the threshold for triggering an implementing power under Article 291(2) TFEU was met, would have been equally convincing. In any event, and as was pointed out in the preceding section in relation to the *Short-selling* ruling, in order to uphold the institutional balance, safeguards should be in place to protect the integrity, in this case, of Article 291 TFEU, even if some commentators downplay the risk that *Spain v Council* presents in this regard.[189] Concretely, then, the legislator ought to adduce objective factors amenable to judicial review (such as the impossibility for Member States to sanction themselves) that identify those cases of implementation that do not come under Article 291 TFEU and motivate the choice why a given implementing power is given to a specific executive actor. To counter the risk that the legislator has an incentive to narrowly conceive implementation under Article 291 TFEU, this could be coupled with transposing the rule and exception under Article 291(2) TFEU also to the type of implementation discovered in *Spain v Council*: if the Commission is the default EU authority for both types of implementation, there is little incentive for the legislator (more concretely the Member States in Council) to expansively interpret the *Spain v Council* type of implementation.

As it is, the Council has adopted further acts qualified as implementing acts for which it is doubtful that they could have been properly adopted by the Member States and for which it is therefore doubtful whether they come under Article 291 TFEU. These powers are also discussed in section 6.III.B, the relevant question in the present section being whether under 'normal' circumstances, these powers would (or could) be exercised by the Member States. Arguably that is not the case for the appointment of EU officials such as the Chair and Vice Chair of the SSM Supervisory Board.[190] The same seems to be the case for

[186] Although such an exhaustive reading was deemed the most natural reading of Art 291 TFEU, resulting in the observation by Türk that 'Given the comprehensive nature of Article 291 TFEU for the adoption of Union implementing acts … it would not seem permissible to pursue the implementation of certain Union acts outside the regime of Article 291 TFEU'. see Alexander Türk, 'Lawmaking after Lisbon' in Andrea Biondi, Piet Eeckhout and Stefanie Ripley (eds), *EU Law after Lisbon* (Oxford, OUP, 2012) 78.

[187] See above n 89.

[188] See above n 186.

[189] Antoine Buchet, 'La réforme des pouvoirs conférés à la Commission européenne, entre métamorphose et réminiscence' (2018) 54 *Cahiers de droit européen* 226.

[190] See above, n 116.

decisions to grant EFSM loans,[191] and the decisions to adopt the macroeconomic adjustment programmes (MAPs) under the two-pack.[192] The fact that the latter replace the economic partnership programmes (EPPs) which are adopted by the individual Member States' themselves should not immediately lead to the conclusion that the adoption of MAPs does come under Article 291 TFEU, since MAPs are qualitatively different from EPPs. The latter are essentially informational replies to the Commission's recommendations, whereas the MAPs are binding instructions, spelling out what economic reforms a Eurozone Member State must adopt. Finally, the measures imposed on rule of law-flouting Member States under the Conditionality Regulation would also seem to come under this exception.[193] After all, it seems difficult to uphold that Member States that breach the rule of law could adopt corrective budgetary measures against themselves. However, in *Hungary v Parliament and Council*, the Court already implicitly accepted that the Council would be implementing, in the sense of Article 291(2) TFEU, the Regulation when it adopts measures. After all, the Court relied on Article 291(2) TFEU to hold that by empowering the Council, the legislator had not undermined the Commission's prerogative to implement the EU budget under Article 317(1) TFEU and it verified whether the choice to empower to the Council was duly justified in line with Article 291(2) TFEU.[194] If anything, this shows that the recognition of enforcement powers as separate from (rather than a subcategory of) implementing powers in Article 291 TFEU in *Spain v Council* was at least problematic.

In any event, assuming that the power to adopt the measures discussed above, following *Spain v Council*, do not come under Article 291 TFEU, it remains unclear whether conferring them on the Council requires any specific threshold to be met (see section 6.III.B.ii). For the reasons set out above, the view professed here is that this should indeed be the case.

V. The Comitology Procedures

Having presented and assessed the Treaty and judicial carve-outs to the Commission's implementing function under Article 291 TFEU, the general framework governing the exercise of its implementing powers can now be analysed. That framework consists of Article 291(3) TFEU and the Comitology Regulation prescribed by it. That Regulation succeeded and replaced the (second) comitology decision.[195] Under the Lisbon Treaty, the horizontal comitology instrument is adopted, for the first time, by the Parliament and Council acting together (pursuant to the ordinary legislative procedure) rather than by the Council on proposal of the Commission. This constituted a significant increase of parliamentary control. However, as will be shown, in terms of what the Parliament subsequently did with its accrued formal powers, the picture is more mixed.

[191] See above, n 113.
[192] See above, n 114.
[193] See above, n 124.
[194] Case C-156/21, *Hungary v Parliament & Council*, ECLI:EU:C:2022:97 [185]–[189].
[195] Council Decision 1999/468 laying down the procedures for the exercise of implementing powers conferred on the Commission, OJ [1999] L 184/23.

A. The Proposal for and Negotiations on the Comitology Regulation

In its 2010 proposal,[196] the Commission provided for the three existing comitology procedures (given that the PRAC largely aligns to Article 290 TFEU, not Article 291 TFEU) be reframed as an advisory procedure and an examination procedure. The first would replace its predecessor of the same name and would change little. That would have been different for the examination procedure, which the Commission proposed would replace the old management and regulatory procedures. In the Commission's proposal, the examination committee would decide on draft measures by qualified majority. A negative opinion would no longer imply a referral to the Council, but the draft would be further discussed in the committee and/or amended by the Commission while in the absence of an opinion, the Commission could adopt the measure. However, in the latter case and even in the event of a positive opinion, the Commission could also decide not to adopt the draft measure. One further major element in the Commission proposal was the lack of any role for Parliament or the Council, other than being kept informed of the work in the committees. The Commission also tried to further strengthen its position by providing binding criteria for the selection of the comitology procedure to be followed.[197] Under the second comitology decision, these criteria already existed, but the recitals explicitly provided that they were not binding.[198] In its case law, the Court had therefore confirmed the non-binding nature of these criteria, but also stated that if the legislator chose a different procedure than the one designated by the criteria, that choice must be properly justified.[199] With this, the Court made it clear that the legislator could opt for a more cumbersome procedure as long as this was justified.[200] The Commission's proposal envisaged binding criteria prescribing that the advisory procedure would be the standard procedure, with the examination procedure only applicable in exhaustively listed cases, but even then, the legislator could decide to apply the advisory procedure.[201]

With its proposal, the Commission remained very loyal to Article 291 TFEU while at the same time it clearly tried to both push forward the simplification and rationalisation of comitology in secondary law and, in doing so, to also strengthen its own position. However, during the legislative negotiations, the Parliament and Council made some key amendments. First, the Council introduced the Appeal Committee in the examination procedure.[202] While a referral to the Appeal Committee is not the same as a referral to

[196] Proposal for a Regulation of the European Parliament and of the Council laying down the rules and general principles concerning mechanisms for control by Member States of the Commission's exercise of implementing powers, COM (2010) 83 final.

[197] See recital 8 of the proposal.

[198] See recital 5 to Council Decision 1999/468. In its proposal for the second comitology decision, the Commission had also proposed binding criteria (which the Council did therefore not accept), just like in its 2002 proposal to adapt the comitology decision in light of the ongoing Convention. See Art 2 of the Proposal for a Council Decision laying down the procedures for the exercise of implementing powers conferred on the Commission, COM (1998) 380 final; Art 1 of the Proposal for a Council Decision amending Decision 1999/468/EC laying down the procedures for the exercise of implementing powers conferred on the Commission, COM (2002) 719 final.

[199] See Case C-378/00, *Commission v Parliament & Council*, ECLI:EU:C:2003:42.

[200] This was no general rule, however, since the Court in *Common Market Fertilizers* also noted that for measures of individual application, the (heavier) regulatory procedure could never be prescribed. See Case C-433/05 P, *Common Market Fertilizers SA v Commission*, ECLI:EU:C:2007:511 [125]–[128].

[201] See recital 10 of the proposal.

[202] See the new recital 5a and Art 5a in the four-column table NEGO_CT(2010)0051 of 11 October 2010.

the Council (under the second comitology decision), let alone that the Appeal Committee might seize a file from the Commission, it can de facto meet at the level of Member States' ministers (although this has not happened yet).[203] The Parliament in turn managed to tighten the requirement for the Commission to inform Parliament and Council. Yet where Parliament proposed that it would be fully and promptly informed,[204] recital 17 of the final Regulation 'only' provides for prompt information. A further partial win for the Parliament may be seen in the *droit de regard*, which the Commission did not originally foresee in its proposal and which the Parliament insisted on,[205] but which it only received for measures implementing acts adopted pursuant to the ordinary legislative procedure.[206] A further partial win for the Council was its insistence that the choice to confer implementing powers would fully come within discretion of legislator,[207] but in the end recital 2 confirms that this choice is still bound by the criteria of Article 291 TFEU. The Council thus unsuccessfully tried to nullify the objective triggering factor for the existence of implementing powers at EU level (see section 6.I).

On four points, the Parliament and Council failed to push through their views: first, the Parliament wanted to include a reference to Article 52 of the Charter, barring implementing measures from interfering with fundamental rights unless this was prescribed by law;[208] second, it had proposed to allow Parliament and Council to send observers to committee meetings;[209] third, it put forward a tweak whereby a no opinion in examination procedure by default would prevent the Commission from adopting the draft measure,[210] whereas under the Regulation's final text this is only so in three (broadly defined) situations.[211] The fourth issue, and the one key issue which the Council failed to push through was its attempt to continue to keep the implementation of the Common Commercial Policy (CCP) out of the horizontal comitology regime.[212] This will be returned to in section 6.V.B.ii. The 'normalisation' of the CCP is important as it illustrates the Parliament's decisive influence in integrating the implementation of the CCP into the horizontal comitology regime. The assessment here is therefore much more positive for the European Parliament than that of Christiansen and Dobbels, who argued that the Parliament lost the implementation game (see chapter 1) in the negotiations on the Comitology Regulation.[213] In a nutshell, the difference in assessment results from a different appraisal of three key points: (i) the present enquiry makes a constitutional distinction between the Member States in comitology committees and the Council, which means that the lack of equality between the Parliament and the Member States is not considered a 'loss' for the Parliament;[214] (ii) it assesses the

[203] See recital 7 of the Comitology Regulation.

[204] See recital 12 in the four-column table NEGO_CT(2010)0051 of 11 October 2010, 5.

[205] See the new recital 12a and Art 8a in the four-column table NEGO_CT(2010)0051 of 11 October 2010.

[206] See Art 8a in the four-column table NEGO_CT(2010)0051 of 17 November 2010 and Art 11 of the Comitology Regulation.

[207] See the new recital 1a in the four-column table NEGO_CT(2010)0051 of 17 November 2010.

[208] See the new recital 3a in the four-column table NEGO_CT(2010)0051 of 17 November 2010.

[209] See recital 5 in the four-column table NEGO_CT(2010)0051 of 11 October 2010, 2.

[210] See Art 5(4) in the four-column table NEGO_CT(2010)0051 of 11 October 2010, 13.

[211] See Art 5(4) of the Comitology Regulation.

[212] See the new recital 14a in the four-column table NEGO_CT(2010)0051 of 11 October 2010, 6.

[213] See Thomas Christiansen and Mathias Dobbels, 'Comitology and delegated acts after Lisbon: How the European Parliament lost the implementation game' (2012) 16 *European Integration Online Papers* Art 13.

[214] By contrast, Christiansen and Dobbels for instance note that 'it was to be expected that the EP was not willing to accept a referral to member state representatives, or else it would demand similar provisions for Parliament in line with the equality between the institutions promised by the treaty'. See ibid 10–11.

outcome of the negotiations based on the opening position of the Parliament, not on potential opening positions;[215] and (iii) it attaches quite some importance to the finding that the Comitology Regulation is overall in line with letter and spirit of Article 291(2) TFEU, which constituted a 'win' for the Parliament. If the Parliament did not make any major gains in the negotiations on the Comitology Regulation, it merely means that the Parliament did not achieve additional victories rather than it losing the implementation game.

B. The Comitology Regulation

Before looking into the basic features of the Comitology Regulation and the most important comitology procedure it is important to properly clarify the Regulation as an act of organic law, ranking above 'normal' legislation, even if Article 291(3) TFEU prescribes the ordinary legislative procedure for its adoption.

i. *The Comitology Regulation as Organic Law*

The EU Treaties do not formally recognise a subset of legislative acts that rank between 'ordinary legislation' and primary law. As noted in chapter 2, post-Lisbon there are only legislative and non-legislative acts, whereby only the latter are further subdivided in categories. By contrast, there is no differentiation between legislative acts, even if the specific procedure for their adoption (ordinary vs special procedures) may vary. Still, there is force in the argument that a special category of 'organic' legislative acts needs to be recognised. The then Director-General of the Commission Legal Service, seized the occasion of the Convention to propose to enshrine these organic or constitutional laws in a hierarchy of norms, below primary law but above regular legislation.[216] Such organic law would take up a special position within the body of secondary law because it governs the EU institutions' and bodies' activities in a horizontal manner. Examples would arguably include the Transparency Regulation,[217] the General Data Protection Regulation,[218] and also the Comitology Regulation.[219]

As regards the latter, its special position in the hierarchy of laws also results from the *LIFE* case (see section 5.IV.B), in which the Court explicitly noted that the comitology decision,

[215] Christiansen and Dobbels rightly note that some Parliamentary committees (and some individual MEPs) had wanted to upgrade the Parliament's droit de regard to a genuine veto. This would indeed have been a significant 'win' for the Parliament, but the Parliament as an institution did not put this forward in the negotiations with the Council.

[216] See Secretariat of the European Convention, Note summarising the meeting of Working Group IX (Simplification) on 17 October 2002, CONV 363/02, 5. However, the Praesidium of the Convention rejected suggestions to introduce the notion of organic laws in the EU legal order. See Secretariat of the European Convention, Draft Constitution, Volume I – Revised text of Part One, CONV 724/1/03, 86–87.

[217] Regulation 1049/2001 of the European Parliament and of the Council regarding public access to European Parliament, Council and Commission documents, OJ [2001] L 145/43. *Contra*, see Case C-404/10 P, *Commission v Éditions Odile Jacob SAS*, ECLI:EU:C:2012:393 [110].

[218] Regulation 2016/679 of the European Parliament and of the Council on the protection of natural persons with regard to the processing of personal data and on the free movement of such data, OJ [2016] L 119/1.

[219] Referring to the Comitology Regulation as 'superlegislative', see Eugenia Dumitriu-Segnana, 'Le nouveau règlement «comitologie»' (2011) *Journal de droit européen* 130.

as an act of secondary legislation, could not 'add' to the Treaties but that the principles and rules set out therein *must* be observed when measures conferring implementing powers on the Commission are adopted.[220] While an IIA cannot alter the status of the Comitology Regulation, the 2016 IIA on Better Law-Making also seems to confirm the organic nature of the Comitology Regulation, since it provides that:

> As regards the Commission's exercise of implementing powers, the three Institutions agree to refrain from adding, in Union legislation, procedural requirements which would alter the mechanisms for control set out in Regulation (EU) No 182/2011 of the European Parliament and of the Council.[221]

As such, this provision in the IIA has also proven to be important for legislative practice. It facilitates inter-institutional negotiations by shutting down any special requests (eg from individual Member States) for ad hoc arrangements to control the Commission: if the legislator opts to prescribe a comitology procedure (see section 6.V.B.ii) it can only rely on the arrangements and procedures foreseen in the Comitology Regulation.

Assuming this reading of the Comitology Regulation (as an act of organic law) is correct, an important (potential) constitutional modification to comitology must be flagged. In 2010, following the financial crisis, the three ESAs, three EU agencies, were established. As has been noted in section 6.IV.A, the Court has recognised that these bodies may be conferred an implementing power, but their intrusion in the Commission's executive domain also goes further. Just as they are involved in the drafting of delegated acts (see section 5.IV.A), the ESAs also draft so-called 'implementing technical standards' which the Commission ultimately adopts as implementing acts. Article 15 of the ESA Regulations prescribe in detail how these implementing acts are adopted. Thus, the area in which this special type of implementing act may be adopted is defined by reference to Article 1(2) of the ESA Regulations which essentially covers all secondary legislation conferring tasks on the ESAs.[222] All these acts may thus provide for the adoption of 'implementing technical standards',[223] in which case the relevant ESA is entitled to 'submit its draft implementing

[220] Case C-378/00, *Commission v Parliament & Council*, ECLI:EU:C:2003:42 [39]–[40].

[221] See point 30 of the Interinstitutional Agreement between the European Parliament, the Council of the European Union and the European Commission on Better Law-Making, OJ [2016] L 123/1.

[222] This is not to say that all implementing acts adopted pursuant to these acts follow are adopted following an atypical procedure. Which procedure applies will be defined in these acts themselves. The capital requirements regulation for instance prescribes an 'ordinary' comitology examination procedure for the adoption of some implementing measures, while prescribing the 'implementing technical standards' procedure for other acts. See Regulation 575/2013 of the European Parliament and of the Council on prudential requirements for credit institutions and investment firms, OJ [2013] L 176/1. Compare eg Art 142(2) on equivalence decisions with Art 451(2) on implementing technical standards on the template for institutions' disclosing their leverage ratio. Of course, given the ESAs' expertise they may also be involved (more informally) in the development of implementing measures adopted pursuant to an ordinary comitology procedure. On the adoption of equivalence decisions, see Pieter Van Cleynenbreugel, 'Accountability Challenges for EU Agencies in the Context of Third Country Equivalence Assessments' in Herwig Hofmann, Ellen Vos and Merijn Chamon (eds), *The External Dimension of EU Agencies and Bodies* (Cheltenham, Edward Elgar, 2019) 147–53.

[223] Following the 2019 revision of the ESA Regulations, Arts 15(4) also require such implementing acts to be identified explicitly as 'implementing technical standards' in their title.

technical standards to the Commission for adoption'.[224] Before doing so, the ESA must in principle hold public consultations and request the opinion of its dedicated Stakeholder Group.[225] The ESA is subsequently required to inform the Parliament and Council of these drafts. The Commission must decide on the endorsement of the draft within a period of three months (which may be extended with one month)[226] and may only deviate from the draft if this is in the Union's interests. Even then, it must justify to the ESA concerned why it does not intend to fully endorse the ESA's draft.[227] The ESA subsequently has a period of six weeks to submit an amended draft to the Commission and must also keep the Parliament and Council in the loop. Only after giving the ESA this opportunity can the Commission adopt the final implementing act itself.

There are some possible variations to this procedure, but its crux remains the same: the Commission cannot autonomously decide on implementing acts but must ask the ESA for a draft or opinion and must dialogue with the ESA if it disagrees with the ESA's drafts or opinions. Ultimately, the Commission remains solely competent (and responsible) for the implementing technical standard, but it must be noted that these implementing acts do not in any stage of the process go through a formal comitology procedure and that therefore also the safeguards and (transparency) requirements of the Comitology Regulation do not apply. Specifically, for the Parliament it may be noted that its *droit de regard* under Article 11 of the Comitology Regulation (see section 6.V.D) is not reproduced in the ESA Regulations for the adoption of implementing technical standards. If the Commission exceeds the limits of its implementing powers, the Parliament may of course always adopt a resolution pursuant to Rule 143 of its Rules of Procedure, but the Commission, unlike under Article 11 of the Comitology Regulation, would not be under a specific obligation to reconsider its measure and inform the Parliament of the outcome of its reconsideration.

Effectively, then, the ESA Regulations have created a carve-out from the scope of application of the Comitology Regulation. In light of the Regulation's status as organic law and paragraph 30 of the 2016 IIA, the question arises whether the framework for adopting implementing technical standards is valid. Taking constitutional avoidance to its extremes, one could argue that the ESA Regulations do not *add* requirements that alter the mechanisms for control provided for in the Comitology Regulation. Instead, the procedure involving the ESAs would be conceptualised as preceding the stage whereby the Commission drafts an implementing act ('upstream').[228] Since the comitology procedures only apply once the Commission has finalised a draft (requiring it to subsequently submit it to a comitology committee, 'downstream'), nothing would be 'added'. The legislator would then simply be conferring implementing powers on the Commission without subjecting the Commission to the control regime set out in the Comitology Regulation (an option which the Comitology

[224] See Art 15(1) of the ESA Regulations as amended by Regulation 2019/2175 of the European Parliament and of the Council, OJ [2019] L 334/1. The original 2010 regulation referred to endorsement rather than adoption.

[225] See ibid.

[226] See ibid.

[227] See ibid.

[228] The Commission itself refers to these arrangements as 'pre-comitology' phases in the exercise of implementing powers which it believes are compatible with the Comitology Regulation in so far as the Commission is not 'bound by the opinions of those bodies and this consultation intervenes before and separately from the comitology procedure.' See European Commission, Delegated and Implementing Acts – Guidelines for the Services of the Commission, SEC(2020) 361, 44.

Regulation gives to the legislator; see section 6.V.B.ii). Practically, there are of course good reasons for not prescribing comitology: when the draft has already been the subject of a back and forth with the ESA (which brings together national authorities), there is no added value (either in terms of drawing expertise or in enabling Member States' control) in another round of scrutiny in a comitology committee.

Legally, however, this procedural set-up remains questionable. If the above reasoning were to be accepted, the legislator would always be able to decide to grant implementing powers that are not subjected to the control regime of the Comitology Regulation, but whereby the Commission would be 'assisted' 'upstream' by ad hoc or *sui generis* bodies composed of national (or other) experts. That would of course amount to completely circumventing the Comitology Regulation.

Unless the ESA Regulations themselves are also to be qualified as organic law (and thus of the same rank as the Comitology Regulation), the special framework created for the adoption of technical implementing standards thus amounts to a constitutional modification.[229]

Arguably, no institutional balance test is required to show this constitutional modification since the legal framework in positive law is clear enough: the power concerned undoubtedly comes under Article 291 TFEU (different from the powers discussed in sections 6.IV.A and 6.IV.B), paragraph 3 of which prescribes that the Commission is controlled by the Member States and that the procedure to do so must be laid down in advance in a general instrument. Those prescriptions do not appear to leave any scope for control by entities other than the Member States (*in casu* EU agencies) and for ad hoc arrangements like those laid down in secondary legislation like the ESA Regulations. What if an institutional balance test would still be pursued just for the sake of the argument and assuming that the letter of Article 291 TFEU is insufficiently clear? Such a test would already give a negative result in its first step: while Article 291(3) TFEU might not require one *single* instrument that is adopted in advance, the purpose would still be to enable control by the Member States (not by EU agencies). Finally, if under a combined historical and teleological reading one would insist that the ultimate purpose of 'control by Member States' is (also) aimed at ensuring that the Commission has access to sufficient expertise (see section 3.I) which may also be understood as 'expert input (from whatever source)', the argument would still fail on the second and last step of an institutional balance test since the requirements imposed on the Commission by the legislator unduly interfere with its institutional autonomy and because the procedures in place lower the level of scrutiny which the Parliament may exercise (compared to the parliamentary scrutiny provided for by the Comitology Regulation).

ii. Basic Features of the Comitology Regulation

Returning to the basic features of the Comitology Regulation, it may be noted that while the legislative negotiations added complexity to the Commission's original proposal, the Regulation still constitutes a simplification and rationalisation of the comitology regime in light of the new Treaty framework (compared to the pre-Lisbon comitology regime).

[229] Also Declaration No 39 to the Lisbon Treaty, would not 'save' this modification.

As noted above, in terms of scope, the implementation of the CCP is now subject to the ordinary comitology regime.

The importance of this for the CCP and for the scope of the Comitology Regulation should not be underestimated. While the Commission in pre-Lisbon times also had to cooperate with the Council and with committees of national experts when adopting or proposing trade measures, these procedures were not formally governed by the horizontal comitology framework.[230] While the incorporation of the CCP in the comitology system may then have been inspired by the Lisbon Treaty itself, it was far from a done deal when the Treaty entered into force. To recall, the (new) wording of Article 207(2) TFEU only foresees the adoption of 'measures *defining the framework* for implementing the CCP', while Article 133(2) TEC and even Article III-317(2) of the draft Constitution provided for 'measures implementing the CCP'. As a result, and following a textual interpretation of Article 207(2) TFEU, the Council (now Council and Parliament) can no longer adopt implementing measures based directly on Article 207 TFEU.[231] Instead, such measures now require a framework instrument (eg the Basic Anti-Dumping or the Basic Anti-Subsidy Regulation) as an enabling act.[232]

Still, it was not a given that measures implementing such framework instruments would also be adopted under the 'default' comitology system. Indeed, the Commission's proposal to this end initially led to a stalling of the negotiations on the new Comitology Regulation in the Council.[233] While the original proposal foresaw a straightforward integration of CCP measures in the horizontal comitology regime, the final regulation effectively lays down a separate regime for CCP measures.[234] Still, the importance of the decision-making in the CCP being brought under the horizontal comitology framework remains significant[235] and the Parliament being a co-legislator under Article 207 TFEU proved to be crucial in securing this rationalisation.[236] The only (remaining) carve-out foreseen in the Comitology

[230] See recital 12 of the preamble of Council Decision 1999/468, OJ [1999] L 184/23.

[231] Rudolf Streinz, Christoph Ohler and Christoph Herrmann, *Der Vertrag von Lissabon zur Reform der EU*, München, Beck, 2010, p. 152. Gosalbo Bono on the other hand found it was 'not clear what the terms "framework for implementation" mean'. See Ricardo Gosalbo Bono, 'The organization of the external relations of the European Union in the Treaty of Lisbon' in Panos Koutrakos (ed), *The European Union's External Relations a Year after Lisbon*, CLEER Working Paper 2011/3, 18.

[232] The only, legally questionable, exception seems to be the adoption of retaliation measures for which Art 14(2) of Regulation 2015/1843 provides that these should be based directly on Art 207 TFEU.

[233] See Frank Hoffmeister, 'Of Transferred Competence, Institutional Balance and Judicial Autonomy – Constitutional Developments in EU Trade Policy Seven Years after Lisbon' in Jenö Czuczai and Frederik Naert (eds), *The EU as a Global Actor – Bridging Legal Theory and Practice* (Leiden, Brill/Nijhoff, 2017) 318; House of Commons European Scrutiny Committee, Nineteenth Report of Session 2010–11, 23. During the trilogues on the new Comitology Regulation, the Belgian Presidency even proposed the following recital: 'This Regulation does not apply to the specific procedures that were not subject to the Council Decision 1999/468/EC, in particular those created for the implementation of the common commercial policy and it does not prejudge the possibility to lay down specific procedures under article 291 TFEU'. See proposed Recital 14a in the four-column table NEGO_CT(2010)0051(REV-11-10-2010).

[234] Birgit Daiber, 'EU-Durchführungsrechtsetzung nach Inkrafttreten der neuen Komitologie-Verordnung' (2012) 47 *Europarecht* 248–51. Noting that this special regime was the price to pay to put the adoption of trade measures under the horizontal comitology regime, see Dumitriu-Segnana, 'Le nouveau règlement' (2011) 130–31.

[235] According to Jinaru, Moroni and Willems, the Commission now even has too much power (in the adoption of anti-dumping measures); see Anamaria Jinaru, Alessandra Moroni and Arnoud Willems, 'Accountability in Antidumping: The Silent Death of Lisbon' (2019) 14 *Global Trade and Customs Journal* 271–72.

[236] For a more elaborate discussion, see Jacques Bourgeois and Merijn Chamon, 'The Integration of EU Trade Defence in the Horizontal Comitology Regime' in Michael Hahn and Guillaume Van der Loo (eds), *Law and practice of the Common Commercial Policy: the first 10 years after the Treaty of Lisbon* (Leiden, Brill/Nijhoff, 2020) 512–30.

Regulation, just like in the comitology decisions, is the implementation of the EU's competition policy.[237] This appears constitutionally defensible given that the Commission has also been vested with important autonomous executive powers for the implementation of that policy (see section 2.II).

Next to the Regulation's scope, a further feature to note is that, in line with Article 291(3) TFEU and differently from pre-Lisbon comitology, the control which it prescribed is a control solely by the Member States since no referrals to the Council are possible anymore.[238] The Regulation does hint, however, that the Member States need not necessarily always control the Commission as recital 6 provides that committees will be set up for those basic acts where control by the Member States is required and Article 2 provides that a basic act '*may* provide for the application of the advisory procedure or the examination procedure' (emphasis added). While the Court has sanctioned the possibility to forego at comitology in the pre-Lisbon *Common Market Fertilizers* case (see section 6.II.A), it is questionable whether doing so in the post-Lisbon setting is still constitutionally sound.

Article 291 TFEU arguably gives a right to the Member States to control the Commission when the latter implements EU law and it is difficult to see how the conferral of this right in specific cases could depend on the discretion of the EU legislator. The important change in wording between Article 202 EC and 291 TFEU must be recalled here (see section 2.III.B). Three textual points stand out. First, Article 291(1) TFEU establishes the rule that the default actors implementing EU law are the Member States, reinforcing a claim that they should be involved in controlling the Commission when the latter is exceptionally conferred an implementing power. Secondly, Article 291(3) TFEU explicitly indicates the Member States as those actors that control the Commission, rather than referring to 'certain requirements in respect of the exercise of [implementing powers by the Commission]' as Article 202 EC did. Thirdly, Article 202 EC explicitly provided that 'The Council *may* impose' (emphasis added) such requirements, whereas Article 291 TFEU does not refer to such an option anymore. As a result, control *must* be prescribed and that control *must* be one by the Member States. A counterargument could be that Article 291(3) TFEU only requires the Parliament and Council to 'lay down in advance the rules and general principles concerning mechanisms for control by Member States', without excluding that those rules and general principles could allow to dispense with Member State control. While this is indeed not explicitly excluded by Article 291(3) TFEU, the three textual changes flagged above, as well as a coherent reading with Article 290 TFEU, suggests otherwise. On this coherent reading there is only one further possible reservation: in section 5.IV.B above it was not noted that it is an outstanding question whether Parliament and Council can decide to delegate powers (in the sense of Article 290 TFEU) without prescribing either the objection or revocation mechanism. The view taken was that Parliament and Council must prescribe control and cannot dispense with it. Should the Court in the future find otherwise, the coherence argument advanced in the present paragraph would of course lose force.[239] In sum, the counterargument to the

[237] See recital 22 of the Comitology Regulation.

[238] This was not a given, however; see Karine Caunes, 'Et la fonction exécutive européenne créa l'administration à son image … Retour vers le futur de la comitologie' (2007) 43 *Revue trimestrielle de droit européen* 329–30.

[239] While the coherence argument would lose force, a finding that no control under Art 290 TFEU is indeed possible does not automatically mean that control may also be dispensed with Art 291 TFEU either – if only because of the textual differences between Arts 290 and 291 TFEU and because under Art 290 TFEU it would be Parliament and Council deciding that they will not make use of the option to control the Commission, whereas under Art 291TFEU they would be making that choice for the Member States.

reasoning developed here does not convince and even if it were accepted, it could in any event at the most result in a finding that Member State control is not always required but that it should still remain the rule. As a result, deviations from the rule would have to be explicitly justified, but even this is not the case in the institutions' current practice.[240] The latter is therefore questionable – if not because comitology must always be prescribed when the Commission exercises implementing powers pursuant to Article 291 TFEU, then at least because deviations from the rule that comitology should apply are not justified. This issue may end up before the Court even though in the typical constellation in which implementing powers are conferred on the Commission it will not pose any political problems (the Member States in Council agreeing to forego at Member State control through comitology). In more atypical constellations however, we have seen in section 6.II.A how dispensing with comitology may prove contentious.

In any event, the advisory and examination procedure are also the only procedures (together with the procedure allowing for immediately applicable measures), even if the examination procedure comes in different variants depending on how basic acts define the consequences of the absence of an opinion in the examination committee (see Figure 6.2).[241]

The examination procedure, then, applies when implementing measures of general scope are to be adopted and for measures relating to programmes with substantial implications; the CAP and CFP; the environment, security and safety, or protection of the health or safety, of humans, animals or plants; the CCP; and taxation.[242] In other cases or in duly justified cases (normally falling within the scope of the examination procedure), the advisory procedure applies.[243] While the Regulation is not explicit on whether these criteria are (non-) binding, the fact that the legislators took out the explicit reference to the criteria's binding nature and changed the prescriptive language (in the Commission's proposal) suggests that just like under the second comitology decision, the criteria remain non-binding.

The advisory procedure has not been altered as such and is rather straightforward: the committee adopts its opinion on the draft measures with a simple majority. The Commission must take the utmost account of the conclusions drawn from the discussions within the committee and of the opinion delivered, but can in any event adopt its draft measure (modified or unmodified). Both procedures applied automatically with the entry into force of the Comitology Regulation since Article 13 prescribes that references to the old comitology procedures under the second comitology decision (apart from the PRAC) are to be read as references to the new procedures of the regulation.

iii. The Examination Procedure

By way of contrast to the advisory procedure, the examination procedure is much more complex than envisaged in the Commission's original proposal. Here the committee adopts

[240] See eg Recital 15 of Regulation 2016/2336 of the European Parliament and of the Council establishing specific conditions for fishing for deep-sea stocks in the north-east Atlantic and provisions for fishing in international waters of the north-east Atlantic, OJ [2016] L 354/1.

[241] For this reason, Craig suggested there are in fact four (rather than two) procedures in the Comitology Regulation, see Paul Craig, 'Delegated Acts, Implementing Acts and the New Comitology Regulation' (2011) 36 *European Law Review* 684–85.

[242] See Art 2(2) of the Comitology Regulation.

[243] See Art 2(3) of the Comitology Regulation.

its opinions with a qualified majority vote. In case of a positive opinion, the Commission *must* adopt its draft. If no opinion is reached in the committee, the Commission may adopt its draft, unless we find ourselves in one of the scenario's listed in Article 5(4) of the Regulation, ie where the draft concerns taxation, financial services, the protection of the health or safety of humans, animals or plants, or definitive multilateral safeguard measures; where the basic act prescribes that a measures may not be adopted based on a no opinion; or where a simple majority in the committee opposes the draft. In those scenarios, the lack of an opinion effectively equates with a negative opinion. Specifically in relation to the second scenario, the Commission has claimed that, 'The inclusion of a no opinion clause in the basic act must respond to a specific need and must be justified by the legislator'.[244] In its internal guidance the Commission relies on the *LIFE* jurisprudence (see 5.IV.B), to substantiate this requirement.[245] While this might make sense if one considers that the legal consequence of a no opinion is thus altered in a way similar to the different legal effects of a no opinion under the management and regulatory procedures (of the second comitology decision),[246] the Commission's reading is not as such supported by the text of the Comitology Regulation.[247] Although the Commission consistently objects when the legislator does not motivate the inclusion of 'no opinion clauses' in legislation,[248] it would indeed seem that this choice is fully within the discretion of the legislator and need not be motivated.[249]

In so far as the non-adoption of the draft measures would not result in significant disruption of the markets in the area of agriculture or a risk for the financial interests of the Union, the Commission may then either redraft its measure and go back to the committee, or it can seize the Appeal Committee. Where there would be such signification disruption or risk, the Commission may still adopt the draft measure (notwithstanding the negative opinion or absence of opinion), but if it does, it must immediately seize the Appeal Committee.

[244] See European Commission, Report on the implementation of Regulation 182/2011, COM(2016) 92 final, 6.

[245] See European Commission, Delegated and Implementing Acts – Guidelines for the Services of the Commission, SEC(2020) 361, 46–47.

[246] Under the second comitology decision, a no opinion under the management opinion meant that the Commission could go ahead but could still be overruled by the Council, whereas a no opinion under the regulatory procedure meant that the Commission needed to submit a proposal to the Council and could only adopt that proposal itself if the Council had not opposed the proposal or acted on it itself.

[247] While the Commission rightly claims that the rule under Art 5(4) of the Comitology Regulation is that a no opinion allows the Commission to adopt the measure, it should be noted that the relevant exception is broadly worded and does not require to basic act (that is implemented) to explain why a no opinion should prevent the Commission from adopting this measure. In addition, it should be noted that the Commission in its original proposal for a Comitology Regulation had suggested that a no opinion would always allow it to adopt the draft measures, whereas in the trilogues the Parliament had proposed to simply prohibit the adoption of implementing measures following a no opinion. The current Art 5(4) of the Regulation then presents a middle ground between both options and was proposed by the Council. See Art 5(4) in the four-column table NEGO_CT(2010)0051 of 11 October 2010.

[248] See for instance the Commission declaration annexed to the European Parliament legislative resolution of 15 December 2020 on the Council position at first reading with a view to the adoption of a directive of the European Parliament and of the Council on the quality of water intended for human consumption, OJ [2021] C 445/219.

[249] In contrast, Corona seems to agree with the Commission's reading of Art 5(4)(b). See Daniela Corona, 'The Adoption of Secondary Legislation through Comitology in the EU: Some Reflections on the Regulation (EU) 182/2011 in Comparison with the Pre-Lisbon Reform' (2014) 2 *The Theory and Practice of Legislation* 106.

This Appeal Committee was a novelty in the post-Lisbon regime and was not foreseen in the proposal of the Commission. As noted above, it was introduced during the legislative negotiations to ensure more opportunities for the Member States to scrutinise draft implementing measures. The Regulation prescribes that the Appeal Committee 'should meet at the appropriate level'.[250] This in principle allows Member States to send representatives ranging from ordinary civil servants, permanent representatives to ministers. However, the rules of procedure of the Appeal Committee also provide that each Member State must 'inform the chair and the other Member States with a view to achieving a level of representation as homogenous as possible at the meeting of the appeal committee'.[251] In practice this means that the Appeal Committee brings together representatives at the level of the Committee of the Permanent Representatives of the Governments of the Member States to the European Union (COREPER).[252] In the Appeal Committee the same logic as in the examination committee applies: a positive or no opinion allows the Commission to adopt (or maintain) its draft since the Appeal Committee can only block a measure if it musters a qualified majority against the draft (or adopted) measure.[253] The exceptions here are draft definitive multilateral safeguard measures, which require a positive opinion in the Appeal Committee before they can be adopted by the Commission. Figure 6.2 sets out the examination procedure as described above.

It is important to point that out, in contrast to what the regulatory procedure under the second comitology decision prescribed, the Commission is no longer required to adopt a measure in case of a no opinion.[254] Indeed, Articles 5(4) and 6(3) of the Comitology Regulation provide that the Commission may adopt the draft measure in case of a no opinion in respectively the committee or Appeal Committee. Surprisingly the Commission has not unequivocally welcomed this extra margin of manoeuver (see section 6.VI).

Finally, as noted in section 6.V.B.i the control over the Commission is genuinely exercised by the Member States and not by the Parliament or Council. Still, Articles 10 and 11 of the Comitology Regulation provide information rights and a (circumscribed) *droit de regard* to both institutions. Article 10(3) prescribes that they shall have access to the information

[250] See recital 7 of the preamble to the Comitology Regulation.

[251] See Art 5(1) of the Rules of Procedure of the Appeal Committee, OJ [2011] C 183/13.

[252] See European Commission, Delegated and Implementing Acts – Guidelines for the Services of the Commission, SEC(2020) 361 57.

[253] An outstanding question is in how far a final negative opinion in the Appeal Committee limits the degree of discretion which the Commission has in redrafting a measure and submitting it before the original committee again. In the *Orphacol* case, the applicant argued that the Commission is 'not entitled to re-initiate the Comitology Procedure with a draft decision substantively the same as the version already rejected by the Standing Committee and Appeal Committee.' See Action brought on 10 July 2012 – Laboratoires CTRS v Commission, OJ [2012] C 250/20. The General Court did not deal with this plea and instead granted the application based on a different plea. See Case T-301/12, *Laboratoires CTRS v Commission*, ECLI:EU:T:2013:346 [79]. In *Hungary v Commission*, the General Court held that even if the operative part of a draft decision is identical to an earlier draft (submitted to the committee), those drafts are not the same if the scientific assessments underlying those drafts are not the same. See Case T-240/10, *Hungary v Commission*, ECLI:EU:T:2013:645 [82]ff.

[254] Art 5(6) of the second comitology decision provided that if the Council did not itself adopt a draft measure (following referral) but did not reject the draft measure either, 'the proposed implementing act *shall* be adopted by the Commission' (emphasis added).

Figure 6.2 The examination procedure

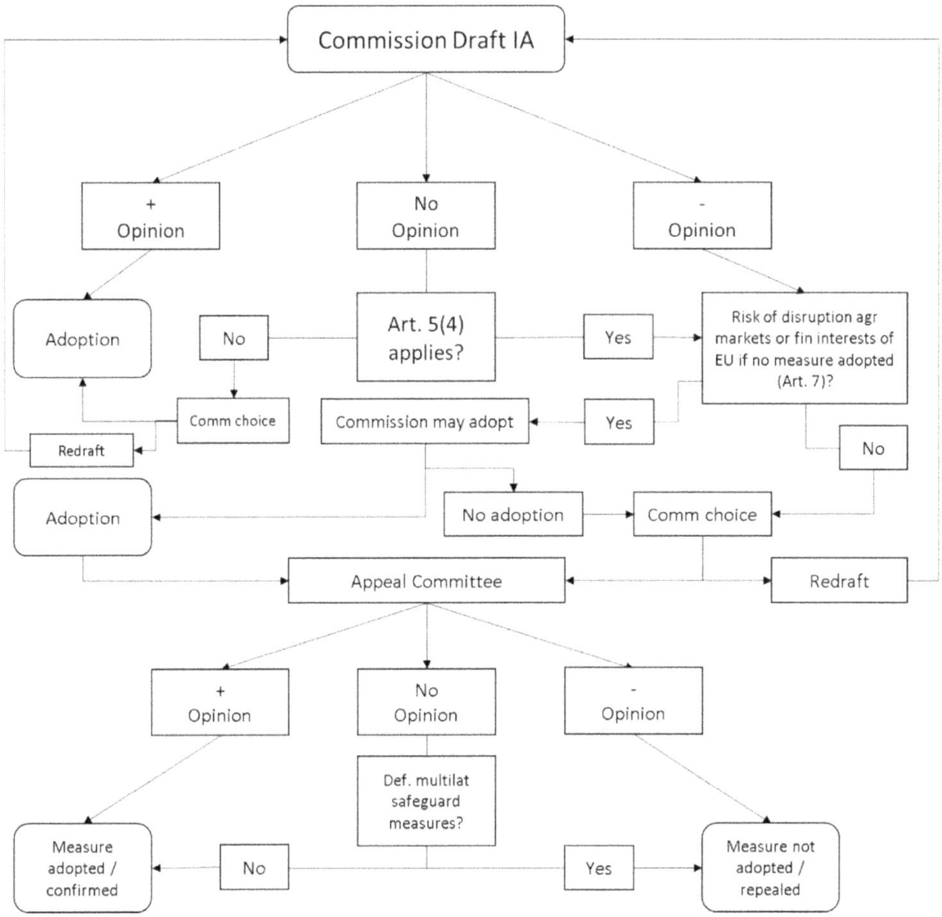

which the Commission is required to keep in the comitology register.[255] Parliament and Council have access to the agendas of the committees, the draft acts presented by the Commission and the final drafts following the opinions of the committees at the same time as the committees themselves.[256] Access to this information allows the Parliament and Council to exercise their *droit de regard* under Article 11 of the Regulation: if a draft act implementing a basic act adopted pursuant to the ordinary legislative procedure 'exceeds the implementing powers provided for in the basic act', the Parliament and Council can notify the Commission thereof. The Commission is then required to review its draft, but may still maintain it.

[255] The register is available at ec.europa.eu/transparency/comitology-register/screen/home. Importantly, Art 10(5) of the Regulation only requires the statistical data with regard to the committees' function to be made public, as well as the *references* of the documents containing the agendas, voting sheets, minutes, etc. As a result, the transparency provided to the public by the Commission goes beyond what is required of it by the Regulation.

[256] See Art 10(4) of Regulation 182/2011.

iv. The Proper Conduct of Comitology Proceedings as Essential Procedural Requirements

Given the origins of comitology (see section 3.I), it was natural for the EU institutions, including the Court, to regard comitology proceedings as an internal affair between the Commission, Council and Member States. The legitimate claim of the Parliament for greater transparency of, if not greater involvement in, comitology first undermined this idea. Post-Lisbon, there may be further signs that the Court is also increasingly recognising the interest which private parties have in the proper conduct of comitology proceedings. In the pre-Lisbon *Common Market Fertilizers* case, the applicant had invoked the rules of procedure of the comitology committee, which prescribed that the Commission should provide the members of the committee with at least 14 days to study its draft measures, to challenge the validity of an implementing measure (for which the committee members had only been afforded 13 days of scrutiny). Both the General Court, the AG and the Court of Justice on appeal found that the relevant rule could not be invoked by a private party since the rule's purpose was 'to ensure the internal working of the Customs Code Committee while fully respecting the prerogatives of its members [and was] not intended to ensure protection for individuals'.[257] By contrast, such rules could be invoked by the Member States.[258]

The adoption of the Comitology Regulation potentially signaled important changes, since some of the provisions hitherto laid down in the committees' rules of procedure were transferred to the Comitology Regulation. The latter, in contrast to the comitology decisions, contains one Article dedicated to the 'common provisions' regulating *all* different comitology procedures and their variants. Thus, Article 3(3) of the Regulation inter alia prescribes that 'Except in duly justified cases, the chair shall convene a meeting not less than 14 days from submission of the draft implementing act and of the draft agenda to the committee'. In the post-Lisbon *Tilly Sabco* cases, the applicant invoked this provision to challenge the legality of a Commission implementing measure that had been communicated to the committee on the same day as its opinion was asked. The General Court explicitly left open the question whether a private party could invoke Article 3(3) of the Regulation,[259] but noted that even if this were the case, the Commission could duly justify an exception *in casu*,[260] and even supposing the Commission had breached Article 3(3), the applicant could not show that the measure could otherwise have been substantially different.[261] On appeal, AG Wahl explicitly addressed the issue of the invocability of Article 3(3) of the Regulation, noting that private parties 'do not have an actionable right under Article 3(3) of Regulation No 182/2011, in the circumstances of the present case, to challenge the way in which the Commission interacts with the Management Committee'.[262] The AG found so after explicitly recognising that the requirement at issue was not just laid down in (internal) rules of procedures anymore, but in a legislative regulation.[263] Still, he noted that Article 3(3) was rather imprecisely worded and

[257] Case C-433/05 P, *Common Market Fertilizers SA v Commission*, ECLI:EU:C:2007:511 [144]–[145].
[258] See Case 278/84, *Germany v Commission*, ECLI:EU:C:1987:2.
[259] Case T-397/13, *Tilly Sabco v Commission*, ECLI:EU:T:2016:8 [83]–[120].
[260] ibid [125].
[261] ibid [126]–[129]. In line with established case law, see Koen Lenaerts, Ignace Maselis and Kathleen Gutman, *EU Procedural Law* (Oxford, OUP, 2015) 371.
[262] Opinion of AG Wahl in Case C-183/16 P, *Tilly Sabco v Commission*, ECLI:EU:C:2017:348 [61].
[263] ibid [58].

> that a risk exists that the line of case-law mentioned in the previous point [on the non-invocability of internal rules of procedure] would be circumvented if the notion were to be entertained that private individuals might be able to extract hard rules from higher-ranking provisions such as Article 3(3) of Regulation No 182/2011.[264]

This in itself is a remarkable observation since it does not seem to consider the possibility that the legislator made the conscious choice of lifting this type of provision out of the rules of procedure and putting them in a binding and directly applicable instrument of EU law.[265] In this respect, the AG simply noted that Article 3(3) 'presumably deliberately, [has] been drafted in vague and malleable terms by the EU legislature';[266] and that from a teleological perspective

> Regulation No 182/2011 aims to ensure that the procedures for control by Member States of the Commission's exercise of implementing power are clear, effective and proportionate to the nature of the implementing acts and that they reflect the institutional requirements of the FEU Treaty as well as the experience gained and the common practice followed in the implementation of [the second comitology decision].[267]

On appeal, the Court sided with Tilly Sabco, finding that the Commission could not justify why it had not respected the default 14-day period for consultation. Crucially, on the issue of the invocability of Article 3(3) it held that it need not consider this, since it is in any case competent to review violations of essential procedural requirements of its own motion.[268] While this is true, it should be remarked that the Court did not indicate whether respect for Article 3(3) of the Regulation is a matter of public policy, which also *requires* the Court to raise the issue of its own motion.[269] The Court seemed to confirm this in *Eurobolt*,[270] where it invalidated a Commission implementing act imposing anti-dumping duties because the Commission had not provided the committee the necessary information, which Eurobolt as an interested party had sent to the Commission, 10 days before the committee's meeting, as prescribed by the Anti-Dumping Regulation. Referring to *Tilly Sabco*, the Court held that this requirement also constituted an essential procedural requirement disregard of which invalidated the measure(s) adopted. *Eurobolt* could therefore be seen to confirm that at least those procedural provisions laid down in the Comitology Regulation may now indeed be invoked by private parties. This development is not just in the interest of private parties, but

[264] ibid [57].

[265] Here it may be noted that the Commission's original proposal for a Comitology Regulation did not contain this prescription and that instead it had been put forward by the Council during the trilogues. See the new Art 3(3) in the four-column table NEGO_CT(2010)0051 of 11 October 2010, 8–9.

[266] Opinion of AG Wahl in Case C-183/16 P, *Tilly Sabco v Commission*, ECLI:EU:C:2017:348 [57].

[267] ibid [55].

[268] Case C-183/16 P, *Tilly Sabco v Commission*, ECLI:EU:C:2017:704 [114]–[116]. Similarly, in a case brought by Hungary (which of course is a privileged applicant) against the Commission, the General Court confirmed that the Commission had breached an essential procedural requirement, which it held involved a question of public policy, by not resubmitting an amended draft to the committee before adopting it. See Case T-240/10, *Hungary v Commission*, ECLI:EU:T:2013:645.

[269] On this requirement for the Court to raise issue of its own motion, see also above, ch 5 n 67.

[270] See Case C-644/17, *Eurobolt*, ECLI:EU:C:2019:555. One important caveat here is that the Anti-Dumping Regulation provides interested parties with certain procedural rights. As a result, it could be argued that the requirement imposed on the Commission to provide the committee with the information sent by interested parties in a timely manner is linked to a right conferred on those interested parties and may therefore also be invoked by them (unlike the typical internal rules of procedures which only aim to ensure the proper functioning of the decision-making procedure).

arguably also in the interest of the EU courts themselves. Where technically or scientifically complex decisions are contested, it is much easier for the courts to quash measures based on procedural irregularities (as part of the *légalité externe*) rather than having to look at the substance of the decision (as part of the *légalité interne*).[271]

C. The Functioning of the Post-Lisbon Comitology Regime

In addition to the annual reports which the Commission adopts on the functioning of the comitology committees pursuant to Article 10(2) of the Comitology Regulation (and before that, Article 7(4) of the second comitology decision), the Commission in 2016 also adopted one report specifically on the implementation of the (new) Regulation as required by Article 15 of the Regulation.[272] In its report the Commission noted that the transition between legal regimes (from the second comitology decision to the Regulation) was ultimately seamless, also because the Regulation partially codified existing comitology practices.[273]

It is nonetheless remarkable that in its report the Commission does not yet envisage any need to amend the Comitology Regulation.

As noted in section 6.V.B.iii, the Commission has discretion to adopt (or not) measures on which committees expressed no opinion. In some exceptional cases, this latitude is not welcomed by the Commission itself. Notably under the EU's GMO legislation, where the 2001 GMO Directive allows for the authorisation of GMOs for cultivation[274] and the 2003 GMO Regulation allows for authorisation of GMOs in food and feed,[275] the Commission is typically faced with no opinions in both the committee and the Appeal Committee, putting it in a difficult position. Indeed, as noted by Poli, when faced with a no opinion on a draft GMO authorisation under the 2003 GMO Regulation, the Commission could decide to grant the authorisation or to refuse it based on 'other legitimate factors' (other than scientific ones).[276] Combined with Articles 5(4) and 6(3) of the Comitology Regulation this means that the Commission has the necessary latitude to take political responsibility to adopt decisions even if they are not backed by a positive opinion in the Appeal Committee. Normally the Commission also amply makes use of the possibility to adopt draft measures in cases of a no opinion. Between the entry into force of the Comitology Regulation and end of 2021, the comitology register lists some 360 dossiers in which measures were adopted following no opinion cases (compared to some 17,500 dossiers where measures were adopted in positive opinion cases). Very rarely, in around 16 cases over the same period, the Commission opted to withdraw (rather than adopt) a

[271] See Case T-240/10, *Hungary v Commission*, ECLI:EU:T:2013:645; Case T-301/12, *Laboratoires CTRS v Commission*, ECLI:EU:T:2013:346.

[272] European Commission, Report on the implementation of Regulation 182/2011, COM (2016) 92 final.

[273] Such as the extensive use of the written procedure. See ibid 3.

[274] Directive 2001/18 of the European Parliament and of the Council on the deliberate release into the environment of genetically modified organisms, OJ [2001] L 106/1.

[275] Regulation 1829/2003 of the European Parliament and of the Council on genetically modified food and feed, OJ [2003] L 268/1.

[276] Sara Poli, 'The Reform of the EU Legislation on GMOs: A Journey to an Unknown Destination?' (2015) *European Journal of Risk Regulation* 561.

draft measure which had not received a QMV for or against. Yet, in heavily politicised or mediatised cases such as typical for GMOs or pesticides (eg glyphosate), this possibility to adopt draft measures following no opinions becomes a curse rather than a blessing for the Commission.

However, in its 2016 report the Commission still envisaged that the 2015 amendment of the 2001 GMO Directive would resolve the politically sensitive issue of no opinions at the level of the committee and the Appeal Committee.[277] The same belief led it to remark that the 2003 GMO Regulation ought to be amended in the same vein as the 2001 GMO Directive without 'depart[ing] from the horizontal procedural rules agreed to implement the EU acquis'.[278] Yet, the amendments to the EU's GMO legislation whereby Member States were granted unilateral opt-outs did not result in smoother decision-making at the authorisation stage as hoped for. This is why, just two years later, the Commission in 2017 changed its point of view and proposed an amendment to the Comitology Regulation (see section 6.VI).

Other than on this issue, comitology has not only continued to function smoothly, but its post-Lisbon functioning is also characterised by a genuine continuity. This becomes clear when a number of key indicators are taken into consideration. All the data in this respect are taken from the Commission's annual comitology reports adopted since 2000.[279] On average, a number of 1,600 implementing acts per year are adopted since the entry into force of the Lisbon Treaty. As Figure 6.3 shows, the decline in total number of acts adopted continues a trend started before that period.

Figure 6.3 Number of implementing acts adopted

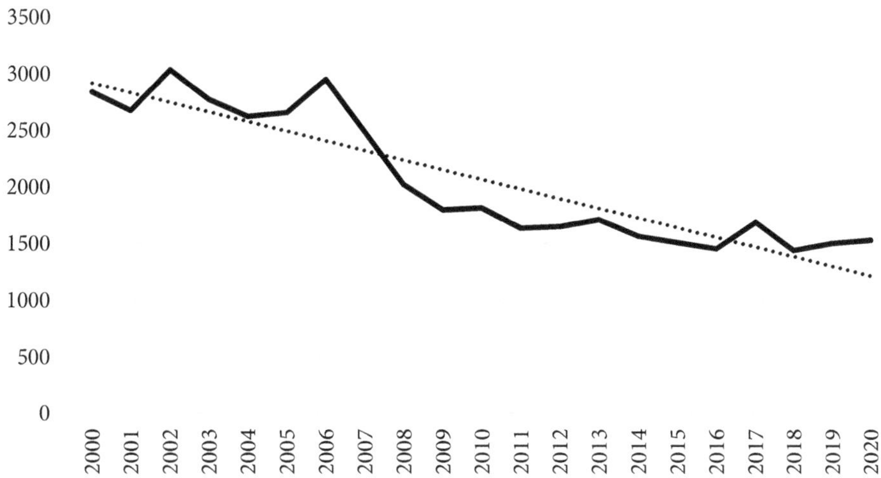

[277] European Commission, Report on the implementation of Regulation 182/2011, COM (2016) 92 final, 6–7.

[278] European Commission, Reviewing the decision-making process on genetically modified organisms (GMOs), COM (2015) 176 final, 8.

[279] The requirement to adopt such a report was first introduced by the second comitology decision (see Art 7(4) of Decision 1999/468) and is now prescribed by Art 10(2) of the Regulation. The annual reports are always accompanied by detailed Commission Staff Working Documents containing the more detailed data.

The Lisbon-split, carving out the delegated act out of the pre-Lisbon implementing acts, has of course contributed to this, but given the overall limited number of delegated acts adopted each year (see Figure 5.3), the main reason for this decline is found elsewhere. Zooming in on specific policy fields, the decline in number of acts adopted is almost completely determined by a collapse in the number of implementing measures adopted in the CAP, as shown in Figure 6.4.

Figure 6.4 Number of implementing acts adopted in the CAP

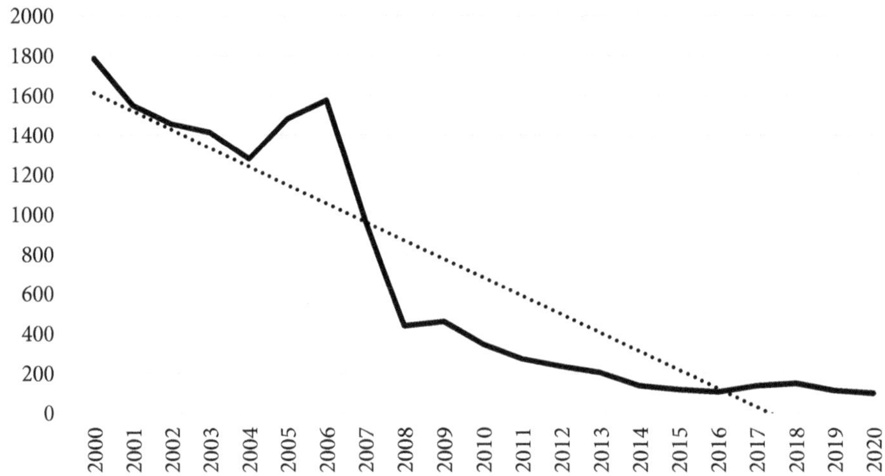

This collapse in the number of CAP implementing acts precedes the entry into force of the Lisbon Treaty, but has only continued since. As noted by Bianchi, this is the result of successive CAP reforms whereby the total number of (basic) legislative acts has dropped, and the policy has become much less interventionist and more laissez faire, requiring fewer implementing measures.[280] A similar, but less drastically, declining trend can be seen in the number of committee meetings (see Figure 6.5),[281] with a parallel continuous increase in the number of files dealt with through the written procedure. The significant increase in the number of written procedures in 2020 is of course explained by the outbreak of the COVID pandemic, but even before 2020 the upward trend was clear (see Figure 6.6). As Article 3(5) of the Comitology Regulation makes clear, this procedure, like the silence procedure in the Council,[282] may be used 'in duly justified cases' and implies that a draft act is deemed adopted when the committee members do not explicitly oppose the measure.

[280] Daniele Bianchi, 'La comitologie est morte! vive la comitologie!' (2012) 48 *Revue trimestrielle de droit européen* 103–04.

[281] After the outbreak of the COVID pandemic, meetings did not take place physically anymore and were instead held remotely online. These remote meetings are still counted as meetings. See European Commission, Report on the working of committees during 2020, COM(2021) 544 final, 1.

[282] See Art 12(2) of Council Decision 2009/337 adopting the Council's Rules of Procedure, OJ [2009] L 325/35.

Figure 6.5 Number of comitology meetings held

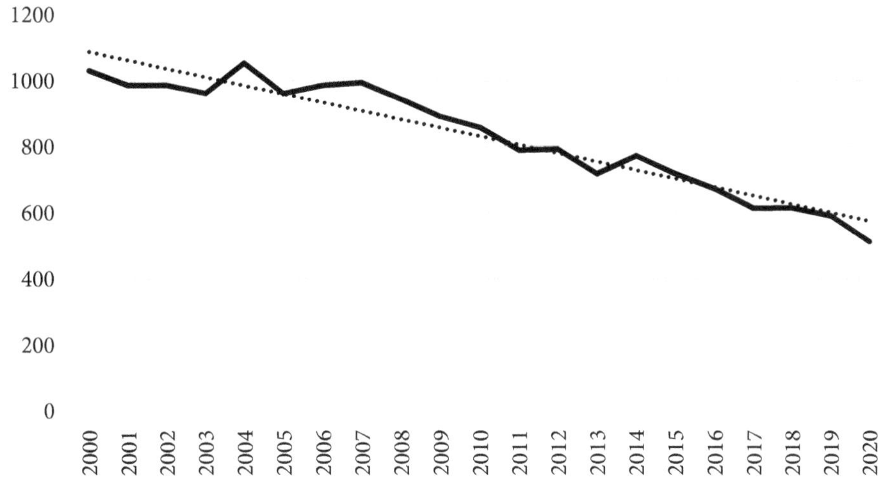

Figure 6.6 Number of files decided through the written procedure

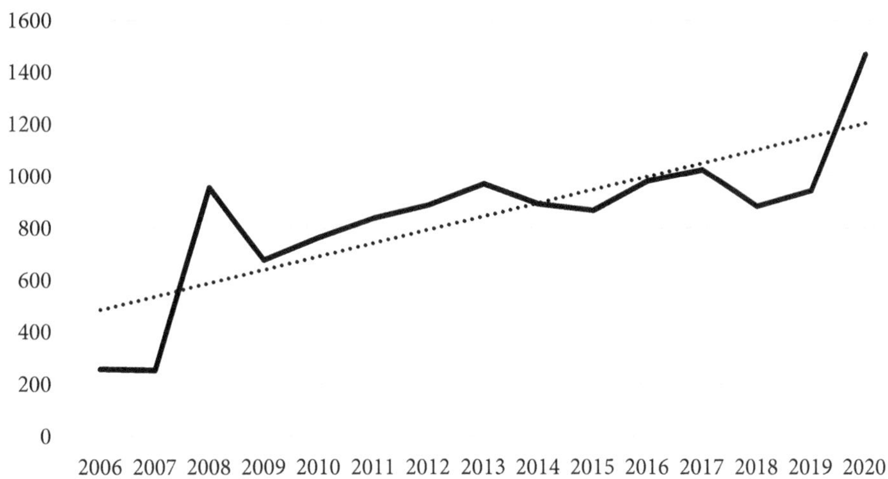

Finally, given the insistence of the Member States in Council on retaining control, exemplified by the inclusion of the Appeal Committee in the examination procedure, it is also useful to look into the statistics specifically for this committee. Based on the figures of the comitology register and the annual reports, the Appeal Committee has on average six meetings a year and before the COVID pandemic did not rely on the written procedure.[283]

[283] To be entirely precise, the Appeal Committee relied on the written procedure once before the pandemic, in 2017.

By and large, the Appeal Committee meets following a no opinion from the Genetically Modified Food and Feed Committee, but referrals typically do not result in breaking any deadlocks. Since its establishment and until the end of 2021 the Appeal Committee adopted 126 opinions, of which 118 were no opinions, seven positive opinions and only one was a negative opinion.[284]

These figures in itself show that the added value of the Appeal Committee (under the current rules) is extremely limited at best. In more than 93 per cent of the cases, a referral to the Appeal Committee does not change anything and therefore simply amounts to a superfluous procedural step. This finding primarily supports a suggestion to simply do away with the referral to the Appeal Committee (in line with the original 2010 Commission proposal for a Comitology Regulation) or to revise the procedure so that it results in fewer no opinion cases. The latter approach can be seen in the Commission's 2017 proposal (see section 6.VI). However, as elaborated in the section devoted to that proposal, most no opinions would stay no opinions, the referral to the Appeal Committee remaining of limited 'added value'.

D. The European Parliament's *Droit de Regard*

Since the second comitology decision, the Parliament has been accorded a limited *droit de regard* for draft implementing acts.[285] Article 11 of the Comitology Regulation provides:

> Where a basic act is adopted under the ordinary legislative procedure, either the European Parliament or the Council may at any time indicate to the Commission that, in its view, a draft implementing act exceeds the implementing powers provided for in the basic act. In such a case, the Commission shall review the draft implementing act, taking account of the positions expressed, and shall inform the European Parliament and the Council whether it intends to maintain, amend or withdraw the draft implementing act.

This *droit de regard*, which originally was only envisaged for the Parliament, has therefore been extended to the Council, but its material scope has remained the same as it only exists in relation to draft acts implementing legislative acts adopted pursuant to the ordinary legislative procedure. Both elements show that Article 11 is no expression of a general democratic control mechanism over executive rulemaking, but instead must be conceptualised narrowly as protecting the prerogatives of the original authors of the act that is being implemented. In this regard, it merits pointing out that, while the same logic could be applied *mutatis mutandis*, the *droit de regard* does not extend to the implementation of acts adopted pursuant to special legislative procedures.

[284] The latter concerned a proposed decision refusing a market authorisation for Orphacol. See also above, n 253.
[285] See Art 8 of the second comitology decision. The *droit de regard* arguably goes back to the 1994 *Modus Vivendi* between the Parliament, Council and Commission which inter alia provided: 'In the context of this *modus vivendi*, the Commission shall take account as far as possible of any comments by the European Parliament and shall keep it informed at every stage of the procedure of the action which it intends to take on them, so as to enable the Parliament to assume its own responsibilities in full knowledge of the facts'. See the *Modus Vivendi* of 20 December 1994, OJ [1996] C 102/1, point 6.

As also noted by Hofmann et al, Parliament 'made sparing use of resolutions objecting to the Commission's implementing measures under Article 8 [of the second comitology decision]'.[286] The six measures objected to as reported by Hofmann et al stand in stark contrast to the post-Lisbon scrutiny of the European Parliament when it adopted objections already more than 80 times.[287] At the moment of writing the ninth parliamentary term was just halfway through and the Parliament had already raised as many objections as in the whole eighth term.[288] Looking into these objections reveals that the Parliament's Environment, Public Health and Food Safety (ENVI) committee is in fact the only committee making use of the objection under Article 11 of the Comitology Regulation.[289] Substantively, the objections relate almost exclusively to highly sensitive files in food safety such as GMOs and plant protection products. Procedurally, objections are adopted by the plenary based on reasoned motions put forward by the responsible parliamentary committee.[290] Analogous to objections pursuant to Article 290 TFEU, the possibility for the Parliament to challenge the legality of an implementing act does not depend on it having exercised its *droit de regard*.[291]

Unlike under Article 290 TFEU, however, there is no period foreseen for the Parliament (and Council) to scrutinise the draft act. While the Parliament is automatically informed of any developments in the drafting of the act, there is therefore potentially little time between the decision on the final draft and its formal adoption (and typically its publication). The 2008 IIA between the Commission and Parliament on procedures for implementing the second comitology decision explicitly provided that the Parliament 'is to have a period of one month in which to do so, beginning on the date of receipt of the final draft of the implementing measures in the language versions submitted to the members of the committee concerned'.[292] While the 2008 IIA has not formally been abrogated, a similar provision is lacking in the post-Lisbon IIAs. Indeed, on several occasions it appears that the Parliament objected not to any draft implementing measure but to the implementing

[286] Hofmann, Rowe and Türk (n 86) 399.

[287] Even in 2014, Corona still noted that the European Parliament was 'not actually using its right of scrutiny'. See Corona, 'The Adoption of Secondary Legislation through Comitology in the EU' (2014) 100.

[288] Objections can be tracked through the Legislative Observatory (OEIL), if one looks for documents adopted pursuant to the provision in the European Parliament's Rules of Procedure putting into effect Art 11 of the Comitology Regulation (Rule 112(2) at the moment of writing).

[289] The only exception seems to be the objection by the Agriculture and Rural Development Committee against the draft subsequently adopted as Commission Implementing Directive 2017/1279 amending Annexes I to V to Council Directive 2000/29/EC on protective measures against the introduction into the Community of organisms harmful to plants or plant products and against their spread within the Community, OJ [2017] L 184/33. See European Parliament resolution of 15 December 2016 on the draft Commission implementing directive amending Annexes I to V to Council Directive 2000/29/EC on protective measures against the introduction into the Community of organisms harmful to plants or plant products and against their spread within the Community.

[290] See Rule 112(2) of the Parliament's Rules of Procedure.

[291] In *Eures network*, the Parliament had challenged a Commission implementing act that had not gone through comitology (see section 6.II.B) to begin with. In the second post-Lisbon case where Parliament challenged a Commission implementing act (see n 87), it is challenging one of several decisions partially authorising the use of chromium trioxide. The decision challenged (Commission Implementing Decision C(2020)8797) is thereby similar to another decision (Commission Implementing Decision C(2020) 8735) on which the Committee on the Environment, Public Health and Food Safety proposed to express an objection (see Motion for Resolution B9-0202/2020) but which was rejected in the plenary in its sitting of 10 July 2020.

[292] See the Interinstitutional agreement between the European Parliament and the Commission on procedures for implementing the second comitology decision, OJ [2008] C 143/1, point 9.

acts as adopted by the Commission.[293] The Parliament's International Trade Committee proposed to reintroduce the requirement to give the Parliament at least one month of scrutiny time at the occasion of the proposed revision of the Comitology Regulation (see section 6.VI),[294] but this was not picked up by the lead committee or the plenary.

Contrasting perhaps even more with the Parliament's post-Lisbon use of its *droit de regard* is that of the Council, which until recently did not once make use of its power to require the Commission to review a draft measure under Article 11 of the Comitology Regulation. The single occasion when the Council then used its *droit de regard* was in June 2021 to object to a measure designed to implement Regulation 2018/1724. The latter, in its relevant enabling clause, prescribes that the Commission had to adopt implementing measures by 12 June 2021,[295] but the Commission only communicated a draft measure to the Council 10 days before this deadline.[296] In its implementing measure it proposed to empower itself to adopt some of the further necessary implementing measure after the deadline of 12 June 2021,[297] which the Council found to exceed the competences originally conferred on the Commission.[298] This one-off case is interesting for a number of reasons. First, it shows how the Commission's 2017 proposal to reintroduce the Council in comitology procedures (see section 6.VI) was politically misguided. The Member States in Council do not need a *droit de regard* since it holds little added value compared to their involvement in the committees, and the Council as an EU institution has no self-standing interest in the implementation of EU law. In this one case, the scrutiny was lifted from the committee to the Council because the central point of contention was not a matter of policy or substance (for which the experts in the committee are best placed to exercise scrutiny) but an institutional problem of the Commission de facto granting implementing powers to itself to circumvent a deadline fixed by the legislator.

The involvement of the Council was therefore necessary, and this case contrasts with the many objections raised by the Parliament in the post-Lisbon era, which amount to an abuse of the procedure under Article 11. To recall, the purpose of the latter is not to voice disagreement with the EU policy (on GMOs, pesticides, etc) as implemented by the Commission as such, but to ensure the Commission respects the limits of the power conferred on it. Finally, the Council's objection in June 2021 is useful to further illustrate the issue of a possible auto-empowerment by the Commission. In contrast to what was discussed in section 6.II.A, the Commission had wanted to confer de facto implementing powers on itself (since it had not qualified the powers as implementing powers) without

[293] See European Parliament Resolution of 6 February 2014, OJ [2017] C 93/103; European Parliament Resolution of 16 December 2015, OJ [2017] C 399/71; European Parliament Resolution of 10 October 2019, OJ [2021] C 202/2; European Parliament Resolution of 26 November 2020 on Commission Implementing Regulation (EU) 2020/1511; European Parliament Resolution of 11 March 2021 on Commission Implementing Regulation (EU) 2021/52; European Parliament Resolution of 10 June 2021 on Commission Implementing Regulation (EU) 2021/621.

[294] See the Opinion of the INTA Committee for the Committee on Legal Affairs on the proposal for a regulation of the European Parliament and of the Council amending Regulation 182/2011, 19 March 2020, PE648.503v01-00, 7–8.

[295] See Art 14(9) of Regulation 2018/1724 of the European Parliament and the Council establishing a single digital gateway to provide access to information, to procedures and to assistance and problem-solving services, OJ [2018] L 295/1.

[296] Council of the EU, Decision to exercise the right of scrutiny, Council Doc 9289/21, 2.

[297] See Art 4(2) of the draft Implementing Regulation in Council Doc 9289/21 ADD 1.

[298] Council of the EU, Decision to exercise the right of scrutiny, Council Doc 9289/21, 3.

subjecting it to the procedure prescribed by the legislator, and this arguably because it could not adopt all the necessary implementing measures before the deadline prescribed by the legislator had lapsed. Such a construction is indeed problematic: implementing acts should be qualified as such for reasons of legal certainty and clarity; the Commission cannot, in principle, pretend to respect a deadline set by the legislator by adopting only a partial set of the necessary implementing measures; and if for some reason only a partial set of measures may be adopted, the remain set of implementing measures must of course be adopted pursuant to the enabling clause in the original legislative act. As a result, both conceptually and contextually this issue is entirely different from a delegated act conferring implementing powers on the Commission.

Since 2014 the Commission (again)[299] mentions the number of objections under the *droit de regard* in its annual comitology reports, but makes no mention of its own follow-up actions. Fortunately, for the objections adopted by the Parliament, the Commission's follow-up is easily retraceable through the Parliament's legislative observatory.[300]

Finally, the question whether the *droit de regard* should be upgraded to a veto right should probably be addressed. That would fit the idea expounded in section 5.IV.B in that the control regime (over executive rulemaking) should be conceived flexibly and that if such flexibility would be given to the co-legislators, there would also be less discussion on whether to grant a power under Article 290 TFEU or 291 TFEU. From a comparative perspective, there would indeed be a number of reasons to give the European Parliament a veto over implementing acts adopted by the Commission, where such a control mechanism does not typically characterise the legislative-executive relationship in national systems.

At the EU level, there is no stable parliamentary coalition supporting the executive as is typical for national parliamentary systems. Secondly, unlike national parliaments, the European Parliament cannot on its own introduce new legislation if it is unhappy with how existing legislation is applied, as is illustrated by the GMO authorisations. Thirdly, unlike national presidential systems, the EU executive does not have its own direct and independent democratic legitimacy. These three reasons could be invoked to argue that, in duly justified specific cases, the Parliament should be able to veto decisions implementing legislative acts adopted pursuant to the ordinary legislative procedure (or a special legislative procedure prescribing Parliamentary consent). Ultimately, however, it seems impossible to square such a veto with the text of Article 291 TFEU, which explicitly restricts the control to a Member State control. Instead, what the Parliament and Commission could do is to beef up the *droit de regard* in an IIA. However, a precondition for this would arguably be that the Parliament exercises its *droit de regard* more responsibly, restricting it to the actual cases in which the Commission disregards the limits to its implementing power rather than ceremonially exercising the *droit de regard* to voice its discontent with the legislation which the Parliament itself adopted as co-legislator.

[299] It is to be noted that the Commission mentioned the number of times the Parliament made use of its *droit de regard* until the 2005 annual comitology report but then stopped doing so. It started doing so again in 2014.

[300] On the database (available at oeil.secure.europarl.europa.eu/oeil/search/search.do?searchTab=y), the Parliament's objections may be found by looking for documents based on Rule 112(2) of the Parliament's Rules of Procedure (this is the current legal basis for exercising the droit de regard). For each objection, the document gateway will also link to the Commission's reply to the objection. For the Commission's reply to the Council objection an access for documents request had to be lodged.

Having looked at the functioning of the comitology system, the final section of this chapter will briefly address the remarkable initiative by the Commission, in 2017, to amend the Comitology Regulation, despite the fact that the system has been functioning rather smoothly since 2011.

VI. No Self-Love, the 2017 Proposal to Amend the Comitology Regulation

The Commission in 2017 submitted a proposal to amend the Comitology Regulation on four key points.[301] According to the Commission, the problems with authorising GMO products and active substances in biocides such as glyphosate, where the committees consistently fail to deliver an opinion, putting the political responsibility for the decision squarely with the Commission, required a targeted amendment of the Regulation. The Commission thus proposed to:

1. change how the qualified majority is calculated in the Appeal Committee by only taking into account votes for or against (ie Member States that are present but abstain are deemed not to have participated in the vote);
2. introduce a second appeal (following a first appeal to the Appeal Committee) whereby the Appeal Committee would be composed of representatives at ministerial level;
3. make the voting behaviour of the Member States in the Appeal Committee public;
4. provide the Commission with a possibility to ask a non-binding opinion from the Council in case the Appeal Committee cannot adopt an opinion.

While the Commission published its proposal on Valentine's Day, it shows limited love for itself and no love at all for the European Parliament. Before looking into the latter issue, it is useful to stress how all four targeted amendments would contribute to the Commission's overall aim of shifting political responsibility for controversial decisions away from itself and to the Member States. Indeed, by disregarding abstentions, it becomes easier to obtain an opinion. That the opinion may also be negative and thus prevent the Commission from authorising products or substances on which the risk assessor gave a positive opinion is worth highlighting: as noted in section 6.V.C most of the no opinion cases would remain no opinions if the abstentions are left out. This is so because there is typically a majority of Member States against the Commission draft, albeit that this simple majority does not attain the qualified majority threshold. Analysis of the publicly available voting sheets of the Appeal Committee uploaded on the comitology register shows that between 1 November 2014 (when the new Lisbon rules on the calculation of the QMV were applied) and March 2022,[302] there were 90 no opinions. Of these, 14 would have turned positive and three would have turned negative if the abstentions had been disregarded.[303] In the other 73 cases,

[301] See European Commission, COM (2017) 85 final.

[302] Account is only taken of the opinions adopted by the Appeal Committee under the Lisbon QMV for ease of comparison.

[303] For an example of a vote that would have turned positive, see the vote of 12/07/2017 on draft measure D050157/06. For an example of a vote that would have turned negative, see the vote of 31/03/2015 on draft measure D038594/04.

the no opinion would still remain a no opinion. Of course, we cannot just apply new voting rules to historic voting records, since the Member States would most probably have strategically changed their voting behaviour. However, forcing Member States to 'pick sides' might still result in a stalemate (if the abstentions are split evenly to votes in favour and votes against) or could result in more negative opinions (if abstaining Member States preponderantly move to voting against).

The Commission thus prioritised the possibility to hide behind the Member States above any policy preferences and ultimately its own institutional interest (since it could also result in more negative opinions in policy areas other than plant protection products and GMOs). Similarly, the second proposed change would force the Member States' representatives at the highest political level to assume political responsibility for controversial authorisation decisions. The third change would add transparency and would allow the Commission to pinpoint blame on individual Member States, preventing the latter from hiding their positions from citizens and civil society. Lastly, the fourth change, like the second, would allow the Commission to put the Member States' representatives at the highest level 'on the spot', making them assume political responsibility for the (non-)authorisation decisions.

While this *political* logic is clear and might be understandable, the Commission's proposal suffers from several legal flaws. Firstly, the Commission's proposal appears completely disproportionate in relation to the 'problem' it aims to address. One may rightly argue that there is no problem in the examination procedure itself to begin with, but simply a political unwillingness on the part of the Commission to take political responsibility. Even if one takes the Commission's analysis as a given and it is accepted that the no opinions in the Appeal Committee show a malfunctioning of the examination procedure, the proposal appears disproportionate, as in not necessary, since it would fundamentally alter the examination procedure not only for the politically sensitive authorisation procedures, but across the board.

Turning to the proposed changes themselves, the assessment is mixed. While it seems doubtful that the Commission's proposal is informed by a concern for the legitimacy of EU decision-making, its third proposed change would significantly strengthen throughput legitimacy of the Appeal Committee's functioning. That said, it is unclear why an amendment of the Regulation would be needed for this. The confidentiality requirement which prevents the Commission from making public the discussions and votes in both the committees and the Appeal Committee[304] is prescribed by the Rules of Procedures of the committees, not by the Regulation. Those rules of procedure can even be changed more easily (through simple majority) than the Comitology Regulation.[305] The input legitimacy of the first proposed change is already more debatable. By excluding absent and abstaining members from those considered 'present', and because of the quorum of 50 per cent, in the most extreme scenario, eight small-to-medium-sized Member States would be enough to carry a QMV in the appeal committee. However, the remaining two proposed changes appear completely constitutionally flawed since the Commission essentially proposes to further undo the Lisbon reform of comitology. This would add to the

[304] See Reply of the European Commission to the Ombudsman's Recommendation in case 2142/2018/TE regarding the European Commission's refusal to grant access to Member State positions on a guidance document concerning the risk assessment of pesticides on bees, 11 November 2019.

[305] See Arts 3(7) and 9 of Regulation 182/2011.

other instances of constitutional modifications identified previously. Through its second proposed change, the Commission de facto would reintroduce the Council in comitology procedures[306] while its fourth proposed change would do so *de iure*. These proposals go against one of the most fundamental innovations brought by the Lisbon, that is excising the Council from comitology, putting it on an equal footing with the Parliament and recognising that the control under Article 291 TFEU follows the logic of the EU's executive federalism. By proposing to reintroduce the Council in the examination procedure, the Commission ignores the constitutional premises underlying Article 291 TFEU. The amendments would reintroduce the pre-Lisbon unequal treatment between the two branches of the EU legislator which made the Parliament contest the comitology system for decades.[307]

At the time the proposal was published, its political and legal sagacity was already being questioned,[308] not least because it is unclear why Member States in Council would agree to the Commission's blame-shifting ploy and because the proposal completely ignores the Parliament (which under Article 291(3) TFEU has to agree to the amendments; see section 2.III.B). It should furthermore be noted that convening the Appeal Committee at ministerial level is in any event already possible under the current framework, since the Appeal Committee meets 'at the appropriate level' (see section 6.V.B.iii). In practice, however, the Appeal Committee has never convened at ministerial level, which again explains why the Commission's proposal (on this issue) was politically misguided.

Indeed, more than five years after the proposal's submission to the co-legislators it is still stuck in first reading. The deadlock in negotiations between the Council and Parliament could have been a reason for the new Commission to withdraw the 2017 proposal. Instead, following its review of the pending legislative procedures, the Von der Leyen Commission identified the revision of the Comitology Regulation as a priority, under the heading of 'A New Push for European Democracy'.[309]

In 2018 the Council Legal Service adopted a negative opinion on the proposal,[310] and the Bulgarian presidency's progress report of the same year noted that a (vast) majority of the Member States was opposed to the Commission's changes. The only exception was the proposed change to increase transparency on which 'many delegations conveyed positive views', without there being sufficient support to move forward.[311] A coalition of 15 Member States even rejected the Commission's endeavour to amend the Regulation, further pointing to the Commission's own positive assessment of the functioning of the Regulation in its 2016 review.[312]

[306] The de facto reintroduction of the Council here only relates to the personalities who would attend the Appeal Committee. Importantly, the body would still be chaired by the Commission and formally be a comitology committee.

[307] Also noting this, and equally critical, see Volpato (n 31) 186–87.

[308] See Daniel Guéguen, 'Comitology reform: Doing, undoing and redoing is still hard work' *Euractiv*, 16/02/2017; Merijn Chamon, 'The Proposed Amendment of the Comitology Regulation – A Constitutional Perspective' *Verfassungsblog.de*, 19 February 2017.

[309] See European Commission, Commission Work Programme 2020, COM(2020) 37 final, 9; Annexes to the Commission Work Programme 2020, COM(2020) 37 final, 24.

[310] See Council Legal Service, Opinion on Questions related to the procedure of the appeal committee, Council Doc 6752/18.

[311] See Council of the EU, Presidency Progress Report, Council Doc 10127/18, 3–5.

[312] ibid 5.

While the Council Legal Service's opinion is only partially public, it is clear that it rightly takes issue with the requirement that the Regulation would prescribe that it should be ministers sitting on the Appeal Committee, with the new voting calculation and with the referral to the Council (which would violate the institutional balance).[313] In contrast to the legal service's analysis, however, it is far from clear how the amendment, giving the Commission a power to determine the appropriate level in which the Appeal Committee meets, would 'unnecessarily encroach … upon the national political structures of the Member States protected by Article 4(2) TEU and [would] go … against the principle of sincere cooperation enshrined in Article 4(3) TEU'.[314] After all, it would be the EU legislator (and not the Commission) creating and prescribing this possibility and national political structures would not be affected as such. Prescribing that it should be the ministers meeting at EU level leaves national political structures intact, unlike other EU legislation that eg requires Member States to establish independent agencies,[315] and is more akin to Article 16(2) TEU and, at the level of secondary law, existing EU legislation which prescribes the requirements which persons sent by the Member States to sit in EU bodies, must meet.[316]

While the Commission in its proposal had tried to convince the co-legislators to keep the amendment *targeted*,[317] it was unsurprising to see that the Parliament seized the proposal to revisit the Comitology Regulation more broadly. After all, following the controversy over the approval of glyphosate as an active substance under the plant protection products Regulation,[318] the European Parliament set up a Special Committee on the Union's authorisation procedure for pesticides.[319] Following the Special Committee's enquiries, the Parliament adopted a resolution in which it inter alia:

> Stressed the need to ensure political accountability for the adoption of implementing acts using the comitology procedure; expresses its concern at the lack of transparency in the PAFF Committee; calls on the Commission and the Member States to increase the overall transparency of the procedures, including by providing detailed minutes on the comitology discussions and the respective positions, in particular by explaining and justifying the PAFF Committee's decisions and by making public the votes of the Member States.[320]

[313] As Jacqué points out, the proposal to convene an Appeal Committee consisting of representatives at ministerial level does not so much breach the principle of sincere cooperation but rather that of institutional balance given the Treaty of Lisbon's clear intent to exclude the Council from comitology. See Jean-Paul Jacqué, 'Chronique Droit institutionnel de l'Union européenne' (2019) *RTDE* 673–92.

[314] See Council Doc 6752/18 17.

[315] On this, see Malte Kröger, *Unabhängigkeitsregime im europäischen Verwaltungsverbund* (Baden-Baden, Nomos, 2020).

[316] For instance, the regulations establishing EU agencies that prescribe the qualities of members of the Management Board of the agency concerned. Generally, see Common Approach on EU Decentralised Agencies, Council Doc 11450/12, para 10.

[317] In the explanatory memorandum to its proposal, it inter alia noted that the no opinion issue should be addressed 'through a few very targeted changes' and that its proposal 'contains four targeted amendments', providing 'for targeted and limited amendments'.

[318] See Regulation 1107/2009 of the European Parliament and of the Council concerning the placing of plant protection products on the market, OJ [2009] L 309/1.

[319] European Parliament Decision of 6 February 2018 on setting up a special committee on the Union's authorisation procedure for pesticides, its responsibilities, numerical strength and term of office, OJ [2018] C463/73.

[320] European Parliament resolution of 16 January 2019 on the Union's authorisation procedure for pesticides, OJ [2020] C411/48 [79].

The Parliament was therefore bound to seize this opportunity to present the Commission and Council with its wish list.

Still, only at the end of 2020 did the Parliament adopt its opinion in first reading,[321] approving the draft by Rapporteur Szájer.[322] The Parliament largely followed the Commission but further proposed three types of amendments: a first set was aimed at safeguarding its (perceived) prerogatives; a second at further promoting transparency; and a third at introducing further changes to the examination procedure as such.

In terms of safeguarding its prerogatives, the Parliament wants: (i) the Commission to also ask Parliament's position, whenever an opinion would be requested from the Council for its opinion; (ii) both co-legislators to have immediate access to the information listed in Article 10(1) of the Regulation; and (iii) a beefed-up *droit de regard* under Article 11 that allows objections not just if the Commission exceeds its implementing powers but also if the implementing act conflicts with the basic act's objectives and that foresees that the Parliament (and Council) can ask the Commission to submit a legislative proposal if it believes certain implementing powers need to be reviewed.[323]

In terms of greater transparency, the Parliament proposes that Member States' voting behaviour is made public generally and not just in the Appeal Committee; that Member States should justify their votes and that also these justifications should be made public; that for decisions in particularly sensitive areas, those justifications have to be case-specific detailed reasons; that the comitology register be improved especially with regards to its search functionality; that drafts of the texts to be decided upon and documents to be discussed should also be uploaded on the comitology register; and finally that also the persons attending committee meetings should be listed in the comitology register.

Dealing specifically with the examination procedure, the Parliament proposes that the second referral to the appeal committee (sitting at ministerial level) could also be decided upon by a simple majority of the Member States and not just by the committee chair; and that the pre-Lisbon regulatory procedure should effectively be reintroduced for the authorisation of products or substances where the basic act concerns the protection of the health or safety of humans, animals or plants in the sense that authorisations could only be granted, following a positive opinion in the Appeal Committee.

Since negotiations on this file seem to be stuck and the prospects of a tangible amendment of the Regulation appear slim to non-existent, the Parliament's proposed amendments will not be fully discussed here. Suffice to note that the Parliament has not seized the opportunity to put forward a more fundamental review of comitology. This is clear when looking

[321] Amendments adopted by the European Parliament on 17 December 2020 on the proposal for a regulation of the European Parliament and of the Council amending Regulation (EU) No 182/2011 laying down the rules and general principles concerning mechanisms for control by Member States of the Commission's exercise of implementing powers, P9_TA(2020)0364.

[322] For a more elaborate discussion, including the positions taken by the other parliamentary committees, see Rafał Mańko, Reform of the Comitology Regulation, EPRS Briefing, PE 689.360, March 2021.

[323] The proposed formal strengthening of the *droit de regard* is arguably only a confirmation: when the Commission adopts an implementing act that goes against the objectives of the parent act, it arguably also exceeds the implementing powers conferred by the parent act and Arts 225 and 241 TFEU cover the possibility for Parliament and Council to ask the Commission to submit legislative proposals (reviewing the conferral of implementing powers).

at its suggestions for Article 11. Prescribing that the *droit de regard* may be exercised also when the Commission acts against a basic act's objectives seems superfluous since under the *Eures network* test (see section 6.II.B), the Commission must already comply with the basic act's essential general aims. Further, Parliament may already, at its discretion, call on the Commission to submit legislative proposals.[324] That said, while the Commission probably has no issues with the first set of changes, the danger posed by Parliament's proposed changes to the examination procedure are clear: even if limited to only a certain type of parent acts (those concerning the protection of the health or safety of humans, animals or plants) the amendment resulting in a no opinion equating a negative opinion is not something the Commission would want to see written in the Regulation.

[324] See Art 225 TFEU.

7

The Practice and Politics of Delegated Legislation

The literature on comitology in political science and EU studies is rich and varied,[1] but since the focus of this enquiry has so far been mainly legal, that literature has featured little in previous chapters. In this final chapter, however, the enquiry will take a rational choice (institutionalist) perspective, engaging with the work of Brandsma and Blom-Hansen.

I. Strategies in Delegating Powers

In their work on post-Lisbon executive rulemaking at the EU level, they surmise that the guiding principle of both Parliament and Council, when they negotiate control structures in the legislative process, will be to obtain the most efficient control position.[2] Concretely this meant that Brandsma and Blom-Hansen expected the Council to push for implementing acts and the Parliament to prefer delegated acts.

In their empirical analysis of post-Lisbon legislative negotiations, Brandsma and Blom-Hansen identify four strategies which the Parliament and Council can pursue in their negotiations.[3] First, both institutions can 'split the difference', accepting the substance of the Commission's proposal, and dividing the enabling clauses between implementing and delegated powers. Second, they can agree to remove enabling clauses, simply refusing to allow the Commission to exercise delegated or implementing powers. A third strategy is to rewrite enabling clauses, making vague provisions more concrete and thus limiting the discretion of the Commission when it exercises implementing or delegated powers. Finally, the fourth strategy identified by Brandsma and Blom-Hansen is using 'side payments', trading off concessions on the control regime with concessions on policy questions. They subsequently find evidence of these strategies, focusing on one legislative file for each strategy,

[1] Among many, see Christian Joerges and Jurgen Neyer, 'Transforming strategic interaction into deliberative problem-solving: European comitology in the foodstuffs sector' (1997) 4 *Journal of European Public Policy* 609–625; Renaud Dehousse, 'Comitology: who watches the watchmen?' (2003) 10 *Journal of European Public Policy* 798–813; Adrienne Héritier, Catherine Moury, Carina Bischoff and Carl Fredrik Bergström (eds), *Changing Rules of Delegation: A Contest for Power in Comitology* (Oxford, OUP, 2013); Nikoleta Yordanova and Asya Zhelyazkova, 'Legislative Control over Executive Law-making: Delegation of Quasi-legislative Powers to the European Commission' (2020) 58 *Journal of Common Market Studies* 345–64; Ana Mar Fernández Pasarín, Renaud Dehousse and Joan Pere Plaza, 'Comitology: the strength of dissent' (2021) 43 *Journal of European Integration* 311–30.

[2] Gijs Jan Brandsma and Jens Blom-Hansen, *Controlling the EU executive? The politics of delegation in the European Union* (Oxford, OUP, 2017) 86.

[3] ibid 92–93.

concluding that their case studies 'confirmed that the European Parliament and the Council have opposing delegation preferences, but that in practice they often find ways to settle their differences. This suggests that daily delegation conflicts do not normally block the legislative process'.[4] While undoubtedly true, that conclusion requires further refinement in light of the analysis conducted in the preceding chapters and in light of the empirical analysis developed below.

A. Adding Levels and Strategies to the Model

First of all, the four strategies identified by Brandsma and Blom-Hansen are not the only ones available to the Parliament and Council. As both authors would agree, they are not mutually exclusive, nor are they complete alternatives to each other. In the negotiations on one legislative file, different strategies can thus be combined by the Parliament and Council. At the same time, the different strategies are not completely interchangeable since they play at different levels.

At the first level, the Parliament and Council will need to decide *whether* they want to initially include enabling clauses in their legislation. This is where strategy 2 of Brandsma and Blom-Hansen plays out. Yet, if and when Parliament and Council agree to include enabling clauses, the subsequent choice is not whether these clauses will be delegated or implementing clauses as suggested by strategy 1 identified by Brandsma and Blom-Hansen.

Instead, and as follows from the analysis in the preceding chapters, the Council and Parliament have a choice at the second level as to *which* executive actor to empower. This choice, which can be played out as strategy 1*a*, also goes beyond a binary choice between the Commission and the Member States, which was the focus of Franchino's study on delegation.[5] Indeed, there is a plethora of executive actors which the legislators can choose from: the Member States (under Article 291(1) TFEU), the Commission (under Article 290 or 291(2) TFEU), the Council (under Article 291(2) TFEU) and EU agencies are only the main, but by no means only, options. Only when the Commission is selected from among these executive actors can strategy 1 be subsequently played out.

Only at a third level, once the Parliament and Council have decided to include enabling clauses in their legislation and have settled for an executive actor, will strategy 3 identified by Brandsma and Blom-Hansen play out whereby the discretion left to the executive actor (whichever one is picked) may be broadened or reduced.

Finally, at all these three levels, strategy 4 may be played out between Parliament and Council: the institutional choices on whether to include enabling clauses, which executive actor to empower, through which procedure and the degree to which discretion is left can all be traded off against substantive policy concessions.

A graphic representation of these levels and strategies can be found at the end of this chapter, refined in light of the case studies devoted to the General Data Protection Regulation (GDPR) and Data Governance Act (DGA).

[4] ibid 115.
[5] Fabio Franchino, *The powers of the Union: Delegation in the EU* (Cambridge, CUP, 2007) 17.

B. Testing the Model

In what follows, those two legislative files will be analysed, comparing the original Commission proposal, the trilogue documents, and the legislative act ultimately adopted to identify further evidence of the strategies identified by Brandsma and Blom-Hansen. In contrast to the analysis of these authors, the files in the present case studies were not randomly selected. Instead, the first legislative file, resulting in the GDPR[6] was selected for analysis precisely because it was politically sensitive and because of the institutional disagreements on the delegation of executive powers. The second file, the DGA, was less politically sensitive, or at least less politicised, but has been selected because, unlike the GDPR, it was proposed, negotiated and concluded after the 2019 IIA, the purpose of which was to facilitate negotiations (see section 4.III.D) and, like the GDPR, comes within the field of data protection, facilitating a comparison.

The choice of these files evidently means that the case studies do not necessarily present a representative picture for legislative negotiations generally, but they can still be expected to reveal the typical preferences and strategies employed by the co-legislators when deciding on enabling clauses for delegated legislation. Most files relied on for the analysis were retrieved from the public domain: Commission proposals and final legislative acts are published on the EU's Eur-Lex website. Trilogue documents are made available by the European Parliament, especially since the 2018 *De Capitani* ruling of the General Court,[7] on its website.[8] Further documents of the institutions, setting out their positions, were retrieved from those institutions' register of documents or by submitting access to documents requests.

II. General Data Protection Regulation

The General Data Protection Regulation (GDPR) which was adopted in 2016 and entered into force on 25 May 2018, hardly needs an introduction. The GDPR governs how personal data of natural persons may be processed, regardless of the purpose of the processing,[9] in order to protect these persons' right to protection of personal data laid down in Article 8 of the Charter of Fundamental Rights.

A. The Commission's Proposal

When the Commission presented its much-anticipated proposal in 2012, it was heavily scrutinised. In the proposal,[10] the Commission included 25 enabling clauses which would

[6] Regulation 2016/679 of the European Parliament and of the Council on the protection of natural persons with regard to the processing of personal data and on the free movement of such data, OJ [2016] L 119/1.

[7] See Case T-540/15, *De Capitani v Parliament*, ECLI:EU:T:2018:167.

[8] On the Parliament's Public Register of Documents page (www.europarl.europa.eu/RegistreWeb), the 'Advanced Search' option can be used to look up specific legislative procedure according to their procedure number (eg 2012/0011(COD) for the GDPR). This will present all the documents related to this procedure whereby the trilogue documents are indicated with 'NEGO_CT'.

[9] The only exceptions to this are laid down in Art 2(2) GDPR.

[10] See European Commission, Proposal for a Regulation on the protection of individuals with regard to the processing of personal data and on the free movement of such data, COM(2012) 11 final.

have granted it an implementing power all of which prescribed the examination procedure. The proposal further contained 26 enabling clauses which would have granted a delegated power to the Commission pursuant to Article 290 TFEU. This high number of enabling clauses must be understood against the backdrop of the Commission's frustration with the implementation of the GDPR's predecessor, the 1995 Data Protection Directive.[11] Already in 2003, in its first report on the implementation of the Directive, the Commission noted problematic divergences in how the Member States had both transposed and were implementing the Directive. Some of the divergences resulted from the very nature of the instrument itself, the Commission recalling that 'the ambition of a Directive is approximation and not complete uniformity and that, in order to respect the subsidiarity principle, the process of approximation should not go further than is necessary';[12] whereas other divergences simply resulted from wrong transposition.[13] In 2010, these problems of divergent national legislation and/or implementation had not improved.[14] The Commission's solution was then twofold: first, by changing the instrument from a directive to a regulation, the transposition problem would be neutralised; and second, the inclusion of several empowerments to adopt delegated or implementing acts would allow the Commission to intervene and refine or uniformly implement legislation where it noticed divergent application of the regulation in the national legal orders.

While a total of more than 50 enabling clauses is exceptional, it should be noted that the Commission's approach was informed by a fully coherent conceptualisation of Articles 290 and 291 TFEU that was furthermore largely in line with the spirit of these Articles. Without discussing each of the proposed enabling clauses in detail, it is useful to highlight that the Commission consistently proposed to provide itself with an implementing power to address the *how* question of implementation (see section 4.III.D.iii), eg to adopt a series of standard forms in which certain information needed to be acquired or presented by data controllers or processors;[15] and standard formats and procedures for performing certain actions.[16] These enabling clauses relate to ancillary matters and do not elaborate on the substantive obligations or rights which the GDPR lays down. They therefore squarely come under the notion of measure that ensure that the GDPR is implemented under uniform conditions. However, for some other implementing enabling clauses this was different.

Indeed, there were further clauses in which the Commission proposed to further detail the substantive requirements imposed by the GDPR through implementing acts. For instance, the Commission proposed that it would be empowered to: (i) adopt technical standards allowing data controllers to meet the requirements of data protection by design and default;[17] (ii) adopt detailed requirements fleshing out the requirement related to the secure processing of personal data, *in particular* (see below) on preventing unauthorised

[11] Directive 95/46 of the European Parliament and of the Council on the protection of individuals with regard to the processing of personal data and on the free movement of such data, OJ [1995] L 281/31.

[12] European Commission, First report on the implementation of the Data Protection Directive, COM(2003) 265 final, 11.

[13] ibid.

[14] See European Commission, A comprehensive approach on personal data protection in the European Union, COM(2010) 609 final.

[15] See Arts 8(4), 12(6), 14(8), 15(4), 28(6), 34(9) of the Commission's proposal.

[16] See Arts 18(3), 31(6), 32(6), 33(7), 34(9), 43(4), 55(10), 62(1)c of the Commission's proposal.

[17] See Art 23(4) of the Commission's proposal.

access and disclosure and ensuring that the lawfulness of processing could be verified;[18] (iii) adopt (non-)adequacy decisions on the legal data protection rules of a third country;[19] and (iv) declare generally valid or adopt standard data protection clauses which controllers or processors must rely on to show that appropriate safeguards are in place when data is transferred;[20] and to decide on the correct application of the GDPR in case of disagreements between the different data supervisors.[21]

These enabling clauses are a mixed bag in terms of the types of measures that could be adopted, but mostly relate to the *what* question of implementation (see section 4.III.D.iii). Most could indeed be qualified as facilitating the uniform implementation of the GDPR, similarly to purely procedural clauses, as discussed above. This goes for the technical standards on data protection by design and default, in so far as they would facilitate controllers and processors in how to meet the substantive requirements under Article 25 of the GDPR. The (non-)adequacy decisions and decisions adopting or sanctioning standard data protection clauses are arguably even absolutely necessary to ensure uniform implementation since in absence thereof data transfers to third countries could be treated differently depending on the EU Member State from which the data is being transferred. Finally, the power to settle disputes through a consistency mechanism allowing the imposition of one application of the GDPR on the different authorities responsible for its implementation also amounts to ensuring the implementation under uniform conditions and is akin to the exceptional power at issue in *Short-selling*: in case of disagreement or ineffective implementation by the national authorities, an exceptional EU power is activated whereby the default implementing actor is set aside and an EU actor takes its place.[22] In these cases, the higher threshold for entrusting such an implementing power to an EU actor (see section 6.I) would indeed seem to be met.

The one remaining enabling clause is the trickiest to assess and to classify as either providing for implementation or supplementation is the provision allowing the Commission to specify the requirements imposed by Article 30 (final Article 32 of the GDPR) on security of processing. The enabling clause would have allowed the Commission to concretise the specific requirements that flow, eg from the general requirement to 'prevent any unauthorized access to personal data'. In addition, the Commission proposed an open list of general requirements which it could flesh out, since it explicitly envisaged this power to apply *in particular* to three general requirements.[23] This clause would arguably have allowed the Commission to work out substantive requirements on any issues coming under the notion of 'appropriate level of security'. However, for these measures (unlike the measures

[18] See Art 30(4) of the Commission's proposal.

[19] See Arts 41(3), 41(5) of the Commission's proposal.

[20] See Arts 42(2)b and 62(1)b of the Commission's proposal.

[21] See Art 62(1)a of the Commission's proposal.

[22] The only decision so far adopted pursuant to this power confirms this. See EPDB Decision 01/2020 on the dispute arisen on the draft decision of the Irish Supervisory Authority regarding Twitter International Company under Art 65(1)(a) GDPR. As will be elaborated below, in the end the legislators decided against empowering the Commission and instead conferred this power on the EPDB. This effectively transposed the *Short-selling* solution: instead of empowering the Commission to implement EU law under uniform conditions, an EU agency was empowered. While the EPDB is not considered an EU decentralised agency by the EU institutions it does meet the definition of a decentralised agency advanced in Merijn Chamon, *EU Agencies: Legal and Political Limits to the Transformation of the EU Administration* (Oxford, OUP, 2016) 10.

[23] See on this, Opinion of AG Cruz Villalón in Case C-364/13, *International Stem Cell*, ECLI:EU:C:2014:2104 [33].

on (non-)adequacy decisions and on settling disputes) it is not immediately clear how they would not supplement the GDPR since the latter's normative density would be increased. In any event, this last enabling clause brings the present discussion neatly to the delegated enabling clauses envisaged in the Commission's proposal. Here again the Commission was largely consistent in in its approach: whenever certain criteria, conditions, requirements or additional rules needed to be fleshed out, it proposed to do so through delegated acts.[24] This consistency in opting for delegated acts makes the single provision in which it envisaged allowing itself to adopt further requirements through implementing acts all the more remarkable.

One notable critique on the Commission's proposal came from the European Data Protection Supervisor (EDPS). In his Opinion he noted that:

> In many provisions of the proposed Regulation the Commission is empowered to adopt delegated or implementing acts. Although such further acts might contribute to the uniform application of the Regulation and allow for further alignment of national practice based on experience gained after the Regulation applies, the EDPS, … has reservations as to an approach that builds so heavily on these acts. Furthermore, the EDPS doubts whether all issues are addressed at the correct legislative level.[25]

Elaborating on this, the EDPS identified three main problems: (i) a risk of the GDPR being inoperative (or being applied in a non-uniform manner) at the time when it should start to apply in those cases where the Commission failed to adopt the delegated and implementing acts that are critical for the GDPR's application; (ii) some enabling clauses granting a delegated power to the Commission possibly touching on the essential elements of the GDPR; and (iii) the Commission's choice between delegated and implementing acts which was not always properly justified. On this latter point, however, the EPDS did not seem too concerned with the provision which was flagged above as problematic, and succumbed as well to the control fallacy since he noted that his reservations to a number of implementing enabling clauses were informed by the Parliament's more limited role in adopting implementing acts. As noted above, however, the nature of an executive power (delegated or implementing) does not depend on the control regime, but rather vice versa. While the EDPS's critical opinion was communicated to the Commission before the latter formally published its proposal, the opinion did not make the Commission revisit its proposal. The opinion did, however, very much inspire the work of the legislators (notably the Parliament) when they started to negotiate on the file.

B. The Trilogues and the Resulting Text of the GDPR

Even before the trialogues started, it was clear that Parliament and Council did not accept the extensive delegation of executive powers which the Commission had envisaged in its original proposal and the GDPR negotiations are therefore mostly dominated by

[24] See Arts 6(5), 8(3), 9(3), 12(5), 14(7), 15(3), 17(9), 20(5), 22(4), 23(3), 26(5), 30(3), 31(5), 32(5), 33(6), 34(8), 35(11), 37(2), 39(2), 43(3), 44(7), 79(7), 81(3), 82(3), 83(3) of the Commission's proposal.

[25] EPDS, Opinion of 7 March 2012 on the data protection reform package, 12 at para 71.

strategy 2 identified by Brandsma and Blom-Hansen. The Parliament's rapporteur for instance noted that:

> The Regulation needs to be comprehensive also in terms of providing legal certainty. The extensive use of delegated and implementing acts runs counter to this goal. Therefore the rapporteur proposes the deletion of a number of provisions conferring on the Commission the power to adopt delegated acts. However, in order to provide legal certainty where possible, the rapporteur has replaced several acts with more detailed wording in the Regulation .... In other instances, the rapporteur proposes to entrust the European Data Protection Board (EDPB) with the task of further specifying the criteria and requirements of a particular provision instead granting the Commission the power to adopt a delegated act.[26]

Limiting the number of empowerments was thus a key issue for the Parliament negotiators.[27] The pre-trilogue discussions in the Council are perhaps even more revealing. The empowerments to the Commission were one of the three horizontal issues which were immediately discussed at political level in the Council.[28] The Cypriot presidency asked the delegations in the Council working group to comment on every delegated and implementing enabling clauses, informing the presidency of whether they agree or disagree with the inclusion of the enabling clause and, in case of disagreement, whether the delegations preferred a simple deletion of the enabling clause, imposing more conditions on the Commission or pursue other options.[29] A very clear consensus emerged from the delegations' replies that there was no support for the Commission's ambition to give it a pivotal role in fleshing out the GDPR.[30] Instead, and turning to strategy 1*a*, the Presidency's compromise text for a general approach[31] substituted a lot of the empowerments for provisions prescribing guidance would be adopted by the European Data Protection Board (EPDB).[32] Faced with this opposition, the Commission quickly signaled that it could be flexible on this point,[33] paving the way for a significant reduction of the extent of its delegated and implementing powers in the ultimate legislative act.

The 10 trilogues[34] held on the GDPR were intense and rather fast, being organised in just around half a year between June and December 2015. More importantly, they fundamentally altered the Commission's proposal in terms of delegated and implementing enabling clauses. Simply comparing the number of enabling clauses in the final GDPR makes this clear: of the 25 proposed implementing enabling clauses, 10 were withheld and one clause was added. Of the 26 proposed delegated enabling clauses, only one survived and a

[26] See the explanatory statement to the report on the proposal for a regulation of the European Parliament and of the Council on the protection of individuals with regard to the processing of personal data and on the free movement of such data, A7-0402/2013. The Commission took note of Parliament's preference to elaborate the GDPR's provisions in more detail, see GRI fiche of 29 November 2012, SI(2012) 551, 5.

[27] See GRI fiche of 1 March 2013, SI(2013) 77/2, 5.

[28] See GRI fiche of 29 November 2012, SI(2012) 551, 4.

[29] Council of the European Union, Questionnaire on administrative burdens, delegated/implementing acts and flexibility in data protection rules for the public sector, Council Doc 12918/1/12 REV 1.

[30] See Council of the European Union, Replies to questionnaire on delegated/implementing acts, Council Doc 14609/5/12 REV 5.

[31] See Council of the European Union, Preparation of a general approach, Council Doc 9788/15.

[32] See GRI fiche of 5 June 2015, SI(2015) 234, 6.

[33] See GRI fiche of 29 November 2012, SI(2012) 551, 5.

[34] See GRI fiche of 14 January 2016, SI(2016) 2/2, 4.

second was maintained but modified. The positions taken in the trilogues suggest that the Parliament and Council mainly relied on strategies 2, 1*a* and 3, in that order of importance.

First, as the simple quantitative comparison of enabling clauses in the proposal and final text reveals, Parliament and Council mainly agreed on strategy 2, throwing out the majority of these clauses, thus opting not to allow for any executive rulemaking to begin with. It probably will not surprise that one of the victims of this exercise was the clause allowing the Commission to specify requirements on security of processing (which was qualified as legally dubious above). However, the actual difference is not as big as a first glance at the numbers ((25+26) in the proposal and (11+2) in the final text) suggest. This is because notably the Parliament heavily relied on strategy 1*a*: in respect of a lot of the proposed delegated enabling clauses, the Parliament proposed to empower the EPDB rather than the Commission.[35] The Parliament was also successful in its endeavour as Article 70(1) of the GDPR makes clear: a lot of the delegated enabling clauses that the co-legislators deleted were recycled by giving soft law powers to the EPDB. In addition, the power to settle disputes under the consistency mechanism which the Commission had claimed for itself was also vested in the EPDB pursuant to Article 65(1) GDPR,[36] although the Commission tried to limit the conferral of binding empowerments to the EDPB by invoking the *Meroni* and *Short-selling* doctrines (see section 6.IV.A.i).[37] The Parliament would have even gone further and entrusted the EPDB with the power to adopt the arrangements for exchange of information between authorities (Article 67 GDPR),[38] and the format and procedures for mutual assistance between authorities (Article 61(9) GDPR)[39] but in the GDPR these are still adopted by the Commission. Finally on strategy 1*a* (choosing the delegate authority) it is important to stress how much it is interlinked with strategy 2 (throwing out enabling clauses) because of the EU's constitutionally engrained executive federalism: when the co-legislators delete enabling clauses empowering the Commission, the legislative act's silence on who adopts further implementing measures means that by default the Member States are empowered (again) pursuant to Article 291(1) TFEU.

In contrast, in the absence of any specific legislative provision, Member States cannot supplement an EU legislative act (see section 4.III). It is therefore interesting to point out that the GDPR also contains such an enabling clause. Where the Commission had proposed that it would adopt delegated acts to specify the safeguards in place for processing data of employees by employers, the Council insisted this would be left (entirely) to the Member States.[40] In an interplay between strategy 1 (splitting the difference) and 1*a* (choosing the delegate authority), the Parliament also proposed to delete an implementing enabling clause

[35] In relation to the enabling clauses in Arts 8(3), 9(3), 30(3), 31(5), 32(5), 44(7), 55(10), see the five-column document of 15 September 2015, 78, 87; the six-column document for the trilogues of 29 and 30 September 2015, 132, 142, 149; the draft compromise text of 15 June 2015, 56; the six-column document of 15 October 2015, 189.

[36] This is also in line with the EDPS opinion, which criticised this element of the Commission's proposal since it would have undermined the independence of data protection authorities. See EPDS, Opinion on the data protection reform package, 40–41 at paras 248–255. Although conferring this power on the Commission is wholly consistent with Art 291 TFEU it would indeed have clashed with the Court's well-developed case law on the importance of the independence of national data protection supervisor as their independence would arguably be threatened if a disagreement between themselves could result in the Commission stepping in and settling the disagreement for them. For the Court's case law, see Case C-288/12, *Commission v Hungary*, ECLI:EU:C:2014:237 [47]–[56].

[37] See GRI fiche of 30 June 2014, SI(2014) 269/2, 5; GRI fiche of 2 December 2014, SI(2014) 463/2, 10.

[38] See six-column document of 15 October 2015, 277.

[39] See ibid, 189.

[40] Compare Art 82(3) of the proposal with Art 88 GDPR and the five-column document of 10 November 2015, 110.

on the definition of the format and procedures on exchange of information for binding corporate rules under current Article 47 GDPR and to allow the Commission to adopt these pursuant to delegated acts,[41] but the final text of the GDPR entrusts this instead to the EPDB (in Article 70(1)i).

Turning to strategy 1, given how most of the enabling clauses were simply deleted (under strategy 2) or recycled to empower the EPDB (under strategy 1*a*), there was limited scope left to change delegated enabling clauses into implementing ones, and vice versa. However, where there was scope left for a strategy of 'splitting the difference' it must be noted that Parliament remained completely empty-handed as virtually all its suggestions were rejected, whereas all the suggestions of the Council made it to the final text. Based on the two institutions' starting positions,[42] going in the trilogues, it is interesting to see that the Parliament retained (or introduced) 10 delegated empowerments[43] and one implementing empowerment. In contrast, the Council suggested 11 implementing empowerments and only one delegated empowerment. The final text of the GDPR contains exactly these 11 implementing powers proposed by the Council, the one delegated empowerment on which Parliament and Council agreed in their opening positions and one delegated empowerment which was suggested by the Parliament, but which only made it to the final text in (significantly) watered down form.[44]

Finally, evidence of strategy 3 being played out can also be retraced in the trilogue documents. Here again the Parliament unsuccessfully tried to procedurally reduce the discretion of the Commission by prescribing, for a series of clauses, that it could only adopt measures after having obtained the opinion of the EPDB.[45]

C. Assessment

Although the GDPR only applies as of May 2018, national judges have already referred, at the moment of writing, an astounding number of 37 requests for preliminary rulings on the proper interpretation of the GDPR's provisions to the Court of Justice. This might incidentally indicate that the legislator has not been sufficiently detailed in its prescriptions and could vindicate the Commission's original case for more delegated empowerments to itself. The unwillingness to empower the Commission may thus result in a greater role for the Court to clarify the meaning and scope of the GDPR's provisions. That said, the

[41] See the draft compromise text of 30 June 2015, 49.

[42] See Council of the European Union, four-column document setting out the Parliament's first reading opinion and the Council's General Approach, Council Doc 10391/15.

[43] According to Parliament sanctioning codes of conduct (Art 40(9) GDPR) and adopting (non-)adequacy decisions ought to have been done through delegated acts, but on this point the Parliament failed as the GDPR prescribes implementing acts for these measures. That adequacy decisions would be adopted by implementing acts was a fundamental point for the Commission (on which it was backed by the Council). See GRI fiche of 10 July 2015, SI(2015) 171/2, 5.

[44] The latter empowerment is Art 12(8) of the GDPR. Compare it to Art 13a(5) of the Parliament's Position in Council Doc 10391/15, 289.

[45] See the five-column document of 14 September 2015, 84; the six-column document of 29 and 30 September 2015, 226, 242; the six-column document of 15 October 2015, 274ff; the five-column document of 10 November 2015, 110.

empowerments that made it to the final text, apart from the hard law empowerments of the EDPB,[46] still largely reflect the letter and spirit of Articles 290 and 291 TFEU.

Starting with the two delegated powers foreseen in the GDPR, the possibility to specify further requirements to be taken into account for data protection certification mechanisms aims at increasing the normative density of the GDPR framework, and should therefore indeed be pursued through delegated acts.[47] The other delegated empowerment in the GDPR is less sound however. 'Determining the information to be presented by icons and the procedures for providing standardised icons'[48] arguably touches on the question of *how* the GDPR should be implemented rather and does not increase the normative density of the GDPR by prescribing further obligations. Unsurprisingly, the latter empowerment found its origin in a suggestion by the Parliament.[49]

Turning to the implementing powers, all put forward by the Council (see above), most relate to the question *how* the GDPR ought to be uniformly implemented,[50] while decisions such as the adequacy decisions relate to the *what* question,[51] whereby there is a necessity in the strict sense that there should only be one (uniform) way of implementing EU legislation. The only problematic implementing power in this regard is to be found in Article 40(9) of the GDPR, which provides that the codes of conduct agreed on by private actors may be endorsed by the Commission following which they will have general validity in the entire EU. The simple act of endorsing and making legally valid pre-existing measures could be said to relate to the *what* question of implementation, but given that the codes of conduct may further flesh out the GDPR, they could also increase the normative density of the GDPR, which would mean that the delegated act is more appropriate.

The case of the GDPR further shows how the empowerment of EU agencies is a functional equivalent to empowering the European Commission (under either Articles 290 or 291 TFEU), but also how there might be overlap between both types of empowerment. At a first level this goes for soft law adopted by both agencies and the Commission. The Commission indeed noted, in vain, before the trilogues that there is little need for explicit provisions on the EDPB's guidance, since the Commission is generally empowered under Article 292 TFEU to adopt any necessary interpretative guidance.[52] This raises the question what happens when soft law adopted by the Commission would conflict with soft law adopted by an EU agency.

At another level, Article 70(1)(e) of the GDPR empowering the EPDB to issue guidelines, recommendation and best practices in relation to *any* question related to the application of the GDPR may also be exercised in relation to issues for which the GDPR has also given a specific empowerment to the Commission to adopted implementing (or delegated) acts. In some cases this also results in conflicting requirements imposed on practitioners. For instance, in its Guidelines 05/2021, the EPDB explicitly notes that a transfer of personal

[46] As discussed in section 6.IV.A, the possibility of empowering EU agencies, while endorsed by the Court in *Short-selling*, fits difficultly with the framework defined in Arts 290 and 291 TFEU.

[47] See Art 43(8) of the GDPR.

[48] See Art 12(8) of the GDPR.

[49] See above, n 44.

[50] See Arts 28(7), 43(9), 47(3), 61(9) and 67. These empowerments inter alia relate to the arrangements, formats and procedures for the exchange of information, standardised formats to provide information, standard clauses, etc.

[51] See Art 45(3) and (5) of the GDPR. In addition to the adequacy decisions, see Art 46(2)c and d.

[52] See GRI fiche of 5 June 2015, SI(2015) 234, 7.

data to a third country qualifies as such irrespective of whether the importer (in the third country) already is subject to the GDPR.[53] This concretely means that for such a transfer, appropriate safeguards would need to be in place (as far as there is no adequacy decision and no derogation applies), such as adequate contractual clauses. The Commission's implementing decision 2021/914 on standard contractual clauses on the other hand provides that they may only be used for transfers for which the processing by the importer does not already come within the scope of the GDPR.[54] These conflicting interpretations are a direct result of the legislator pursuing strategy 1*a* and (preferring to) empower(ing) the EDPB rather than the Commission.

The preceding section already reflected on the strategies identified by Brandsma and Blom-Hansen being pursued in the negotiations on the GDPR and these reflections will be further developed after the assessment of the DGA, below.

III. Data Governance Act

In 2020 the Commission presented its proposal for a Regulation on European data governance,[55] aimed at facilitating the use of certain protected (but not necessarily personal) data held by public authorities. Looking into the fate of this more modest legislative initiative is interesting in light of the discussion of the GDPR above, since the proposal was presented after the major clarifications by the Court of Justice of the Lisbon framework and after the institutions agreed on the different IIAs discussed above (notably the 2019 IIA). At the same time, and while it is a much less high-profile case, it also constitutes a part of the EU data *acquis* which facilitates comparisons.

A. The Commission's Proposal

In its proposal, the Commission only envisaged three empowerments. In terms of implementing powers, the Commission proposed it be granted the power to adopt: (i) adequacy decisions; and (ii) uniform consents forms through the advisory procedure.[56] In terms of delegated powers the Commission envisaged further defining the conditions which need to be met before certain sensitive data can be transferred to third countries.[57] Much like its GDPR proposal, these proposed empowerments were in line with the letter and spirit of Articles 290–291 TFEU: adequacy decisions need to be uniform for the entire

[53] See EDPB, Guidelines 05/2021 on the Interplay between the application of Art 3 and the provisions on international transfers as per Chapter V of the GDPR, 18 November 2021, point 7.

[54] See recital 7 of the preamble to Commission Implementing Decision 2021/914 on standard contractual clauses for the transfer of personal data to third countries pursuant to Regulation (EU) 2016/679 of the European Parliament and of the Council, OJ [2021] L 199/31.

[55] See European Commission, Proposal for a Regulation of the European Parliament and of the Council on European data governance, COM(2020) 767 final.

[56] See Arts 5(9) and 22(1) of the Commission's proposal for a Regulation on European data governance, COM(2020) 767 final.

[57] See Art 5(11) of the Commission's proposal for a Regulation on European data governance, COM(2020) 767 final.

EU (see section 7.II.A) and consent forms are typical instruments setting out *how* legislative prescriptions must or may be complied with. The conditions to be met before data can be transferred adds substantive obligations for which it is more appropriate to adopt delegated acts.

B. The Trilogues and the Resulting Text of the Data Governance Act

As could be expected, Parliament and Council did not leave these three empowerments unamended but, in addition and remarkably, they also introduced further delegated empowerments to the benefit of both the Commission and a further body to be established by the DGA.

Starting first with the three originally envisaged empowerments, Parliament and Council immediately agreed on allowing the Commission to adopt uniform consent forms through the advisory procedure, but pursued strategy 3 by adding a pre-comitology phase (see section 6.V.B.i) by giving an advisory role to the European Data Innovation Board (EDIB) and the EDPB.[58]

Regarding the adequacy decisions and the conditions for transfer, Parliament and Council succumbed (again) to the control fallacy by proposing to change the nature of the empowerment to that which gives them the greatest control. As in the GDPR trilogues, the Parliament proposed that adequacy decisions be adopted through delegated acts.[59] Conversely, the Council proposed that the conditions for transfers would be defined through implementing acts adopted pursuant to the examination procedure,[60] which incidentally meant that the Council did not want the legislative act to delegate (in the sense of Article 290 TFEU) any powers to the Commission.

Where Parliament and Council did not suggest to change the nature of the executive power to be granted, they still proposed amendments that would reduce the Commission's discretion, relying on strategy 3. Procedurally, for the Council that meant prescribing the examination, rather than advisory, procedure for adequacy decisions and a pre-comitology phase involving the EDIB.[61] For the Parliament this meant a requirement for the Commission to adopt the delegated acts following a recommendation from the EDPB.[62] Substantively, it resulted in further circumscribing the power granted. For instance, Parliament and Council quickly agreed that when the Commission defines the conditions for data transfers to third countries, this should be limited to those cases where the data 'transfer to third countries may put at risk Union policy objectives, such as safety and public health, or may lead to the risk of re-identification of non-personal, anonymised data'.[63]

Turning to the additional empowerments advanced by Parliament and Council, both institutions proposed an implementing power to lay down standard contractual

[58] See proposed Art 22(1) in three-column document of 19 October 2021 NEGO_CT(2021)10769(2021-10-19)_XL, 150 line 268.
[59] See ibid, Art 5(9), 92–93 line 121.
[60] See ibid, Art 5(11), 96–97 line 129.
[61] See ibid, Art 5(10b), 95–96 line 128c.
[62] See ibid, Art 5(11), 96 line 129.
[63] See ibid, Art 5(11), 96 line 129.

clauses, albeit that Parliament suggested to prescribe the advisory procedure[64] while the Council preferred the examination procedure and a pre-comitology advice by the EDIB.[65] Parliament also proposed an implementing power (exercised pursuant to the advisory procedure) to adopt common logos for data intermediation and data altruism.[66] Finally, the Council proposed that the Commission would adopt 'codes of conduct' for data altruism organisations. These would be adopted in close cooperation with data altruism organisations and relevant stakeholders in the form of implementing acts following the examination procedure.[67] The Council's suggestion to use implementing acts for these codes of conduct was problematic, since substantively they would clearly build on the content of the legislative act in the sense of the 2019 IIA[68] and would constitute new substantive prescriptions, which suggest they should be adopted in the form of delegated acts.[69] In addition, the Commission rightly noted that qualifying these measures as 'codes of conduct' would suggest they are merely non-binding and it also pushed back against the attempts to introduce 'pre-comitology phases' in the drafting of the codes of conduct and the consent forms.[70]

Lastly, the Parliament also pursued strategy 1*a* by suggesting additional empowerments which would not grant further powers to the Commission. Instead, the Parliament proposed to significantly expand the tasks of the EDIB, explicitly prescribing that the EDIB would advise and assist the Commission when the latter drafts guidelines, but also that the EDIB would propose guidelines itself.[71] Unsurprisingly, the Commission also pushed back against this idea.[72]

Before the final trilogue, one of the outstanding disagreements related to the question of delegated legislation.[73] For the contractual clauses both institutions agreed that an implementing act should be used, but they disagreed on the procedure (advisory or examination) to be used.[74] Parliament further wanted delegated acts (rather than implementing acts like the Council) for the adequacy decisions, for defining the conditions for transfers to third countries and for the codes of conduct.[75] In the end, seven enabling clauses made it to the final text,[76] and the four outstanding issues were solved by splitting the difference. Under the

[64] See ibid, Art 5(10a), 94–95 line 128a.

[65] See ibid, Arts 5(10a) and 27(1)(ea), 95 line 128b and 164 line 300d.

[66] See ibid, Arts 9(2b) and 15(3), 110–11 line 160b and 131 line 213.

[67] See ibid, Art 19a, 144–45 lines 253a–253g.

[68] See the 2019 IIA, criterion C.

[69] The Commission also preferred delegated acts for inter alia these reasons; see GRI fiche of 26 November 2021, SI(2021) 352/2, 5.

[70] See GRI fiche of 15 October 2021, SI(2021) 289/2, 7.

[71] See Art 27(1) in three-column document of 19 October 2021 NEGO_CT(2021)10769(2021-10-19)_XL, 158–64 lines 295–300d.

[72] See GRI fiche of 15 October 2021, SI(2021) 289/2, 9.

[73] See GRI fiche of 26 November 2021, SI(2021) 352/2, 3.

[74] See Council of the European Union, Preparation for the trilogue, Council Doc. 14021/21, 4–5.

[75] Interestingly, the Commission seemed willing to compromise on the use of implementing acts to define the conditions for transfers to third countries. See GRI fiche of 15 October 2021, SI(2021) 289/2, 9. By contrast, it opposed the reliance on delegated acts for adequacy decisions, also citing this would be inconsistent with the GDPR where implementing acts are used for adequacy decisions. See GRI fiche of 26 November 2021, SI(2021) 352/2, 4.

[76] Regulation 2022/868 of the European Parliament and of the Council on European Data Governance, OJ [2022] L 152/1.

DGA, the Commission is granted an implementing power to adopt: (i) model contractual clauses;[77] (ii) adequacy decisions;[78] and (iii) common (recognisable) logos for data intermediation services and data altruism organisations,[79] and uniform consent forms to facilitate the collection of data based on data altruism.[80] The DGA also grants two delegated powers to the Commission: the codes of conduct initially suggested by the Council will be adopted as a 'rulebook' in the form of delegated acts;[81] and the Commission may adopt delegated acts setting specific conditions for the transfer of certain sensitive data to third countries.[82] The Commission is thereby required to draft these implementing and delegated acts with the assistance of other bodies.[83]

C. Assessment

The three enabling clauses in the Commission's original proposal thus made it to the final text, and the Commission received a further four empowerments, whereby all empowerments properly reflect the distinction between implementing and delegated acts set out above: the clauses allowing the Commission to substantively increase the normative density of the legal framework (the conditions for transfers to third countries and the rulebook) foresee delegated acts; the clauses targeting the question of *how* implementation is to be done in a more uniform manner provide for implementing acts (model contractual clauses, common logos, consent forms), as do the clauses where by necessity there should only be one uniform way of implementing the DGA (adequacy decisions).

That the Commission thus received more delegated (in a generic sense) powers than it asked for is a bit of a conundrum from a rational choice perspective. After all, it is typically assumed that the Commission will try to maximise its powers and will strategically assess as to what would be acceptable for the co-legislators. That the Commission underestimated the Parliament and Council's willingness to delegate may then be the result of incomplete information on the preferences of the latter or could also have to do with the constraining factor of time. Compared to the GDPR, the DGA was quickly decided on and this may have to do with a sense of urgency of the EU legislator to be seen to be acting in the public interest.[84] When the EU institutions feel the need to be seen to be addressing public concerns, this might lower the political threshold for the co-legislator to delegate executive powers to the

[77] See Art 5(11), which prescribes the examination procedure.

[78] See Art 5(12), which prescribes the examination procedure.

[79] See Arts 11(9) and 17(2), which prescribe the advisory procedure.

[80] See Art 25(1), which prescribes the advisory procedure.

[81] See Art 22. The co-legislators thus followed the advice of the Commission to refer to the codes of conduct as a rulebook to reflect the binding nature of the implementing acts. See GRI fiche of 26 November 2021, SI(2021) 352/2, 4.

[82] See Art 5(13).

[83] Pursuant to Art 27, the EDIB does 'advise and assist' the Commission in drafting the consent form and it 'advises and assists' the Commission when the latter evaluates whether model contractual clauses or adequacy decisions are needed. Conversely, pursuant to Art 19a(2), the rulebook must be prepared 'in close cooperation with data altruism organisations and relevant stakeholders'.

[84] It should be noted that also the GDPR only gained serious momentum after the revelations of Edward Snowden created a need to be seen to act; see Elena Sánchez Nicolás, '2013: Snowden was "wake-up call" for GDPR', *EUObserver*, 29/12/2020.

Commission to decide on regulatory issues rather than having to take the time to come to an agreement on these issues themselves in the legislative act.

The pattern followed by these enabling clauses is also largely the same as that for similar, parallel, clauses in the GDPR. This makes it all the more remarkable that before agreeing on the final text, both Parliament and Council, seemingly informed by the control fallacy, proposed to change the nature of some of these empowerments. On this, the trilogue documents even show that on several clauses there was complete agreement on the actual provision, the only issue left to decide on in the end being the form (delegated or implementing) the power would be granted in.[85]

While it has been noted above that the non-binding criteria of the 2019 IIA may not yet have produced their full effect because of the different context in which legislative negotiations had to be conducted during the pandemic (see section 4.III.E), it thus seems that they at least do not immediately have any preventive effect. Indeed, Parliament and Council still put forward changes to the nature of enabling clauses with the aim to maximise their control. Of course, this may largely boil down to strategic posturing, the Parliament/Council putting forward changes with the intention to use it in a trade-off with other issues. Disregarding the 2019 IIA when defining the initial position *before* trilogues are entered into may, then, paradoxically, be conducive to reaching a compromise if it facilitates the exchange of tradeoffs *during* trilogues.

That said, some attempts by the co-legislators to increase their control over executive rulemaking cannot simply be reduced to them succumbing to the control fallacy, and instead point to a latent tension (or, some might say, anomaly) in the (primary) legislative framework. The issue of the adequacy decisions seems a case in point. Legally, they are unilateral decisions on the part of the EU, following an assessment of the relevant regulatory framework and practices of third countries. In reality, however, as the 2022 privacy shield decision with the USA shows,[86] they often come about as a result of a series of bilateral negotiations with such third countries, in which case they would de facto boil down to international agreements. Yet, where the European Parliament has the formal power of consent (and thus veto) for (most) international agreements concluded by the EU by virtue of Article 218(6)(a) TFEU, it at the most has a *droit de regard* (see section 6.V.D) when an adequacy decision is adopted in the form of an implementing act. This issue becomes even more focused when the regulatory area to which the adequacy decision relates has important fundamental rights implications such as in the area of the transfer of (personal) data. And while the Court has accepted that unilateral decisions may constitute (part of) an international agreement for which Parliamentary consent is required,[87] that solution cannot be applied when an implementing act is prescribed as the instrument in which that unilateral decision is contained. Cases likes this do show that it could be useful to rethink the control regime which applies to implementing acts (see section 6.V.D).

[85] This was so for the rule book, the conditions for transfers to third countries and the adequacy decisions. See, in the column on the draft agreement in the four-column document of 30 November 2021 NEGO_CT(2021)10769(2021-11-30)_XL, recital 16, 19 and 35 and Art 19a(1) at lines 26, 29, 46 and 253b.

[86] See Vincent Manancourt, 'EU, US strike preliminary deal to unlock transatlantic data flows', *Politico.eu*, 25 March 2022. At the time of writing the agreement between the EU and US was still to be translated into a new Commission decision.

[87] Joined Cases C-103/12 and C-165/12, *Parliament & Commission v. Council*, ECLI:EU:C:2014:2400.

IV. Refining the Model

In light of the two case studies, the refined model presented above (section 7.I.A) may be further refined and can be graphically represented as in Figure 7.1. First of all, it may be noted that based on the GDPR and DGA, the evidence for the first strategy identified by Brandsma and Blom-Hansen is limited since it was completely absent from the GDPR. While it was applied in the DGA, this was only so after Parliament and Council disregarded the 2019 IIA by prescribing their politically preferred control regime (rather than the legally correct one). Indeed, it is not clear whether 'splitting the difference' may be sustainable as a strategy since it largely comes down to a generalisation of the control fallacy: assuming rational actors that want to maximise their preferences, 'splitting the difference' would see a Parliament that always suggests delegated acts and the Council always suggesting implementing empowerments for every enabling clause, regardless whether this makes legally sense or not. The institution not pursuing that approach would otherwise lose out in the zero-sum approach of 'splitting the difference'. Yet, as the cases studies above show, while Parliament and Council indeed at times succumb to the control fallacy, it is not as dominant as a 'splitting the difference' strategy would suggest.

The case studies have also shown that strategy 2, ie whether enabling clauses should at all be included, should be refined with a sub-strategy whereby a choice may be made between giving soft law or hard law executive powers. While the Commission contests this (see section 4.III.D), it is at least part of the co-legislators practice to consider 'soft law enabling clauses' in the form of implementing measures as a genuine option. This of course broadens the range of options open to the legislator and may facilitate the choice to delegate (in a generic sense) powers. While undoubtedly more problematic from the perspective of legal certainty and accountability, the co-legislators may be more willing to delegate powers if the delegate authority can only adopt soft law measures.

This brings us to strategy 1*a*, where especially the case of the GDPR (but also the DGA) has shown how the Commission and EU agencies (or other EU bodies and offices) as well as Member State authorities may be alternative delegate authorities from the perspective of the co-legislators. Finally, a further refinement may be applied to strategy 3 since 'restricting the delegate authority's discretion' can be done in two main ways. Discretion may not just be curtailed by including more detailed substantive conditions, but also by tinkering with the procedure prescribed to adopt executive acts. This not only within the framework of what is explicitly foreseen in the comitology regulation (eg the choice between the advisory or examination procedure), but for instance also by prescribing pre-comitology consultation requirements.

One potentially important aspect which largely remains a blind spot of the model relates to the factor of time. The case studies above may suggest that lack of (perceived) time might also determine patterns of delegation whereby the co-legislators are willing to delegate more powers than they would otherwise (in 'normal' conditions) be willing to.[88]

[88] Noting that 'decision makers under time constraint have been shown to switch to simpler strategies', see Lisa Ordóñez, Lehman Benson and Andrea Pittarello, 'Time-pressure Perception and Decision Making' in Gideon Keren and George Wu, *The Wiley Blackwell Handbook of Judgment and Decision Making* (Chichester, Wiley, 2016) 521.

Figure 7.1 Delegation strategies

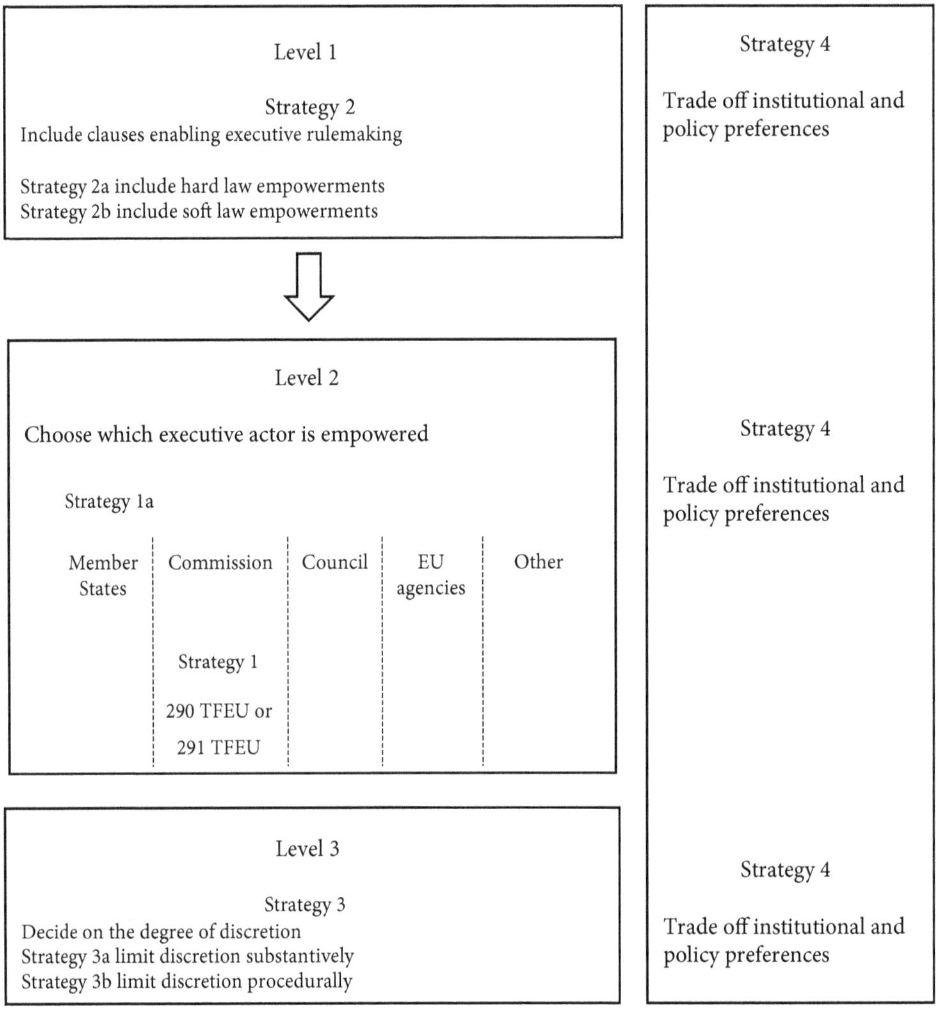

8

Conclusion

I. Looking Back …

The preceding chapters have focused, in some detail, on the many issues that have been raised by the Lisbon Treaty's shaking-up of the institutional balance in executive rulemaking and delegated legislation. The challenge for this conclusion is to take a step back and try to present a coherent picture of both the interstitial change that has occurred post-Lisbon, as well as to find whether such change has been to the benefit or detriment of the European Parliament, and whether it amounts to a constitutional modification of the institutional balance. Clearly there is no immediate direct link between these last two questions: interstitial change may or may not be in the European Parliament's favour, but the fact that it is not is not in itself proof of there being constitutional modification. Conversely, there may also be infringements of the institutional balance that benefit the European Parliament. Typically, however, and since the Lisbon Treaty in general strengthened the Parliament's position, deviations from the Lisbon institutional balance will tend to be at the Parliament's expense.

The main finding of this enquiry is that the post-Lisbon institutional practice and jurisprudence has meant that the Lisbon reform has been deradicalised since the relations between the institutions in the area of executive rulemaking have been redefined to resemble the pre-Lisbon status quo. The EU institutions have exploited much of the textual ambiguity of the Lisbon Treaty to develop a post-Lisbon framework that goes against the spirit of the Lisbon reform and that on a number of points undermines the institutional balance.

The institutional balance has thus been altered since Articles 290 and 291 TFEU require a certain distinction between both types of acts which has been reduced to a bare textual minimum by the Court in *Biocides* and *Visa reciprocity* as well as by the political institutions in the 2019 non-binding criteria. The lack of a sufficient distinction further translates into the standard applied to executive powers under Article 291 TFEU, which a fortiori (because of the delegation carve-out) should be different from the pre-Lisbon standard applicable under Article 202 EC, but which has remained the same following *Eures network*. The reason for this alteration is clearly political: the spheres of normative activity governed by Articles 290 and 291 TFEU have not been clarified by the political institutions precisely because the control regimes applicable to both have been (interpreted as being) set in stone. Both control regimes are defined horizontally, one in an act of organic law (Article 291 TFEU), one in primary law itself (Article 290 TFEU). The latter textually and teleologically allows for different control mechanisms, but has been interpreted as exhaustively defining the control mechanisms available to the co-legislators. To compensate for this rigidity on the control side, the primordial issue of *which* executive power is being controlled has been blurred. The choice regarding which power is being delegated is thus informed by the institutions' preferred control regime, instead of adapting the control regime to the requirements which a specific delegated power poses. This has been referred to as the 'control fallacy' in this enquiry and it has resulted in protracted disagreements on the form (delegated or implementing) which an executive power should take.

Of course, reversing this logic back to the end intended by the Treaties (ie requiring the institutions to first determine which power they are delegating and letting the control regime depend on the type of power that is delegated) would not itself be a panacea for facilitating legislative decision-making. To put it bluntly: Parliament and Council might no longer bicker over which power they are delegating, but if the control regime of Article 290 TFEU is flexible (as suggested in section 5.IV.B), the discussion would shift to the type of ad hoc control mechanisms which may be imposed on the Commission when a delegated power is being granted. Still, this would be constitutionally sounder, and a greater variety of control mechanisms would obviate the political 'urge' of imposing ongoing control mechanisms which interfere with the autonomy of the Commission. From this perspective, confirming that Article 290(2) TFEU lays down a non-exhaustive list of control mechanisms does not mean that the Lisbon split is undone, and neither would it give *carte blanche* to the legislators to impose any and all kinds of control mechanisms. Instead, it would uphold the Lisbon split by giving the legislators the necessary discretion in crafting the control mechanisms appropriate for a given delegation while staying within the institutional balance.

A further (potential) alteration of the institutional balance, even if these instances cannot be said to constitute regressions into the pre-Lisbon status quo, result from the Court's findings in *Short-selling* and *Spain v Council*. While Articles 290 and 291 TFEU could have been interpreted as constituting a coherent and exhaustive framework for delegated legislation, capturing all executive rulemaking outside the autonomous executive powers resulting directly from the Treaties, that has not been the interpretation settled upon. In *Spain v Council* the Court could have ruled that decisions which the Member States could not adopt themselves by necessity come under Article 291(2) TFEU, but it did not. In *Short-selling* it was unrealistic for the Court to rule that no implementing powers may ever be granted to EU agencies, but it could realistically have prescribed an objective factors test or set a clearer threshold that the legislator must respect when it wishes to empower an agency rather than the default authority (ie the Commission). These constitutional modifications are, in the first place, at the expense of the Commission. Conferring implementing powers on the Commission (rather than on an agency) now seems to depend on the goodwill of the legislator. Conversely, by carving out the enforcement of EU law against Member States from Article 291 TFEU, there is no immediate legal reason to consider the Commission the default authority for this normative activity. Indirectly this weakens the Parliament's position as well since the Parliament has the greatest institutionalised control over the Commission.

Focusing on Article 291 TFEU, the EU institutions have again returned to the pre-Lisbon status quo: the conferral of implementing powers is (still) not determined by objective factors, allowing the legislators to claim that the decision *whether* to confer implementing powers comes within their discretion. Further, the implementation by the Council under Article 291(2) TFEU has not been subjected to an objective factors test and neither has it become more exceptional, since the Court in *National Iranian Oil Company* and *Hungary v Parliament & Council* accepted and applied the pre-Lisbon standard. Two key textual differences between Articles 202 EC and 291 TFEU have therefore been ignored and remain dead letter. As noted above, this has been at the expense of the Commission, but it also has indirect consequences for the Parliament since none of the alternative actors that may implement EU law are subject to the institutionalised control applicable to the Commission.

Georgiev predicted that 'it is unlikely that the ECJ will interfere in a significant way in order to reduce the uncertainties [in the Lisbon reform]'[1] and the above cases confirm that prediction.[2] More generally, the Court on many occasions let an opportunity slip to transpose its 'objective factors' test as it had done in *SBC*. Thus, no objective factors which are amenable to judicial review need to be adduced to show that uniform conditions in implementation are required; or that the Council needs to be exceptionally empowered; or that an EU agency needs to be exceptionally empowered; or that a delegated rather than an implementing power (or vice versa) is at issue; etc. Clearly, the lack of such 'objective factors' standards does not itself undermine the institutional balance, but introducing them would have allowed to Court to consolidate the rationalisation of the Lisbon reform. Expecting this from the Court of Justice has been criticised as taking 'a rather optative notion of the role of the Court in constitutional litigation'.[3] This may be a valid critique, depending on which role the reader believes the Court ought to play. Still, proposing that the Court sets out an 'objective factors' test for these questions would not result in judicial overreach. The Court can posit such a test and decide a case without definitively and exhaustively settling what those objective factors can (or cannot) be. This leaves room for initiative to the political institutions to agree on what those specific objective factors could be. In addition, as even the legal basis test shows, an 'objective factors' test does not equate with rigidity or judicial micromanagement.[4] Instead, it primarily contributes to a constitutionalist ethos by requiring authority to justify its choices, relying on a vocabulary and grammar which we recognise as conferring legitimacy on those choices.

Turning specifically to the European Parliament, the present enquiry would not go as far as claiming it has simply lost the implementation game. Still, the three factors identified by Christiansen and Dobbels to shed light on the Parliament's position in the post-Lisbon constitutional framework do indeed hold. These factors are: (i) resources; (ii) politicization; and (iii) Parliament's interaction with the intergovernmental bargaining in the Council.[5] The first two, interlinked, factors in particular seem to explain why the Parliament, so far, has not exploited the potential of the Lisbon Treaty, in addition to the Court's conservative reading of the Lisbon Treaty (over which the Parliament of course has little to no control). Even if the Parliament has invested extra resources to upgrade its capacity to scrutinise delegated legislation, time remains a scarce resource and

[1] Vihar Georgiev, 'Too much executive power? Delegated law-making and comitology in perspective' (2013) 20 *Journal of European Public Policy* 544.

[2] With the exception of *Spain v Council*, where the Court arguably interfered by creating an uncertainty.

[3] Kieran Bradley, 'Delegation of Powers in the European Union – Political Problems, Legal Solutions?' in Carl Fredrik Bergström and Dominique Ritleng (eds), *Rulemaking by the European Commission – The New System for Delegation of Powers* (Oxford, OUP, 2016) 60.

[4] On some occasions, even the choice of legal basis test is 'not determined by objective factors but by the subjective will of the Council' with which the Court does not interfere. See Merijn Chamon, 'Op-Ed: The Court's Opinion in Avis 1/19 regarding the Istanbul Convention', *EU Law Live*, 12 October 2021.

[5] Thomas Christiansen and Mathias Dobbels, 'Comitology and delegated acts after Lisbon: How the European Parliament lost the implementation game' (2012) 16 *European Integration Online Papers*, Art 13, 5.

substantive policy issues (rather than the form a delegated empowerment is granted in) are the prime target for politicisation. Both issues combined means that ordinarily, MEPs do not prioritise the institutional prerogatives of the Parliament, or at least not above the policy considerations of a given file. The only time where they seem to do so is when there are no substantive policy issues to focus on, eg when the Comitology Regulation is amended or when IIAs are negotiated. Because of this, the discretion which the Court left to the legislator to choose between empowering the Commission under Article 290 TFEU or 291 TFEU, and which formally benefits both co-legislators equally, is arguably more advantageous for the Council.

Conversely, the objective factors test in *SBC* works more to the advantage of the Parliament since it exclusively reserves an area to (typically) the ordinary legislative procedure. Apart from this case, however, the Court's post-Lisbon case law has not further advanced the Parliament's institutional position. While, from the Parliament's perspective, this may be politically regrettable, the Court's case law is not necessarily legally unsound. For instance, the Court's conservative reading of the formal legislative sphere (ie when is an act *legislative* in nature) and its refusal to read a hierarchy between legislative legal bases and autonomous executive legal bases may be deplored by Parliament, but cannot be criticised on legal grounds. The Court's findings in these cases are a rather faithful reading of the Treaty text itself, and any criticism should thus be directed at the Treaty authors. The same goes for the Court's finding in *Hungary and Slovakia v Council* that an autonomous executive act may create exceptions to legislative acts. As noted above, the legally more questionable rulings which also politically disadvantage the Parliament are the Court's refusal to fundamentally revise the implementation notion in *Eures Network* and its refusal to establish institutional balance safeguards in *Short-selling*.

Still, none of this detracts from the fact that the Lisbon Treaty's potential of further parliamentarisation is still there. While some doors have been closed through post-Lisbon case law and inter-institutional convention, the 'implementation game' is a continuous one and is played with every new policy initiative or legislative act being negotiated. Each time, choices will have to be made on how policy will be developed and given effect, each time giving an opportunity for the Parliament to ensure greater parliamentary control over executive rulemaking or delegated legislation.

II. … to Move Forward

In light of the previous section, it need not surprise that the suggestions presented in this final section will not call for any major Treaty revision. Indeed, the premise of the present enquiry has been that, in theory, the Lisbon Treaty's most fundamental reform in executive rulemaking, ie splitting delegated acts from implementing acts, was constitutionally sound, and this premise arguably still stands. In the longer term, both the legal bases foreseeing in special legislative procedures as well as in autonomous executive powers should ideally prescribe the ordinary legislative procedure (or simply taken out of primary law and be transferred to secondary legislation), but these do not pose fundamentally pressing issues. The same applies to delegated legislation adopted by EU agencies following *Short-selling*. While it is an anomaly that this possibility is not foreseen in primary law, and ideally

Article 291 TFEU should foresee that EU agencies may implement EU law,[6] this again is not an immediately pressing issue, since agencification is largely kept in check through political convention.[7]

As a result, it would also not seem appropriate to simply undo the Lisbon split in primary law. This would not solve the issue of protracted negotiations in trilogues, since undoing the Lisbon split would require the reintroduction of a procedure resembling the PRAC, in the comitology regulation. Discussions in trilogues would then simply become protracted on the issue of which of the different comitology procedures to prescribe. Alternatively, one could argue that the Lisbon split should be redrawn and that delegated acts should be restricted to amendments only.[8] However, that would not nullify the risk of protracted negotiations either because it would result in the Parliament insisting that 'implementing' measures be fixed in annexes to legislative acts.[9] In addition, it would result in a step back in the process of EU primary law parliamentarising the EU's functioning.

Instead, the Lisbon split should be kept intact and the political institutions should continue to build on the 2016 and 2019 IIAs. Without revisiting the Court's post-Lisbon clarifications to date, it should be clear that there is ample potential for the Court to take a less deferential approach to executive rulemaking and delegated legislation. This means that an objective factors test would be prescribed for those issues where post-Lisbon jurisprudence still leaves room for such a test. Conversely, even if it is accepted that the legislator has discretion in choosing between Articles 290 and 291 TFEU, which excludes an objective factors test from being applied, that discretion can still be restricted. After all, the Court also held that 'that discretion must be exercised in compliance with the conditions laid down in Articles 290 and 291 TFEU'.[10]

Much then depends on what those (implicit) conditions are. As noted above, the Court can (initially) leave it to the political institutions to flesh out those conditions, building on the existing IIAs. As discussed above, those IIAs allow the institutions to converge on the idea that executive acts that increase the normative density of the legislative framework should take the form of delegated acts, while ancillary provisions that facilitate putting into effect that framework should be provided for by implementing acts. The distinction between Articles 290 and 291 TFEU and the meaning of implementation should thereby also be integrated with the Court's established jurisprudence on the scope of normative activity left to Member States when they implement EU regulations. Focusing on Article 291(2) TFEU, the threshold to be reached to trigger an implementing power at EU level should thereby be lower for the question of *how* EU law should be implemented compared to the

[6] For proposals, see Miroslava Scholten, *Political Accountability of EU and US Independent Regulatory Agencies* (Leiden, Brill, 2014) 339–41; Merijn Chamon, *EU Agencies: Legal and Political Limits to the Transformation of the EU Administration* (Oxford, OUP, 2016), 376–81.

[7] Indeed, the political institutions have not seized the full potential of *Short-selling*; see Merijn Chamon and Nathan de Arriba-Sellier, 'FBF: On the Justiciability of Soft Law and Broadening the Discretion of EU Agencies' (2022) 18 *European Constitutional Law Review* (forthcoming).

[8] A precursor to this argument can be found with Kortenberg, who noted at the occasion of the revision of the first comitology decision that the equality between Council and Parliament proposed by the Commission only made sense for those cases in which comitology is resorted to amend legislation adopted under the co-decision procedure. Helmut Kortenberg, 'Comitologie: le retour' (1998) 34 *RTDE* 322.

[9] On the 'strategic' use of annexes, see point 4 of the 2019 IIA and section 4.III.D.i above.

[10] Case C-88/14, *Commission v Parliament and Council*, ECLI:EU:C:2015:499, [28].

threshold that needs to be reached if an EU actor is to decide on *what*, in a given situation, the result is that EU law prescribes. Both scenarios require EU intervention to be *necessary*, but in the first, 'necessary' may be understood as useful, while in the second, 'necessary' is to be understood as indispensable. As also noted above, having the EU institutions' minds converge on this may be facilitated by accepting that the different possible control mechanisms for delegated acts are not exhaustively defined by Article 290(2) TFEU.

Without having to fundamentally revise some of its post-Lisbon rulings, the Court still has leeway to further clarify issues such as the notion of implementation, restricting its overly generous *Eures network* test and more rigorously distinguishing essentiality and specificity, giving the latter an independent role. Admittedly, these are limited suggestions, but given the developments described and analysed in this study, they are already quite ambitious, since they depend on a change of heart at the Court. Until now, it has allowed the political institutions to exploit the ambiguity left in the Lisbon Treaty to have the legal framework governing delegated legislation develop in the direction of the pre-Lisbon status quo. One important aspect of this trend is the Member States' attempts to intergovernmentalise supranational decision-making. This intergovernmentalisation takes many forms, discussed throughout chapters five and six: agencification of the EU administration; unjustified recourse to Council implementation under Article 291(2) TFEU; the involvement of the European Council in the implementation of EU law; the introduction of a formal role for the Member States under Article 290 TFEU, etc. This creeping intergovernmentalisation is one specific, but important, way in which the Member States and Council have sought to reverse (some of the most supranational features of) the Lisbon Treaty's redefinition of the institutional balance in delegated legislation. Continued vigilance of the Court to resist against these attempts is therefore warranted, even if the main lines of force of the post-Lisbon framework governing delegated legislation and executive rulemaking have now crystallised.

The conclusion that the Lisbon Treaty's promise of further parliamentarising that framework has not been fully realised may be sobering, but should not distract us from the fact that the present framework is still an improvement (both democratically and in terms of the Parliament's role) on the pre-Lisbon framework, and that the system has continued to function effectively. In any event, and even if the constitutional framework is now largely fixed, 'implementation' is also a continuous game that is played with every legislative, and even executive act, that is adopted. The future therefore holds many battles which the Parliament can win, honouring the promise of the Lisbon Treaty.

Annex: Overview of Autonomous Executive Legal Bases[1]

	Legal basis	Author	Proposal	Consent	Consultation	Information
1	Arts 44(2), 45(3)d, 105(2), 105(3), 106(3), 108(2), 108(4), 114(6) and 143(3) TFEU	Commission	/	/	/	/
2	Arts 143(2), 143(3), 243 and 337 TFEU	Council (QMV)	/	/	/	/
3	Art 342 TFEU	Council (unanimity)	/	/	/	/
4	Arts 132(1) first indent, 132(1) second indent TFEU	ECB	/	/	/	/
5	Arts 236(a) and 236(b) TFEU	European Council	/	/	/	/
6	Arts 31, 42(2), 43(3), 75(2), 107(3)(e), 112, 122(1), 126(6), 126(9), 126(12), 213 and 300(5) second sentence TFEU	Council (QMV)	Commission	/	/	/
7	Art 203 first sentence TFEU	Council (unanimity)	Commission	/	/	/
8	Arts 65(4), 108(2) and 331(1) TFEU	Commission	MS (request/ notification)	/	/	/
9	Arts 65(4) and 108(2) TFEU	Council (unanimity)	MS (request)	/	/	/

(continued)

[1] This table is largely based on the overview presented in Nicholas Otto, *Die Vielfalt unionaler Rechtsetzungsverfahren: Eine verfassungs- und verfahrenstheoretische Rekonstruktion der Funktions- und Organisationslogiken des Rechtsetzungsverfahrensrechts der Europäischen Union* (Tübingen, Mohr Siebeck, 2022) 112–16. Some legal bases were added. Legal bases related to purely organisational matters (such as the composition of committees) have been omitted.

(Continued)

	Legal basis	Author	Proposal	Consent	Consultation	Information
10	see Art 252(1) second sentence TFEU	Council (unanimity)	Court	/	/	/
11	Art 255(2) first and second sentences TFEU	Council (QMV)	President of the Court	/	/	/
12	Arts 150(1) and 160(1) TFEU	Council (QMV)	/	/	European Parliament	/
13	Art 242 TFEU	Council (simple majority)	/	/	Commission	/
14	Arts 95(4) and 96(2) TFEU	Commission	MS (request) or Commission (own initiative)	/	MS	/
15	Arts 78(3), 103(1) 109, 125(2), 126(14)3 and 349(1) first sentence TFEU	Council (QMV)	Commission	/	European Parliament	/
16	Arts 122(2), 155(2) and 126(11) TFEU	Council (QMV)	Commission	/	/	European Parliament
17	Art 352(1) first sentence TFEU	Council (unanimity)	Commission	European Parliament	/	/
18	Art 315(2) TFEU	Council (QMV)	Commission	European Parliament (negative consent/veto)	/	/
19	Art 128(2) second sentence TFEU	Council (QMV)	Commission	/	European Parliament and ECB	/
20	Art 144(3) TFEU	Council (QMV)	Commission	/	EFC	/
21	Art 134(3) TFEU	Council (QMV)	Commission	/	EFC and ECB	European Parliament

	Legal basis	Author	Proposal	Consent	Consultation	Information
22	Arts 66, 138(1) and 138(2) TFEU	Council (QMV)	Commission	/	ECB	/
23	Art 322(2) TFEU	Council (QMV)	Commission	/	European Parliament and Court of Auditors	/
24	Art 140(2) TFEU	Council (QMV)	Commission & QMV of Euro area MS (recommendation)	/	European Parliament and European Council (discussion)	/
25	Art 70 TFEU	Council (QMV)	Commission	/	/	European Parliament and national parliaments
26	Art 95(3) and 188(1) *iuncto* 187 TFEU	Council (QMV)	Commission	/	European Parliament and EESC	/
27	Art 81(3)2 TFEU	Council (unanimity)	Commission	National parliaments (negative consent/veto)	European Parliament	/
28	Art 14(2)2 TEU	European Council (unanimity)	European Parliament	European Parliament	/	/
29	Art 153(2)4 TFEU	Council (unanimity)	Commission	/	European Parliament and social partners	/

(continued)

(Continued)

	Legal basis	Author	Proposal	Consent	Consultation	Information
30	Art 192(2)2 TFEU	Council (unanimity)	Commission	/	European Parliament, EESC, CoR	/
31	Art 140(3) TFEU	Council (QMV)	Commission	MS adopting the euro, Euro area MS (unanimity)	ECB	/
32	Art 129(4) TFEU	Council (QMV)	Commission or ECB		European Parliament and ECB or Commission	/
33	Arts 82(2)2, letter d and 83(1)3 TFEU	Council (unanimity)	Commission or ¼ MS	European Parliament	/	/
34	Art 86(4) TFEU	European Council (unanimity)	Commission or ¼ MS	European Parliament	Commission	/

INDEX

NB–page locators in *italics* indicate information in figures, and those in **bold** indicate information in tables

www.ingramcontent.com/pod-product-compliance
Ingram Content Group UK Ltd.
Pitfield, Milton Keynes, MK11 3LW, UK
UKHW050944290926
15470UKWH00005B/1627

9 781509 931859